LAW AND PRACTICE OF INTERNATIONAL FINANCE

PRINCIPLES OF
INTERNATIONAL INSOLVENCY

AUSTRALIA
The Law Book Company
Brisbane * Sydney * Melbourne * Perth

CANADA
Carswell
Ottawa * Toronto * Calgary * Montreal * Vancouver

AGENTS:
Steimatzky's Agency Ltd., Tel Aviv;
N.M. Tripathi (Private) Ltd., Bombay;
Eastern Law House (Private) Ltd., Calcutta;
M.P.P. House, Bangalore;
Universal Book Traders, Delhi;
Aditya Books, Delhi;
MacMillan Shuppan KK, Tokyo;
Pakistan Law House, Karachi, Lahore.

LAW AND PRACTICE OF INTERNATIONAL FINANCE

PRINCIPLES OF
INTERNATIONAL INSOLVENCY

By

Philip R Wood
BA (Cape Town), MA (Oxon)

Solicitor of the Supreme Court

Visiting Professor, Queen Mary
& Westfield College,
University of London

LONDON
SWEET & MAXWELL
1995

Published in 1995 by
Sweet and Maxwell Limited of
South Quay Plaza, 183 Marsh Wall,
London E14 9FT
Computerset by Interactive Sciences, Gloucester
Printed in Great Britain by
Butler & Tanner, Frome and London

No natural forests were destroyed to make this product:
only farmed timber was used and re-planted

**A CIP catalogue record for this book is
available from the British Library**

ISBN 0 421 54290 X

©
PHILIP R WOOD
1995

To my wife Marie-elisabeth, my twin sons
John Barnaby and Richard,
my daughter Sophie and my son Timothy

PREFACE

This book is one in a series of six works on international financial law which, taken together, are the successor to my *Law and Practice of International Finance* which was published in 1980 and which was reprinted eight times.

The works now cover a much broader range of subjects, with substantial additions in the fields of comparative law, insolvency, security, set-off, netting payments, and title finance, as well as specialist subjects like netting, securitisations and swaps and derivatives. But the works have the same objectives as the original book. However great a gap there may be between the aim and the actuality, the objectives I have sought to achieve are to be practical as well as academic, to provide both a theoretical guide and legal source-book as well as a practitioner's manual, to be international, to provide serious comparative law information, to get to the point as quickly as possible, to simplify the difficulties, to find the principles underlying the particularity, to inform, and, most of all, to be useful.

The six works are separate but they are nevertheless related. Together the books are intended to form a complete library for the international banking and financial lawyer, as well as for specialists in related areas such as insolvency, leasing, and ship and aircraft finance. The topics covered by each volume are summarised on the inside of the front cover.

These books offer what I hope is a fundamentally new approach to comparative law in this area and, for the first time perhaps, provide the essential keys to an understanding of the world's jurisdictions, the keys to unlock the dark cupboard of financial law so that the light may shine in. These keys are not merely functional; they are also ethical and they are driven by history. The ideas are really quite simple, once discovered, but this should not obscure the difficulty of their application to the variety of circumstances. The core of the first book, entitled *Comparative Financial Law*, is a classification and snap-shot of virtually all the jurisdictions in the world – more than 300 of them – according to various financial law criteria. These criteria are developed in succeeding books in the series and applied to particular transactions. I believe that this also is the first time that a classification of this type has been done in this detail; but it has to be done because comparative law is no longer an academic luxury: it is a practical necessity if we are to have an orderly international legal regime.

My hope is that my voyage of discovery into what is really going on in world financial law will help to mitigate international legal surprises and legal risks and, in the wider context, that jurisdictions will be better equipped to make essential choices as to what their legal systems should achieve. This is particularly important in view of the fact that at least 30 per cent of the world's population live under legal systems which are still emerging and that the remainder live in jurisdictions divided into camps which often do not agree on basic policies. There is no reason why we should not agree on the basic policies: we do not have to have a muddle. The law is our servant, not our master. It must set us free, not tie us down. It must satisfy our sense of justice.

This book on insolvency is one of the centre-pieces of the series. Insolvency law is fundamental to commercial and financial law in all its departments and is the most piercing indicator of the doctrines that divide the world's legal systems in the context of financial law. It is the destructive force of bankruptcy which has moulded the central tenets of commercial law and it is bankruptcy which is the ultimate test of a jurisdiction's ability to realise its own views of fairness, equity and legal civilisation.

The books also contain lists of about 250 research topics in total which might be appropriate for further research and which I hope will be useful to prospective writers.

I am acutely conscious of the fact that, in writing about legal systems other than my own (which is England), I will often have committed some real howlers and I hope that my foreign colleagues will be tolerant of my ignorance. Obviously one must always confirm the position with competent local lawyers.

As regards style, I have endeavoured to be as economical as possible. The citation is selective: there are now millions of cases and it is hopeless to try and list even a proportion of them. I am easily terrorised by footnotes and therefore, if material is good enough to go in the footnotes, it is good enough to go in the text: as a result there are no footnotes in these works. At least one does not have to read the text in two places at once. Tables of cases and statutes seemed less sensible in a work endeavouring to cover hundreds of jurisdictions where there is an avalanche of names and numbers and dates and acts and statutes and decrees, and, in view of this, I decided to omit them.

I have endeavoured to reflect the law round about the middle of 1994 based on the international materials then available to me, although some subsequent changes were introduced in the course of publication.

Philip R Wood
One New Change
London

Request for Information

Works on the law in the jurisdictions of the world must rely heavily on information from private sources. With a view to improving the information in any subsequent editions there may be, I would be very pleased to receive papers of all kinds on subjects covered by this and other works in this series – seminar papers, essays, articles, client briefings by law firms, memoranda, notices of book publications, and the like. Material should be sent to me at the following address:

Philip R Wood
Allen & Overy
One New Change
London EC4 9QQ

Fax: 0171 330 9999

ACKNOWLEDGEMENTS

I owe to many a debt of gratitude in the help they gave me in preparing this work.

I am grateful to numerous partners and colleagues at Allen & Overy for their advice and assistance. In particular Paul Philips worked with me on some aspects and Bridget Harris and Lisa Mullen did background research on prejudgment attachments. Osamu Nomoto of Mitsui, Yasuda, Wani & Maeda, Tokyo, contributed much Japanese case law and comment while he was on secondment to my firm.

I owe a particular debt to the authors of the works listed in the bibliography and of a very large number of articles and books not listed without which it would not have been possible to write this book: if I have used their words, as I believe I often have, this is because they said it much better than I ever could.

There are many others – practitioners, students, academics, bankers and others – who have contributed to this work in one way or another: it would be impossible for me to thank them all individually.

None of the above is of course responsible for the defects in this work.

I am most grateful to my secretary Sue Wisbey and to the Allen & Overy word processing department who laboured so magnificently to type this work.

I am thankful to my publishers for their hard work and patience in bringing this work – and the other books in this series – to fruition and also for their support through all the years.

My brother John, my sister Melanie and my mother all encouraged me and were tolerant of my efforts.

Finally, I owe an enormous debt to my wife and children and can only express my affection for them by the token of dedicating this book to them.

CONTENTS

	Page
Preface	vii
Acknowledgements	x
Table of Abbreviations	xix

Chapter	Page

1. General Principles of Insolvency

Choice	1

Classification of world jurisdictions

Three broad groups	2
Pro-creditor and pro-debtor labels	3
Scaling of jurisdictions	4
Key determinants	5
Illustrative table	6
Comments on the ranking	6
Summary survey of jurisdictions	7

The bankruptcy hierarchy

Ladder of payment	10
Super-priority creditors	10
Priority creditors	23
Pari passu creditors	26
Deferred creditors	27
Equity shareholders	29
Expropriated creditors	29

Individual and corporate bankruptcies

No bankruptcy of non-merchants	31
Exempt assets	31
Limitations on security	32
Discharge and rehabilitation	32
Community of matrimonial property	32

Chapter	Page

Classes of corporation	33
Causes of bankruptcy	33

2. Bankrupt's Property: False Wealth and Trusts

Introduction

Main criteria of jurisdiction attitudes	35
Trusts and false wealth	36
Napoleonic and Germanic view	38
Examples of apparent owner being treated as absolute owner	39
Deposits for safe-keeping: custodians	40
Unjust enrichment generally	41
Special purpose payments	41
Wrongful takings of money	43
Mistaken payments and accidental commingling	44
Tests of whether asset is held in trust	45
Fungibility	47
Custodianship of securities	48
Tracing of trust property	50

Deposits of property for sale or collection

Illustrations	53
Property held by insolvent in specie	54

Chapter	Page
Receipt of proceeds by insolvent	55
Deposits and sale proceeds in civil countries	58
Assignment of debts	58

3. Contracts, Leases and Forfeitures

Contracts and leases

Interested parties	60
Rights of insolvent estate to accept or reject	60
Disclaimer of contracts	61
Performance by debtor's estate	63
Rights of solvent counterparty	63
Statutory nullification of ipso facto clauses	65

Forfeitures

Examples of forfeitures	68
Increased liabilities on bankruptcy	70
Exceptions to rule against forfeitures	71

4. Preferences: Introduction

Introduction

Policies	72
Terminology	73
Outline of preference law	74
Main issues	75
English-based jurisdictions	75
Franco-Latin jurisdictions	78
United States law	79

Actio Pauliana: fraudulent transfers	82

5. Preferences: Prejudice to Creditors

Prejudice to creditors generally	85

Chapter	Page
Prejudice to creditors: undervalue transactions	
Gifts and transactions at an undervalue	87
Guarantees as undervalue transactions	88
Subordinations as undervalue transactions	89

Prejudice to creditors: payments

Payment of existing debts	89
Negotiable instruments	90
Ordinary course of business payments	91
Current accounts	92

Prejudice to creditors: security

Security for new money	93
Secured loans to pay off existing creditors	93
Security for pre-existing debt	94
Roll-over of secured current accounts	96
Security over after-acquired assets	97
Floating charges for pre-existing debt	98
Late registration of security	99
Late notification of assignments	100
Purchase of unsecured claims by secured creditor	101

Prejudice to creditors: set-off and netting

Set-off generally	101
Countries disallowing insolvency set-off	101
Countries allowing insolvency set-off	102
Compensating contracts	103
Settlement netting	104

Prejudice to creditors: transfer of business	104

Chapter	Page	Chapter	Page
Prejudice to creditors: transactions with shareholders		Belgium	123
		Brazil	124
		Czech Republic: Slovak Republic	124
Maintenance of capital	105	France	125
Financial assistance to purchase company's own shares	106	Italy	126
		Japan	127
Prejudice to creditors: preferment of guarantors	106	Netherlands	128
		Peru	130
		Russia	130
Prejudice to creditors: judicial executions	107	Spain	131
		Sweden	132
		Switzerland	134
6. Preference: Other Aspects		Ukraine	136
Actual insolvency of debtor	109	**8. Veil of Incorporation: Introduction and Director Liability**	
Length of suspect period	109		
Insiders and connected persons	110	**Introduction**	
Composition proceedings	111	Candidates for personal liability	137
		Policies	137
Defences		Private and public companies	139
Summary	111	**Scale of jurisdictions**	141
Preferential intent	112		
Creditor ignorance of the insolvency	115	**Director's personal liability for debts of insolvent companies**	
Avoidance and recapture		Summary of heads of liability	142
		Fraudulent trading	142
Avoidance procedure	116	Wrongful trading	142
Recapture	116	Director's duty to petition for insolvency or call shareholders meeting	145
Revival of guarantees	117		
Revival of security	118	Duty to petition for insolvency	145
Protection of third parties	118	Duty to call shareholders' meeting on serious loss of capital	146
Security over after-acquired assets	118	Negligent management	149
Preferred transferee insolvent	119	Director's liability for breach of company law	155
Set-off against repayment claim	119		
Deterrence and penalties	120	Director's liability for preferential claim	157
7. Selected Preference Laws		Director's tort and environment liability	158
Argentina	122	De facto directors	158
Belarus	122		

Chapter	Page
9. Veil of Incorporation: Shareholder and Lender Liability	
Shareholder liability	
Generally	160
Commingling, undercapitalisation and informalities	161
Shareholders as de facto directors	164
Group liability	165
Group liability for tax	166
US equitable subordination	166
Consolidation on insolvency	170
Lender liability	171
Interference in management	171
Abusive support of insolvent company	173
10. Judicial Rescue Proceedings: Introduction	
Introduction	
Rescue proceedings and private restructurings	174
Short history of rehabilitations	175
Classification of proceedings	
Voluntary compositions	177
Traditional compositions and moratoriums	178
Country examples	179
11. Corporate Rehabilitation Proceedings: England, France, Japan, US	
General	182
Key issues	183
Eligible debtors	185

Chapter	Page
Grounds for petition and ease of entry	186
Debtor incentives to commence proceedings	188
Stay on legal proceedings	189
Security interests	189
Title finance	198
Set-off	200
Contract cancellation and lease forfeitures	201
Disclaimer and abandonment powers	203
Avoidance of pre-commencement transactions: preferences	204
Replacement of management	204
Financing the business	206
The reorganisation plan	207
Liability of administrators	210
Exit from the proceedings	210
12. Judicial Rescue Proceedings: Other Country Summaries	
Countries covered	212
Australia	212
Canada	215
Italy	219
New Zealand	222
Spain	222
Central and Eastern Europe	224
Insurance companies, banks and other public interest entities	226
13. Insolvency Conflict of Laws: Introduction	
Reasons for lack of comity	227
Territorial and universal theories	228
Advantages and disadvantages of single forum	228
Examples of foreign assets	229
Classification of jurisdictions	230
Organisation of the topic	230

Chapter	Page

14. Insolvency Conflict of Laws: Jurisdiction

Insolvency jurisdiction

Introduction	231
Local company and local branch	231
Long-arm jurisdictions: summary	231
The grounds for opening proceedings	234
Compositions and rehabilitations	234
Insolvency jurisdiction in England	234
Insolvency jurisdiction in Continental Europe	236
Insolvency jurisdiction in the United States	237
Insolvency jurisdiction in Japan	237
Insolvency jurisdiction in Scandinavia	238
Insolvency jurisdiction in Latin America	239

Whether principal bankruptcy covers global property — 240

15. Insolvency Conflict of Laws: Recognition of Foreign Insolvencies

Main options	242
Recognition of home forum proceedings	243
Conditions of recognition	246
Concurrent proceedings in foreign local forum	249
Recogition in England and English-based countries	250
Recognition in Switzerland	258
Recognition in the United States	259
Recognition in Continental Europe	264
Recognition in Scandinavia	267
Recognition in Japan	268
Recognition in Latin America	269

Chapter	Page

16. Insolvency Conflict of Laws: Particular Aspects

Equalisation and other direct remedies

Generally	271
Equalisation	271
Examples of excess receipts	272
Enforcement of equalisation	272
Country survey of equalisation	272

Discovery of foreign assets — 274

Insolvency set-off

General	275
Home forum rules	276
Attitude of foreign local forum to home forum rules on set-off	278

Security and title finance — 279

Rescission of executory contracts and leases

Generally	280
Home forum	280
Attitude of foreign local forum to home forum	280

Priority, pari passu and deferred creditors

Priority creditors	281
Pari passu creditors	281
Deferred creditors	282
Equity shares	282

Preferences

Home forum	282
Attitude of foreign local forum to home forum's avoidance	284

Involuntary gap creditors — 286

Bankruptcy procedure — 286

Chapter	Page
Moratoriums and discharges	
Home forum	286
Foreign local forum attitude to home forum	287
Veil of incorporation	289
Home forum	290
Foreign local forum attitude to home forum rules	290
Bankruptcy penalties and disqualifications	290

17. International Insolvency Treaties

General	291
French conventions	292
Nordic Bankruptcy Convention of 1933	293
Montevideo and Bustamente Conventions: Latin America	293
Bankruptcy treaties not in force	296

18. Private Restructuring Agreements: Introduction

Introduction	297
Advantages and disadvantages	297
Final liquidation compared to private restructuring	298
Judicial rehabilitation proceedings compared to private restructuring: generally	299
Advantages of judicial rehabilitation	300
Disadvantages of judicial rehabilitation	302
Other factors	304
Jurisdictional attitudes	305

Chapter	Page
Participants in a work-out	
Banks	307
Bondholders	308
Secured creditors	309
Lessors	309
Factors	310
Trade creditors	310
Litigants	310
Tax authorities	310
Employees	310
Management	311
Shareholders	311
Types of corporate debtor	
Public and private/large and small	311
Public interest businesses	311
Asset-based companies	312

19. Standstill and Support Agreements

Standstill agreements	313
Informal standstill	313
Steering committee	313
Terms of standstill agreement	314
Management changes	316
Review of debtor's position	317
London Approach	318
Support agreements	
Override and consolidated agreements compared	318
Restructured debt	319
Terms of support agreements	319
Security for restructured debt	322
Maximising the security	322
Loss sharing agreements	
Loss sharing agreements compared to pro rata sharing clauses	323
Sharing formula	324

Chapter	Page	Chapter	Page
20. Private Restructuring Agreements: Debt/ Equity Conversions		Breach of contract to lend money	337
		Abusive credit and false wealth	342
		Bank as adviser	343
Conversion of debt into equity		Credit references	344
		Misrepresentation liability	345
Introduction	325	Control of debtor	346
Debt eligible for conversion	325	Liabilities of secured creditor	347
Advantages of conversion	327		
Disadvantages of conversion	329	**Lender liability for environmental pollution**	
Other implications of conversion	330		
Types of securities	335	Introduction	347
		Categories of environmental liability	348
Transfer to bank holding company	336	Involvement in management	348
		Occupation	349
21. Insolvency and Lender Liability		Ownership	349
		Operational control or responsibility	349
Lender liability generally		Priority of environmental clean-up orders and costs	350
Generally	337	CERCLA	351

	Page
Select Bibliography	353
List of Research Topics	355
Index	359

ABBREVIATIONS

ABGB	Austrian General Civil Code
Art	Article
BA	Bankruptcy Act
BC	Bankruptcy Code
BGB	German Civil Code
BL	Bankruptcy Law
c	chapter (of laws)
CC	Civil Code
CCP	Code of Civil Procedure
CO	Code of Obligations
ComC	Commercial Code
Conflicts Restatement	Restatement of the Law, Conflict of Laws 2d, by the American Law Institute
Dicey	Lawrence Collins (general editor), *Dicey and Morris on the Conflict of Laws* (12th ed 1993) Sweet & Maxwell
EISO	Philip Wood, *English and International Set-off* (1989) Sweet & Maxwell
IA	Insolvency Act
ICSID	International Centre for the Settlement of Investment Disputes
IR	Insolvency Rules (England)
Mann, Money	FA Mann, *The Legal Aspect of Money* (5th ed 1992) Clarendon Press, Oxford
Ord	Order
PILA	Private International Law Act 1987 (Switzerland)
Restatement	Restatement of the Law by the American Law Institute
RSC	Rules of the Supreme Court (England)
s	section
Sched	Schedule
UCC	Uniform Commercial Code (United States)
ZPO	Code of Civil Procedure (*Zivilprozessordnung*)
Zweigert/Kötz	KA Zweigert and H Kötz, *An Introduction to Comparative Law* (2nd ed 1987)

CHAPTER 1

GENERAL PRINCIPLES OF INSOLVENCY

Choice

Insolvency law is the root of commercial and financial law because it obliges   1–1
the law to choose. There is not enough money to go round and so the law
must choose who to pay. The choice cannot be avoided or compromised or
fudged. The law must always decide who is to bear the risk so that there is
always a winner and a loser. On bankruptcy it is difficult to split the difference. That is why bankruptcy is the most crucial indicator of the attitudes of
a legal system and arguably the most important of all commercial legal
disciplines.

Further, bankruptcy has a profound effect on normal legal relationships.
Bankrupts and their directors are disqualified from working and their basic
freedom and liberty compromised and controlled. Property is seized and
sequestrated, including that of creditors. Assets are expropriated without
compensation. Contracts are shattered and their terms interfered with or
negated. Security interests are frozen or avoided or debased below priority
creditors. People lose their jobs. The economy of the state itself may be
sapped. Bankruptcy is a destroyer and spoliator.

Nowadays it is not possible to avoid the international impact of bankruptcy. Many routine dealings in markets are global and no state is an
island.

This work primarily concerns the insolvency of large corporations, and
not individuals or family companies which tend not to be participants in
international finance. Hence there is no need here to review whether the
slant of bankruptcy law should be different for individuals or small businesses. The insolvency of sovereign states is discussed in another volume in
this series of works on financial law.

Bankruptcy is a collective procedure for the recovery of debts by creditors. It also protects individuals who have become overburdened by their
debts. Corporate bankruptcies are, in terms of size and impact upon
people's lives, of much greater significance now than individual bankruptcies and this book will therefore deal almost exclusively with corporate
bankruptcy.

1–2   The three essential features of bankruptcy are often said to be the following:

1.   Actions by individual creditors against the bankrupt are frozen. The piecemeal seizure of assets by disappointed creditors through the levying of distress, or attachment or execution are stayed and replaced by a right to claim for a dividend against the pool.

2.   All assets of the bankrupt belong to the pool which is available to pay creditor claims.

3.   Creditors are paid pari passu, i.e. pro rata out of the assets according to their claims.

The first proposition – that judicial actions by creditors are stayed – is universally true with only very few exceptions on the fringes. The second proposition – that all of the assets of the bankrupt are available for creditors – is so eroded by exceptions as to be doubtful. The third proposition – that creditors are paid pari passu – is a piece of ideology which is nowhere honoured.

This book deals with the substantive law of bankruptcy, not the detailed procedure. The reason is that the procedure is routine and obvious and not interesting to those entering into transactions who wish only to know how bankruptcy will affect their transaction.

1–3   Of course, there must be a petition or application for bankruptcy to this or that court. Of course there must be an insolvency administrator – a liquidator, a trustee, a receiver, a curator, a syndic. Of course the bankruptcy must be advertised so that creditors know the play is over and so that persons are advised they may no longer deal with the bankrupt and of course this publication is often late or not sufficiently public. Of course creditors must file their claims and provide this or that supporting evidence. Of course the liquidator must get in the assets, investigate the bankrupt's affairs, verify creditor claims, realise the assets and distribute the proceeds to creditors by way of dividends. Of course, there must be creditor committees and judicial supervision. Naturally bankruptcy laws must deal with procedure, just as rules of court must deal with the procedure and the papers and the filings and the applications and the time within which. Essential though they are for the conduct of proceedings, one cannot spend time on these matters.

Classification of world jurisdictions

Three broad groups

1–4   The world's jurisdictions can be roughly divided into three groups:

1.   Pro-creditor

2.   Pro-debtor

3.   Not interested. These are mainly former communist states, fundamen-
talist Muslim states and states without a commercial tradition. There
are also a few "don't knows".

A pro-creditor jurisdiction allows a creditor to protect himself against an
insolvency, e.g. by security or set-off. A pro-debtor jurisdiction aims to
maximise the defaulter's assets so as to increase the assets available for distribution. The main criterion which is used is the extent to which the law
increases the debtor's estate, but this is not the only criterion.

The pro-creditor argument is that people should be able to avoid losses
resulting from a debtor default. If this is impossible, the insolvency creates
risks for everybody and perhaps even risks for the system. The pro-debtor
argument is that defaulters (and their employees) ought to be saved and that
all creditors ought to contribute to this rescue. They also say that increasing
the debtor's estate improves the lot of unsecured creditors.

Pro-creditor and pro-debtor labels

The pro-creditor and pro-debtor labels are very ambiguous. For example, a   1–5
pro-debtor system may aim at a judicial business rescue, but the availability
of a statutory rescue procedure might push more businesses earlier into the
trauma and destructiveness of a formal insolvency instead of encouraging a
private consensual restructuring: most practitioners agree that a private restructuring is by far the best, if it is attainable. If that is correct, a pro-creditor opposition to easy rehabilitation proceedings which cram down
creditors is instead pro-debtor.

Pro-debtor states may, by destroying creditor and owner rights, increase
the insolvent estate, but it may be argued that this merely results in greater
returns to the priority creditors (the taxman, employees) and not a materially increased return to other unsecured creditors. This would be the case if
bankruptcy returns were very small – and the evidence is that they usually
are. In that case the regime favours a class of unsecured creditors.

Another example of the ambiguity of a pro-creditor protection is the
universal floating charge espoused by systems based on English law which
enable the capital-provider to be paid ahead of just about everybody else.
Pro-debtor countries say that this prejudices unsecured creditors, especially
trade. Those in favour of the floating charge would say that this security
facilitates the financing of business enterprises which would not otherwise
see the light of day, that the bank's secure position encourages it to allow
the business to continue longer (so that more short-term creditors get out),
and that the floating charge is a successful survival technique because the

business can be sold as a whole. If that is correct, the most monopolistic pro-creditor protection in the world best serves the interests of debtor survival.

A further illustration is insolvency set-off. Dealer A and dealer B owe each other 100. Dealer B becomes bankrupt. If dealer A could set off the 100 against the 100, his exposure is zero. If he cannot set off, his exposure is 100 – because he must pay in 100 to dealer B's insolvent estate and prove for 100 on which he will very likely receive a trifling dividend as an unsecured creditor. Some legal systems, such as England, insist on the set-off. Others, like France, reject it. Since exposures in money and foreign currency markets can run into vast amounts and since set-off can dramatically reduce exposures, this reduces the risk to a fraction of the original risk. If one had a 90 per cent better chance of staying alive, for some people the choice is clear. But still many legal systems do not agree with that approach. They say there is a higher principle – the pari passu payment of debts.

These are all matters for debate and many differing views have been and no doubt will continue to be expressed. All one can say is that the argument requires a subtle approach and that there are no easy answers. It is not the present object to express a view on which is best, but merely to attempt to present the opposing policies and the facts – what the law is, not what it ought to be.

But there is one aspect which cannot be a subject for debate. This is that bankruptcy law should aim at satisfying the sense of fairness to individual debtors and creditors. It should not be a machine to serve some dirigist state economic policy or override the paramountcy of a legal order based on justice and equity.

Scaling of jurisdictions

1–6   One may attempt to rank some of the senior jurisdictions on a scale according to whether their corporate insolvency laws are pro-debtor or pro-creditor. **One** on the scale is extreme pro-creditor. **Ten** on the scale is extreme pro-debtor. The suggested and tentative scale is as follows·

1. Hong Kong, Singapore and other English-influenced states (at least 60 of them)

2. Australia, England, Ireland

3. Germany, Netherlands (and former Dutch states like Indonesia), Sweden, Switzerland

4. Scotland, Japan, Korea, New Zealand, Norway

5. United States, Canada (Quebec more pro-debtor)

6. Austria, Denmark, South Africa (and related states like Botswana and Zimbabwe)

7. Italy

8. Greece, Portugal, Spain, most of Latin America

9. Belgium, Luxembourg, many former French colonies

10. France.

Apart from those at the extreme ends of 1 and 10, it would be quite legitimate to move others up or down a rung or two in the scale.

Key determinants

The scale is highly impressionistic and is bound to be unreliable. Extensive comparative research would be required to authenticate it and it is probably true that accuracy is unattainable. Quite apart from the size of the task, it is not enough to compare bare legal rules: one must also compare how they are applied and this would require immersion in each individual legal system. Legal civilisation is different from legal rules. And, as mentioned, the labels themselves are deceptive. Nevertheless, despite these essential qualifications, even the casual observer is aware of broad legal differences and there is some utility in proposing an empirical analysis, however imperfect, however broad-brush, to record those trends. 1–7

The scale is based on key indicators used as litmus paper. Each country is scored from 1 to 5 on the major criteria. A special weighting is given to the more important criteria, namely security, rehabilitation proceedings and set-off. These are scored from 1 to 10. A more sophisticated weighting would be bound to lead to substantial reorderings.

The key determinants are:

1. The scope and efficiency on bankruptcy of security and title financing (such as retention of title, factoring and financial leasing)

2. Insolvency set-off (enabling the reciprocal unsecured creditor to be paid ahead of other unsecured creditors)

3. Corporate rehabilitation statutes

4. Ownership of assets in the possession of the debtor (trust, tracing)

5. Honouring the veil of incorporation and protection of directors against personal liability. This is an ambiguous factor since arguments can be made that a weak veil is either pro-creditor or pro-debtor. But unquestionably a strong veil shows a business orientation.

6.   Preferential transfers

7.   Contract and lease rescission

Other indicators could be added, e.g. priority creditors, protection of good faith post-petition creditors and direct actions (e.g. undisclosed principal), but the above list will do.

1–8   The relevance of these indicators individually and a more detailed analysis of their make-up appears as follows:

1.   Security: reviewed in another volume in this series of works on international finance, but summarised very briefly at para 1–16 *et seq.*

2.   Insolvency set-off: reviewed in another volume in this series, but summarised at para 1–21 *et seq.*

3.   Corporate rehabilitation statutes: chapters 9 to 12

4.   Ownership of assets: chapter 2

5.   Veil of incorporation: chapters 8 and 9

6.   Preferential transfers: chapters 4 to 7

7.   Contract and lease rescission: chapter 3

A general grouping of most of the world's jurisdictions (307 of them) appears in another work in this series of books on international financial law.

Illustrative Table

1–9   Set out opposite is a table illustrating the method of scoring, for a few selected countries or groups.

Even allowing for a very substantial margin of error, it is plain that the jurisdictional differences on those criteria are very great.

Comments on the ranking

1–10   Three important points may be noted about this ranking.

First, the traditional division between common law and civil code states is unimportant. The pro-creditor side includes code states, like Germany, and the pro-debtor side includes common law states, like Canada and the United States. The civil code/common law division is now an uninteresting classification, except in relation to the trust. It is not particularly relevant how a country writes its laws down. It is much more interesting to know what those laws say.

Scoring (10 or 5)	Trad. English	England	Germany	Japan	US	Italy	Trad. French	France
Security (10)	1	2	5	6	2	8	8	8
Title finance (10)	1	1	1	1	2	5	8	7
Set-off (10)	1	1	2	2	3	2	10	9
Rehabilitation (10)	1	3	1	3	8	9	2	10
Trust (5)	1	1	4	2	1	5	5	5
Veil (5)	1	2	1	1	2	2	3	5
Preferences (5)	1	1	2	2	5	2	3	3
Rescission (5)	1	1	1	1	4	2	2	5
TOTAL	8	12	17	18	27	35	41	52

Second, there is no correlation between degree of industrialisation and overall legal slant, e.g. that pastoral or lesser developed countries can be expected to be pro-debtor and developed countries pro-creditor. Industrialised countries can be found in both groups, and so can pastoral countries. There appears to be no correlation between economic performance and bankruptcy bias. Thirdly, the ranking is based on legal rules. The current culture of a state may be, and often is, wholly different. For example, it is absurd to allege that the culture of France and England are at the opposite ends of the scale: it is self-evident that this is not so. Hence the legal rules and the actual experience are separate matters.

Summary survey of jurisdictions

One may take a bird's eye view of jurisdictions before dealing with topics in detail.   **1–11**

In terms of the strictly legal rules, France seems to be the most pro-debtor jurisdiction of all the major commercial states, followed closely by related countries like Belgium, with Luxembourg trailing along with misgivings. For example, in France business security is very limited in scope and is primed by preferential creditors, but in England a single creditor can take a universal floating charge. In France the veil of incorporation is weak and directors are easily liable on insolvency, but in traditional English jurisdictions, fraud must usually be shown. In France, insolvency set-off is prohibited, but in English-based states it is not only allowed, but is mandatory. In France, the "false wealth" doctrine excludes the trust and makes the assignment of debts difficult, but in Anglo-American jurisdictions secret ownership is trumpeted as a protection. In France, the rehabilitation law is probably the toughest in all the leading nations – on paper at least.

England shifted a bit east as a result of the introduction of the administration procedure in 1986, as did Australia in 1992, leaving Hong Kong (plus most other English-based insolvency jurisdictions such as the Cayman Islands, India and others) still in the extreme pro-creditor mould.

For historical reasons, the United States does not have a homogeneous legal culture and there is an acute conflict between pro-debtor and pro-creditor attitudes. This may help to explain why US case law often seems so confusing and contrary. In 1978 the pro-debtor view was predominant in the Bankruptcy Code of that year: many of the pro-debtor concepts showed great similarity with ideas subsequently intensified in France in 1985. Since then the pro-creditor tradition has been reasserting itself and has achieved some successes. But still the United States seems more pro-debtor in its legal rules overall than, say, Germany and England.

Italy was pro-debtor as a result of the Napoleonic conquest. But in 1942 Italy adopted German bankruptcy ideas. Italy was thereby restored to the mercantilist tradition established by Venice and the other Italian city states, but overlaid it with an extreme pro-debtor rescue statute in 1979.

Canada and the Republic of Ireland were extreme pro-debtor in the old English style but both changed around 1990. Ireland adopted a mild rehabilitation statute in 1990, and Canada a tough one in 1992, but not as tough as France or Italy or the United States. New Zealand has since 1934 had an optional government-initiated procedure which is almost as extreme as France, although this was used only twenty times between 1958 and 1990.

1–12   Germany and the Netherlands are solidly pro-creditor, but Germany has enacted new bankruptcy laws to come into force in the late 1990s. Japan is less so, but is still in this camp, having taken over the German Civil Code and the German bankruptcy legislation of 1877, subsequently followed in 1952 by the mildly pro-debtor old Chapter X from the pre–1978 US bankruptcy legislation. Korean bankruptcy laws appear to be similar to those in Japan.

Scotland's banking tradition enabled it to transmute the pro-debtor culture of mediaevalised Roman law which it inherited. For some reason the same did not happen in the equally Roman jurisdiction of South Africa. The Scandinavians walked a parallel path to Germany although with less conviction – at any rate away from the Romanism which was pastoralised by the pre-Revolution jurists and which formed the basis of the Napoleonic code.

Most of the countries of Central and Eastern Europe had a developed bankruptcy law before it was smothered by communist ideology. But this creed did not succeed in obliterating the original laws which were resurrected, usually in line with previous traditions. Thus Poland reverted to its bankruptcy laws of the mid–1930s, based on the German model. The Czech and Slovak Republics refined their Austrian-based pro-creditor legislation in the early 1990s. Hungary struck out on its own with a fiercely independent statute.

In Latin America, most countries have remained in the mild pro-debtor mould, with Panama reflecting its financial status (shipping, banking, tax haven corporations) by a courteous but slight bow in the direction of the pro-creditor table (insolvency set-off, possessory management of mortgaged ships by mortgagee).

As to Africa, most of the North African countries are French-influenced, 1–13 such as Egypt. At the other end of the continent, South Africa's Roman Dutch system was not anglicised and surprisingly Cecil Rhodes and his fellow-colonists carried that medium pro-debtor system through to Zimbabwe, but not to Zambia which was wholly imperialised in legal terms by lex Britannica. The countries in between the tips more or less adopted what the colonisers gave them, so that, for example, the insolvency laws of Kenya and Nigeria are English-based, those of Zaire are Belgium-based and those of the Ivory Coast are French-based. Liberia is a vacuum country without insolvency laws.

In the Middle East, Israel received the old English system and is therefore a strong pro-creditor country. Arabian countries, such as Kuwait and Qatar, have got along without developed bankruptcy laws, not altogether surprising for cultures which have historically stigmatised usury and hence credit as sinful.

In the Far East, India and Pakistan are English-based but with an interesting dichotomy between city and provincial bankruptcy laws. Indonesia is Dutch pro-creditor. Thailand and the Philippines are mixed. China's bankruptcy laws are still somewhat inchoate.

The former countries of the USSR disbanded themselves before the projected Soviet draft bankruptcy law prepared in the late 1980s could come into force. The new statutes in such countries as Russia, Belarus, the Ukraine and Khazakstan are too skeletal and untested to perceive bias.

The bankruptcy hierarchy

Ladder of payment

1–14   It is often said that the most fundamental principle of bankruptcy is the pari passu or pro rata payment of creditors – each proportionately out of the pool of the bankrupt's estate pro rata according to his debt.

In practice even the most cursory examination of bankruptcy internationally shows that the pari passu rule is nowhere honoured. On the contrary creditors are paid according to a scale or hierarchy or ladder of priorities, which usually comprises at least six main ranks or steps, as follows:

1.   Super-priority creditors

2.   Priority creditors

3.   Pari passu creditors

4.   Deferred creditors

5.   Equity shareholders

6.   Expropriated creditors

These may be briefly summarised in turn.

Super-priority creditors

1–15   Super-priority creditors are creditors who are paid in full (or up to the amount of their asset) and who are broadly outside the bankruptcy in the sense that they can take assets out of the estate, free of the pari passu rule. They are separatists. There are usually six sub-groups in this main group:

(i)   Secured creditors
(ii)   Creditors with a set-off
(iii)   Title finance creditors
(iv)   Owners wrongfully deprived of their property
(v)   Creditors with a direct action
(vi)   Creditors with rights of rescission

These are explained below.

1–16   **Secured creditors** Creditors with security over an asset of the debtor can pay themselves out of the asset to the extent of its value by realising it. The international attitude to security – a huge topic – is surveyed in another volume in this series of works on international financial law and only a few comments are made here.

Secured creditors are super-priority creditors on insolvency. Security must stand up on insolvency which is when it is needed most. Security which is valid between the parties but not as against the creditors of the debtor is futile. Bankruptcy laws which freeze or delay or weaken or de-prioritise security on insolvency destroy what the law created. Hence the end is more important than the beginning.

Rationale of security The main purposes and policies of security are: protection of creditors on insolvency; the limitation of cascade or domino insolvencies; security encourages capital, e.g. enterprise finance; security reduces the cost of credit, e.g. margin collateral in markets; he who pays for the asset should have the right to the asset; security encourages the private rescue since the bank feels safer; security is defensive control, especially in the case of project finance; security is a fair exchange for the credit.

Main objections to security The objections to security are mainly historical, 1–17
but they resurrect and live on. The hostility may stem from: debtor-protection stirred by the ancient hostility to usurers and money-lending and now expressed in consumer protection statutes; the prevention of false wealth, i.e. the debtor has many possessions but few assets – this is usually met by a requirement for possession (inefficient because not public) or public registration; unsecured creditors get less on insolvency and this is seen as a violation of bankruptcy equality, although more often it is motivated by desire to protect unpaid employees and small creditors; security disturbs the safety of commercial transactions because of priority risks, e.g. the purchaser of goods; the secured creditor can disrupt a rescue by selling an essential asset, e.g. a factory.

Deep policies are involved, but choices have to be made. The international tendency seems to be to encourage security, but sometimes this is half-hearted, as where the secured creditors' rights are frozen on formal insolvency rescue proceedings.

Meaning of security The essence of security is twofold:

– the creditor can force a sale of the property and use the proceeds to pay the secured debt ahead of other creditors;

– the debtor can insist on a release of creditor's rights of realisation on payment of the secured debt.

There is much confusing terminology: mortgage, pledge, charge, hypothecation, lien, fiduciary transfer, assignment. The confusion is often deepened by the old notion that security is a transfer of title by debtor to creditor and a re-transfer back when the secured debt is paid. But most jurisdictions distinguish absolute transfers and leases, e.g. sale and repurchase, finance leases though many recharacterise these as mortgages.

1–18 **Jurisdictional classification** One may rank jurisdictions according to whether a country is sympathetic or hostile to security.

Key criteria in ranking jurisdictions include:

– The **scope of assets** which may be mortgaged, e.g. the availability of floating charges or other general business charges over all assets of a corporate debtor; the availability of non-possessory chattel mortgages, of security over receivables without notification to the debtor, and of security over future or after-acquired property.

– The **perfection** of the security; whether the security must be publicly registered or protected by a public filing and whether the registration must be periodically renewed; whether the creditor must take possession of the asset or (in the case of debts) notify the debtor or (in the case of investment securities) be registered as the holder in the books of the issuer.

– The degree of **formalities** acting as a hindrance to the grant of security, notably whether the security must be notarised or in writing or in other formal form or can be created orally or informally by deposit of title deeds, share certificates or other indicia of ownership or paper representing the asset; whether the contents of the security document are prescribed.

– The scope of the **debt which may be secured**; whether there are any limitations on secured debt, such as exclusions for future debt (affecting current accounts, revolving loans and currency convertibles) or for damages (i.e. only liquidated sums); whether a maximum amount must be specified; whether foreign currency mortgages are possible; whether there are any limitations on interest; and whether junior priority debt secured on the same asset (a second mortgage) is possible.

1–19 – Any **limitations on the creditors** entitled to the security, e.g. domiciliaries or nationals only, or non-recognition of trustees holding security for several creditors, or restrictions limiting the grant of security to banks or other financial institutions.

– The scope of the **remedies** of the secured creditor, including any limitation of remedies, such as public auction only (as opposed to a private sale or temporary receivership or possession), compulsory grace periods on enforcement rights, or sale only to nationals or in local currency; and the costs of enforcement. Self-help is a feature of common law jurisdictions, but judicial protectionism is the general rule elsewhere, subject to wide exceptions.

- Whether there are any **bankruptcy freezes** on enforcement of the security or a moratorium on secured debt; whether the insolvency administrator can use the secured asset or substitute security in the event of insolvency rescue proceedings.

- Whether the insolvency administrator of the debtor in an insolvency rehabilitation can raise **super-priority moratorium loans** to finance the rehabilitation but which prime existing security.

- Whether there are reasonable safe harbours in favour of the creditor against the security being avoided as a **preference** on insolvency and the length of the suspect period.

- The certainty and predictability of the creditor's **priority** over competing interests, especially preferred creditors on bankruptcy (e.g. taxes, employees, bankruptcy administration costs), attaching creditors, subsequent purchasers, subsequent mortgagees, liens (especially ships and aircraft); whether the creditor can claim subsequent accessories and fixtures; the creditor's position with regard to lessees, charterers and licensees of the asset.

- Whether the creditor may **restrict redemption** of the security, e.g. by a restriction on prepayments, or by prepayment penalties, or by insisting on the consolidation of mortgages (a doctrine which insists that the debtor redeem both mortgages or neither).

On this basis, a suggested broad ranking is as follows: 1–20

- **Very sympathetic:** Most English-based common law countries and (to a lesser extent) Sweden, Finland and Norway (but not Denmark); most states in the US, though with lesser enthusiasm than traditional English countries. Examples are the universal business charge enforceable by self-help possessory management through a receiver in English-based countries and the Scandinavian equivalents – although the latter do not contemplate possessory management through a receiver. In the English-based countries, formalities for security over personal property are few and, although there is a system for public registration of certain corporate charges, the taking of security over personal property is quite informal. The security can secure all future money owing without specifying a maximum amount. A trustee is available to hold security for several creditors. If so provided, the secured creditor can realise by a private sale, without court order.

- **Quite sympathetic:** Some Germanic countries, such as Germany, Japan, Netherlands, Switzerland, Scotland, South Africa. An example is the

Germanic fiduciary transfer which is about 50 per cent as wide as the English floating charge. One reason for the more restricted approach is the absence of a public registration system for security, except land, ships and aircraft, in the Germanic countries. But the South African notarial bond is registrable in a Deeds Registry.

— **Quite hostile:** Belgium, Luxembourg, most Latin American countries, Greece, Spain. Some have a cautious business charge, which does not usually approach anything like the scope of the English floating charge.

— **Very hostile:** Austria, France, Italy. These countries object to non-possessory chattel mortgages and to non-notified assignments of debts. The doctrine of specificity limits the ability to charge future generic assets, e.g. investment securities or inventory or receivables: they have to be individually specified. A trustee to hold security is not available. The principal remedy is judicial public auction: a private sale is unusual. Security is overridden by priority unsecured creditors in France. But in 1994 Italy widened the scope of security to include a non-possessory business charge over goods and inventory – if specified and identified (not generic) – and their proceeds of sale.

But most countries allow mortgages of land, ships and aircraft.

1–21 **Set-off** Creditors who also owe a debt to the bankrupt and who are entitled to set off the debt owed to them by the bankrupt against what they owe are paid to the extent of the set-off. Thus if the bankrupt owes the creditor 150 but the creditor owes the bankrupt 100, and if the creditor can set off, he is "paid" 100 out of his claim of 150. Set-off – a remedy of some complexity which is therefore studied in detail in another volume in this series of works on international financial law – is one of the leading, and most accurate, indicators of pro-debtor or pro-creditor attitudes to insolvency: it is a litmus test of jurisdictions. For example, in English-based countries, set-off is restricted between solvent parties (favouring payment to creditors like banks, lessors and sellers who wish to be paid without deduction so as to maintain cash-flow and to support the "pay now, litigate later" principle) and compulsory on insolvency (favouring payment to creditors who are thereby paid by the defaulter, even though they are unsecured), while in most Franco-Latin jurisdictions solvent set-off is liquid between solvent parties (favouring debtors) but prohibited on insolvency (augmenting the debtor's estate and hence favouring debtors). The contrast could not be more complete.

1–22 **Security function of set-off** Set-off avoids circuity of payment and achieves the aim of judicial economy by avoiding multiplicity of proceedings. But the main effect of set-off is that a debtor with a set-off is in substance "secured" in that the debtor's cross-claim can be paid or discharged by setting it off against the creditor's claim. Thus a bank can discharge a loan owed to it by setting it off against a deposit owed by the bank. The set-off discharges both claims.

Since claims are a major form of property nowadays and since creditors are often also debtors to the same counterparty, the law of set-off is of paramount importance in international financial affairs – almost as important as the law of security interests. The most common cases of set-off in other contexts include set-off by banks of loans against deposits; set-off between institutions in financial markets such as the inter-bank deposit market; netting of foreign exchange, swaps, futures, securities and repo contracts; and set-off in centralised payment systems. The amounts involved are immense and the reduction in exposures achieved by set-off, with resulting reduction in credit costs, and cascade risks threatening the integrity of the financial system, are correspondingly large.

But this short list should not disguise the persuasiveness of set-off in financial and business affairs: wherever there are a series of contracts between parties, there is a potential for set-offs, and even single contracts containing reciprocal obligations give rise to a set-off possibility – banking, sales, insurance, leasing, custodianship, transportation, services.

Policies of insolvency set-off The old classical view espoused by the Franco-   1–23
Latin jurisdictions is that insolvency set-off is a violation of the pari passu principle because a creditor with a set-off gets paid in full, and that the set-off is like an unpublicised security interest causing assets to disappear on bankruptcy.

The arguments in favour of set-off are: (a) it is unjust that the defaulter should insist on payment, but not pay himself; (b) set-off helps creditors escape the debacle and hence mitigates the knock-on or cascade effect of bankruptcy; (c) set-off reduces exposures and hence the cost of credit; (d) set-off avoids circuity and hence reduces costs; (e) set-off prevents the debtor from being bankrupted on a debt he does not owe, if the overall position is taken into account; if he has this admittedly legitimate relief, he should not be in a better position than the creditor.

As to the view that set-off is effectively an unpublished security interest, it is not practical to require creditors who have reciprocal claims to publish this fact. There are many other cases where it is accepted that it is not realistic to publicise the fact that assets will be removed or depleted on insolvency, e.g. repossessions of leased assets, cancellation of contracts and forfeitures of mortgaged assets where it is too expensive or burdensome to require filing or registration. Financial statements themselves are based on the necessary assumption that the enterprise will continue as a going concern: a bankruptcy break-up sale results in a dramatic collapse of values and extinction of goodwill, so that creditors dealing with an enterprise must accept that bankruptcy is a spoliator of value, a devastation far in excess of anything that set-off can inflict. The "secrecy" argument therefore appears unconvincing.

In any event, whatever view one may take about the policies, the fact of the matter is that if set-off is to be of any value as a form of "security" it must stand up on insolvency which is the time that the protection is really needed.

1–24 **States allowing insolvency set-off** The majority of international opinion favours the grant of wide insolvency set-off of mutual claims incurred prior to bankruptcy, although there is variation in the detail. States allowing insolvency set-off by statute include the following.

> **Europe:** Austria, Czech Republic, Denmark, England, Germany, Guernsey (but only if the parties have contracted for it), Ireland (North and Republic), Isle of Man, Italy, Jersey, Liechtenstein, Netherlands, Poland, Scotland (case law – no statute), Slovak Republic and Switzerland

> **North America:** Canada (including Quebec since the Federal bankruptcy legislation overrides the Napoleonic bar on insolvency set-off), and the United States (including Louisiana which is also a Napoleonic state where the Bankruptcy Act 1978 s 553 overrides, although there are contrary decisions). Note that there is a stay on set-off under the Canadian Bankruptcy and Insolvency Act 1992 s 65.1(1) amending the insolvency set-off in BA s 75(3)

> **Scandinavia:** Finland, Norway, Sweden

> **Latin America:** Panama

> **Middle East:** Cyprus, Israel

> **Asia and Pacific:** Australia, China, Hong Kong, India, Japan, South Korea, Malaysia, New Zealand, Pakistan, Singapore, Sri Lanka, Thailand

> **Africa:** Liberia (probably, although there is no statute), Nigeria, Zambia and probably some or all of the former British colonies (except South Africa and surrounding states)

> **Caribbean:** Bahamas, Bermuda, Cayman Islands

The position in the Arabian states in the Middle East, such as Saudi Arabia, is often uncertain because of the absence of a developed bankruptcy law.

The position in the new states following the collapse of the Soviet empire appears unclear. It is believed that the new bankruptcy laws in Russia, Belarus, Khazakhstan and the Ukraine do not mention insolvency set-off.

States refusing insolvency set-off In those jurisdictions which do not permit 1–25
insolvency set-off, the general principle, subject to local variations, is that the reciprocal claims must satisfy the conditions of the solvent set-off rules prior to the relevant insolvency date, e.g. in the case of independent set-off both claims must be mutual, liquidated, matured and legally payable, or they must have been set off by contract prior to the insolvency date under a contract entered into prior to the preferential suspect period. Generally a contract which removes an obstacle to set-off such as illiquidity, multi-currency or immaturity, must remove the bar prior to the suspect period and the claims must be eligible for set-off before the relevant insolvency date pursuant to the contract.

If the claims do not satisfy these requirements by the relevant date, there can be no set-off and the creditor must pay the cross-claim into the insolvent's estate and prove for the claim owed to him by the insolvent. Hence if a bank owes a term deposit maturing after the insolvency date and is owed a term loan accelerated before the insolvency date, there is no set-off and the bank must pay in the term deposit and prove for the accelerated loan – something of a disaster. The bar is also unfortunate for netting agreements.

The group of non-allowing states comprises:

Europe: France (Art 107 of the Decree of December 27, 1985), Belgium, Luxembourg, Spain, Greece, Portugal

Middle East: Egypt, Kuwait (probably, but there is no statutory provision), Bahrain (Art 86 of the Banking and Composition Law No 11 of 1987)

Latin America: Argentina (CC Art 862, Art 134 of the Bankruptcy Law 1955), Brazil (but this is worth checking), Chile, Colombia, Mexico (Art 128 of the Bankruptcy Law)

Africa: South Africa and (probably) various other states originally part of the French or Belgian dominions, e.g. Francophone north, west and central African states

Exceptional insolvency set-offs in refusing states

1–26　There are two main exceptions to the general bar on insolvency set-off in the refusing states.

(a) **Current account set-off** It seems to be universally true that current account set-off is available in the refusing states on the rationale that debits and credits are but one account eligible for compensation on termination of the banker-customer relationship on insolvency. This is true in France and Luxembourg. See also, for example, Art 784 of the Argentine Civil Code and Art 36 of the Bahrain Bankruptcy and Composition Law No 11 of 1987.

(b) **Transaction set-off** There appears to be wide acceptance of the notion in the non-allowing states that transaction set-off is permitted because it would be intolerable that, for example, an insolvent should be able to claim the price without bringing into account damages for delay or defective performance.

Under the pre–1985 bankruptcy legislation, France allowed set-off between an insurance premium and policy proceeds, between reciprocal claims arising out of supply contracts, between the price owing to the insolvent for goods or services supplied and a damages claim for defective performance or delay, and between an invoice payable by a consumer to a gas company and caution money due to the consumer. This was so even if the debt owing by the insolvent matured after the relevant insolvency order. These decisions were codified in a 1994 amendment to the 1985 French bankruptcy legislation. The principle is that the *lien de connexité* justifies the set-off. See also, for example, Art 69 of the Chilean Bankruptcy Law and Art 128 (IV)(a) of the Mexican Code of Commerce.

If the reciprocal claims are not in fact connected by virtue of the same transaction, it appears that generally an attempt by contract to create a set-off on insolvency will fail as contrary to the policy of the bankruptcy laws.

The impact on contractual set-off of preferential doctrines and long suspect periods is particularly relevant. Long suspect periods are typical of French-based bankruptcy regimes.

1–27　**Title finance creditors** These are creditors who, instead of taking security in the form of a mortgage or charge, entered into a quasi-security transaction with the bankrupt which was not security in form but has a similar effect in substance. Examples of such transactions are financial leasing, hire purchase, sale and lease-back, sale and repurchase, the recourse factoring of debts and retention of title. The lessor or other owner takes possession of his own property free of the claims of the bankrupt.

If the jurisdiction recharacterises these as in substance mortgages, then the transaction may fail on bankruptcy, either on the ground that the transaction was not published by public registration or on the ground that a non-possessory mortgage of the asset is impossible. For example, if hire purchase is recharacterised as a mortgage, then, on the bankruptcy of the lessee, the equipment is deemed to belong to the lessee and the lessor is effectively expropriated. Some jurisdictions, which are otherwise suspicious of security, encourage title finance, not because they blindly refuse to see that these transactions often in substance have the effect of mortgages (the form over substance approach), but simply because the law of mortgages over personal property is seen as obsolete and out-of-date and title finance is a splendid opportunity, supported by the judiciary, to escape these tiresome restrictions.

In any event, title finance is a large subject and is reviewed in another volume in this series of works and nothing more will be said about it here.

Owners wrongfully deprived of their property This class comprises credi- 1–28 tors who have been deprived of their property, usually money, by the delinquency of the bankrupt. Typical examples are restitutionary claims by companies against their directors for misfeasance and claims by principals against their agents for misapplied money. If the law allows the wronged creditor to trace his money into the hands of the bankrupt or is given a prior charge on the insolvent estate, then effectively the creditor is paid ahead of other creditors and has a super-priority claim. Included in this class are mistaken payments by the creditor as where a bank mistakenly pays a customer when they become bankrupt. These claims are peculiar to common law countries and are briefly discussed in chapter 2.

Creditors with direct action: summary Generally creditors in this sub- 1–29 group are permitted to leapfrog the insolvent and to claim direct from a third party and thereby get paid. Some of the most common examples are:

1. The undisclosed principal
2. Third party liability insurance
3. Building sub-contractors
4. Lifting the veil of incorporation
5. Product liability

In addition, unjust enrichment claims often allow a leapfrog over an insolvent to the person who has been unjustly enriched.

1–30   **Direct action: undisclosed principal** English-based jurisdictions and the United States common law jurisdictions allow the undisclosed principal. Where a person contracts with a third party apparently as principal but in reality as agent and the agent becomes insolvent, the undisclosed principal can intervene on the contract and claim from the third party direct: e.g. *Cooke v Eshelby* (1887) 12 App Cas 271; US Restatement of the Law of Agency ss 306 *et seq*. This is so unless the contract is of a personal nature where the identity of the principal is critical, as in *Said v Butt* [1920] 3 KB 497 (the unwanted spectator in the theatre ticket case) – unusual in market transactions. The agent is deemed to hold the claim against the third party in trust for the principal and so it does not form part of his insolvent estate. The effect is that the undisclosed principal is protected against the agent's insolvency and becomes a super-priority creditor: he takes away for himself the agent's claim against the agent's counterparty.

This situation is common in organised markets where brokers may act sometimes for their own account as principals, sometimes as agents for outside clients but without disclosing this. The rule protects the outside client against his broker's insolvency, especially as brokers are often undercapitalised.

The third party is protected by being able to raise, against the intervening creditor, set-offs and other defences he could have raised against the agent if the agent had remained sole holder of the transferred claim, although, as regards set-offs, the third party is less well off than he would otherwise have been for various technical but important reasons.

One must distinguish situations where the agent discloses to the third party that he acts as agent, whether or not he names the principal. Here, the principal can claim direct everywhere, it seems.

1–31   English-based jurisdictions and United States common law jurisdictions readily allow the undisclosed principal to intervene.

According to Zweigert-Kötz, vol II chapter 9, many civil code systems sometimes reach the same result, notwithstanding the general rule, based on the objection to false wealth (see para 2–2 *et seq*) that if the principal is to have the contract, the contract must be in the principal's name: France CC Art 1984 (the mandatory must act for the principal and in his name); Italy CC Art 1388. These jurisdictions get round this by the direct action. By the French CC Art 1994(2), the mandatory has a direct action against the third party to whom the mandatory has delegated the execution of the mandate. The position is similar in Italy (CC Art 1705 (2)) and Switzerland (CO Art 399(2)). See also the Swiss CO Art 32(2). Thus a customer of a bank could bring a direct action against another bank to which his own had entrusted the carrying out of the mandate: Paris October 17, 1934, Gaz Pal 1934.2.781. The depositor of goods could sue a warehouseman chosen by the mandatory: Rouen, February 2, 1950, Gaz Pal 1950 1. 345. Whether those were insolvency cases is a matter for investigation. Germany is more reluctant to allow this claim, but it appears to be possible under BGB s 328 if the agent, though transacting in his own name, was intending to create rights not only for himself but also for his principal: see OLG Hamburg, MDR 1948, 52.

Further, special provisions in civil countries give principals direct rights   1–32
against the third party on the insolvency of the agent. This situation usually arises where an agent has sold the principal's property and become bankrupt before receiving the proceeds from the buyer. The principals can step in and claim direct from the buyer so as to escape the agent's insolvency: e.g. Germany HGB s 392(2) (commission agents); Greece ComC Art 669(2), Netherlands CC 7: 412 Austria ABGB s 392(2), Portugal CPC Art 1237(3); Turkey CO Art 393; Mexico Bankruptcy Law Art 159 VI e; Philippines CC Art 1455. In Switzerland CO Art 401 provides that a principal can take over the agent's claim against the third party as soon as the principal has discharged his contractual obligations towards the agent even if the agent is bankrupt and even if the agent acted in his own name. In Sweden the principal of a commission agent has a direct claim against the third party if the agent is in breach of his obligations under the agency: Art 57(2) of the Law on Commission Agency of April 18, 1914 (also in force in Denmark and Norway).

The position is different however as regards direct actions by the third party against the principal if the agent is insolvent. The Anglo-American jurisdictions allow this, subject to detailed case law if the third party mistakenly sues the agent first: see the English textbooks on agency and the US Restatement on Agency s 210. But the general view in the German, Franco-Latin and Scandinavian countries is that the third party has no such claim: the third party could attach the right of indemnity owed by the principal to the agent and get through to the principal that way, but he is too late if the agent is insolvent. The civilian view may be based on the proposition that the third party bargained only for the credit of the agent and should not be able to look to a third party he had never heard of when the contract was made: he should not be able to remove an asset from the agent's estate. But, whatever the ethics of the matter, it is plain that the English-based systems are determined to protect creditors against an insolvency.

Direct action: third party liability insurance Under third party liability   1–33
insurance, a third party injured by an insured may be able to claim compensation direct from the insurer on the insolvency of the insured. The policy is to protect that involuntary creditor, especially if he has suffered personal injury, against the insolvency of the debtor causing the injury. If a direct

action were not allowed, the bankrupt estate would acquire a windfall insurance payment for the benefit of creditors generally and the injured victim would get only a paltry dividend.

This direct liability is often created by statute and is common in developed jurisdictions. Examples are the British Third Parties (Rights Against Insurers) Act 1930 and the French CC Art 2102–80; Code Assurance Art L 124–3.

1–34   **Direct action: building sub-contractors** Workmen of an insolvent building contractor may have direct leap-frog claims against the ultimate employer. The policy is to protect workers against the insolvency of building contractors and is part of the traditional policy of giving a degree of priority to employees.

No such right exists under English law. In some countries the worker may have a mechanics lien over tools and materials on site. For example, in Canada, Mechanics Liens Acts provide in effect that sums received by a builder or contractor on account of the contract price are a trust fund for the benefit of the proprietor, builder, contractor, sub-contractor, workman's compensation board, workmen and persons who have supplied materials on account of the contract. The object is to ensure that these moneys would reach suppliers and workmen. In France the worker has in certain cases an imperfect direct action against the ultimate employer: CC Art 1798.

Sub-contractors may have direct rights against the employer, leap-frogging the head building contractor. No such implied right exists under English law, but standard forms of building contact often give the sub-contractor direct rights by trust or assignment of the benefit of the payment of retentions moneys held by the employer.

Often the object of the employer in paying the sub-contractor direct is to ensure that the work is completed despite the insolvency of the head contractor. In pursuit of this policy, the English courts have upheld clauses in the head contract allowing the contractor to do this, even though strictly this involves taking away the bankrupt's claim and hence stripping his estate: *Re Wilkinson* [1905] 2 KB 713.

In France a sub-contractor has certain direct rights against the master of the works (*maitre de l'ouvrage*): Law of December 31, 1975 Art 12 *et seq.*

Direct action: lifting of veil of incorporation Direct actions by a creditor of a bankrupt company against the shareholders or directors are achieved by lifting the veil of incorporation: chapters 8 and 9.

Direct action: product liability The buyer of a product can avoid the bankruptcy of his seller if he can claim in tort from the manufacturer direct by leap-frogging over the seller.

Creditors with rights of rescission These are creditors who are entitled to   1–35
rescind, cancel or terminate a contract, lease or licence with the bankrupt
and thereby potentially deprive the insolvent estate of a profitable right for
the benefit of the creditor. One example is the rescission by the seller of
goods or foreign exchange of the sale contract with the bankrupt buyer
before delivery in circumstances where the seller can resell the goods at a
profit. Another example is the termination of a exclusive patent licence in
favour of the bankrupt by the owner of the patent who is as a result able to
licence the patent more profitably elsewhere. These are super-priority creditors because they effectively take away an asset of the insolvent estate for
their own profit and advantage. Of course the contract could be at a loss in
which event it is the counterparty who loses. These situations are discussed
in chapter 3.

Priority creditors

This group – ranking second in the hierarchy of seniority – comprises credi-   1–36
tors who are paid next out of the available pool of assets after deduction of
the claims of the super-priority creditors. The main classes are:

   (i)   Expenses of the insolvency proceedings
   (ii)   Taxes
   (iii)   Employee remuneration
   (iv)   Others

Expenses of the insolvency proceedings These include the remuneration of   1–37
the insolvency administrator, lawyers, agents, auctioneers and employees;
costs of premises and insurance; costs of storage and realisation; costs of
contracts adopted by the liquidator; litigation costs. In England these costs
are ranked on 16 rungs: IA 1986 ss 115, 156; IR 1986, r 4.218. In the US
there are six rungs of administrative expenses: see BC 1978 ss 507, 726. The
expenses of the insolvency proceedings must come first because insolvency
administrators do not work for nothing and because otherwise the insolvency administration could not take place without those involved knowing
that they would be paid. Unlike judges, the expenses of bankruptcy are not
treated as a governmental expense to be borne by the taxpayer, but rather as
an expense to be suffered by those interested in the estate. In the case of
judicial rehabilitation proceedings, this class is often expanded to involve
the post-commencement contracts, including financing loans.

Taxes This priority claim is usually subject to limits, e.g. English IA 1986   1–38
Sched 6. The arguments put forward by tax authorities for the priority of
their claim is traditionally that the public interest comes before the private

interest and that they are involuntary creditors (but so are tort claimants) or that if they were not reasonably secure, they would be obliged to bankrupt companies earlier than necessary and hereby incur much opprobrium. There is great international variation in the acceptance of these views.

1–39   **Employee remuneration and benefits** These are also usually subject to limits. The reasons that employees are preferred is three-fold: (1) otherwise they might not man the ship in the storm; (2) sympathy for the employee (on the bankruptcy, they are left without means of livelihood), and (3) some-times, a political philosophy which puts the interests of the workers first. In any event, everywhere they merit a measure of priority.

In the 1898 US case of *The John E Stevens*, 170 US 113, 118 (1989) Justice Gray described the seaman's claim for his wages as a "sacred lien, and so long as a plank of the ship remains, the sailor is entitled, against all other persons, to the proceeds as security for his wages." In *Re Lawsam Electric Co Inc*, 300 F 736 (SDNY 1923), Judge Learned Hand observed:

> "Priority of payment was intended for the benefit of those who are dependent upon their wages, and who, having lost their employment by the bankruptcy, would be in need of such protection.
>
> The statute was intended to favour those who could not be expected to know anything of the credit of their employer but must accept a job as it comes, to whom the personal factor in employment is not a practicable consideration."

1–40   **Others** In some jurisdictions there are dozens of other claimants whom the law has decided to prefer for this or that reason.

Often depositors with banks and policy-holders with life insurance companies may be preferred in order to protect the public and to maintain public confidence. In England bank depositors rank equally with other secured creditors but are protected by a compensation fund up to certain limits: see the Banking Act 1987. Some US states confer a super-priority lien for environmental clean-up expenses.

1–41   **Priority creditors and secured creditors** In most jurisdictions, secured creditors prime the priority unsecured creditors and hence are paid out first out of the proceeds of realisation of the assets over which they have security. But there are a number of exceptions.

1.   In some states, certain priority creditors rank ahead of secured creditors, or some secured creditors. Thus in France, the priority claims of employees and the expenses and costs of the insolvency proceedings rank ahead of secured creditors. In England and English-based countries, the preferential creditors (basically taxes and wages) rank ahead of floating charges, by reason of the monopolistic scope of the floating

charge. These are special cases and most countries recognise that if security is to have predictable value, the secured creditor must be able to look only to the value of his security and not be burdened with speculation about the amount of unpaid taxes, wages and the like which might erode the value of the security. The topic is reviewed in more detail in the book on international security in this series of works.

2. It is often the case that certain claims associated with an asset which is the subject of security are paid in priority out of the proceeds of sale of that asset. These claims tend to fall into two main classes. The first is the costs of realisation of the asset incurred by the secured creditors, or, if the insolvency administrator has a right to implement a sale himself, by the insolvency administrator (e.g. court costs, auction costs, legal costs, advertising, selling commissions to agents), plus the costs of preservation in the meantime (e.g. insurance, warehousing, watchmen). Even if the jurisdiction does not by statute insist that these costs are paid first, in practice they have to be since the secured creditor could not implement a realisation without ensuring that they are paid. The other priority group are prior liens on the asset for the benefit of privileged creditors. The most prominent examples are maritime liens in favour of, for example, collision and salvage claimants and the crew.

Subrogation to priority claims If a third party finances the payment of a   1–42
priority claim, the question arises as to whether he is subrogated to the priority of the creditor who has been paid by the third party. The question typically arises where a bank finances the payment of wages.

In England and related jurisdictions, a bank which makes an advance to pay wages is by statute subrogated to the priority of the paid creditor: no doubt this is to encourage banks to support the employees of companies in financial difficulties. Hence banks financing companies in difficulties establish separate wages accounts to identify the loans concerned and operate them so that payments go to reduce other advances on the general account first: *Re EJ Morel (1934) Ltd* [1962] Ch 21.

Generally, this is the only English subrogation. There appears to be no subrogation to taxes, for example.

In the United States subrogation to priority is permitted only for adminis-   1–43
trative claims (the cost and expenses of the insolvency proceeding) and claims incurred during the "involuntary gap" period between presentation of the insolvency petition and the insolvency order. An entity that is subrogated to the rights of a holder of any other claim in the priority list in s 507(a) is not subrogated to the right of the holder of the claim to priority.

Thus in the US a bank which finances wage claims is not subrogated to the priority of wages. But the same effect of subrogation can be achieved if the wage-earner assigns his claim to the bank in return for payment of the price of the assignment, as opposed to the bank making a loan to the debtor to pay the wages. Wage claims do not lose their character merely because they have been assigned: see *Re Missionary Baptist Fund of Am*, 667 F 2d 1244, 5 CBC 2d 1462 (5th Cir 1982). Note that in many countries wages are not assignable, in which case this technique to achieve priority is presumably not available.

Apart from the above examples, there is no US subrogation to the priority of wages, contributions to employee benefit plans, consumer credit, or taxes.

Pari passu creditors

1–44   This group – ranking third after the super-priority and priority creditors – are the true pari passu creditors and are generally the unsecured creditors of the bankrupt. Their lot is not a happy one since experience has shown that the dividends payable to this group, after payment of super-priority and priority creditors, is either nil or some small percentage – rarely more than 20 per cent and usually much less. This melancholy result demonstrates the emphasis which bankruptcy law in many jurisdictions places upon protecting other prior claimants and also, of course, the low value of the assets of a failed and broken-up business.

The largest of these creditors are commonly unsecured bank creditors and trade creditors for goods sold or work done.

The general rule is that all unsecured creditors can claim, whether their debts were liquidated or unliquidated, mature or immature, contingent or unascertained, present or future, provided that they were incurred prior to the commencement of the insolvency proceedings. A claim for damages resulting from the administrator's repudiation of a contract is usually treated as incurred prior to the proceedings because the damages flow from a pre-insolvency contract: see, e.g. the English IR 1986, r 13. 12 (1). But certain comments may be made.

1–45   **Discounting** Unmatured credits may have to be discounted. In England, IR 1986, r 11.13 provides that the creditor's entitlement to dividend is to be calculated by reducing the amount of the proof by a percentage (5 per cent) calculated by reference to the length of the period between the date on which a dividend is declared and the date on which payment of the debt would otherwise be due. The balance of the amount is recoverable as a deferred debt. In Germany a future debt is discounted back at a rate varying between 4 per cent to 6 per cent p.a. In the Netherlands, claims with a fixed maturity of one year are provable at their full value; if after that year, their value is estimated. In Japan and Korea unmatured debts are available for proof subject to discounting. Other countries which discount are Panama, Italy, Switzerland, Denmark, Finland, Norway and Sweden.

In jurisdictions which do apply discounting to unmatured debts, it would be for consideration whether discounting applies if the creditor has a right to accelerate the unmatured credit. If not, discounting would depreciate the value of a term deposit, term loan or deferred purchase credit even though the credit does not contain an interest element (as would be the case with equipment rentals under finance leases or single sum notes bundling up both principal and interest).

Assignments for less than full value It is not unusual for persons to pur-   1–46
chase claims against a potential insolvent for much less than their nominal value as a speculation in the hope that the debtor will survive so that the purchaser recovers more than he paid for the debt. He may also buy a debt because he owes a debt to the debtor and hopes to achieve a set-off on the insolvency.

In England, a creditor who has purchased a debt at a discount can never-theless claim the full nominal amount in the insolvency: *Re Humber Iron-works Co* (1869) LR 8 Eq 122. The debt would have been claimable at its full value if there had been no purchase and there is no reason to penalise the purchaser who, after all, has lost on his speculation and will only receive a tiny dividend.

Where a debtor to the insolvent debtor purchases debts owed by the insolvent in order to achieve an insolvent set-off in those jurisdictions which allow insolvency set-off, the effect is that the purchasing debtor achieves a preferential payment, by means of the set-off, ahead of other creditors. It appears that most, if not all, states which sanction insolvency set-off, also have rules inhibiting this transaction: this topic is pursued in detail in another work in this series.

Deferred creditors

The fourth-ranking group – ranking after super-priority, priority and pari   1–47
passu creditors – comprises creditors who for some reason are deferred. They usually receive nothing on the insolvency. Depending on the jurisdiction, there are at least six sub-groups in this group as follows:

(i)   Equity creditors
(ii) Equitably subordinated creditors

    (iii)   Post-insolvency interest
    (iv)   Creditors without an *escritura publica*
    (v)   Consensually subordinated creditors

1–48   **Equity creditors** These are creditors whose debts so resemble equity shares that they should be treated as such and subordinated to all other creditors. An example is a loan where the interest varies with profits.

    Section 3 of the English Partnership Act 1890 applies to loans (whether to companies or partnerships or anybody else – see IR 1986, r 12.3(2A) of the Insolvency Rules (1986)) if interest varies with the profits of the borrower or if the lender is to receive a share of profits: the lender is not entitled to receive anything in respect of his loan until the other creditors have been satisfied. This rule is widely adopted in other common law jurisdictions based on English law, such as common law Canada.

    In Germany if a shareholder of a company with limited liability (GmbH) grants a loan to the GmbH when shareholders acting as prudent business-men would have granted equity capital to the company, then, in the event of the bankruptcy of the GmbH or court composition settlement proceedings, the claim for repayment of the loan is excluded pursuant to s 32 (a) of the German GmbH Law. In Denmark, a lender enjoying a right to profits has been subordinated on the debtor's bankruptcy: Ugeskrift for Retsvaesen 1978 p 205.

1–49   **Equitably subordinated creditors** These are creditors whose claims are subordinated on account of their wrongful or oppressive conduct in relation to the bankrupt, e.g. creditors who are subordinated in the US on the grounds of culpable interference in the management of the debtor corpor-ation to the prejudice of its other creditors. This is almost an exclusively US doctrine: see BC 1978 s 510(c) and chapter 9. It has been adopted elsewhere only in special situations. For example, the concept is partially reflected in s 215(4) of the British Insolvency Act 1986 which allows the court to direct that a person who is liable for fraudulent or wrongful trading in relation to a company and who is also a creditor is to be subordinated to the payment of all other debts owed by the company plus interest. A person who controls the management of the company, e.g. an over-intrusive bank, could be a "shadow director" (see s 741 of the Companies Act 1985) and, if so, could be liable for wrongful trading and be postponed by this section.

    Certain claims for disgorgement of profits resulting from the carrying on of an unauthorised investment or deposit-taking business are subordinated by statute in Britain: see IR 1986, r 12.3(2A), as amended, and s 49 of the Banking Act 1987.

Post-insolvency interest Interest which accrues post-insolvency is almost 1–50
invariably postponed to ordinary unsecured creditors. In England it is payable out of the surplus before equity creditors: IA 1986 s 189. In practice, this means it is not paid.

No escritura publica In Spain and certain related jurisdictions, such as the Philippines, a creditor who formalises the document evidencing his debt – usually a loan – in the prescribed manner before a notary or other official and pays a documentary tax or fee, ranks ahead of other creditors who have not gone through the process. The latter are therefore junior creditors payable after those diligent enough to ceremonialise themselves.

Consensually subordinated creditors Finally in this group of deferred creditors are those who have agreed to subordinate themselves to other creditors. Consensual subordination is discussed in another book in this series of works.

Equity shareholders

In the fifth rank – ranking after super-priority, priority, pari passu and 1–51
deferred creditors – are the shareholders of a company whose claims are generally recoverable only on dissolution of the company, subject to wide exceptions. They are the cushion on which all other creditors rest and may be internally ranked as, for example, preferred, ordinary and deferred shareholders. They receive nothing on insolvency.

Expropriated creditors

The final group are not creditors at all since their claims are not eligible for 1–52
proof against the bankrupt estate: in effect they are expropriated. The main classes to be found, sometimes patchily, in the various jurisdictions are:

   (i)   Late claimants
  (ii)   Foreign revenue and penalties
 (iii)   Foreign currency creditors
 (iv)   Tort claimants

Late claimants Creditors who file their claims too late, e.g. because they are 1–53
foreign and are not given adequate notice of the insolvency or of the time limits, are deprived of a dividend if the late claim is excluded, as under the French Law of January 25, 1985 Art 53. The ineligibility of foreign creditors merely because they are foreign is now very rare and was mainly a Latin

American xenophobic doctrine analogous to the Calvo doctrine, e.g. in Argentina. Foreign creditors can prove in England: *Ex p Melbourne* (1870) LR 6 Ch App 64. Ditto in France. Foreign creditors are more likely to be effectively excluded because they do not have adequate notice of the insolvency and of the time limits for the filing of their claims. In many countries, foreign creditors have extra time to file their claims, e.g. France.

1–54   **Foreign revenue and penalties** Many jurisdictions do not permit the claims of foreign revenue authorities or foreign penal demands. In England the unenforceable foreign claims include penal claims, e.g. fines for crimes committed within the jurisdiction of a foreign state: see especially *Huntington v Attrill* [1893] AC 150; Dicey Rule 3; as to the US, see Restatement of the Conflict of Laws, Second (1971) s 89. In England, domestic penalties are not provable either: IR 1986, r 12.3(2). Penal claims include foreign judgments which include a penal demand. An award of punitive or exemplary damages may not be penal within the rule where it is payable to a private plaintiff and not to a state: see *SA Consortium General Textiles v Sun & Sand Agencies Ltd* [1978] QB 279, 309, *per* Lord Denning MR, *obiter*. But an award of treble or other multiple damages, e.g. in an anti-trust action in the United States, may be regarded as penal at common law (consider *Jones v Jones* (1889) 22 QBD 425), and usually cannot be enforced in England under the various statutory provisions for the recognition of foreign judgments in England: see Dicey Rule 35.

1–55   **Foreign currency creditors** It would appear to be a near universal rule that foreign currency debts owing by the insolvent are provable (subject to any exchange controls) and are converted into local currency on the relevant insolvency date. This is so, for example, in England (IR 1986, rr 4.91, 6.111), France, Germany, Italy, Austria, Denmark and the United States: see s 502(b) of BC 1978.

The effect therefore is that if the local currency is depreciating, the proof is reduced and the creditor expropriated. This has been a serious problem in countries with runaway inflation, e.g. 1000 per cent per year – these are countries which have often also been insolvent thereby throwing local companies with foreign currency liabilities into bankruptcy. Although there appears to be little case law, it is perhaps the case that top-up clauses covering currency losses typical of bank term credit agreements would often not be effective because they override a mandatory bankruptcy policy of equality of ordinary creditors.

1–56   **Tort claimants** In some countries, notably those basing themselves on the pre–1986 English model, tort claims, e.g. for product liability, libel, personal injury or negligence, are not provable or claimable against the bankrupt estate, unless they can alternatively be framed in contract, e.g. negligence or misrepresentation under a contract. The original justification may have been that tort claims delay the proceedings and are often extremely large or alternatively were personal to the bankrupt and hence not discharged. This rule has disappeared in England: see IR 1986, r 13.12. Tort claims are allowable in the US.

Individual and corporate bankruptcies

It is worth noting some of the most important substantive differences   1–57
between individual and corporate bankruptcies. Some of these tend to stem from greater sympathy felt for the bankrupt individual overburdened with debt than for the bankrupt corporation. More often, the divergence stems from the fact that individual insolvency law remained unchanged from the old forms, while corporate insolvencies took the centre of the stage in terms of economic importance and therefore attracted reformist legislative attention.

No bankruptcy of non-merchants

In numerous jurisdictions, mainly in the old Franco-Latin civil code group, it is not possible to subject an individual non-merchant to the bankruptcy procedure. The effect is that these non-merchants cannot seek the protection of the bankruptcy freeze on creditor harassment and subsequent discharge even if they are consumers running up much consumer credit or in arrears on home mortgages.

Exempt assets

In order to protect the individual from being thrown on to the streets with   1–58
nothing to keep him alive, insolvency laws invariably exempt some assets from seizure. For the US Federal exemptions, see BC 1978 s 522 (which is vetoed in at least 36 states and which is usually replaced by state exemptions which are often, but not always, more liberal).

For example, the family home may be safeguarded under homestead legislation to promote the stability and permanence of family life as a higher social end than payment of creditors. The bankruptcy of a spouse can ruin the whole family. There is a homestead exception under most US state laws.

In England there is a very limited family home immunity under IA 1986 s 337 which merely leads to a possible stay of a sale for up to a year. But the bankrupt's spouse may have the beneficial interest and so to that extent be entitled to the proceeds of sale.

In New Zealand the spouses may register a house under the Joint Family Homes Act 1964 in which event only rarely will the court order a sale for the benefit of creditors of either spouse and even then not all the proceeds go to creditors.

Commonly, the law may exempt pension and salaries from seizure or provide for the judicial making of limited income payment orders out of earnings in favour of the estate: see the British IA 1986 s 310. Tools of the trade are usually exempt so that the bankrupt may continue to earn his living: IA 1986 s 283.

The law may also exempt claims of the bankrupt which are personal to himself, e.g. for a libel damaging his reputation or for personal injury.

Limitations on security

1–59   Bankruptcy rules applying to individuals are often less protective of security given to creditors in order to safeguard the bankrupt from his own imprudence or impecuniosity. The classic example is the hostility of English-based jurisdictions to non-possessory chattel mortgages given by individuals and to general assignments by individuals of all future receivables owing to them, including wages. The chattel mortgage problem was circumvented in England and its related jurisdictions by the device of hire purchase.

Discharge and rehabilitation

1–60   The concept of the discharge of the bankrupt from his former debts and his consequent rehabilitation is well-rooted in bankruptcy law, though usually subject to time periods and exceptions in the case of fraud or misfeasance. The aim of rehabilitation has only latterly been espoused by corporate insolvency policies.

Community of matrimonial property

1–61   The concept of the community of matrimonial property of course finds no counterpart in corporate bankruptcies. Under a community system, spouses are deemed to share matrimonial property from the date of the marriage, subject to opting out. This system is practised in most European countries and their associated jurisdictions. Community prevails in at least nine US states: Arizona, California, Idaho, Louisiana, Nevada, New Mexico, Texas, Washington and Wisconsin. For details, see 1 Collier Bankruptcy Manual s 541 and BC 1978 s 541.

The liability of one spouse for the other's debts and the availability of the community property for the creditors of a bankrupt spouse varies from jurisdiction to jurisdiction. Subject to wide exceptions, community property usually belongs to the bankrupt estate of the manager of the community, usually the husband. There is no community in England, but often the wife is deemed to have a 50 per cent interest in the matrimonial home by virtue of her contributions to the household.

Classes of corporation

A brief word may be said regarding the differing treatments accorded to the type of corporation concerned. In advanced jurisdictions, a special regime may apply to financial institutions, insurance companies and other institutions where the maintenance of public confidence and the protection of the public is of crucial national importance.   1–62

For example, bank bankruptcies are covered by separate legal regimes in the United States, the Netherlands and Austria, amongst others.

In England, special rules apply to the insolvency of insurance companies, especially life insurance companies.

Apart from those cases, it is almost everywhere true that public corporations and municipalities either enjoy special immunities or are subject to official management arrangements in the event of insolvency.

Causes of bankruptcy

Bankruptcy is caused by misfortune or mismanagement or a combination of both.   1–63

Mismanagement includes poor product, over-borrowing, too many employees, inadequate financial controls, unpreparedness for business cycles, uncommitted short-term borrowings vulnerable to business downturns instead of long-term committed finance, and Byzantine corporate structures.

Misfortune outside the control of the bankrupt company can be an important contributing factor, e.g. increased interest rates, currency depreciations, unforeseeable economic slumps, natural disasters and the like.

Some bankruptcies are caused by fraud of the management or senior officials in the form of embezzlement or looting the company or financial non-disclosure or overstatement or invention of non-existent assets.

Others are caused by a one-off event, such as the failure of a major debtor or a fire which is inadequately insured against.

CHAPTER 2

BANKRUPT'S PROPERTY: FALSE WEALTH AND TRUSTS

Introduction

This chapter and the next are mainly concerned with a category of super- 2–1
priority creditor who can take assets out of the insolvent estate before anybody else other than the other super-priority creditors. Often, the creditors
are not strictly creditors – they are the third party owners of property which
is held by the bankrupt.

Main criteria of jurisdictional attitudes

If the legal system allows a wide class of third party owners to claim their
property held by the bankrupt ahead of other creditors, then the jurisdiction
is broadly pro-creditor: it helps claimants to achieve a super-priority ahead
of other creditors. If on the other hand, the legal system limits the class of
third party owners, it is broadly pro-debtor: it seeks to aggrandise the
debtor's estate for the benefit of its unsecured creditors and ultimately for
the benefit of the debtor himself.

Apart from exempt property for individuals (such as the homestead
exemption), the following are among the main criteria in this regard:

1. **Trust** Whether the law recognises the trust or whether it insists that the
    apparent, titular, legal or nominal owner is to be deemed the real
    owner so that the asset reputedly owned by him goes to his creditors.

2. **Unjust enrichment** Whether the law divests the debtor's estate of assets,
    of which the real owner has been mistakenly or wrongfully deprived,
    on the grounds of unjust enrichment, or whether the state insists that
    the apparent owner of these assets transferred to him by mistake or
    delinquently taken by him is deemed the real owner so that the mis-
    taken or deprived owner loses his asset to the creditors of the recipient.

3. **Assignments** Whether an assignment of a debt must be notified to the
    debtor to be effective on the assignor's insolvency.

4. **Contract and lease rescission** Whether a party is entitled to rescind or cancel a contract or lease with the insolvent on the grounds of his insolvency alone.

5. **Deprivation on insolvency** The strength of the rules preventing the divestment of the bankrupt's property on his bankruptcy by cancellation or forfeiture clauses or the like.

Trusts and false wealth

2–2   The most fundamental division between jurisdictions in this context is between those which insist that the apparent owner is the real beneficial owner, on the one hand, and, on the other, those which accept that the apparent owner may hold the asset for the benefit of another – the beneficial owner. Legal systems which accept a different beneficial ownership from the apparent ownership adopt the concept of the trust – the trustee is the legal, titular or nominal owner but he holds the property for a third party, who is the beneficial or equitable owner.

The acceptance or otherwise of the trust is one of the few remaining points which divide jurisdictions more or less uniformly into the civil code/common law groups with only a few exceptions. In many other areas this classification is much less useful than it used to be. For example, civil code countries such as the Netherlands and Germany which share many English attitudes about who to protect on insolvency remain relatively hostile to the trust and to the tracing of money. They each have exceptions, but they are only exceptions.

The key difference lies in the impact of the insolvency of the apparent owner, trustee or titular holder. If the jurisdiction does not recognise the possibility of the apparent ownership not being the real ownership, then, when the apparent owner becomes insolvent, the entire asset – which he is holding for the benefit of the real owner – goes to pay his creditors. The true owner is expropriated. If the trust is accepted, then the property does not belong to the trustee's estate and the beneficial owner can claim the asset as a super-priority claimant. The concept espoused in continental Europe from at least the time of Napoleon was that anybody who wanted a real right or rights in rem enforceable against everybody, including creditors, must not acquire it privately or secretly, but the right must be patent and published to the world.

The main reasons for the rejection of the trust may now be reviewed.

2–3   **False wealth** The principle root of this extraordinary doctrine that one person's property should be taken to pay another's debts lies in the deep objection in non-trust countries to false wealth or false credit based upon apparent riches, apparent possession, apparent assets: the principle that creditors might be misled into giving credit to the debtor on the basis of his ostensible wealth when in fact his assets belong to a secret third party who takes all on the debtor's insolvency. The hostility is so powerful that it survives even in individual bankruptcies in English-based countries in the form of "reputed ownership" bankruptcy provisions. These never applied to corporate bankruptcies, only to individual bankruptcies, were reduced by case law almost to vanishing point by 1820 and were finally abolished in England in 1986.

Priorities The second objection in non-trust countries is that the presence of   2–4
secret hidden ownership rights might destabilise transactions, especially commercial transactions, and give rise to unpredictable priority disputes: how could a buyer or mortgagee be sure of getting good title or a safe mortgage if some third party might come out from behind the arras and claim the property as his and upset the sale or mortgage?

The common law answer to this is to protect purchasers, mortgagees and the like from the hidden owner if they gave value, acted in good faith and had no notice of the true owner. But because notice might be extended to facts which would have come to light if the purchaser made diligent enquiries or if he had followed up suspicious circumstances, commercial transactions in common law countries are more vulnerable to priority disputes. Hence the protection of true owners from the insolvency of the possessor has thrown up greater complexity as regards priority. The solution is to support the trust on insolvency but to subordinate the interests of the secret owner as against purchasers and mortgagees by ensuring that the latter are not prejudiced by a secret interest if they are not actually aware of it, for which purpose businesssmen are not required to act as amateur detectives: this in fact is the solution which the English courts, at least, have been striving towards. But in the end a choice has to be made between protecting owners and protecting commerce by predictable priorities.

The "false wealth" proposition is considered by the common law countries to be a weak basis for taking one man's property to pay another's debt – in effect expropriating him. A large slice of the assets of the modern corporation is in the form of invisible property – claims, receivables, debts which creditors cannot see in any event so that one cannot say that they are deceived by false appearances. Creditors of companies rely on the fact that, on the whole, companies do own their assets and, if they do not, that their financial statements exclude property held in trust. The fraud risk is regarded in these countries as insufficient to overpower the unconscionability of expropriation.

On the other hand, the common law countries have enthusiastically embraced the false wealth doctrine in their attitude to publicising security interests by registration in a public bureau, e.g. Art 9 of the UCC, the equivalents in some Canadian provinces, and the English-based registration of corporate charges.

2–5   **Other factors** There may be other reasons for the rejection of the trust in many of the civil code countries. One surmises that among the most important of these reasons were the demands of the taxman who insisted on taxing the user and possessor of assets and who might be confused and perhaps thwarted by the presence of the secret owner. Another reason – probably crucial in the eyes of creditors – may have been the fear of fraud and fraudulent preferences, and yet another (a weak one) a desire to prevent property being tied up by trusts and inalienable forever.

Napoleonic and Germanic view

2–6   It is clear that the classical Romans had developed a principle whereby one person could hold property for the benefit of another and it is also clear that this system was accepted in pre-Napoleonic times in Europe.

But the idea of divided ownership was rejected by the Napoleonic code. Apart from false wealth, the reasons for the adoption of the unitary theory of ownership apparently also included a desire to simplify the law, to define ownership as the absolute right to the enjoyment and disposition of a thing, to rid property of the feudal burdens of the ancient regime, to facilitate capitalism, to exalt the individual's power over things and to satisfy the emotional desire to have and to hold – a melange of well-meaning aspirations. But whatever the real reason, the espousal of this doctrine in the Napoleonic code had enormous influence elsewhere by virtue of the international success of the code.

When the German BGB was drafted, the same solution was adopted, notwithstanding a leading lawyer's lament that it was "a horrible legal blunder – a scientifically unmotivated notion". Nevertheless, the systematic view was this: (1) rights in rem which were good against creditors had to be publicly registered, (2) the code set out the available rights in rem; *ergo* (3) only publicly registered rights could be asserted in rem and the number of *in rem* rights was closed.

Notwithstanding this somewhat dogmatic view, there are numerous examples of equivalents of the trust in German law, and indeed in the Franco-Latin systems. Apart from old family examples, such as the administration of the matrimonial community property by the husband, the usufruct of a parent or guardian of a child's property and inheritances, other instances are the *Kommissionär* in German law and the co-ownership of a fungible mass of securities held by a bank custodian and created by the

Custody Act 1937 (*Depotgesetz*), originating in 1846 legislation (echoed in the Austrian *Depotgesetz* 1969), the claim which a principal has for unpaid sale proceeds on a sale of the principal's property by a commission agent who has become bankrupt under HGB s 392 (for the equivalent in other countries, see para 1–32) and the *Treuhand* introduced by the occupation authorities in the late 1940s to administer the property of those who could not do so themselves.

In Franco-Latin systems, there are fewer examples of divided ownership,   2–7 except those created specifically by statute, such as the co-ownership of fungible securities held by central depositories, as in Belgium, Luxembourg, France itself, and Portugal. This co-ownership of fungible securities also appears in the Netherlands and Denmark. Similarly, statutes in Latin American countries and elsewhere have constituted banks or stock exchange companies as trustees of securities deposited with them for safe custody, as in Argentina, Brazil, Mexico, the Philippines, Portugal.

But all of those are special positive carve-outs from the general prohibition on divided ownership and together do not significantly change the overall view.

The trust affects an extraordinarily wide range of daily transactions and it is worth citing some of them to give an idea of the impact of the rule.

Examples of apparent owner being treated as absolute owner

In the pure non-trust countries in the classical mould, the person named in   2–8 the land register is deemed to be the owner. The possessor of goods in a warehouse or held under custodianship is the real owner, unless the goods are segregated and marked as belonging to another. The registered holder of registered securities is deemed the owner even though he is a custodian, clearing-house or nominee. The possessor of bearer negotiable instruments is the owner unless they are segregated and marked in the same way as goods belonging to another. The owner of a claim who has assigned it is deemed to remain the owner until the debtor has been notified so as to take it out of the assignor's apparent ownership. Money in a bank account in the name of the apparent owner is his on bankruptcy: if this result is to be avoided, the client must be named as the account-holder at the bank. The moneys may, for example, be the proceeds of sale received by an agent or the proceeds of a collection or money received by mistake or delinquency.

In all these cases, if the apparent owner becomes bankrupt and if the prescribed steps to take the asset out of his reputed ownership have not been taken, the property goes to his creditors and the real owner is left with a mere debt claim in bankruptcy on which he will commonly receive only a paltry dividend, if anything.

In the trust countries, a warehouse keeper or other bailee of goods can hold them on trust and the trust is recognised on insolvency without the necessity for segregation or marking. The custodian of securities can hold them as nominee without the necessity for registration in the name of the beneficial or real owner. The assignment of a debt is effective in the assignor's bankruptcy on the agreement to assign, even though the debtor has not been notified of the transfer. If an agent or fiduciary, such as a selling agent or an estate agent or a securities broker or a lawyer, holds money owing to a client on trust in the agent's bank account, the money belongs to the client, even though the client is not named as the holder of the account at the bank. In none of these cases can the asset be consumed by the creditors of the apparent owner.

There has been some erosion, by statute and by case law in civilian countries, of the false wealth principle, initially in relation to custodianship of goods and more recently in relation to investment securities held by custodians or clearing-houses.

Deposits for safe-keeping: custodians

2–9 If the owner of property deposits them with a custodian for safe-keeping and the custodian becomes bankrupt, then in the common law jurisdictions the property does not fall into the debtor's estate even if it is not marked or identified as belonging to the real owner.

The point is of particular importance in relation to investment securities. It is the practice for pension funds, investment trusts, insurance companies and others to deposit their securities held for beneficiaries or for their own account with custodians. Often securities of a particular issuer may be deposited with a custodian in the country of the issuer so that the custodian can conveniently collect payments on the securities.

The custodian may hold their securities in the name of a nominee company and they may be registered in the books of the issuer in the name of the nominee or the custodian – not the ultimate owner. They may be held on a fungible basis. If the custodian becomes insolvent, then in common law jurisdictions the securities are held in trust and do not belong to the custodian's estate even though, so far as the outside world is concerned, the custodian is the apparent owner. But in many civil code jurisdictions, the securities are deemed to belong to the custodian and hence go to the custodian's creditors. In order to avoid this result, bearer securities must be bundled together and marked with the true owner's name and registered securities must be registered in the books of the issuer in the name of the true owner (not the custodian) or, sometimes, registered in the name of the custodian with an indication that they belong to third parties – many registration systems do not permit notice of the owners to appear on the register, mainly to avoid confusion as to who to pay.

Unjust enrichment generally

In the case of cash in particular, the trust countries have gone a step further 2–10 and been prepared to extend the trust idea in order to prevent unjust enrichment. Typical examples are: special purpose payments; expropriated money; mistaken payments; and accidental commingling.

In the trust countries, the law compels the debtor's estate to hand back the money which the recipient could not use as his own because it was to be used for a special purpose (e.g. to pay the recipient's creditors), or the secret profits or other delinquent proceeds which the wrongdoer should never have had in the first place, or the mistaken payment which would otherwise be a windfall to the payee and his creditors. To give effect to this claim, the trust countries allow the complicated remedy of tracing the asset through its various permutations. But in non-trust countries, the law insists that if the money is not reserved or identified as being the real owner's, it is lost, and the real owner is left with a non-proprietary unsecured claim which is commonly worthless. The result is that the creditors of the debtor receive a windfall and are enriched at the expense of the hapless real owner. Note that the real test of whether a jurisdiction is serious about unjust enrichment is whether the real owner can get its money back on the insolvency of the holder: a rule which entitles it to get it back only if the holder is solvent is futile because the recipient is commonly insolvent.

Special purpose payments

A trust may be fixed on money paid to a recipient for a special purpose 2–11 which is not satisfied, e.g. payments to a fiscal agent to pay bondholders (consider *Henderson v Rothschilds* (1886) 33 Ch D 459), payments of a loan to a borrower for a special purpose and payments of cash to a bank issuing a letter of credit. The category also includes advance payment deposits (for consumer goods or holidays), caution money to landlords and margin deposits in organised markets. In each case the test is whether the recipient was entitled to use the money as his own. If not, there is a trust. If he is entitled to use the money as his own, he becomes a mere debtor to the payer, and the proprietary trust claim is lost.

Case law examples are: 2–12

In *Gibert v Gonard* [1884] 54 Ch D 439, a lender lent £4,000 to a borrower on terms that the loan was to be applied by the borrower in purchasing a property

---

which the borrower was then to mortgage to the lender. The borrower paid the money into his own account, spent some on himself and then became bankrupt. *Held*: the lender had a super-priority claim for what was left in the bank account.

In *Re Australian House Finance Pty Ltd* [1956] VLR 1 (Victoria S Ct), participants paid instalments to a company on terms that, once the instalments had reached a certain amount, the money would be used to finance a house for the payer. The company went into insolvent liquidation. *Held*: the benefit of its bank account into which the instalments had been paid was held in trust for the payers. It was clear that the company was not to use the money as its own since it was earmarked for a purpose.

In *Carreras Rothmans Ltd v Freeman Mathews Treasury Ltd* [1985] 1 All ER 155, a company which was an advertising agency was in financial difficulties. The employer of the company considered that some of the company's creditors with whom the employer's advertisements had been placed would put commercial pressure upon the employer to pay their debts. The employer accordingly paid money into a separate bank account at the company's bank on terms that the money was to be used only to pay those creditors. The company went into liquidation. *Held*: the arrangement created a trust of the benefit of the bank account in favour of those creditors.

In *Barclays Bank Ltd v Quistclose Investments Ltd* [1970] AC 597, HL; [1968] 3 All ER 651, a lender lent money to a company in financial difficulties for the specific purpose of enabling the company to pay a dividend which it had declared. The company paid the money into a separate account at its bank. Before the dividend was paid the company went into liquidation. *Held*: the terms on which the loan was made were such as to impress on the money a trust in favour of the lender in the event of the condition not being met or the dividend not being paid. The benefit of the bank account belonged to the lender.

In *Re Kayford* [1975] 1 All ER 604, a mail order company in financial difficulties credited all advance payments received from customers for goods to a separate bank account on trust for the customers, so that if the company failed the customers should be refunded their money. *Held*: a trust was validly created even though the instructions to the bank were oral and even though the account was not headed a trust account.

In *Re Nanwa Goldmines Ltd* [1955] 3 All ER 219, a prospectus stated that subscribers money for new shares would be placed in a special account pending passing of the resolutions approving the issue. The issue did not proceed. *Held*: the establishment of a separate account gave the subscribers a property right to a refund and they were not simply creditors of the company. The reason was that the inference to be drawn from the separate account was that the company could not use the moneys as its own. Contrast *Re HB Hain & Associates Inc* [1978] DLR (2d) 262.

In *Re Chelsea Cloisters Ltd* (1980) 41 P&Cr 98, CA an insolvency accountant was supervising the affairs of a company in financial difficulties. Tenants had paid deposits to the landlord company (who were strictly managing agents) to cover the cost of repairs and replacements for which the tenants were responsible. Although previously the landlord had used the deposits as its own, the insolvency accountant decided to place them in a separate account although this was unknown to the tenants. The landlord went into liquidation. *Held*: the segregation indicated that the money was trust property not available to the general creditors of the landlord company.

But the creditor receiving the advance payment or deposit may simply be indebted to the debtor in which event the debtor has a mere debt claim against the creditor if the money is not segregated.

In *Moseley v Cressey's Co* (1865) LR 1 Eq 405, the prospectus stated that deposits would be returned to subscribers if no shares were allotted, but there was no segregation of the deposits. *Held*: since nothing was said in the prospectus as to the depositors having a lien on the deposits or as to the setting apart of the deposits as a trust fund in the name of trustees, no trust was created and the subscribers were merely creditors of the company.

Section 86(6) of the Companies Act 1985 requires a separate account for subscribers money and it is clear that this account would be held in trust.

Wrongful takings of money

Another category of unjust enrichment comprises claims against fiduciaries   2–13
and others who abuse beneficiaries by obtaining improper benefits from the beneficiary's property, such as secret profits by delinquent directors. The property claim may extend to those who receive property from the delinquent, such as banks receiving a company's money paid by a director into his private bank account. The classical English label used for this type of property claim is that of the constructive trust.

But in many civil code states, the deprived owner loses his property if the taker has become bankrupt and the money falls into the estate of the bankrupt available to his creditors. This seems a somewhat illogical extension of the false wealth doctrine, since a delinquent bankrupt will naturally have done his best to keep the proceeds of his wrongdoing secret.

For example, in England where a mortgagee wrongfully disposes of mortgaged securities the mortgagor has a super-priority property claim for their value even though the mortgagee no longer has the securities.

In *Ellis & Co's Trustees v Dixon-Johnson* [1924] 1 Ch 342, affd [1924] 2 Ch 451, affd [1925] AC 489, HL, a client deposited shares with brokers as security and the brokers wrongfully sold the shares. The brokers became bankrupt. *Held*: the brokers or their trustee in bankruptcy were bound to hand over either the securities themselves or their money equivalent as a super-priority proprietary claim ranking ahead of unsecured creditors.

Austria has created a similar priority claim by statute in special cases, but this is unusual in civilian countries; see the Custody Act (*Depotgesetz*) 1969 s 23.

Mistaken payments and accidental commingling

2–14   A third group comprises moneys paid by mistake of fact or of law which unjustly enrich the insolvent's estate. If the recipient becomes insolvent, his creditors would receive a windfall unless the payer can recover his property as a super-priority creditor.

> In *Chase Manhattan Bank v Israel-British Bank (London) Ltd* [1979] 3 All ER 1025, Chase mistakenly paid Israel-British twice. Israel-British knew of the error and went into insolvent liquidation. *Held*: Chase was entitled to a proprietary remedy for the return of the money. In this case there was no initial fiduciary relationship which is usually necessary to give rise to a constructive trust: the money was returnable in order to prevent unjust enrichment.

The category also includes accidental commingled assets which are fungibles, such as oil in a ship's hold or bags of coffee or wheat. Each owner has a super-priority property claim, not a debt claim, for his share or its traceable product.

> In *Gill & Duffus (Liverpool) Ltd v Scruttons Ltd* [1953] 2 All ER 977, a ship carried a large quantity of chestnuts in separate bags which were consigned to each of three buyers and which were separately marked so as to be identifiable. On opening the hatches, it was discovered that some of the bags had burst and the chestnuts had become commingled. *Held*: the mingled chestnuts belonged to the three buyers pro rata.

Conversely, where one owner deliberately mixes his property with another's without the consent of the other, under English law the other does not lose his property. Indeed, the entire property may belong to the wronged owner as a punitive remedy to deter fraud, except to the extent the wrongdoer can identify his own property.

> In *Indian Oil Corp Ltd v Greenstone Shipping Co SA* [1987] 3 All ER 893, a shipowner mixed a cargo-owner's oil with the shipowner's own oil in the ship's tank. *Held*: where H wrongfully mixes goods of O with goods belonging to H of a similar nature and quality so that they cannot be separated, the mixture is held in common and O is entitled to delivery of a quantity equivalent to his original contribution. Any doubt as to quantity must be resolved in favour of O. O can also claim damages from H for any loss he might have suffered, in respect of quality or otherwise, by reason of the mixture. The court did not vest all the goods in O since it was not the function of civil justice to punish or discourage crime by awarding the victim more than he had lost. But, if it was

totally unknown how much of the innocent party's goods went into the mixture and the mixing party had acted wrongfully, the whole would belong to the innocent party.

Tests of whether asset is held in trust

In common law countries, where an owner of money, securities, goods or other property lawfully pays or delivers the property to a holder, the main test of whether the recipient holds the money or other property as trustee or bailee is whether the recipient is on the facts entitled to use the property or its proceeds permanently as his own. If he is, the owner ceases to be the owner and does not have a property claim for the money or other property and ceases to be a super-priority creditor.   2–15

The principle of ownership is that the owner may use the property permanently as his own. Thus a bank to whom notes or coins are paid may use the legal tender as its own and becomes a debtor to the depositor, not a bailee or custodian of the notes or coins. There is much international case law establishing this elementary proposition, e.g. England: *Joachimson v Swiss Bank Company* [1921] 3 KB 110 at 126–7; Ontario: *Royal Trust Co v Molson's Bank* [1912] 27 OLR 441; Philippines: *Gullas v The Philippine National Bank*, 62 Phil 519 (1935).

Express trusts of money Where an owner of money lawfully pays the money to a recipient on express trust, clearly the recipient may not use the money as his own and, if the recipient becomes bankrupt, the beneficiary has a property claim for the money or its traceable product. He is a super-priority creditor, provided he can trace his money. The trust may be imposed by statute or rule. There are now many cases where the legislature has intervened to protect clients of agents against the loss of their money on the agent's insolvency. Examples in England are solicitors client accounts, deposits received by estate agents (see the Estate Agents Act 1979 whereby money received in the course of estate agency work by way of pre-contract or contract deposit is held on trust and must be paid into client account: ss 12, 13 and 14), clients' money received by investment dealers under rules made pursuant to the Financial Services Act 1986, and subscriptions received for the issue of securities: see s 86(6) of the Companies Act 1985. A more abstruse example is where a company director receives unauthorised compensation in connection with a transfer of its business or on a take-over contrary to ss 313 and 314 of the Companies Act 1985: the compensation is held on express statutory trust for the company, or, in case of s 314, in trust for selling shareholders.   2–16

2–17   **Presumptions if no express trust of money** Where there is no express trust of money, the position of the third party is more imponderable and unpredictable. English and US law has recourse to various presumptions, notably the "interest test", and the "segregation test", to ascertain whether the recipient was entitled to use the money as his own and hence constitute the third party as a mere creditor.

2–18   **Interest test** An agreement to pay interest on money received is usually evidence that the relationship is debtor-creditor because it connotes that the holder may use the money as his own. In *Re Broad, ex p Neck* (1884) 13 QBD 740, Cotton LJ said at 746: "If a man pays interest for money he must be entitled to the use of it".

On the other hand if the recipient agreed to invest the money and pay so much interest as is actually earned, there should generally be a property claim and not a debt claim. There should be a debt claim if the agreement was to pay fixed interest. But even here it is possible that the payee agreed that the investment will yield a minimum return in which event a property claim should not be excluded. The recipient may make an advance to the payee against money or property received on which interest is paid: the money received or its product may still be held on trust if that is the agreement. This point has notably arisen in cases where a customer has deposited instruments for collection with his bank and the bank has credited the customer with the amount of the instruments prior to collection of the proceeds by the bank.

2–19   **Segregation test** Another test – and probably the most important test in England – is whether it was agreed that the money would be segregated in a separate account because this is presumptively an indication that the recipient may not use the money as his own. If he was not obliged to segregate, then this is an indication that the money is not held in trust. There is much English case law involving trading agents, stockbrokers, lawyers, advance deposits for goods by consumers, sub-sale proceeds under retention of title clauses, shipping agents, fiscal agents and collecting banks.

> See, e.g. *Wilsons & Furness-Layland Line Ltd v British & Continental Shipping Co* (1907) 23 TLR 397 (agency account not to be kept separate, no trust); *Re Nanwa Gold Mines Ltd* [1955] 3 All ER 219 (proposals stated that subscription for shares would be placed in separate account, trust of subscription on company's insolvency); *Re Kayford* [1975] 1 All ER 604 (separate account for advance payments of customer deposits for goods: trust of advances on payee's insolvency); *Hancock v Smith* (1889) 41 Ch D 456 (separate stockbrokers accounts for client's money: trust of moneys); *Neste Oy v Lloyds Bank PLC* (1983) 2 Lloyds Rep 658 (no separate agency account: no trust of principal's money on agent's insolvency); *Henry v Hammond* [1913] 2 KB 515; *Lyell v Kennedy* (1889) 14 AC 437.

Fungibility

Many assets are fungible in the sense that they enjoy the same qualities, e.g. grain, securities of the same issue, gold bullion and money. In many (but not all) civilian countries, it is not possible to transfer ownership of a fungible without identifying the actual asset, but in common law countries it is possible to create a trust of fungibles. The true owner loses ownership only if the recipient is entitled to use the fungible property as his own.

2–20

The question has often arisen in practice of whether an owner of non-money fungibles who delivers them to a custodian for storage or safekeeping on the basis that the custodian may return equivalent property leaves the owner with a mere debt claim on the custodian's insolvency. The problem is that on storage the fungibles may become indistinguishable from those of others. The general test is the same, i.e. whether the custodian or other bailee can use the deposited property permanently as his own.

Thus where the owner delivers fungibles or near-fungibles, such as negotiable bonds to a clearing house, wheat to a warehouse keeper, gold bullion to a bullion dealer, oil to a warehouse tanker, on terms that the recipient can redeliver equivalent assets, the essential requirement for loss of property is that the recipient can permanently use the original property and its proceeds as his own, in the same way that a bank may use deposited money as its own.

2–21

> In *South Australian Insurance Co v Randell* (1869) LR 3 PC 101, farmers deposited corn with a miller who mixed it with a common bulk and held the whole stock on the terms that a farmer could claim at any time a quantity of grain of the same quality equal to that which he had delivered, or in lieu thereof the market price of an equivalent quantity and quality ruling on the day on which he made his demand. *Held*: the miller was the owner of the corn. As there had been no obligation to preserve the identity of each consignment of corn delivered and to return it intact upon demand and as the miller could use the corn as his own (e.g. by milling it and selling it), the transaction was a transfer of property for value, and not a bailment. The farmer did not have the right to an equal quantity of wheat, but only money.

This decision has been followed in many cases concerning the bulk handling of commodities for the purposes of storage, processing or marketing.

> See, e.g. *Re Inglis* [1932] 5 ABC 255 (South Australia); *Lawlor v Nicol* [1898] 12 Man LR 224 (Manitoba); *Chapman Bros v Verco Bros & Co Ltd* [1933] 49 CLR 306 (Australia); *Farnsworth v Federal Commissioner of Taxation* [1949] 78 CLR 504 (Australia). The position is now regulated by statute in many jurisdictions (see, e.g. UCC Art 7–207(2); Canadian Grain Act (1977), Bulk Handling Act 1967–76 (Western Australia); Bulk Handling of Grain Act 1955–77 (South Australia).

But the mere fact that the recipient can return an equivalent item does not necessarily confer on the recipient the property in the original item: he must be able to use the original item permanently as his own.

Custodianship of securities

2–22   The variety of possible types of ownership under English law and other common law jurisdictions is demonstrated by the position with regard to the deposit of securities with clearing-houses or custodians – such as bearer bonds, certificates of deposits, government bonds, commercial paper or share certificates. The impact of the deposit on the beneficial ownership varies and has corresponding implications in relation to the question of whether the depositor has a debt or a property claim against the clearing house. Thus:

(a) The clearing house may become beneficial owner of the securities. This will be the case if the clearing house has a right to deal with the securities permanently as its own. The clearing house agrees to deliver equivalent securities or cash to the depositor or to his order. It would normally be inappropriate for a clearing house to be beneficial owner, unless local law does not recognise the trusts described below (even though they are bare trusts) but in such a case the depositor has a mere debt claim against the clearing house for damages for non-delivery and takes a credit risk on the clearing-house. The clearing house is similar to a bank and should record those debt obligations on its balance-sheet.

(b) The clearing house may hold the specific deposited securities, identified by number, as trustee or bailee for the depositor on terms that the clearing house must return the specific securities, not equivalent securities. The clearing house is a pure custodian and has no beneficial ownership and the depositor has a super-priority property claim against the clearing house for those specific securities. This arrangement is inconvenient in that it prevents the fungibility described below.

(c) The clearing house may be trustee or bailee of other securities of the same class and, by the clearing house regulations binding on all members, is authorised by each depositing member to transfer to the depositor a proportionate interest in all the securities of that class. If the depositor has an interest as beneficiary under a trust of those securities as a pool without having a specific interest in each specific security, the arrangement is similar to a unit trust. The clearing-house is not owner of the securities but holds the whole bulk or pool as the property of the depositors. The securities are fungible and the clearing-house can return equivalent securities. The depositors have a super-priority claim against the clearing-house.

(d) The depositor may be granted a proportionate beneficial interest in *each* security of that class. Hence if the depositor deposits 500 bearer bonds and the clearing house holds 5000 securities of that class, the clearing house is authorised to grant to the depositor, in exchange for his 500 securities, a 10 per cent interest in *each* of the 5000 securities as tenant in common with the other depositors of those securities. This procedure therefore achieves a limited fungibility. The depositor has a super-priority property claim against the clearing house.

Austria, Germany and the Netherlands are among the countries which by statute have created similar specific deposits and collective co-ownership of fungible securities in special (and limited) cases – the German *Sonderverwahrung* and *Sammelverwahrung*, as compared to irregular deposit where property in the securities passes to the custodian. There are similar systems in Belgium and the Netherlands, especially for the securities custodians Euroclear and Cedel.   2–23

Similar principles apply in England to commodities – whether precious metals or primary commodities, such as produce (wheat, sugar, cocoa) or non-precious metals, such as copper, zinc, aluminium or tin. The metals are commonly physically held by a custodian. The custodian may, in accordance with the above principles, (a) be beneficial owner of the metals and be a debtor to depositors, (b) hold specific segregated lots for each depositor, in which event the custodian is bailee of the depositor who has a property claim for these specific lots, or (c) hold all the metals of the same quality in trust for all depositors depositing metal of that quality as tenants in common, in which event each depositor has a property claim against the custodian as beneficiary under a trust.

Trust of part of fungibles An owner may declare a trust of part of a fungible mass without defining which part.   2–24

> In *Hunter v Moss* [1994] 1 WLR 452, CA, Moss had 950 shares in a company. He declared a trust of 50 of them in favour of Hunter, without specifying which 50. *Held*: Moss had effectively transferred 50 shares.

The position would have been different if the shareholder had not declared a trust, but had merely purported to sell 50 shares out of his 950, without appropriating them: *Re London Wine Co (Shippers) Ltd* [1986] PCC 121 (wine in cellar – no appropriation); *Re Wait* [1927] 1 Ch 606 (grain on ship – no appropriation). Hence the trust is used in English law to whittle down the old doctrine of specificity to vanishing point.

As mentioned, co-ownership of fungible securities held by a central depository has been created by statute in a number of countries which otherwise do not permit the trust (because of the false wealth doctrine) or ownership of part of a mass of fungibles (because of the false wealth doctrine). Examples are Austria, Belgium, Germany, Luxembourg and the Netherlands. The rule applies only to the securities and to the central depositories concerned and so is purely an exception to the usual principle, motivated by necessity and convenience.

There is a detailed review of fungibility and custodianship of securities generally in another volume (on international security) in this series of works on financial law.

2–25 **Loans of fungibles** The principle also applies to loans of fungibles. Where the owner of fungibles lends the fungible to a borrower to be returned at the end of the loan period, the question is whether the owner has a property claim or a debt claim. Loans of fungible securities, such as stocklending to cover short positions, are routine by dealers in organised securities markets. The test is whether the "borrower" must return the specific securities or can use them permanently as his own and return other equivalent securities: in the latter case, the "lender" has a mere debt claim for damages for non-delivery. Whether or not this is strictly characterised as a loan or as a sale and repurchase transaction is immaterial to this question. The same tests should equally apply to loans of other fungibles, such as gold or oil.

2–26 **Property claim converted into damages claim** In certain circumstances the English courts may order a bailee of goods to return the value of the goods which he has interfered with wrongfully instead of delivering the specific goods themselves: s 3 of the Tort (Interference with Goods) Act 1977. This will often be the case where the goods are commercial and have no idiosyncratic or unique value. But where the court orders the payment of the value of the article, the owner's claim to his property is ordinarily not converted into a debt claim: he does not lose his right of ownership to his property and hence his super-priority claim until the value is actually paid. This is so even if he sues for the value of the property – he only loses his property claim if he actually proves as an unsecured claimant in the bankruptcy of the bailee. If the position were otherwise, the owner's property claim would be converted into an unsecured debt claim in the bailee's insolvency. If the bailee had granted a floating charge to a third party, the owner's money claim would rank as an unsecured claim subject to the floating charge.

Tracing of trust property

2–27 Where property or money is commingled or exchanged so that it is not possible to identify it any longer *in specie*, common law jurisdictions are very astute in maintaining the property right of the original owner and identifying the money or its traceable product and have developed a number of methods of locating the asset on which the property claim can fix so as to preserve the super-priority claim of the true owner if the holder should become insolvent. These methods include mainly (a) tracing, (b) appropriation, (c) charging property, (d) imposition of a tenancy in common, and finally (e) a straight order for a super-priority payment on insolvency. As a general rule, the civil code countries do not recognise any of these remedies and regard the money as gone unless it is actually identified and segregated as belonging to another, subject to a (usually futile) unsecured claim for a dividend out of the insolvent estate.

Tracing essentially involves the following of money through its various permutations and is a process of tracking the genealogical descent of the money into its ultimate product. Thus if a trustee or other person holding the money of another pays trust money into his bank account, the proportionate benefit of the bank account is the trust property. If he uses the trust money to buy shares, the trust property is the shares. If he sells the shares and pays the money into his bank account, the bank account again becomes the trust property. If he buys a car out of the bank account, the car is the trust property.

An example is the following:

> In *Banque Belge pour L'Etrange v Hambrouck* [1921] 1 KB 321, a clerk fraudulently obtained cheques of his employer drawn in favour of himself and paid them into his bank, i.e. his bank collected the proceeds from the employers' bank. The clerk drew out the money by cheque and paid it to his mistress, Mademoiselle Spanoghe. She paid the cheque into her own bank account. *Held*: the employers' bank could trace the proceeds of the money into the mistress' bank account. Although money has no earmark, it was immaterial that strictly the actual bank notes could not be pointed to and the money had lost its identity since it was possible to ascertain the descent of the money into its product. The mistress could not keep the money because she gave no consideration or alternatively the consideration was immoral and therefore illegal.

Tracing is not available against a bona fide purchaser for value without   2–28
notice, e.g. where the trustee pays the money into his bank account which is overdrawn and the bank has no notice of the true ownership of the money and gives value. The degree of value can be quite slight such as forbearing to call in a loan: *Thomson v Clydesdale Bank Ltd.* [1893] AC 282, HL.

Tracing ends when the ultimate product is consumed so as to disappear completely as where the car is destroyed or where the bank money is spent on a dinner. There is no identifiable asset which can be followed: see *Re Diplock* [1948] Ch 465.

2–29   **Appropriation** The second method of identification of money employed by common law states is by appropriation or imputation so as to preserve the owner's property. The classic example is the mixing of trust moneys in the trustee's private bank account. The trustee (e.g. a selling agent, or estate agent, or broker or other person holding client's money on trust) is deemed to draw out his own moneys first so as to preserve the trust moneys: *Re Hallett's Estate* (1880) 13 Ch D 696. The trust property is the appropriate proportion of the credit balance held by the trustee. Thus if the trustee pays 20 of trust moneys into his bank account containing 80 of his own money and then draws out 80, the credit balance of the remaining 20 is the trust property undisturbed. If he draws out a further 5, then inevitably the trust property has shrunk and remains at 15 even if the trustee pays in another 5, unless the trustee intended to treat the 5 paid in as replacement trust moneys. This is the "lowest intermediate balance" test. The same principles apply to a company's money expropriated by a director, secret profits wrongfully taken by a director and mistaken payments.

2–30   **Charge** The third method is by imposing a charge, e.g. where a trustee buys shares for himself out of trust money on a wrongdoer's property for an amount equal to the deprived owner's property. In effect the charge is a grant of judicial super-priority interest over non-money property to secure the amount owing to the wronged victim and confers a proprietary interest which attaches to the property and its proceeds of sale: see *Re Oatway* [1903] 2 Ch 356; *Re Tilley's Will Trusts* [1967] Ch 1179. Various protections have been afforded to innocent volunteers, e.g. where it would be unjust to compel them to sell their property to realise the charge. Difficulties arise if the property appreciates in value.

2–31   **Tenancy in common** The fourth method is by imposing a tenancy in common, i.e. shared beneficial ownership. In the case of non-money fungibles, this may occur where one owner's property (e.g. grain, bullion, fungible securities) is, by accident or the unauthorised acts of third parties, commingled with the property of another innocent owner so as to be indistinguishable: the two owners are deemed to own the commingled mass as tenants in common according to their contributing shares: para 2–14 *et seq*. In the case of moneys of two trusts intermixed in the same bank account, a similar result is achieved by treating the two sets of beneficiaries as having a pro rata claim.

2–32   **Priority claim** Finally the English courts may simply order the insolvency representative of a party owing a property claim to repay an amount equal to the property as a super-priority claim on his insolvency. In this case there is no attempt to identify any trust asset and the order is made on the basis of equitable principles applying in the administration of an insolvency in order to prevent the unsecured creditors of the insolvent from receiving a windfall.

For example, the application of traditional tracing rules and the search for a traceable asset can be quite impossible in the case, e.g. of banks where there may be many thousands of transactions happening in quick succession. As a result in certain cases the courts have simply treated a property claim as a right of the owner of the claim to be paid in priority to other creditors of the insolvent without too prim a hunt for the thimble.

> In *Chase Manhattan Bank v Israel-British Bank (London) Ltd* [1981] Ch 105: [1979] 3 All ER 1025, Chase mistakenly paid Israel-British twice. Israel-British knew this but failed to return the money and went into liquidation. *Held*: Chase could recover the mistaken payment. One of the arguments advanced on behalf of Israel-British was that Chase had failed to identify any property to which Chase's interest could attach. The court said at 1034 "when equitable rights are in question, the court does not encourage fine distinctions founded on the technicalities of financial machinery."

> In *Space Investments Ltd v Canadian Imperial Bank of Commerce Trust Co (Bahamas) Ltd* [1986] 3 All ER 75, PC, a bank trustee opened a trust account in favour of the trust but without segregating the money or identifying it, e.g. by depositing it with another bank. *Held*: although quite clearly no asset could be identified, the court was prepared to impose a charge on all of the assets of the bank and to order the bank's estate to pay the beneficiaries ahead of the general unsecured creditors. As it happened however, the trust instrument had authorised the bank to do what they did and the beneficiaries accordingly had to prove as unsecured creditors.

Deposits of property for sale or collection

Illustrations

The same question – of whether a claim is a debt or super-priority property   2–33 claim – arises where a principal deposits property for sale or collection with an agent who may use the services of a sub-agent. Some examples are as follows:

1. A customer may deposit instruments for collection with his bank, such as bonds, shares, cheques, bills or other paper. The transaction is that the deposit bank is to convey the paper to the person liable, present it, collect the proceeds or the income on the instrument and remit these to the customer. The deposit bank may use a correspondent bank for the collection. These transactions are very frequent, as where a custodian of securities deposits them with a sub-custodian in the country of the

currency of the security or the country of the issuer or a paying agent so that the sub-custodian can collect interest, dividends and redemption payments on the securities.

2.   A seller of goods may deposit goods with an agent with instructions that the agent sell them on his behalf and remit the proceeds. The agent may, for example, be a broker on a commodities market or a bullion dealer. The agent may deal through a sub-agent.

3.   A seller of securities, such as shares or bonds, may deposit them with a broker to sell them on the market. Again the broker may employ a sub-agent to effect the sale.

In each of these cases the principal deposits his property with the agent who may deposit it with a sub-agent who sells or collects, and remits the proceeds to the agent who in turn remits the proceeds to the principal. Property goes down through the chain and money comes back up the chain.

The position primarily depends on who becomes insolvent and at what point during the chain of disposals down and remittances back. Everything depends on particular circumstances, but the guiding English principles may be summarised as set out below.

Property held by insolvent *in specie*

2–34   So long as the property – the goods, the securities, the instruments – on the way down through agent and sub-agent are *in specie*, the normal rule is that the property belongs to the principal who has a super-priority property claim for it. This is so even if the property is not specifically marked as belonging to the principal so as to take it out of the reputed or apparent ownership of the agent or sub-agent. Hence if the principal, agent or sub-agent becomes insolvent, the insolvency will generally freeze further deal-ings (by termination of agency or by avoidance of post-petition disposals of the principal's property) and the principal will have a super-priority property claim for his property against the agent or sub-agent who holds as bailee or trustee, subject to any available lien: see, e.g. *New Zealand and Australian Land Co v Watson* (1881) 7 QBD 374, CA (sale of wheat through sub-agents).

If a customer deposits negotiable paper for collection (such as a prom-issory note, a bond, a draft or a cheque) with his bank, presumptively the beneficial interest in the paper is retained by the customer until collection and the deposit bank holds the paper as bailee or trustee for the depositor. If prior to collection, the deposit bank becomes insolvent, the customer should be entitled to the return of the paper as a super-priority property claim subject to any lien of the deposit bank. There are many cases on this subject, going back to *Giles v Perkins* (1807) 9 East 11.

> In *Giles v Perkins* (1807) 9 East 11, a customer deposited bills with bankers for collection. The bankers credited him with the amount of the bills and charged him interest. But the bankers did not purchase the bills. The bankers become bankrupt and thereafter they received payment of the bills. At the time of the bankruptcy the bankers owed a credit balance to the customer excluding the amount of the bills. *Held*: the bills and hence the proceeds were the property of the customer. The bankers did not have a lien on the bills because the customer did not owe the bankers any money and the bankers had not advanced money on the security of the bills. If on the other hand the account had been over-drawn, then the bankers would have had a lien by custom on the bills.

> In *Thompson v Giles* (1824) 3 B&C 422, a customer deposited term bills with his bankers for collection. The bankers credited the proceeds to the customer's account and charged interest. The bankers became bankrupt. The bankers owed the customer a credit balance which was independent of the bills. *Held*: the bills and the proceeds belonged to the customer. The bankers had not pur-chased the bills.

Similarly if the collecting sub-agent bank fails before collection, the deposit bank agent is entitled to the return of the bills. The same applies to collections on investment securities through agents and sub-agents.

There are two main qualifications to the proposition that the principal is entitled to the return of his property so long as it remains *in specie*. These are: (a) the agent has purchased the property, e.g. has bought the cheque or the goods; and (b) the agent or sub-agent has a lien. Again, there are numer-ous English cases discussing these situations, often turning upon delicate factual distinctions.

In any event in many civil code jurisdictions, the property usually falls into the estate of insolvent agent or sub-agent unless it is identified as not belonging to the agent or sub-agent.

Receipt of proceeds by insolvent

The position is more complicated after the proceeds have been received and are on the way back up the chain.   **2–35**

In common law countries, the position depends upon whether the agent or sub-agent was entitled to use the money as its own, i.e. by crediting it to its own bank account for its use, on the basis that the agent or sub-agent is merely indebted for that amount to his superior. If on the other hand, the agent or sub-agent was not entitled to use the money as his own, the money or its traceable product belongs to the superior. A prohibition on using the money as his own can arise either because the principal expressly so required, or because the money is in fact segregated, or because the sub-agent, agent or principal becomes insolvent, thereby freezing further dealings with the money.

In many civil code countries, there is no question of a trust of the proceeds arising unless the proceeds are banked in an account which is marked in the bank's books as belonging to the principal.

2–36   **Proceeds received by sub-agent** In common law countries, if the sub-agent receives the proceeds *before* the insolvency of the sub-agent, agent or principal, the sub-agent is a debtor to the agent if he is entitled to deal with the proceeds as his own, e.g. because he is a bank. If he may not do so, e.g. because of an obligation to segregate or because of an express trust, he holds the proceeds or their traceable product on trust for the agent. The agent in turn may at this point merely be a debtor to the principal, or the agent may hold his money claim against the sub-agent on trust for the principal, or (if the sub-agent holds the proceeds on trust for the agent) the agent may hold this property claim against the sub-agent on sub-trust for the principal, thereby conferring a property claim on the principal directly against the sub-agent.

On the whole, where the sub-agent is a debtor to the agent, the English courts have not favoured the proposition that the agent holds this claim on trust for the principal: see *New Zealand and Australian Land Co v Watson* (1881) 7 QBD 374, CA. See also the US Supreme Court decision of *Jennings v United States Fidelity and Guaranty Co*, 294 US 216 (1935).

If the sub-agent receives the proceeds *after* the insolvency of the sub-agent, agent or principal, then property rights are generally frozen by reason of the fact that the insolvency either terminates the power of the sub-agent or immediate agent to use another's money as his own, or the fact that any appropriation of the money involves a void post-petition disposal of an insolvent's property (in the case of the principal's insolvency). Again there will be the question of whether the principal has a mere debt claim against his immediate agent as opposed to a direct claim against the sub-agent, or whether his immediate agent holds his property claim for the proceeds against the sub-agent on sub-trust for his principal so that the principal has a direct property claim against the sub-agent for the proceeds or their traceable product.

> In *Re Farrow's Bank Ltd* [1923] 1 Ch 41, CA, involving a typical clearing arrangement for cheque collections, the agent bank collecting a customer's cheques via a sub-agent bank became insolvent *before* the sub-agent bank received the proceeds of the collection of the cheque through the clearing. *Held*: the agent bank could no longer deal with the proceeds as its own and the trust of those proceeds crystallised at once in favour of the customer, i.e. the sub-

agent could no longer pay the proceeds for the benefit of the insolvent agent bank. The agent bank's liquidator was ordered to pay the amount of those proceeds as a super-priority claim to the customer as principal.

In *Kaltenbach v Lewis* (1885) 10 App Cas 617, HL, involving the sale of goods by a sub-agent, the sub-agent received the proceeds of sale from the third party buyer *after* the insolvency of the agent. *Held*: the sub-agent held these in trust for the ultimate principal. The sub-agent could clearly not pay the proceeds to the insolvent agent and hence the money belonged to the principal and did not become an asset of the estate of insolvent agent.

Proceeds received by agent Where the proceeds have been remitted by the   2–37
sub-agent to the agent (by instrument or credit to a bank account) similar principles apply. If the agent receives the proceeds *before* the insolvency of principal or agent, the principal's claim may be a debt or property claim, depending on whether the agent had power to deal with the proceeds as his own.

Thus if the agent receives the proceeds *before* the cut-off point (usually petition against the principal or insolvency or cessation of business by the agent) and he was entitled to use the proceeds as his own, e.g. because he is not obliged to segregate them, the principal has a mere debt claim for the proceeds. If not, the principal's claim is a super-priority property claim: consider *Castendyck & Focke v McLellan* (1887) 6 NZLR 63, where an agent sold property of the principal but did not have authority to use the proceeds as his own. In the case of banks, it will almost invariably be the case that the agent bank can use the money as its own since that is the ordinary course of business of banks.

In *Re West of England and South Wales District Bank, ex p Dale* (1879) 11 Ch D 772, a deposit bank sent orders to its agent bank for collection. The agent bank received the proceeds of the collection partly in cash and partly in the form of a cheque and then went into liquidation. *Held*: the deposit bank had only a debt claim for the cash because there was no agreement to segregate it. But (although the point was conceded) the deposit bank had a proprietary claim for the cheque.

If the agent receives the proceeds *after* the insolvency of the *principal*, the agent holds them in trust for the principal because he can no longer deal with the insolvent's property as his own. The principal's insolvency would generally terminate the agent's authority to act on normal principles of agency and post-petition disposals of the insolvent principal's property will be void unless protected: *Elgood v Harris* [1896] 2 QB 491 (insurance proceeds received by broker).

If the agent receives the proceeds *after* his own insolvency, the agent will invariably hold them on trust for his principal because he is not entitled to deal with the proceeds as his own by appropriating them for the benefit of his general creditors and because generally his insolvency cancels the agency. There is much English case law on this, often involving insolvent banks and auctioneers, e.g. *Tennant v Strachan* (1829) 4 Carr & P 30.

Deposits and sale proceeds in civil countries

2–38   In civil countries objecting to the trust, the background position is that the deposited property must be segregated and marked to take it out of the reputed ownership of the custodian or agent. They must be individualised and specifically identified, so that any fungibility is fatal to ownership unless this is changed by statute.

If the agent sells securities deposited with him, receives the proceeds and then becomes bankrupt, then the proceeds belong to his estate and go to his creditors unless he has placed them in a segregated bank account in the name of the principal (merely opening an account in his own books is insufficient). The principal is left with an unsecured claim for those proceeds.

But if the agent has sold, but has not received the proceeds before becoming bankrupt, then in a large number of civil countries, the principal can by statute claim the proceeds direct from the third party. For the statutory references, see para 1–31 *et seq.*

Assignment of debts

2–39   A diminishing number of jurisdictions insist that, if a creditor assigns a debt owed to him and becomes insolvent, the assignment is ineffective if notice of the assignment is not given to the debtor, often in formal manner. The other group of jurisdictions upholds the sale notwithstanding the absence of notice to the debtor, although notice is desirable for other reasons, e.g. to determine priorities, to ensure that the debtor owing the debt pays the assignee and to exclude further set-offs and other defences available to the debtor.

The insistence that notice of the assignment be given if the assignment is to be effective on the insolvency of the seller appears to be primarily an extension of the "false wealth" doctrine, i.e. so long as the assignment is not notified, the original assignor remains the apparent owner, thereby potentially inducing credit on the basis of many possessions but little property. In the context of debts, the rule is artificial since receivables are intangible property and so are not available to be viewed and, even if a creditor is entitled to assume a merchant's receivables are owned by him, the creditor can hardly know whether or not notice has been given of the assignment.

The survival of the rule in various countries may also be attributable partly to a pro-debtor policy of discouraging situations where a debtor is potentially exposed to a multiplicity of creditors as assignees, who may be more hostile than the original creditor, and partly to a desire to restrain an individual debtor from denuding himself of his income.

On the other hand, the necessity for notice has two objections in the eyes of those states which concede that notice is not necessary to take the assignment beyond the reach of the seller's creditors. The first is that property for which the assignee or buyer may have paid is used to pay the debts of the seller. The second is that the requirement for notice impedes the free marketability of receivables and the ability of a business to finance itself by factoring or discounting or charging its receivables.

The international position is examined in more detail in another work **2–40** (on international security) in this series of books on international financial law. Countries which do not insist on notice include England and English-based countries, the United States (except Louisiana), Austria, Germany, the Netherlands and Switzerland. Countries which do require notice for validity include France (subject to exceptions), Luxembourg, various French-related jurisdictions, Italy, some Latin American countries, Portugal and Spain (possibly), Thailand, surprisingly Japan and Korea. The rule was abolished in Belgium in 1994. In some countries, the notice must be formal, e.g. in France the notice must be served by a court official, the *huissier*, or the assignment must be accepted by the debtor under a formal *acte authentique*. In France, the inconvenience can be side-stepped by subrogation whereby the assignee pays the creditor and is thereby subrogated to the claim paid. In traditional English countries adopting pre–1986 versions of English bankruptcy statutes, the doctrine of reputed ownership may require the notice in the case of the bankruptcy of individual assignors. This doctrine never applied to companies and was finally abolished in England in 1986.

The strength of the English policy in favour of the marketability of debts is demonstrated by the upholding of very informal means of assigning debts which thereby escape the clutches of the assignor's execution creditors or insolvency representative. An example is a mere direction by the creditor to his debtor to pay a third party, which direction is communicated to the third party, so long as the court can find an intention that this was intended to transfer the debt, not merely to constitute the third party as an agent for collection on behalf of the creditor. For the cases, see *Halsbury's Laws* 4th ed vol 6, "Choses in Action", para 38.

CHAPTER 3

CONTRACTS, LEASES AND FORFEITURES

Contracts and leases

Interested parties

3–1 Where a bankrupt has contracts and leases, the interests claiming protection are:

— the **solvent counterparty** who is left with a useless claim for damages if the debtor is unable to perform;

— the **debtor** who may wish to keep alive contracts and leases which are profitable or which are essential to a successful rehabilitation;

— **mortgagees** of the contracts or leases who lose their security if the rights are cancelled: they may be mortgagees of the debtor or the solvent counterparty;

— **sub-contractors** and others claiming derivative rights, e.g. sub-buyers, building sub-contractors, sub-lessees of land or equipment, sub-licencees of intellectual property rights, sub-distributorships, sub-franchisees, sub-agents and sub-creditors (such as sub-participants in loans). Their rights may depend on the continued existence of the head contract. The failure of the head contractor or their immediate contractor may, by domino effect, precipitate their own insolvency. To protect themselves against the insolvency of the middle party, head contractors may take security assignments of sub-rights and sub-contractors may seek to negotiate substituted direct contracts or leases from the head-contractor.

Rights of insolvent estate to accept or reject

3–2 The usual position is that the debtor's estate has a power to disclaim, abandon or reject contracts, leases or onerous property or to call for performance by the counterparty. Examples are:

Austria	BA 1914 s 21 (power to reject or perform contracts)
Belgium	CC Art 1184 (power to apply for contract termination)
Denmark	BA 1977 ss 54–61 (power to reject or perform contracts)
England	IA 1986 (disclaimer of contracts and property ss 178–182 for corporates; s 186 for rescission of corporate contracts by the court; performance rights by case law)
Germany	BA 1879 s 17 (power to call for contract performance)
Italy	BA 1942 Art s 72 (similar to Germany)
Japan	BA 1922 s 59 (power to perform or reject contracts); see para 11–34 for the position under the Corporate Reorganisation Law of 1952
Netherlands	BA 1893 s 37 (similar to Germany)
Sweden	Sale of Goods Act ss 39–41 (relating to sale of goods)
Switzerland	Federal Law on Execution of Debts and Bankruptcy of 1889 (power to perform obligations)
United States	BC 1978 s 365(c) (trustee may assume or reject any executory contract or unexpired lease).

Disclaimer of contracts

As regards disclaimer, a bankrupt estate must have power to abandon con- 3–3
tracts and obligations since the business must cease and the estate must be
wound up. If a counterparty were entitled to performance, he would secure
priority over other creditors.

Invariably the counterparty is entitled to prove for his damages flowing
from the rejection as an unsecured claim alongside other ordinary creditors
and bankruptcy acts usually so provide expressly, presumably to clarify that
the claim is provable even though technically it arose after the declaration of
the bankruptcy.

The insolvency administrator may have a time limit within which to
accept or reject or to respond to a counterparty's request for a decision.

The main exceptions in bankruptcy laws to the ability of the estate to dis- 3–4
claim are:

Bankrupt sellers of land In England and the United States, where the
seller of land becomes insolvent after contract but before completion, the
purchaser can insist on a transfer and possession on payment of the price.
For England, see *Re Taylor* [1910] 1 KB 562, CA. For the United States,
see an exception in BC 1978 s 365 which entitles a purchaser of land in
possession to insist on the delivery of title by the bankrupt against
payment.

Bankrupt lessors Under the US BC 1978 s 365(h) a lessee of real property (but not equipment) can stay in possession even if the bankrupt lessor rejects the lease and can set off damages against the rent (but not claim for them separately). Similar provisions in that section protect the buyer of a timeshare interest and a licensee of intellectual property (the licensee has no right of set-off but does have a right of proof for damages). In England, a lessor of land probably could not disclaim the lease without also disclaiming the entire property (consider *Re Bastable* [1910] 2 KB 518) and, if he could, the lessee could apply for a vesting order in his favour under IA 1986 s 181.

Disclaimer is all or nothing The debtor's estate cannot disclaim part only of a contract: disclaimer is all or nothing. For example, he obviously cannot disclaim the obligation to pay the price of goods and yet claim delivery of the goods. He cannot disclaim an onerous or inconvenient covenant in a lease, such as a covenant to repair, without also disclaiming the lease itself. He should not be able to disclaim an arbitration clause in the contract, without rejecting the whole contract. He should not be able to disclaim some adverse restrictive covenant attached to land without also disclaiming the land itself, as where the land cannot be used for building or is a burial ground subject to rights in favour of various personages to have themselves buried there and to have erected tombs, tabernacles and temples over their interred remains: see *Re Nottingham General Cemetery Co* [1955] Ch 683.

> In the English case of *Re Bastable* [1910] 2 KB 518, a seller-lessee agreed to sell a lease to a purchaser and then became bankrupt before the conveyance of the title to the purchaser. The trustee in bankruptcy purported to disclaim the contract of sale. *Held*: he must also disclaim the lease itself. The inconvenient sale contract could not be disclaimed without also disclaiming the property.

> In *Re Fussell, ex p Allen* (1882) 20 Ch D 341, CA, the trustees of a lessee wanted to disclaim the lease of a tool mill but wished to keep various loose tools and machinery which had been leased together with the mill itself. *Held*: disclaimer must be of the entirety of the property subject to the lease and the trustee could not keep the tools and disclaim the rest of the lease.

Polluted property Whether a debtor could abandon polluted property subject to environmental clean-up costs is a matter for investigation.

Mortgagees and underlessees may lose their rights if property is disclaimed. In England, they can apply for the disclaimed property to be vested in them: see IA 1986 ss 181–182.

Performance by debtor's estate

The debtor's estate can usually call for performance by the counterparty, 3–5
either by statute (para 3–2) or by case law. Thus in England, insolvency on
its own does not terminate contracts: e.g. *Mees v Duffus & Co* (1901) 6
Com Cas 165 (sale contract). But the claim of the estate may be met by a
right of the solvent counterparty to cancel: see below.

If the estate does perform, then invariably any moneys payable by the
estate (such as the sale price or rentals) are a priority claim since the estate
could not properly claim performance but not pay: for England, see for
example *Re Anchor Line Henderson Bros* [1937] Ch 1, CA; *Stead Hazel &
Co v Cooper* [1933] KB 840.

One ignores in this short review the lavish case law in many jurisdictions
concerning sales of *specific* assets where the buyer and seller become bankrupt after contract but before delivery, and the question arises as to who has
got the property. Most sales of assets – securities or goods – are of generic
assets which are not specifically identified on contract, e.g. 100 Republic of
Austria Bonds, as opposed to 100 bonds numbered 245 to 344.

One may only note that the case law has tended to focus on two issues: 3–6
(1) whether the asset is sufficiently identified so that property has passed to
the seller if the buyer is bankrupt, especially where part of a specified bulk is
sold (grain on a ship, wine in a cellar, bullion in a vault) and (2) whether the
seller can recover the asset if the buyer is bankrupt, e.g. by virtue of a vendor's lien or the Franco-Latin right of revendication for a limited period, e.g.
30 days, if the goods are still unchanged and still in the bankrupt's possession. The latter rule has been introduced into Canadian law by BIA 1992.
These rules are all intended to protect trade suppliers and result in a super-
priority over the holders of general enterprise charges.

But these rules can be important in securities clearance systems where, in
order to achieve payment against delivery, a financing bank participating in
the system pays for securities on behalf of its customer the buyer, and wishes
to take a charge over the securities to secure any loan to the customer for
that payment. To have a charge, property must pass on payment. The
amounts concerned can be very large, e.g. in relation to transfers of government debt securities through centralised clearing-houses.

Rights of solvent counterparty

The solvent counterparty is unlikely to be able to insist that the debtor per- 3–7
forms, either on the ground that specific performance is not available, or, if
it is, on the ground that the debtor's estate has a statutory right of disclaimer
or rejection: see *Holloway v York* (1877) 25 WR 627. If the debtor's estate

could be compelled to perform, the counterparty would be preferred ahead of other creditors.

The solvent party will however usually wish to cancel since there is no point in going on with the bankrupt.

Generally the solvent party can cancel in four main cases:

1. The debtor has breached the contract.

2. The debtor's insolvency is an anticipatory repudiation.

3. The contract is personal.

4. The creditor has a contract right to cancel.

These may be reviewed in turn.

3–8 **Breach of contract** Where the debtor has breached the contract and the breach entitles the other party to cancel under applicable non-bankruptcy law, the creditor may cancel, e.g. *Re Nathan, ex p Stapleton* (1879) 10 Ch D 588; *Powell v Marshall Parkes & Co* [1899] 1 QB 710.

Anticipatory repudiation Where the debtor's insolvency constitutes an anticipatory repudiation, i.e. where it is obvious that the debtor will not be able to perform on account of the insolvency, the creditor may cancel. This is an application of ordinary non-bankruptcy contract law.

> In the New Zealand case of *Re Premier Products Ltd* [1936] NZLR 368, the company undertook to supply certain paint products at fixed prices for a period of five years. It became unable to pay its debts and went into voluntary liquidation before the expiration of that period. *Held*: the company had been guilty of a breach of contract when it went into liquidation and so disabled itself from performing its undertaking.
>
> See also: *Ogdens v Nelson* [1905] AC 109, HL; *Re Plumbly, ex p Grant* (1880) 13 Ch D 667, CA (stockbrokers); *Re Edwards, ex p Chalmers* (1873) 8 Ch App 289 (buyer insolvent; seller entitled to refuse to make further instalment deliveries until outstanding payments are made and future payments secured); *Morgan v Bain* (1874) LR 10 CP 15; *Jennings Trustee v King* [1952] 1 Ch 899; *Telsen Electric Co v JJ Eastick & Sons* [1936] 3 All ER 266 (breach of contract by receiver of contracts entered into by receiver); *Baker v Lloyds Bank Ltd* [1920] 2 KB 323 (insolvency of indorser was repudiation of contingent liability to pay holder of bill); *Re National Benefit Assurance Co Ltd* [1924] 2 Ch 339 (insolvency of insurer was repudiation of life insurance policy); *Re Asphaltic Wood Pavement Co, Lee & Chapman's Case* (1885) 30 Ch D 216 (liability to repair street for 15 years); *Official Receiver v Henn* (1981) 40 ALR 569.

3–9 **Personal contracts** Where the contract is of a personal nature, the creditor may cancel. Thus a trustee in bankruptcy cannot require performance of a personal contract e.g. requiring personal skill or service by the bankrupt himself or relying on some special relationship of trust and confidence: see, e.g. *Knight v Burgess* (1864) 33 LJ Ch 727; US BC 1978 s 365. There is case law in many jurisdictions on agency contracts to similar effect.

Express right of cancellation Where the contract contains a provision per-   3–10
mitting the counterparty to cancel on the insolvency of the other – an "*ipso facto* clause", the creditor may cancel. The objects of these clauses are (a) to recognise the fact that it is unlikely that an insolvent will be able to perform, (b) to avoid the uncertainty and potential greater losses while the insolvency administrator considers whether to accept or reject, and (c) to prevent the debtor's estate from cherry-picking contracts, i.e. claiming selective perfor-mance of profitable contracts and rejecting the non-profitable contracts.

But these cancellation rights under *ipso facto* clauses may be overridden or restricted in three principal situations:

– Where the cancellation is a **penal forfeiture** or a forfeiture of protected rights under applicable non-bankruptcy law. The most usual example is the forfeiture of a land lease; see, e.g. English Law of Property Act 1925 s 146. Other examples in the case law of many jurisdictions relate to the cancellation of sale contracts where the buyer has paid a deposit or instalments, and the cancellation of equipment leases or hire purchase contracts where the hirer has paid for most of the equipment.

– Where the cancellation results in the **forfeiture of a vested asset** of the estate contrary to the bankruptcy principle that the assets of the debtor are to be available to his creditors generally. One cannot walk into the bankrupt's home and remove the furniture. Typical examples are attempts in building contracts to divest the bankrupt builder of his materials brought on site or to retake goods sold but not paid. The party seeking to divest must have a vendor's lien, valid retention of title clause, right of revendication, or mortgage.

– Where the counterparty is a **monopoly utility** which has overwhelming bargaining power in order to get paid in full – the utility threatens to switch off: see, for example, the restraints on utilities in British IA 1986 s 233; the US BC 1978 s 366.

– Where an **ipso facto clause** is specifically nullified by bankruptcy legis-lation. This topic requires further discussion.

Statutory nullification of *ipso facto* clauses

As mentioned, an *ipso facto* clause entitles the solvent counterparty to can-   3–11
cel the contract or lease on the insolvency of the other party. The objects are: it is unlikely that the bankrupt will perform; the solvent party should

not have to wait, especially in volatile markets; selective performance by the debtor would prevent netting – netting and the cancellation of executory contracts so as to dramatically reduce exposures in markets for foreign exchange, securities, commodities and the like; and the insolvent should not be able to cherry-pick the profits and cancel the losses. Netting is discussed in detail in another volume in this series of books on international financial law.

The contrary policies are that the cancellation may deprive the debtor of a profitable contract producing a gain for the estate, that the ability to cancel may give the contractor too much bargaining power in order to get paid ahead of other creditors, and that the asset may be essential for a rescue of the debtor via a rehabilitation proceeding, e.g. essential supplies, a lease of buildings, computers or other important assets, or a licence of intellectual property rights. The difficulty with nullifying contract termination clauses is to balance these interests, having regard to the enormous variety of contracts, e.g. sale contracts (land, goods, securities, foreign exchange); building contracts; agency and broker contracts; custodianship contracts for commodities or securities; employment contracts; insurance and reinsurance contracts; transportation contracts; contracts of lease or hire of land or equipment; licences of intellectual property; franchises and distributorships; concessions; loans, subscription and underwriting commitments.

3–12   Apart from the special cases of penal forfeitures, of forfeitures of vested assets and of restraints on utilities, few jurisdictions outlaw *ipso facto* clauses in executory (unperformed) contracts, e.g. contracts of sale, building contracts, licences and financial contracts. Although conventionally the debtor's estate has the right to insist on performance, or to disclaim if the counterparty requires performance, this is subject to the creditor's express rights of cancellation unless the contractual right is void – which usually requires an express statutory direction in the case of most executory contracts.

The few countries which do expressly utilise *ipso facto* clauses include:

  –   Canada: see s 65 BIA 1992
  –   France: see below
  –   New Zealand (under the special statutory management)
  –   United States: see below

3–13   In **France**, s 37(5) of the Bankruptcy Act 1985 nullifies rescission clauses by providing that "Notwithstanding any contractual clause", no termination or cancellation of a contract can result from the sole fact of the opening of the *procédure de redressement judiciare*. The administrator has the option to require performance of or to renounce executory contracts but must decide within a month (compare the German "without delay" on demand). Further, if the administrator claims continuation, the co-contractor must perform in spite of a default in execution by the debtor of engagements prior to the opening judgment. But the co-contractor need not perform if the administrator does not perform obligations under the contract arising after the opening of bankruptcy proceedings.

In the **United States**, s 365(c) of BC 1978 provides that the trustee may assume or reject any executory contract or unexpired lease of the debtor but subject to the court's approval. **3–14**

If there has been a default under the executory contract or lease, then the trustee may not assume unless at the time of the assumption the trustee cures the default or provides adequate assurance that the trustee will promptly cure the default, compensates the other party for any loss suffered and provides adequate assurance of future performance under the contract or lease. In effect therefore the trustee can keep the contract in being provided that he cures any defaults and, where there is a default, provides adequate assurance for future performance. This curing has to be provided only when the trustee assumes, and it will be seen below that a considerable time-gap can elapse before the trustee has to make up his mind.

There are special stipulations as to what is adequate assurance in the case of shopping centre leases where, for example, tenant mix and the status of the tenant are important for the overall scheme.

Section 365(e) nullifies default clauses which permit the other party to terminate on the insolvency of the debtor. The section provides that, notwithstanding a provision in an executory contract of unexpired lease or in applicable law, an executory contract or unexpired lease of the debtor may not be terminated or modified at any time after the commencement of the case solely because of the insolvency or financial condition of the debtor, or the commencement of the case or the appointment of the trustee, i.e. standard contractual events of default which spark off on insolvency and the institution of insolvency proceedings are nullified. Further they do not count as events of default which the trustee has to cure as mentioned above.

There is a similar provision in s 541 which provides that an interest of the debtor in property becomes property of the estate notwithstanding an *ipso facto* clause on the above lines so that the trustee can use, lease or sell property even though there is a termination clause.

The effect therefore is to provide the trustee with an extended grace period during which the other party's rights are frozen.

As to timing, in a liquidation case under Chapter 7 the contract or lease is deemed rejected if the trustee does not assume or reject the contract, or a lease of residential real property or a lease of personal property (e.g. equipment) of the debtor within 60 days, extendible by the court for cause.

Extensions are common. But in the case of a rehabilitation under Chapter 11 (and also in a case under Chapters 9, 12 or 13) the trustee has until the confirmation of the plan to decide, unless the court orders a shorter time. This could theoretically be many months, if not longer.

If the trustee assumes a contract or lease, then effectively any sums payable on the debtor's side are a priority expense as an administrative cost.

3–15   Because of the savage effect upon contracts of the statutory freeze, exceptions have had to be carved out by the Bankruptcy Code. Examples are:

– The traditional indulgence in favour of personal contracts and leases which are based on the personal skill or character or on a special relationship of trust and confidence. Section 365 forbids the trustee from assuming a contract or lease if applicable law excuses the other party from accepting performance from or rendering performance to the trustee and the other party does not consent to the assumption.

– Contracts to make a loan or extend other debt financing or financial accommodations for the benefit of the debtor or to issue a security of the debtor: s 365(c). This does not apply to other contracts which involve credit, e.g. instalment sales or leases.

– Certain close-outs in commodity broker and stockbroker liquidations; certain sale and repurchase agreements in relation to securities; certain financial swaps, such as interest and currency swaps. The latter are described in detail in another volume in this series, a volume which includes a discussion of netting.

Some of the above are designed to prevent cherry-picking and to avoid the risk of domino insolvencies in the financial and commodity sectors of the economy. The effect is to take out of the scope of the freeze large numbers of contracts between institutions in organised markets and between financial counterparties.

Although not strictly within the scope of the freeze in s 365, there are exemptions in favour of the enforcement of certain security interests in US ships and aircraft and railroad rolling stock.

For a review of the position on judicial rehabilitation, see para 11–32 *et seq*. For Canada, see para 12–7 *et seq*.

Forfeitures

Examples of forfeitures

3–16   After the commencement of proceedings, the bankrupt's property may not be forfeited since it is available for creditors generally. In order to forfeit an asset of the debtor, the creditor must have valid security over the asset. Examples of invalid forfeitures may be given.

A provision in a sales contract that, on the buyer's bankruptcy, the ownership of the goods will revert to the seller if the price has not been paid is void. The seller must either take a valid non-possessory mortgage over the goods or must have a valid retention of title clause whereby ownership does not pass to the bankrupt until the price is paid.

A provision in a building contract whereby, on the builder's bankruptcy, all plant, machinery and materials on the employer's land and belonging to the builder, will vest in the employer is void: e.g. *Re Winter* (1978) 8 Ch D 225; *Re Harrison* [1880] 14 Ch D 19.

A provision in a contract whereby a creditor's right to a loan, deposit, deferred credit or the like is cancelled on the creditor's insolvency is void.

In *ex p Mackay* (1873) LR 8 Ch 643, A sold a patent to B in consideration of B paying royalties to A. B at the same time lent A £12,500 and it was agreed that B should retain one-half of the royalties as they became payable towards satisfaction of this loan. It was further provided that if A became bankrupt or made an arrangement with his creditors, B might retain the whole of the royalties in satisfaction of the loan. A became insolvent. *Held*: B had a good charge upon one-half of the royalties but the provision that B might retain the whole of the royalties in case of A's bankruptcy, etc., was a fraud upon the bankruptcy laws and void. The court pointed out that, if this were not the case, then a party could for example sell an asset to a buyer on terms that the price would be doubled in the event of the buyer becoming insolvent.

A non-mutual set-off is void. This affects multilateral clearing systems.　**3–17** Under these systems, let us suppose a triangle of A, B and C. A owes 100 to B who owes 100 to C who owes 60 to A. The clearing rules provide that, on maturity of the debts, A should owe 100 to C instead of B so that A pays C direct instead of A paying 100 to B, and C owes 60 to A. The 100 and the 60 are set-off, so that A owes 40 to C. The result is that, instead of three large payments, only one small payment is necessary, i.e. the payment of 40 by A to C. But if B becomes bankrupt before the clearing, the effect of the clearing is to deprive B of the 100 owed to him by A and hence to divest B of this claim. This is a forfeiture of an asset of B's estate and hence is void: see *British Eagle International Airlines Ltd v Air France* [1975] 2 All ER 390, HL. In order to avoid this result, it is necessary to establish a central clearing house which acts as principal.

A provision in a joint venture agreement that, on the bankruptcy of one of the joint venturers, his share in the assets will be transferred for nil or inadequate value to the other joint venturers, is void. Thus a trustee in bankruptcy is not bound by a partnership agreement which provides that, on the bankruptcy of a partner, his share is vested in the other partners or may be acquired by them for less than its full value: *Whitmore Mason* (1861) 2 John & H 204; *Re Williams, ex p Warden* (1872) 21 WR 51. Whether an insolvency representative is bound by a clause entitling the other parties to sell the bankrupt's share for full value is unclear in England, although often the insolvency representative will be prepared to sell if he is satisfied with the method of valuation. On the other hand a provision in a company's articles that a shareholder is compelled to transfer his shares at full value to the company's nominees on his bankruptcy is valid, provided the price is fair and is fixed equally for all shareholders alike: *Borland's Trustee v Steel Bros & Co Ltd* [1901] 1 Ch 279.

A provision on a bond whereby the debtor agrees that on his bankruptcy, his property will be forfeited and will vest in some third party is void. A debtor cannot defeat his creditors in this way: *Re Johnson* [1904] 1 KB 134. This obvious rule may defeat springing trusts which have in the past been employed by some companies to transfer their assets automatically to another company in another jurisdiction, e.g. in the event of a threatened expropriation locally.

Increased liabilities on bankruptcy

3–18 Apart from forfeitures, any provision whereby the bankrupt's liabilities are increased on his bankruptcy is also void. For example, a provision whereby the sale price is doubled on the buyer's bankruptcy or a loan is increased on the borrower's bankruptcy is void.

> In *Re Johns, Worrell v Johns* [1928] 1 Ch 737, a mother made a somewhat unaffectionate loan to her son of £1,650 on terms that out of the first advance of £1,010, £1,000 was to be retained by the mother as a bonus and that the remaining £640 would be advanced by monthly instalments of £10 each. The loan was secured by a mortgage on the son's interest under a will. The deed further provided that, if the son did not charge his property or become a bankrupt, then on the death of the mother, the son need pay only £650 plus interest, but if the son became bankrupt, the mother could retain the £1,000 plus the advances plus interest. The son became bankrupt and the mother claimed the benefit of the mortgage for £1,650 plus interest. *Held*: the deed was a device to avoid the bankruptcy laws because it was intended to procure that something more was to come to the mother if the son became bankrupt than if he did not. The mother was entitled only to the monthly advances of £10 actually made plus interest. See also *ex p Williams* [1877] 7 Ch D 138.

In the United States, BC 1978 s 541(c) invalidates restrictions on the transfer of property of the debtor. These include provisions in an agreement, transfer instrument, or applicable non-bankruptcy law that restrict or condition transfers by the debtor, or that are conditioned on the insolvency or financial condition of the debtor, on the commencement of a bankruptcy case, or the appointment of or taking possession by a trustee in a Chapter 11 case or a custodian before such commencement, and that effects or gives an option to effect a forfeiture, modification, or termination of the debtor's interest in property.

Exceptions to rule against forfeitures

The main common exceptions in the commercial context to the rule against   **3–19** forfeitures are:

1. **Direct actions**: para 1–29 *et seq*

2. **Contract and lease rescissions** For example, if a seller can cancel an unperformed contract for the sale of goods on the buyer's bankruptcy before the delivery date and keep the profit on a resale, the bankruptcy buyer's estate is deprived of the profit. If a lessor of land can cancel the lease on the lessee's bankruptcy, the lessee is deprived of the benefit of the lease. See above.

3. **Rescission** If a seller has been induced to sell an asset by reason of a fraudulent misrepresentation by the buyer, who has become bankrupt, then in England the seller can disaffirm the sale and retake possession of the property: *Re Eastgate* [1905] 1 KB 465.

CHAPTER 4

PREFERENCES: INTRODUCTION

Introduction

Policies

4–1 All developed bankruptcy laws provide for the recapture of assets transferred by the debtor in the twilight suspect period prior to the commencement of formal insolvency proceedings.

The fundamental and universal requirements qualifying a transaction as preferential are that the transaction:

- prejudices other creditors of the debtor;
- occurs while the debtor is actually insolvent or renders him insolvent;
- occurs in a suspect period prior to the formal opening of insolvency proceedings.

The first item is always required. The other two are usually required but there are exceptions, e.g. in the case of deliberate concealment.

4–2 The objectives are as follows:

- **Fraud** The main and original object is to prevent the debtor from fraudulently concealing or transferring his assets beyond the reach of his creditors when he knows that his own insolvency is looming. This is the true fraudulent conveyance or transfer and often carries an element of dishonesty.

- **Equality** The second object is that, if the debtor is in fact insolvent, he ought to treat his creditors equally even though formal insolvency proceedings have not yet begun. Other creditors should not be prejudiced by a preferential payment or transfer to one of them, thereby diminishing the assets of the estate available to creditors generally.

- **Debtor harassment** Finally, the rules against preferences are designed to discourage creditors with special leverage or who are specially diligent from harassing the debtor in financial difficulties to pay them off or secure them in priority to the others.

These policies are everywhere espoused, more or less. However there are 4–3 other policies which may on occasion conflict with the above objectives.

— **Predictability** The first is the need for the predictability and certainty that transactions with a party will be inviolable and be upheld in favour of third parties dealing with the party in good faith and for value. If all transactions could be unwound if they took place in the suspect period regardless of guilty participation or lack of value given by the third party, there would be no safety in commercial and financial transactions. The preference rules impose the theory of equality at some uncertain date long before the formal insolvency proceedings have already begun and therefore back-date the guillotine.

— **Avoidance of insolvency** The second policy mitigating against an over-broad recapture is the need on occasion to permit the debtor opportunity to trade out of his difficulties. If the debtor and its directors are potentially exposed to penalties or disqualification if they do prefer creditors, then the debtor may be pressurised into shutting up shop prematurely to the likely detriment of his creditors generally. Insolvency proceedings generally have a catastrophic effect upon the value of a company's assets and usually destroy its goodwill, even if euphemistically dressed up as a rehabilitation. This contrary policy illustrates the tension which always exists between encouraging debtors to stop before it is too late and allowing them to continue so as to rescue both themselves and their creditors.

— **Honouring commitments** Finally, there is a conflict between the bankruptcy policy of equality of distribution and the policy that debtors should honour their obligations, e.g. the payment of matured debts.

Whilst nobody objects to the avoidance of the intentional dissipation of assets, the reach of preference laws to catch the more ordinary transaction has always been unpopular and the massive international case law reflects this hostility by creditors called upon to disgorge

Terminology

The transactions under review enjoy no common universal terminology. In 4–4 common law states they are referred to as preferences (or fraudulent preferences or fraudulent transfers, even though the transaction may not be dishonestly fraudulent) and may include the "relation back" doctrine whereby the bankruptcy is deemed to relate back to actual insolvency so as to recapture transfers in that period. In French-based jurisdictions they are often termed transactions inopposable to the mass of creditors (now in France a nullity). In South Africa, they are impeachable transactions. In this study, the transactions will collectively be called "preferences".

Outline of preference law

4–5   In developed jurisdictions, the preference rules may be grouped into broad categories as follows:

1. **Intentionally prejudicial transfers** The first category comprises transfers by the debtor which are intended to prejudice or defeat creditors by removing assets otherwise available to them on insolvency. This is the original Actio Pauliana and is reflected in all developed bankruptcy laws. Its hallmark is a deliberate intention to defraud creditors. Commonly there is no suspect period and the transaction is vulnerable whenever made.

2. **Gifts** The second category comprises the avoidance of gifts by the debtor since these must clearly reduce the assets available to creditors. This category also generally includes transactions at an undervalue where there is an element of gift, such as a sale of the debtor's assets at an undervalue or a guarantee for no commensurate return. The rule may be extended to other types of undervalue transactions, such as excessive remuneration to insiders and extortionate credit transactions. There may or may not be a suspect period for gifts.

3. **General preferences** The third category comprises a general provision attacking all payments and transfers by the debtor which prejudice creditors by depleting the debtor's assets or improve the position of the preferential creditor by placing him in a better position than he would have been on the insolvency of the debtor in the absence of the transfer.

Almost invariably, these general preferences in class (3) must occur within a specified suspect period prior to the commencement of insolvency proceedings at a time when the debtor was actually insolvent.

There may in addition be specific statutory provisions dealing with involuntary transfers by the debtor, such as creditor executions over the debtor's property and trafficking in claims between debtors of and creditors of the debtor to build up set-offs.

There may also be provisions controlling transfers of the debtor's business (commonly called bulk sales laws), and provisions restricting the payment of shareholders before creditors, such as the payment of dividends out of capital or various direct and indirect forms of repayment of share capital, e.g. giving financial assistance for the purchase of the company's own shares.

There is a further category, namely the timely publication of security granted by the debtor, which is sometimes treated as within the scope of the preference rules but is more properly a matter pertaining to the avoidance of apparent wealth undercut by a secret lien.

Main issues

The main issues in determining where a jurisdiction's corporate insolvency **4–6** law (ignoring individuals) is pro-creditor or pro-debtor in the matter of pre-ferences include: the extent of creditor protections for general preferences, notably whether the transaction is saved if the debtor had no intent to prefer or if the creditor did not know of the debtor's insolvency at the time of the transfer; the protection of ordinary course of business payments; the validity of security for pre-existing debt (the main litmus test); and the length of the suspect period.

The main factor in ranking jurisdictions is probably the presence of creditor protections, such as the requirement for debtor intent to prefer which, it will be seen, significantly emasculates the preference doctrine in the interests of the favoured creditor as against the bankruptcy estate. The second chief factor is the length of the suspect period, but in this case the comparison is unsafe by reason of the presence of numerous suspect periods for different types of preference, e.g. one for gifts, another for general preferences and a third for insiders, and the presence of parallel and overlapping grounds of avoidance.

The pro-creditor jurisdictions include the English-based countries, the Netherlands and Switzerland. Traditional French countries take a middle position. The United States is pro-debtor as regards preferences, largely because of the absence of creditor safe-harbours.

Before discussing the comparative approach to particular issues, it is proposed briefly to summarise the statutory provisions in English-based and Franco-Latin jurisdictions and in the United States. A representative sampling of preference laws is summarised in chapter 7.

English-based jurisdictions

The chief features of the English-based approach are set out below and will **4–7** be found in similar form in numerous English-based jurisdictions, although significantly altered in Australia, Canada and New Zealand.

Corporate and individual bankruptcies In traditional English countries, the bankruptcy preference rules applying to individuals are generally applied to companies by cross-reference in Companies Act sections relating to liquidations. But there remain significant differences between the rules applying to individuals and those applying to companies: in the interests of commerce, many corporate transactions are not invalidated where they would be invalidated if done by an individual.

For example, the following traditional English rules for individuals do not apply to companies:

— relation back of the trustee's title to first available act of bankruptcy on which the petition was based, e.g. inability to pay debts. This was introduced in 1571 and abolished in England in 1986;

— avoidance of general assignments of book debts (commercial receivables), introduced by BA 1913 s 14 and now appearing in IA 1986 s 33 (applying also to any class of book debts);

— avoidance of uncompleted executions after notice of an available act of bankruptcy (introduced by BA 1849 and abolished in England in 1986).

Actio Pauliana – fraudulent conveyances This catches transactions made with intent to hinder, delay or defraud creditors: para 4–19 *et seq.*

4–8 **Gifts** It is generally provided that gifts (i.e. transactions in favour of a transferee without reasonably equivalent value or in favour of a transferee acting in bad faith) are voidable if (see the old BA 1914 s 42 based on BA 1869 and BA 1883 s 91):

— made within (usually) two years of the commencement of the bankruptcy, regardless of the solvency of the debtor; or

— made within (usually) 10 years of the commencement of the bankruptcy unless the donee can prove that the debtor was able to pay all his debts (liability/asset test) without the aid of the gift and that the donee received the full interest of the debtor (i.e. no rights retained).

4–9 The English insolvency legislation of 1986 made substantial changes to these rules by introducing the concept of a transaction at an undervalue and a requirement of insolvency in all cases. Transactions at an undervalue are voidable on insolvent corporate liquidation and individual bankruptcy, and on corporate administration: IA 1986 ss 238, 240 and 241 for companies; ss 339, 341 and 342 for individuals.

The present English tests for avoidance are (1) a transaction for no value or significant undervalue; (2) the debtor is insolvent (widely defined to include excess of liabilities over assets – see s 123) at the time of the transaction (or becomes insolvent as a result of the transaction); (3) suspect period of two years for companies; five years for individuals. The onus is on the insolvency representative to prove insolvency, except in the case of transactions with connected persons and associates when the onus is on the transferee. Connected persons include directors, shadow directors and associates of directors, such as those with close family ties, controllers and associated companies: IA 1986 s 435.

Under IA 1986 it is a defence if the company transacted "in good faith and for the purpose of carrying on its business" and at the time there were "reasonable grounds for believing that the transaction would benefit the company". Note that "reasonable grounds" is an objective test, and the debtor's or creditor's bona fide belief in reasonable grounds is irrelevant. This defence does not apply to individuals.

The court may restore the position to what it would have been if the transaction had not occurred. This generally means that the transaction is avoided.

Transactions at an undervalue and preferences are badges of unfitness for the purposes of the disqualification of directors from acting as a director.

Preferences Under the usual traditional English provision, a disposition is 4–10
voidable if (a) the debtor is unable to pay his debts as they fall due out of his own money, (b) the disposition is made in favour of a creditor, (c) the disposition is made "with a view to" giving the creditor or any guarantor for a creditor a preference over other creditors; (d) three or six month suspect period. Transferees from the preferred creditor are protected if they acted in good faith and for valuable consideration. The provision was first introduced in BA 1869 s 92 codifying common law, adapted in BA 1883 s 48, repeated in BA 1914 s 44 and extended to companies by successive Companies Acts.

The chief feature of the English preference doctrine distinguishing it from the traditional French model is that the debtor's factual intent to prefer must be proved: the onus is on the insolvency administrator. The intent must be the dominant intention. Intent is negated by pressure.

The main lines of this preference rule were preserved in the English Insolvency Act 1986 except that the "dominant intent" motive was replaced by the motive that the debtor was merely "influenced" by a desire to put the preferred creditor in a better position: IA 1986 s 239 (for companies); s 340 (for individuals). But the creditor's knowledge or otherwise of the insolvency or of the intent remains irrelevant.

A two-year suspect period for connected persons was also introduced in 1986. Connected persons include directors, shadow directors and associates of directors or of the company – associates are defined to include those with close family ties, controllers and certain associated companies: IA 1986 s 435. The company is presumed to be influenced by a desire to put the preferred creditor in a better position in the case of connected persons unless the contrary is proved, ie the onus of proof is reversed in the case of insiders.

4–11 **Floating charges** Special rules apply to the avoidance of floating charges on insolvent corporate liquidations and (now in England) corporate administrations. They do not apply to individuals since bankruptcy law generally prevents floating charges by individuals, at least over receivables and goods.

The present English tests are (IA 1986 s 245): (1) the company is insolvent at the time of the creation of the charge or insolvent as a result of the transaction – but insolvency at the time of the creation of the charge is not a requirement for charges to connected persons (such as directors and close family of directors and associated companies); (2) suspect period of 12 months (two years for connected persons); but (3) the charge is valid for money paid, value of goods and services supplied or the discharge or reduction of a debt, at or after the creation and in consideration of the charge (meaning "by reason of" or "having regard to the existence" of the charge), plus contractual interest.

In traditional English countries based on previous English law, there is commonly no time extension for connected persons, and the validation is permitted only for new money (not other new value) after the creation of the charge plus interest at a prescribed rate, e.g. 5 per cent.

Franco-Latin jurisdictions

4–12 The basic Franco-Latin model is followed, though with numerous detailed differences, by the central Napoleonic group (France, Belgium and Luxembourg) together with former French dominions (such as the Dominican Republic, Egypt and Haiti) and a large number of Latin American countries, including Argentina, Brazil, Chile and Venezuela. The law in countries like Denmark, Norway, Sweden and Greece is influenced by this approach. Spain and Portugal appear to be distinctive.

The main lines of the approach were substantially settled in the bankruptcy law in the third Book of the French Commercial Code of 1807 promulgated in 1808 – see Arts 443 to 447 – and modified in 1838. The changes since then have been at the edges. The chief features are set out below.

Actio Pauliana All intentionally fraudulent transfers by the debtor are void regardless of their date and regardless of insolvency. The creditor must generally be aware of the damage to creditors. See para 4–19 *et seq.*

4–13 **Transactions automatically void** The following are generally automatically void if within a suspect period commencing on the date the debtor became insolvent (cessation of payments) as determined by the bankruptcy judge in the bankruptcy order, plus (sometimes) a period of 10 days prior to that date or even longer:

— gifts and transactions at a significant undervalue;

— prepayments (in cash or by assets, set-off or otherwise) of unmatured debts, sometimes only if they fall due after the date of the declaration of bankruptcy (Argentina);

— payments of matured debts, except in cash or by negotiable instruments or other normal mode of payment. There is usually an exception for the payment of negotiable instruments;

— security granted to secure existing debts.

The transferee's knowledge of the insolvency or the preferential intent of the debtor are irrelevant.

General preferences Other payments and dispositions may be declared void if made during the suspect period and the transferee knew of the insolvency (cessation of payments) of the debtor. Preferential intent is usually not relevant.

United States law

The US Federal preference rules are contained in ss 547, 548 and 550 of the **4–14** Bankruptcy Code of 1978 as amended.

Preferences: s 547 The trustee in bankruptcy (including a Chapter 11 debtor-in-possession) may avoid any transfer of an interest of the debtor in property if the following tests are met: the transfer (which includes involuntary transfers, executions, arrestments, retention of title and foreclosure of the debtor's equity of redemption) is:

1. to or for the benefit of a creditor;

2. for or on account of an antecedent debt owed by the debtor before the transfer was made;

3. made while the debtor is insolvent (balance-sheet test – s 101);

4. made within 90 days before the filing of the petition (or one year if the creditor was an insider – e.g. relative, affiliate, director, controller of debtor); and

5. enables the creditor to receive more than he would otherwise have received in a Chapter 7 case (i.e. distributive liquidation).

The intent of the debtor is irrelevant. The debtor is presumed to have been insolvent during the 90-day suspect period, but this is rebuttable by the transferee. The onus of proving the above elements is on the trustee.

4–15　　The trustee may not avoid in the following main cases (the burden of proof usually falling on the transferee):

1.　the transfer was in substantially contemporaneous exchange for new value (defined to include money, goods, services, new credit, releases), e.g. cash sales (including cheque payments) and security against new loans;

2.　the transfer (a) was payment of a debt incurred by the debtor in the ordinary course of business or financial affairs (which includes consumer finances) of the debtor and the transferee, (b) was made in the ordinary course of business and (c) according to ordinary business terms;

3.　the transfer creates a perfected security interest to secure new value to enable the debtor to acquire the property used as collateral for the security interest (subject to conditions), e.g. loans to acquire property after the loan is made;

4.　the transfer is after-acquired inventory or receivables or proceeds covered by a perfected security interest if **either** the creditor's position is not improved or if the creditor's improvement did not prejudice unsecured creditors. This is intended to cover floating liens catching after-acquired property of the debtor;

5.　payment of tax liabilities (unless paid after penalty incurred);

6.　certain statutory liens (except to the extent avoidable under s 545);

7.　set-off, even though preferential, if it occurred more than five days before the case, unless it is a set-off under circumstances which would invalidate it under s 553. If set-off is within the five-day period, it is avoidable only if the trustee may use, sell, or lease the property so recovered.

If the creditor and the debtor have more than one exchange during the 90 day period, the exchanges are netted out in accordance with a formula in s 547(c)(4). The netting out only applies to transfers after the preferential transfer. To the extent the new value that the creditor advances is unsecured, that value qualifies under this exemption. This applies notably to running trading accounts.

4–16　**Fraudulent transfers: s 548** The trustee may avoid a transfer of the debtor's property or any obligation incurred by the debtor voluntarily or involuntarily where:

1. the transaction took place within one year of the filing of the petition, and

2. (a) the transaction was with actual intent to hinder, delay or defraud any creditor (the *actio pauliana*), or
    (b) (1) the transfer was at an undervalue, and (2) the debtor was insolvent (or became insolvent as a result of the transfer–balance sheet test, not inability to pay debts as they fall due), or the debtor was left with unreasonably small capital for a business or transaction, or the debtor intended to incur debts beyond his ability to pay as they matured.

The transferee has a lien or other appropriate protection for any value given in good faith.

Both the Uniform Fraudulent Transfer Act (applying in 50 states with limitations) and the Uniform Fraudulent Conveyance Act are to similar effect. The UFTA generally has a four-year suspect period.

Liability of transferee of avoided transfers: s 550 As to transferees, the   4–17
initial transferee is not protected, regardless of his good faith, or absence of knowledge of insolvency. A subsequent direct or indirect transferee from the initial transferee is protected if he takes for value (not necessarily the fair equivalent), in good faith and without knowledge of the voidability of the transfer. Good faith transferees are entitled to a lien on the property for the net value of improvements.

Time limits The trustee must avoid within two years of his appointment or (if earlier) closure or dismissal of the case. For debtor-in-possession in Chapter 11 rehabilitation proceedings, the authorities are split as to two years from Chapter 11 filing or closure or dismissal of the case. Recovery action in both cases must be commenced within one year of avoidance of transfer or (if earlier) before closure or dismissal of the case. There are different periods under state laws, typically four years or more.

Other protections: s 564 The trustee's rights are subject to a right of a seller   4–18
of goods to reclaim the goods if received by a debtor within 10 days of the insolvency and the request is made in writing within 10 days (or the court may grant the reclaiming creditor a lien or priority as an administrative expense in lieu of turning over the property).

The trustee may not avoid a transfer if it is a margin payment or a settlement payment made by or to a commodity broker, stockbroker, or financial institution before the commencement of the case (unless there is intent to defraud other creditors and it is not made in good faith).

The trustee may not avoid a margin/settlement payment to a repurchase agreement participant or a swap agreement by or to a swap participant made before the commencement of the case.

State law Most states have additional rules and the trustee can use these: s 544(b). Note especially the Uniform Fraudulent Transfer Act which is similar to s 548. State laws often also allow attacks on dividends by insolvent corporations.

Actio Pauliana: fraudulent transfers

4–19　　This is the fraudulent transfer where the debtor intends to defeat, delay or hinder his creditors and is known as the Actio Pauliana, stemming from Roman law and now codified in one form or another in probably all commercial jurisdictions.

> See Austria BA s 28; Belgium CC Art 448; Denmark BA Art 74; England IA 1986 s 423; France CC 1167; Greece CC Arts 939–945; Italy CC Arts 2901–4; Netherlands CC Bk3 ss 45–48; South Africa IA 1936 s 31; Sweden BA s 5; Switzerland Federal Debt Collection and Bankruptcy Act 1889 s 288; United States BC 1978 s 548.

The notion evidently first surfaced in Rome in the second century BC and was largely rediscovered in Europe in the eleventh century. Paulus was a compiler of Roman law who described the content of the doctrine. For a short history, see Dalhuisen, *International Insolvency and Bankruptcy* (1982) vol 1, para 1.02[2] n 10; 2.02[1] n 4.

The Pauliana has been used to avoid a wide range of transactions with much case law in the developed jurisdictions, such as gifts, concealment of assets, secret conveyances to spouses, secreting the proceeds of sales of property, the surrender of a right of inheritance, the repayment of advances by the transfer of goods to a creditor aware of the debtor's parlous financial state (Belgium), the grant of a mortgage for pre-existing debt or the transfer of assets to a dummy company owned by the debtor or his relatives. There is case law in many jurisdictions on transfer of a business, e.g. in Belgium, the United States and England: *Arbuthnot Leasing International Ltd v Havelet Leasing Ltd (No 2)* [1990] BCC 636. In the US security interests granted in leveraged buyouts have been caught by the US Pauliana in BC 1978 s 548.

4–20　　The English version stems back to an Elizabethan Act of 1571 which, though changed in England, continues to apply in many English-based jurisdictions. The statute generally provides that every conveyance made with intent to hinder, delay or defraud creditors is voidable at the instance of any person thereby prejudiced. This applies to any transfer of property, including (probably) payments. Insolvency at the time of the transfer need not be proved. There is an unlimited suspect period. Actual intent to deprive creditors must be proved – but deceit is not necessary. Any prejudiced creditor can theoretically apply for avoidance. Innocent transferees in good faith for valuable consideration and without notice of intent to defraud are protected. Bona fide transferees from bad faith transferees are also protected. This version of the Actio Pauliana applies to both companies and individuals.

The 1571 Act was replaced and recast in England in 1925 (by s 172 of the Law of Property Act 1925) which in turn was replaced by IA 1986 s 423 to similar effect. The 1986 version now applies to all transactions at an undervalue (not just dispositions of property) entered into for the purpose of putting the assets beyond the reach of creditors or potential creditors or otherwise prejudicing such creditors. The victim can apply for an avoidance order and the company debtor need not be in financial difficulties. Transferees from the transferee are protected if they acquire the property in good faith, for value and without notice of the undervalue *and* the evasive or prejudicial intention: IA 1986 s 425.

Although the various versions differ, the authentic Actio Pauliana has a   **4–21** number of features which, cumulatively, distinguish it from the mainstream of ordinary preference doctrines, and which are most truly exhibited mainly in the civil code countries in the non-Germanic group.

In all cases, prejudice to creditors is a requirement, which in practice means a diminution of the debtor's assets. The differences from other preferences are:

– **Available outside bankruptcy** The debtor need not be a bankrupt before a creditor can initiate the action, although in practice he generally is. The availability of the action outside actual bankruptcy is the position in England under IA 1986 s 423 and many English-based countries in the Traditional English group. Any injured creditor can bring an action against the debtor: it is not necessarily a collective action brought by a representative of the creditors generally. Hence the court could theoretically order reparation to the injured creditor alone. The objection to this is that one creditor is paid ahead of the others when, once insolvency proceedings have begun, all creditors should submit to the collective proceeding and all recoveries should fall into the estate available for creditors generally.

– **No actual insolvency** The debtor need not be insolvent when he enters into the transaction. The intent to defeat is enough. Hence there is commonly no suspect period of specified length. But, if a debtor is not insolvent or not rendered insolvent as a result of the transaction, prejudice to creditors is inherently more difficult to prove.

– **Creditor collusion** At least in many civil code countries such as Austria, Belgium, Greece and Switzerland, the creditor must be aware of the prejudice to creditors and also (often) the fraudulent intent of the debtor. This makes the Pauline action more difficult to use in these countries when compared to the deemed avoidance of certain transactions, such as security for pre-existing debt, gifts, prepayments and payments of matured debts by abnormal means.

Commonly transferees are protected if they acted in good faith and gave commensurate value.

CHAPTER 5

PREFERENCES:
PREJUDICE TO CREDITORS

Prejudice to creditors generally

The basic requirement of all preferences is that other creditors of the debtor   5–1
are prejudiced. This usually means that the assets of the debtor available to
pay his debts are reduced or depleted.

Sometimes the case law reveals a further form of prejudice, namely, that,
although the assets remain the same in nominal terms, one illiquid asset is
exchanged for cash which can be more easily dissipated, e.g. a sale of a factory or a mortgage over a factory for cash or a sale of an entire business.
Apart from bulk sales, this form of prejudice is rarely stigmatised because it
would endanger ordinary sales and loans for new value. The issue usually
arises when the debtor in desperation sells land or plant at the last moment
and immediately uses the cash to pay the most pressing creditor.

In some countries, e.g. in England and the United States, the test of prejudice to the bankrupt estate is the other way round and provides that the position of the creditor concerned in the transaction is improved in the sense
that the transaction puts him in a better position than he would have been
on the insolvency of the debtor if the transaction had not taken place.

In most cases it makes no difference which test is adopted. But in at least
one situation, there is a difference, namely a substitution of creditor. For
example, if a bank pays a creditor of the debtor at the request of the debtor
and thereby increases the overdraft of the debtor, the bank becomes a creditor in place of the paid creditor. The net assets of the debtor are not diminished and remain the same. However, the position of the paid creditor is
improved because he has been paid in full when he would only have got a
dividend on the bankruptcy. This will affect novations of debt and triangle
schemes whereby one lender makes a new loan which the debtor uses to pay
off another lender. These transactions prejudice creditors only where the
incoming creditor has greater recovery powers than the outgoing creditor,
e.g. because the incoming creditor has a set-off or security.

5–2   International case law shows that there is no prejudice to creditors if:

- The debtor pays a fully secured debt, because the creditor could realise the security for that debt on insolvency. Case law in many jurisdictions so holds, e.g. Denmark, the US and Germany: BGHZ 90212. If the creditor is only partially secured, the payment ought to be applied to the unsecured portion and US case law so presumes.

- The debtor pays a priority debt, e.g. taxes or wages, which would be paid in any event.

- The debtor pays out of money lent to him on trust which he never had the power to use as his own or which was paid by the lender to the other party directly. The debtor never had the money: *Coral Petroleum v Banque Paris-Bas London*, 797 F 2d 1351 (5th Cir 1986).

- The deposit of money by the debtor to a bank account in credit (the debtor still has the asset).

- Substitutions of equal security, e.g. *Roy's Trustees v Colville & Drysdale*, 1903 5F 769 (Scotland), because there is no change in position unless the creditor's security is improved.

- Realisation of security unless at an undervalue: see *Durrett v Washington National Insurance Co*, 621 F 2d 201 (5th Cir 1980) – 70 per cent of market value is reasonably equivalent value.

- Transfers by the debtor of property held by him in trust or as custodian or the return of property held by the debtor in trust, e.g. a mistaken payment.

- Sales for full value, because the debtor's position is unchanged. The United States BC 1978 s 547 exempts contemporaneous exchanges of value.

- Security for contemporaneous new money: para 5–15

- Cancelling a contract profitable to the debtor if the creditor could have cancelled on insolvency in any event and kept the profit.

What follows is an analysis of some typical situations from the point of view of this test, it being remembered that, even if a transaction fails on the prejudice test, it may nevertheless be protected by some other defence, e.g. it was outside the suspect period, or was granted without intent to prefer, or was validated by a safe harbour rule in favour of a good faith creditor unaware of the insolvency.

Prejudice to creditors: undervalue transactions

Gifts and transactions at an undervalue

A gift of assets by an embarrassed debtor will always satisfy the test of   5–3
prejudice to creditors because it involves a diminution of assets without
equal return: less assets will be available to the bankrupt estate on insolvency.

The doctrine commonly extends to transactions at an undervalue where
there is a significant element of gift. Only the gift element is voidable.

Outright gifts will pertain primarily to individuals who, for example, give
their house or other assets to their spouses or children while often nevertheless continuing to enjoy possession and use.

Corporate gifts would sometimes be ultra vires or, if protected against
ultra vires by safe harbours for third parties, be a misfeasance by the directors for which they are liable. The ultra vires doctrine is partly an investor
protection and party a creditor protection. Examples of corporate gifts are
charitable donations, substantial non-contractual gifts to long-standing
retired employees, "golden parachutes" (excessive pay-offs) to retiring
directors or inter-company transfers without full value being payable.

Other examples of undervalue transaction or gifts might include: 5–4

- a voluntary release or cancellation of a debt or surrender of a lease;

- the surrender of security held by the debtor for an obligation owed to the
  debtor by the creditor;

- the release of an option to purchase another's property;

- the sale of assets at a material undervalue, such as supplying goods
  cheaply to a pressing creditor;

- the release by the creditor of an invalid security in return for a payment
  by the debtor (the debtor is paying for nothing);

- collusive judgments whereby the debtor allows the creditor to enter a
  judgment against him for more than the creditor is entitled to or where
  the debtor has a good defence or where the debtor allows creditor application to the court to register security out of time in circumstances where
  the debtor could have opposed the application;

- excessive remuneration to managers. Some states have specific provisions – see Denmark BA Art 66 (if to closely-related persons); Norway
  s 5–4 of the Debt Recovery Act 1984; Sweden BA s 8;

- extortionate credit bargains whereby the return to the creditor far exceeds the market return in the circumstances. These transactions may in any event be caught by specific provisions directed against usury or against extortionate credit transactions. An example in the English insolvency legislation is the power to set aside or vary extortionate credit bargains.

5–5   "Value" usually means any kind of benefit. In South Africa it has been held to include the intangible expectation of the continued financial stability of a group of companies: *Langeberg Koöperasie Bpk v Inverdoorn Farming & Trading Co Ltd*, 1965 (2) SA 597(A).

There are often exceptions in favour of charitable gifts and normal and reasonable gifts, e.g. as in Italy, Sweden and Switzerland.

Some jurisdictions stigmatise gifts as preferential regardless of the insolvency of the debtor if they are made within a fixed suspect period. These countries appear to include Austria, Denmark, Japan, Norway, Sweden, Switzerland and traditional English countries, but not England or Australia (where the transaction is referred to as an "uncommercial transaction" under s 588 of the Corporate Law Reform Act 1992).

Others stigmatise the gift only if it occurs after (or a short time before) the suspension of payments or when the debtor is insolvent. These include traditional French and Latin countries, South Africa and the United States (one year suspect period, but often longer periods under state law).

Guarantees as undervalue transactions

5–6   A perennial problem is the corporate guarantee of another's debt and the question of whether the guarantee is granted for an adequate return. This issue arises also under doctrines of corporate law which forbid directors from giving away assets of the company – there must be corporate benefit. The "corporate benefit" doctrine is partly intended to protect shareholders against an improper depletion of the assets – an investor protection – and is partly intended to protect creditors for the same reason – a creditor protection.

Where a parent guarantees a loan made by a lender to a subsidiary, the benefit will often be the improvement in the value of the shares held by the parent in its subsidiary by virtue of additional finance put to profitable ends or the on-lending of the proceeds to finance the parent or the rest of the group. But the corresponding return will often be more difficult to prove where one subsidiary guarantees a sister-subsidiary or guarantees its own parent, unless the guaranteeing company receives a market rate of commission for the guarantee or other corporate benefit, such as an on-lending of loan proceeds or a tangible enhancement of its trading position by virtue of the financing of the group as a whole.

In England, corporate guarantees (and other transactions) which do amount to a transaction at an undervalue during the relevant suspect period when the debtor is insolvent are saved if the guaranteeing company acted in good faith and for the purpose of *its* business and also at the time of the transaction there were reasonable grounds for believing that the transaction would benefit the company – an objective test: IA 1986 s 238(5). It can be difficult, if not impossible, for banks and others receiving corporate guarantees to establish these essentially commercial benefits with complete certainty and so the safe harbour is not as safe as it should be. The defence does not apply in the bankruptcy of individuals and hence would not protect guarantees given by individuals.

Similar principles apply to collateral security given by one party to secure the debt of another (in substance a guarantee with recourse limited to the collateral).

In the United States "upstream" and "cross-stream" guarantees and pledges among related corporate entities have been successfully avoided because the guarantor or pledgor did not receive reasonable equivalent value for the transfer. Some courts have expanded avoidance to "downstream" guarantees and pledges when the relevant transfer did not actually increase the value of the subsidiary on a balance sheet basis or otherwise.

Subordinations as undervalue transactions

If a creditor agrees to subordinate his existing debt to a debt owed to 5–7 another creditor of the common debtor on terms that the junior creditor agrees to pay dividends and other recoveries on his junior debt to the senior creditor until the senior creditor is paid in full, the junior creditor is effectively giving assets to the senior creditor, just as if the junior creditor had granted the senior creditor collateral security over the junior debt owed to him by the common debtor. This transaction could, as in the case of guarantees, constitute a transaction at an undervalue prejudicing creditors, unless a defence is available.

Prejudice to creditors: payments

Payment of existing debts

Where the debtor pays an existing debt owed to a creditor – such as a sup- 5–8 plier creditor or a bank lender – but without paying other creditors pro rata, the position of the paid creditor is improved because he is paid in full when on insolvency he would only rank for a dividend and the position of the other creditors of the debtor is prejudiced because the payment of the debt in full diminishes the assets otherwise available to them. This is not an undervalue transaction because the debt is owing for full value and the net assets of the debtor in accounting terms are unchanged.

Payment generally includes all methods of discharge – including set-off or payment in kind by a transfer of assets, such as the return of goods sold on credit, or the delivery of bonds.

Indirect or triangular payments are also generally caught. An example is where the debtor is owed money and instructs his debtor to pay his creditor. The transfer is made by the other debtor but it is the debtor's property which is used and he initiated the transfer by his instruction.

A feature of the Franco-Latin jurisdictions, as well as Denmark, Sweden and Norway, is that certain payments are deemed to be preferential if made in the suspect period, regardless of the creditor's knowledge of the debtor's insolvency so that there is no defence. These are (1) prepayments of debts which are not yet due – somewhat unusual in practice since needy debtors are disposed not to prepay unless in favour of some particularly favoured or particularly pressing creditor – and (2) payments of debts which are due by some abnormal means or otherwise than as contracted for. Abnormal measures would include the return of goods by a buyer to a seller sold on credit, because the buyer-debtor cannot pay for them, and the delivery of securities. Payment by credit transfer or cheque would not be abnormal and nobody appears to dissent.

Negotiable instruments

5–9   Payments to holders of negotiable instruments are often specially protected, either by specific provisions (as in a Franco-Latin countries) or by case law (as in the English-based countries): see *Re Clay & Sons* (1895) 3 Mans 31, DC. The reasons are (a) the importance of predictability for mercantile instruments, (b) the policy in favour of ordinary course of business payments, pre-eminently exhibited by commercial paper, and (c) the need to protect the subsequent holder. If a subsequent holder either refuses payment or is paid, he loses his rights against previous holders liable on the instrument. Hence the Franco-Latin countries and various others (including Sweden, Norway and South Africa) render the payment of a bill of exchange or promissory note preferential only if the *first* holder knew of the insolvency when the instrument was issued to him by the debtor and the recovery is only permitted against him.

Ordinary course of business payments

If a debtor is prevented from paying his debts in the ordinary course of busi- 5–10
ness, that might immediately precipitate enforcement action by disappointed creditors so that the debtor would have no means of trading out of
the difficulty. The usual policy of preference law is to discourage unusual
action by debtor or creditors during the slide into bankruptcy but not
routine transactions.

Typical examples of ordinary payments would be payment of commercial
debts for goods or services in the ordinary course of trading (otherwise there
will be no more supplies), payment of rent (otherwise the landlord will forfeit the lease), payment of telephone and other utilities (otherwise the debtor
will be cut off), payment of royalties for industrial property rights or franchises (otherwise the rights will be terminated), and routine payments on
debenture issues or term loans (otherwise the loan will be accelerated).

As a result of the above, it is often the case that the payment is not preferential if it is in the ordinary course of business.

In the **United States,** a specific exemption favours the payment of a debt 5–11
to the extent the debt was incurred in the ordinary course of business or
financial affairs of the debtor and the creditor (including a private individual's personal financial affairs), and the payment was made in the ordinary
course of business according to ordinary business terms – a tight test. See
BC 1978 s 547(c). The courts have focused on the prior conduct of the parties, usual industry practice, knowledge of the financial state of the debtor
by the creditor, and whether the payment resulted from any unusual action
by the debtor or the creditor. Litigation settlements are often not treated as
incurred or paid in the ordinary course of business. Switching from credit to
cash payments in knowledge of the debtor's financial difficulties may be outside the ordinary course, as may sudden and substantial increases of loan
repayments. A payment made after the debtor has closed down its business
may or may not be in the ordinary course.

In **England** and many English-based jurisdictions, there is no specific
statutory exemption in favour of the ordinary course of business payment.
But these will rarely be made with the necessary preferential intent by the
debtor – a basic requirement for a preference in those jurisdictions. In *Abell
v Daniell* (1829) Mood & M 370 NP, the court was prepared to validate a
gift of £200 by a father to his son made on the eve of the father's bankruptcy
where it was shown that the gift was in the ordinary course of maintaining
the son. But a prepayment will almost invariably be treated as made with
intent to prefer: *Re Fleming Fraser & Co* (1888) 60 LT 154. The position in
Switzerland is similar.

In **South Africa** the payee must prove the double test not only that the disposition was made in the ordinary course of business but also that it was not intended to give the creditor a preference: IA 1936 s 29.

5–12 **Netherlands** law is particularly favourable to payments of matured debts. There is no preference unless the transaction was without legal obligation: see BA Art 42 and HR 10 Dec 1976, NJ 1977, 617. Hence if the debtor pays a debt which is due, the payment cannot be avoided. But the creditor can avoid the payment if the payee knew that the bankruptcy of the debtor had been applied for (the post-petition transfer) or there was collusion between the debtor and the creditor to the prejudice of other creditors: BA s 47.

Case law in **Denmark** enquires whether the payment is excessively large in relation to the available cash assets of the debtor, e.g. the debtor uses all his current revenues to pay a single creditor. In **Sweden**, where there is an exception for ordinary payments, payments exceeding 10 per cent of the debtor's assets are in practice regarded as extraordinary – but this is said to be a practitioner's rule of thumb.

In some jurisdictions the more indulgent approach drops away in a short period immediately preceding the insolvency so that even normal cash payments or payment of due debts are caught.

5–13 Typically the **Franco-Latin** jurisdictions automatically avoid prepayments and payments by abnormal means (e.g. by assets, not cash) in the suspect period, regardless of creditor knowledge of the insolvency, so that these are always characterised as outside the ordinary course (and often would be elsewhere). Usually in these countries the payment of matured debts by normal means are unprotected only if the creditor knew of the debtor's insolvency so that there is a safe harbour for ordinary course of business payments but not if the insolvency is notorious.

In **Scotland**, a transaction in the ordinary course of trade or business is generally protected by IA s 243(2), unless there was creditor collusion to prejudice creditors. The mere fact that the creditor knows of the insolvency is not enough to establish collusion: *Nordic Travel Ltd v Scotprint Ltd*, 1980 SC 1.

Current accounts

5–14 In the case of bank current accounts where the debtor makes payments into the account followed by the bank making payments out so that the net position is the same, it would be unfortunate if the jurisdiction treated only the payments in as preferential and ignored the fresh advances – one ought to look at the overall net position to see if there is an improvement.

In *Richardson v The Commercial Banking Co of Sydney Ltd* (1951–52) 85

CLR 111, the bank operated the debtor's current account knowing that he was insolvent. Cheques paid in reduced the overdraft, but were followed by payments out increasing the overdraft. At the end of the suspect period, the overdrawn balance exceeded that at the beginning. *Held*: the net result should be looked at, and since the net overdraft had increased, the payments in were not to be regarded as preferential.

This net improvement test is now statutory in Australia: Corporate Law Reform Act 1992. The US has a net improvement test in BC 1978 s 547(c)(4).

Prejudice to creditors: security

Security for new money

Security granted by the debtor for new money paid at or about the time the security is granted is usually not treated as prejudicial to creditors: e.g. *Re Conn*, 9 Bankr 431 (Bankr ND Ohio 1981). There is an equivalent exchange of value, like a cash sale. This factor should protect new money mortgages, purchase money mortgages, initial margin deposited in connection with trading in organised markets and possessory liens arising by operation of law (though the US position on liens is complex – see BC 1978 s 545). But collateral mortgages to secure the debt of third parties may amount to transactions at an undervalue: para 5–6.

    5–15

The US has a specific exemption in favour of contemporaneous exchanges for new value in BC 1978 s 547. There are numerous US cases on whether a delayed grant of security is substantially contemporaneous, each turning on the length of the delay and the circumstances, e.g. whether the delay was administrative or inadvertent or usual, or was intentional.

Secured loans to pay off existing creditors

Triangle transactions or indirect security, where a debtor borrows money from a new lender against security in order to pay off an existing unsecured creditor have often been treated as a preference of the paid creditor in the US to the extent of the security granted to the new creditor: *Re Hartley*, 825 F 2d 1067, 17 CBC 2d 550 (6th Cir 1987).

    5–16

> In *Re Beerman*, 112 F 663 (ND Ga 1981), the creditor got a third party to lend money to the debtor secured by a mortgage and the loan was used to pay the creditor's claim, with the creditor indemnifying the lender against any loss the lender might suffer. *Held*: preferential.

In *Kellogg v Blue Quail Energy*, 831 F 2d 556, 17 CBC 2d 987 (5th Cir 1987), a third party issued a letter of credit to an existing creditor in return for a pledge by the debtor. *Held*: the issuance of the letter of credit was an indirect preference of the existing creditor who was the beneficiary of the letter of credit.

The economic result of the combined transactions substituting one new secured creditor for the old paid creditors is that the debtor has granted security for pre-existing debt: see below. Similar principles have been applied in England to floating charges: see para 5–21 *et seq*.

Although the payment to the third party creditors may be caught by the ordinary preference rules in BC 1978 s 547, the mortgage would not be – in the US because of the s 547 exemption in favour of contemporaneous exchanges of value unless it is caught by the Actio Pauliana, as in BC 1978 s 548 (actual intent to hinder, defraud or delay creditors by an insolvent debtor): *Coleman American Moving Services, Inc v First National Bank & Trust Co*, 5 CBC 2d 410, (B Ct D Kan 1981).

Security for pre-existing debt

5–17 Generally the grant by the debtor of security for an existing unsecured debt is regarded as prejudicial to creditors: otherwise the pari passu treatment of creditors might be thwarted by creditors harassing the debtor into granting security in the twilight period and the race would go to the most pressing.

The availability of security for pre-existing debt is one of the leading litmus tests of the pro-creditor or pro-debtor bias of a jurisdiction. The international attitude may be summarised as set out below:

- **Deliberate intent** In most developed countries the Pauline action is available but this generally requires the debtor's intent to prejudice creditors and creditor collusion, both of which may be difficult to prove. Para 4–19.

- **Automatically void** In a large group of countries, security for pre-existing debt by an insolvent debtor in the suspect period is automatically void, regardless of the creditor's knowledge of the insolvency. These countries include the Franco-Latin jurisdictions, Denmark, Norway and the United States. The Franco-Latin jurisdictions treat this as on the same footing as gifts. Some shorten the suspect period – e.g. Norway (three months).

- **Not void if intent negated** In the English-based countries, security for pre-existing debt is void only if the debtor had intent to prefer, which will often be negated if there is pressure or a desire to keep the business going by maintaining the goodwill of the bank and the hope of future credit or the bank's forbearance. The *quid pro quo* is keeping the debtor alive.

In *Re M C Bacon Ltd* [1990] BCLC 324, a company in financial difficulties granted security to its bank for existing debt and went into liquidation eight months later. *Held*: the security was not preferential because the directors were not influenced by a positive desire to improve the bank's position on liquidation by granting the security. They were motivated only by the desire to retain the bank's support for the company.

— **Valid if pursuant to previous obligation** In another group of jurisdictions, security granted pursuant to a pre-existing obligation is saved provided that the debtor undertook the obligation outside the suspect period or, more usually, the obligation was entered into when the debt was incurred and was therefore part of the consideration for the loan. This group includes Switzerland (BA s 287) and, more hesitantly, the Netherlands: see BA ss 42, 43. Sweden might be in this group: see BA s 12. But in all cases the security may be caught by the Pauline action, although here the safe harbours in favour of the creditor are generally more protective so that it is more difficult for the estate to avoid.

5–18

One argument is that the obligation to secure on request was part of the original consideration for the loan. The contrary argument is that the creditor is reserving to himself the power to be preferred. In England security granted pursuant to a legal obligation to do so may negative intent which is an English requirement e.g. where the debtor agreed to grant the security as part of the original deal – as in *Re Bent* (1873) 42 LJ Bcy 25, LJ (security granted a year after debt incurred and six weeks after the creditor's requirement for the security); *Re Softley* (1875) LR 20 Eq 746 (security granted pursuant to a previous undertaking to the bank to grant security); *Bulteel & Colmore v Parker & Bulteel's Trustee* (1916) 32 TLR 661. But in other cases the grant of security pursuant to an obligation entered into at the time of the initial advance has been struck down as an agreement to prefer.

In *Re Eric Holmes (Property) Ltd* [1965] Ch 1052, the security was granted to secure a director's advances pursuant to an agreement to grant the security. *Held*: this was an agreement to prefer on request. But the result was probably influenced by the fact that it was an insider who was preferred and by the fact that the company got no advantage from the security.

The point is important in relation to the validity of variation margin in organised markets. Initial margin (ie collateral or cash deposits) is generally given by the trader to the market clearing house at the inception of trading and variation margin is called when the debtor's exposure on his existing trades is increased by reason of market fluctuations. It is crucial to the safety and integrity of markets that the variation margin should be valid and certain. But only the increase in collateral value should be vulnerable.

Both the United States and Britain have special statutory protections for security given in certain organised markets and in certain other cases. In the US, BC 1978 s 546 provides that, the trustee may not avoid a transfer if it is a margin payment or a settlement payment made by or to a commodity broker, stockbroker, or financial institution before the commencement of the case (unless there is intent to defraud other creditors and it is not made in good faith). Also the trustee may not avoid a margin/settlement payment to a repurchase agreement participant or a swap agreement by or to a swap participant made before commencement of the case. In Britain, Part VII of the Companies Act 1989 protects margin and certain other security given to secure obligations under market contracts in connection with various recognised investment exchanges and clearing-houses: s 165.

— **No knowledge of insolvency** In the final group, the creditor may be protected if he did not know of the insolvency of the debtor (Italy, Japan, it seems). This does not help rescues of companies obviously in difficulties.

Roll-over of secured current accounts

5–19   In England security given to secure an existing overdraft on current account will be whitewashed by subsequent payments in and payments out on the current account on the FIFO basis of *Clayton's Case* so that all payments out of the current account by the bank after the creation of the security are treated as new advances and therefore are not pre-existing debt: *Re Yeovil Glove Co Ltd* [1965] Ch 148. But an artificial roll-over will not achieve this result.

In France and Belgium, the case law has adopted three solutions to the question of whether a current account which continues to be operated after the grant of the security can constitute new money. For Belgium, see Cloquet, *Droit Commercial* (3rd ed) vol IV para 539 *et seq*; for France, see Ripert/Roblot, *Traite de Droit Commercial* (11th ed) vol 2 para 2344. The older, more conservative, cases decided that, if the balance on the current account at the date of the final closure of the account exceeded the balance when the security was granted, then the excess must be new money advanced after the date of the security and hence the security would not be avoidable under this head to the extent of the excess. But if the balance on final closure was equal to or less than the balance on the security-date, the whole security was automatically void as security for pre-existing debt.

Subsequent decisions in both countries introduced the refinement that the protected excess was the excess of the final balance over the lowest balance after the security-date.

More recent decisions have, it seems, adopted the *Clayton's Case* analysis that any payments into the account by the debtor are imputed to the oldest payments out so as to operate to repay those oldest advances. Hence new advances after the security-date are capable of being treated as new money regardless of the account balance. It does not seem unfair that post-security advances should be protected: they are given in return for the security and the bank could instead have closed the accounts at once. Hence there is commonly a real *quid pro quo*.

Security over after-acquired assets

Where security covers future assets, then when the future asset comes into   5–20 existence, the effect is that the security over the future asset secures pre-existing debt. Examples are floating charges covering all future assets, buildings added to mortgaged land, and engines fixed to aircraft (usually an exempt substitution).

The capture of after-acquired assets by a floating charge is not treated as preferential in England even though the after-acquired assets were acquired in the suspect period. Other creditors are forewarned by registration of the security.

In the United States the Bankruptcy Code of 1978 preserves the power of a floating lien over after-acquired property, but only if the "two-point net improvement" test in s 547(c)(5) is satisfied. A security interest in inventory or receivables is protected against avoidance to the extent that the secured party either does not improve his position during the preference period (e.g. inventory collateral increases without an increase in the debt) or can show that his improvement in position was not "to the prejudice of other creditors holding unsecured claims".

The question often arises in those countries (mainly those outside the common law group) which prohibit the grant of security over future unidentified assets by reason of the doctrine of specificity. For example, a pledgor who has pledged investment securities may substitute securities in order to trade them, provided the margin of cover is maintained: the new substituted securities are effectively newly pledged. In the Netherlands, the non-possessory pledge over inventory or receivables may cover future assets and the practice is for the pledgor to send "pledge forms" from time to time to the pledgee covering those new assets. Strictly these new pledges are now security for pre-existing debt, but they ought not to be treated as such to the extent that the value of the collateral is not improved, e.g. where the new inventory replaces old inventory or the new receivables replace old receivables which have been paid, or the new securities replace old securities. This is believed to be the solution adopted in Belgium, for example, and is paralleled by the US approach. The English-based approach is much more favourable to the creditor: if after-acquired assets are specified in the original charge, even if generically, there is no preference even if the value of the collateral is thereby improved.

Floating charges for pre-existing debt

5–21   Floating charges receive specially stringent treatment in English-based jurisdictions by reason of the fact that they are a monopolistic security. Ordinarily the floating charge is invalid if created while the company is insolvent (widely defined in the English IA 1986 s 123) in a suspect period of one year except to the extent of cash received by the company for the charge at or about the time of the creation of the charge and interest thereon at a maximum prescribed rate, e.g. 5 per cent. It is not a defence that the company had no intent to prefer or granted the charge under pressure. The object is to allow floating charges only for new money received when the charge is created and to prevent creditors calling for subsequent floating charges for existing debts. In England the concept of new money in cash was widened in 1986 to include the market value (objectively ascertained) of goods or services supplied and the reduction of debts of the company and the allowable interest is at the contractual rate, not a prescribed rate: see IA 1986 s 245.

Guarantees are not protected because they do not result in the injection of new money into the guaranteeing company so that floating charges by insolvent companies to secure guarantees must survive the one year period.

5–22   But if the charge secures an existing current account, payments out following payments in after the charge may "purify" the floating charge because the payments out are treated as new money even though the level of debt remains the same: *Re Yeovil Glove Co Ltd* [1965] Ch 148.

The new money cannot be created by a transparent subterfuge as where the lender rolls over his loan, nor does the company have new money if it never has the use or control of the money because it must immediately be used to pay other creditors under the terms of the loan: *Re Destone Fabrics Ltd* [1941] Ch 319. The effect here is purely to substitute a secured debt for an unsecured debt: *Re GT Whyte & Co Ltd* [1983] BCLC 311.

> In *Re Orleans Motor Co* [1911] 2 Ch 41, a bank pressed directors for payment on their guarantee of the company's overdraft. The directors paid the company

and the company immediately paid the bank and issued a floating charge to the directors. *Held*: the payment was not new money in return for the charge since the company had no benefit from the transaction.

The invalidation does not have retrospective effect so any recoveries on a pre-liquidation enforcement are not recoverable from the chargee: *Mace Builders v Lunn* [1985] 3 WLR 465.

In England, in order to attack mainly inter-company floating charges effectively putting shareholders monopolistically ahead of unsecured creditors, charges to insiders must survive for two years and are invalidated even though the company was not insolvent at the time of the creation of the charge. This was a 1986 innovation.

Simultaneity is not essential provided that the new money was reasonably contemporaneous. A gap of a fortnight has been validated where it was always intended that the charge would be given in consideration of the advances: *Re Columbian Fire-proofing Co* [1910] 2 Ch 120, CA. But later case law has narrowed this time-gap.

In order to avoid the rigours of the 12–month avoidance rule, it is common in English-based jurisdictions to convert the floating charge into a fixed charge over as many assets as is practicable having regard to the company's need to be able to deal with its trading assets, e.g. inventory. The fixed charges would then be subject to a six month suspect period instead of 12 months and the additional requirement that prejudicial intent by the debtor be proved. The fixed charges could apply, for example, to land, buildings, shares in subsidiaries, intellectual property rights, goodwill, major contracts and receivables.

Late registration of security

The usual position for security requiring public registration is either that it 5–23 must be registered within a prescribed time or, if not, is treated as constituted when it is registered so that, if this is in the suspect period, it is potentially void as security for pre-existing debt. In many French-based and Latin American countries, registration of non-possessory chattel mortgages, including over ships and aircraft is constitutive and hence the time of registration determines the time when the security is created for the purposes of the preference rule. Commonly there is a grace period, e.g. 15 days. In Denmark, for example, failure to file the particulars of a mortgage in the appropriate public registry without undue delay renders the security liable to be set aside. When the filing takes place within three months of the commencement of bankruptcy proceedings, undue delay is presumed.

In numerous English-based countries, failure to register corporate security within the 21-day (or 30-day) period generally invalidates the security against creditors (since the object is to prevent the secret lien from deceiving creditors), but it is possible to apply for registration out of time if the non-registration was through inadvertence or other sufficient cause. But the court will not permit late registration if liquidation proceedings have commenced or, usually, if the company is in fact insolvent. The English position was altered by the Companies Act 1989 (provision not yet in force), but the effect remains substantially similar.

5–24   In England, the replacement of a void security by a valid security has been held not to be preferential because the object of the debtor was not to prefer but rather to undo an error.

> In *Re FLE Holdings Ltd* [1967] 3 All ER 553, a company granted a charge to its bank over the company's factory. The charge was void for inadvertent lack of registration. The bank repeatedly required a valid charge and this was granted when the company was insolvent. *Held*: the charge was good because the company's dominant motive was to keep on good terms with the bankers in the hope of future advances, not to confer an advantage on the bank. Similar facts arose in *Peat v Gresham Trust* [1934] AC 252, HL, where the company did not oppose a creditor application to the court to register a void charge out of time even though the company was insolvent. *Held*: the liquidator failed to produce evidence showing an intent to prefer and the court would not infer such an intent.
>
> In *Re Tweedale* [1892] 2 QB 216, a debtor created a chattel mortgage over furniture to secure advances made by his wife. The mortgage was void because it covered after-acquired property. Immediately before his bankruptcy, the debtor corrected the error by a fresh chattel mortgage over the identical furniture. He believed himself under an obligation to create this security. *Held*: the correction of the initial blunder negated the intent to prefer.

In the United States, on the other hand, the intent doctrine does not apply. Hence the absence of continuous perfection of a security interest, as where the filing lapses or the creditor temporarily gives up possession of the collateral, means that the transfer is deemed to take place when the creditor cures the position by a second filing: the second filing does not relate back: see BC 1978 s 547(e) and *Re Abell*, 66 BR 375 (B Ct, ND Miss 1968).

Late notification of assignments

5–25   In many countries, the assignment of a debt is invalid on the seller's bankruptcy (subject to various exceptions) if the assignment is not notified to the debtor, often in some formal manner. These countries include France, Luxembourg, Italy, Portugal, Japan and Korea, but not the English-based countries (at least for in the case of assignments by companies as opposed to individuals), Germany, Belgium (since 1994) or the United States.

In the nullifying countries, notification within the suspect period may be treated as preferential in the same way that late registration of security is preferential because the notification is effectively constitutive of the security assignment.

> In a Danish Supreme Court decision (U 1986, p 508), a bank financed the purchase of goods by a company which intended to resell the goods. The company pledged the resale price to the bank on August 26. The bank issued a guarantee for the purchase. The bank's pledge was notified to the ultimate purchaser of the goods by a notice in an invoice sent with the goods on September 2. *Held*: the notice was unduly delayed and the pledge was set aside. A stringent view.

Purchase of unsecured claims by secured creditor

If a secured creditor with security for all moneys purchases an unsecured   5–26
claim or is an assignee of the security, the effect is that an unsecured debt of the lender becomes secured. This transaction will usually escape because the debtor is not involved unless he participated in the assignment, e.g. by giving a necessary consent to the assignment.

Prejudice to creditors: set-off and netting

Set-off generally

Jurisdictions are sharply divided on the availability of set-off on the insol-   5–27
vency of a debtor, with some jurisdictions allowing the set-off and others prohibiting except to the extent that the claims arise under the same transaction or are otherwise connected or arise on the same current account. Insolvency set-off internationally is described in detail in another volume in this series on financial law and is summarised at para 1–21 *et seq.*

Countries disallowing insolvency set-off

In the countries which refuse insolvency set-off (including most Franco-Latin countries), a set-off in the suspect period is treated as a payment (because it is a discharge of a debt) and is therefore subject to the rules for the avoidance of payments, e.g. in Franco-Latin countries, the automatic avoidance of payments of unmatured debts in the suspect period (by a contractual set-off) and of payment by abnormal means or otherwise than as originally contracted for. A set-off which is automatic, e.g. because the debts are liquidated and mature, is not an abnormal payment because the set-off occurs by operation of law, nor is a payment by set-off in a bank current account since this is part of the routine operation of a current account. If the set-off is artificially created by contract during the suspect period, it is abnormal, but not if the contract was entered into prior to the suspect period. If a set-off of a matured debt owed by the debtor is not abnormal, then in these countries the creditor is generally protected unless he knew of the debtor's insolvency.

Countries allowing insolvency set-off

5-28   In those countries which allow insolvency set-off (most English-based countries, the United States, Japan, Scandinavian and Germanic countries), the position is more complicated. A mere set-off prior to insolvency is not in itself preferential because a creditor does not improve his position or worsen the position of other creditors if he achieves before insolvency what he would be entitled to achieve on insolvency: *Re Washington Diamond Mining Co* [1893] 3 Ch 95, CA. Rather, the test is whether the transaction giving rise to the debt eligible for set-off was preferential.

Typical examples of transactions giving rise to a debt eligible for set-off are: payments into a bank account which is in overdraft; channelling of sale proceeds through an agent of the debtor who owes money to the agent (*Re Hardy* [1901] NZLR 845 (New Zealand)); payment by the debtor to his bank where the account is overdrawn in order to improve the position of a guarantor of the debtor (e.g. *Re R B Shea Ltd* (1977) 25 CBR (NS) 109 (Quebec)); and sales by or to the insolvent with a view to a set-off of the price. In principle it ought to be the transaction giving rise to the set-off which must occur in the suspect period, not the set-off itself (which might take place during the suspect period or on the bankruptcy itself under the insolvency set-off section) and it is that transaction which must satisfy the elements of the preference, e.g. debtor insolvent, debtor intent to prefer, creditor knowledge of insolvency, as the case may be.

In the United States, BC 1978 s 553 provides in effect that (subject to exceptions) a set-off on insolvency is not permitted if the bankruptcy trustee can prove that the creditor incurred a debt in the 90–day suspect period for the *purpose of obtaining a right of set-off*, ie creditor intent, not debtor intent. In addition, the creditor's set-off is limited so as to exclude any improvement in the creditor's position during the 90–day suspect period. Unless the set-off is caught by s 553, an otherwise preferential set-off occurring more than five days before the case is protected and an otherwise preferential set-off within the five-day period is voidable only if the trustee may use, sell or lease the property recovered as a result of the avoidance.

Denmark (BA s 42), Norway (BA s 8) and Finland expressly disallow insolvency set-offs if effectively the set-off resulted from a preferential transaction within their preferential rules.

If the creditor sets off a debt in the suspect period and the set-off would not have been available on the insolvency of the debtor, e.g. because the liability of the creditor is for calls on shares (*Re Land Development Association, Kent's Case* (1888) 39 Ch D 259) or because the set-off is not mutual, then that set-off must be treated as any other payment for the purpose of the preference rules so that here it is the set-off which is relevant, not the transaction giving rise to the set-off.

In countries allowing insolvency set-off, a debtor to the insolvent debtor can acquire a set-off by buying a claim owed by the insolvent debtor to another creditor. Since the insolvent debtor is not involved, there is no preferential action by him. As a consequence, jurisdictions allowing insolvency set-off almost invariably have special rules to avoid the preferential effect of these build-ups. These are reviewed in another volume in this series of works.

Compensating contracts

The reception accorded to compensating contracts, particularly in jurisdictions which allow insolvency set-off, is patchy. These are sale contracts where the price is extinguished by a set-off against a pre-existing debt.   5–29

For example: the debtor owes 100 to a creditor. The debtor sells goods to the creditor for 100 on credit so that the creditor owes 100. On bankruptcy, the reciprocal debts are set off and the creditor gets the goods without paying for them. Effectively the debtor is paying a pre-existing debt by the transfer of goods. In England and English-based jurisdictions, where the debtor must have an intent to prefer, so that mere objective improvement in position on its own is insufficient, compensating contracts will usually be saved by the absence of intent, as where the debtor's dominant motive, uninfluenced by preferential desire, was to do a deal and make a profit on the sale. It might be different if the transaction was an intended camouflage for a payment.

> In the Australian case of *Donaldson v Couche* (1867) 4 WW & AB(L) 41 (Victoria), a debtor owed £70 to his creditor. The debtor held a meeting of his creditors and on that day the creditor bought goods for £50 from the debtor. The debtor insisted on cash but let the goods go without receiving the cash. Subsequently the debtor assigned his assets to trustees for his creditors. *Held*: the creditor could set off the £50. There was no fraud or preferential intent.

But in those jurisdictions which treat payment by abnormal means as a deemed preference, the tendency is to treat the transaction as a payment of a debt by goods and hence abnormal, e.g. in Denmark and the Franco-Latin jurisdictions, such as Belgium. Abnormal payments in the suspect period are usually automatically void in those countries, regardless of creditor knowledge of the insolvency.

Alternatively, the creditor owes 100 to the debtor. The creditor sells goods to the debtor for 100 on credit. On the debtor's insolvency, the two debts are set-off. In this case, provided the sale is at market value and the debtor has received the goods, the estate is not worse off after the set-off, so no case for a preference arises.

Settlement netting

5–30   Settlement netting is the "set-off" of reciprocal delivery obligations for fungible commodities, securities or common currency foreign exchange payments or interest swaps payments where the obligations are to be performed on the same day. The object is to reduce gross settlement exposures if one party should deliver and the other party fail before delivering his side of the bargain. The rationale of settlement netting and the application of the preference rules are discussed in another volume in this series of works on financial law.

Prejudice to creditors: transfer of business

5–31   Creditors may be prejudiced if a company transfers its assets to another company for a consideration left outstanding on loan account. If the transfer is for full value, it is true that there is no gift and the transferor's balance sheet is the same, but nevertheless the productive capacity of the assets is replaced by a possibly worthless claim against another company or the debtor may in the meantime dissipate any cash proceeds without using them to pay his debts. Transfers of assets in this way, including partial transfers of the best assets leaving the worst behind, have been held to be preferential in Belgium.

An example in England is *Arbuthot Leasing International Ltd v Havelet Leasing Ltd (No 2)* [1990] BCC 636, but there must be an intent to defeat creditors.

> C had a judgment debt against D. D then transferred the bulk of its business to T, which was an associated company, on terms that T would pay an annual management fee and certain quarterly payments. The effect was to put the busi-

ness assets beyond the reach of C and to replace them with the fee and quarterly payments. The transaction was at an undervalue. *Held*: the transaction was intentionally preferential and should be set aside under the English equivalent of the Actio Pauliana (IA 1986 s 423).

Many states have express rules governing the sale of a business – bulk sales – e.g. the United States (see UCC Art 6), the Philippines (Act 3592) and South Africa (IA 1936 s 34) but not England. Usually advance notice of the bulk sale must be given to creditors: otherwise the sale is ineffective against them.

In Brazil, the sale or transfer of a business without the consent of creditors is revocable, even if the debtor did not intend to defraud creditors.

Attempts to hide behind the veil of incorporation are commonly fruitless where the debtor is attempting to hide his assets.

In *Kinsela v Russell Kinsela Pty Ltd* (1986) 4 ACLC 215 (New South Wales CA), a company granted a lease to two of its directors immediately prior to its collapse. The aim was to put the property beyond the reach of creditors. *Held*: voidable transaction. See also the English case of *Re A Company* [1985] 1 BCC 99, 421 (elaborate English and foreign corporate structure to hide assets); *Creasey v Breachwood Motors Ltd, The Times,* July 29, 1992 (sale of insolvent company's business to sister company; the sister company was liable to original company's creditors); *Re Nimbus Trawling Co Ltd* (1986) 3 NZ CLC 99,646 (sale of vessel to sister company).

In the German *Tivoli Case*, RG May 5, 1932 (1933) *Höchstrichterliche Rechtspruching* No 299, a company operated a theatre. The building had been lent to it by its sole shareholder who was also its managing director. Creditors obtained judgment against the company for unpaid debts. The shareholder terminated the contract with the company, took over the theatre and thereby deprived the company of its chief asset. *Held*: the creditors could enforce against the theatre. The shareholder had abused the corporate form to defeat the creditors.

Prejudice to creditors: transactions with shareholders

Maintenance of capital

A fundamental principle of company law is that the share capital of the   5–32
company should not be paid before creditors. A repayment of share capital before creditors may therefore in substance be a preference of the shareholders as subordinated claimants.

This policy as to maintenance of capital is met by various company law provisions restricting the redemption of shares, the issue of shares at a discount, the issue of shares for a non-cash consideration which is not properly valued, the payment of dividends out of capital, and financial assistance given by a company to a person acquiring shares in the company. Loans to shareholders and directors may also be specifically restricted.

Financial assistance to purchase company's own shares

5–33   Where a company whose shares are acquired gives financial assistance to the acquirer, the effect can be to prefer the shareholder to the prejudice of creditors and hence offend the rule as to maintenance of capital. The typical illustration would be the take-over of a company, financed by a bank loan for the acquisition, where the acquired company subsequently guarantees the loan or gives security for the loan. The commercial effect is not dissimilar to a repayment of share capital so that the acquiring shareholder receives financial benefit from the company ahead of the company's creditors. The payment of share capital is intended to be subordinated to the payment of creditors.

Financial assistance in these circumstances is controlled by specific company law provisions in a wide range of jurisdictions, including England and the numerous English-influenced countries, South Africa and Continental European countries, usually pursuant to an EC Directive of 1976. In England the transaction is a criminal offence: Companies Act 1985 s 151. But financial assistance is permitted for private companies, provided that they are solvent as proved in the manner prescribed by the Companies Act 1985 s 155. This shows that the doctrine is fundamentally an insolvency policy.

In the United States, "leveraged buyout" financings, whereby the buyer of a target company uses the value of the target to finance the cost of the purchase, have been successfully attacked under state and bankruptcy fraudulent transfer rules when the financing rendered the target insolvent or (perhaps) significantly undercapitalised: *US v Tabor Court Realty Corpn*, 803 F 2d 1288 (3d Cir 1986) – a particularly blatant case where the court could hardly have decided otherwise; compare *Credit Managers Association of Southern California v The Federal Company*, 629 F Supp 175 (CD Cal 1985).

Prejudice to creditors: preferment of guarantors

5–34   If a company pays a creditor a loan which is guaranteed by a third party guarantor, the effect may be to prefer the guarantor. The guarantor's position is improved because, if the company failed, he would have to pay the creditor under his guarantee and be left with a mere right to a dividend on the insolvency of the company. Other creditors are prejudiced because the assets of the company are diminished by the payment in full.

Cases in many jurisdictions stigmatise this as preferential. The payment of the guaranteed credit is often made at the instance of directors of the company who have guaranteed a loan by the bank to the company: they are preferring themselves.

> In *Re M Kushler Ltd* [1943] Ch 248, CA, a director in sole control of a company guaranteed the company's overdraft at the bank. During the run up to liquidation, the director paid all the company's receipts into the bank to reduce the overdraft, but the company did not pay any trade creditors. *Held*: the company through its director intended to prefer the director as guarantor. But the mere fact that payments in fact prefer the guarantor is insufficient without the necessary intent, as where payments of trade receivables are made to the bank in the ordinary course of business: *Re Lyons* [1935] 51 TLR 24.

> In *Re Conley* [1938] 2 All ER 127, the wife and mother of a debtor deposited shares with his bank by way of collateral to secure his overdraft. Just before his bankruptcy, the debtor paid off the bank loan to release his family's security. *Held*: fraudulent preference of the collateral sureties.

For the US see, e.g. *Herman Cantor Corp v Central Fidelity Bank*, 15 BR 747 (B Ct, ED Va 1981) where it was held that a payment to a creditor which discharged the guarantor is a preferential transfer for the benefit of the guarantor. For South Africa see, e.g. *Roussouw v Hodgson*, 1925 AD 97.

Presumably there can be no preference of the guarantor if the guarantor has no recourse to the debtor or his recourse is limited to the net worth of the debtor, i.e. any surplus.

An analogous situation occurs where insiders have made a junior secured loan to the company. If the company pays off the senior secured creditor so as to increase the value of the junior collateral, which was previously partially unsecured, the junior creditors are effectively preferred: see *Re Prescott*, 805 F 2d 719 (7th Cir 1986).

Prejudice to creditors: judicial executions

Where a creditor levies judicial execution over assets of the debtor, he is paid out of the proceeds of the execution and hence is paid ahead of other creditors. Whether an execution is voidable as a preference meets with a mixed reception.   5–35

The arguments against avoidance are that the debtor is not involved (unless he colluded or stood idly by) and that the avoidance of a judicial order of execution undermines the authority and finality of court judgments. Further, once creditors start execution, it is open to other creditors to petition for insolvency and hence call a halt. While in small cases a particular creditor may be first past the post, this is less likely to happen with large corporate debtors where the prospect of a substantial execution diminishing the assets is small. The argument for avoidance is that the creditor may be paid preferentially and the mechanics of that payment ought to be irrelevant.

5–36   In **England,** an execution judgment will not be avoided in the absence of collusion by the debtor since no action by the debtor is required and in any event the requirement for debtor intent to prefer will not be satisfied unless the debtor acts voluntarily. The guillotine of creditor enforcement comes down only on insolvency petition and the remedy of other creditors who wish to forestall individual enforcements is to petition for insolvency and hence freeze judicial proceedings and uncompleted executions. However in traditional English countries (not England), the old doctrine of "relation back" of the bankruptcy to the first "act of bankruptcy" of the debtor connoting actual insolvency may avoid executions uncompleted after the executing creditor has notice of an act of bankruptcy, at least in the case of *individual* bankruptcies. Relation back was abolished in England in 1986.

In **Franco-Latin** countries, it seems that some creditor enforcements actually resulting in payment in the suspect period may be liable to avoidance. It is for investigation whether this applies generally or only to summary enforcement by a bailiff or other court official, without court order, on the basis of a duly protested bill of exchange or "executive title", such as a notarised agreement.

In the **United States,** voidable transfers include involuntary transfers (BC 1978 s 101(48)) and case law has held that execution levies, e.g. under state laws, are within the scope of the preference s 547.

In **Denmark** executions (legal seizures) made within the three months before the commencement date are voidable: BA Art 71. A similar provision applies in **Norway** (BA s 5–8), and **Sweden,** BA s 13.

CHAPTER 6

PREFERENCES: OTHER ASPECTS

Actual insolvency of debtor

The first test of a preference is prejudice to creditors: this has been discussed above. The second main test of a preference is that the debtor was insolvent when he granted the preference or was rendered insolvent by the transaction, e.g. by the gift or the guarantee. The reach-back applies because it is insolvency which crystallises the equality principle and the collective proceeding. 6–1

Insolvency may be defined for this purpose as inability to pay debts as they fall due, or the balance sheet test of excess of liabilities over assets, or both, and commonly includes other indicia of insolvency, e.g. unsatisfied judgments.

The test of inability to pay debts as they fall due is more protective of creditors since there is at least some chance of their learning of the financial difficulties. The balance sheet test is uncertain for creditors since they may have no means of valuing the assets except by financial statements which may be out-of-date. The balance sheet test also poses problems for directors who may incur misfeasance liability or other penalties for granting preferences – assets can be difficult to value precisely and may fetch much less on a break-up them on a going-concern basis. There are obvious evidential obstacles. England applies both tests: see IA 1986 s 240. 6–2

As already mentioned, the test of insolvency is not generally applicable to the Actio Pauliana – the intentional or fraudulent preference. Here it is enough that the available assets are intentionally diminished, thereby weakening the debtor's ability to pay: para 4–19.

Length of suspect period

Except for the Pauline action, it is generally true that the transaction must have taken place in a prescribed period prior to the commencement of the formal insolvency proceedings. The object of a suspect period is to give 6–3 tainty to transactions which outlive the period concerned, even though on occasion the period may turn out to be too short. Fixed periods also recognise the practicalities of the matter that, in most cases, an actual insolvency is swiftly followed by a formal insolvency and that, the longer the period, the more formidable the evidential problems.

Everybody has a different idea on how long the suspect period for particular preferences should be and one simply has to look it up in each case. See chapter 7 for some examples.

Commonly there are different suspect periods for different classes of preference, with the more culpable meriting the longest, e.g. gifts, with no suspect period at all in the case of culpable fraud.

6–4   The traditional English approach is to fix a period of generally three or six months – so that transactions outside that period are saved, apart from the special rules for intentional fraud and gifts. Apart from these situations, the Franco-Latin rule back-dates the suspect period to the time the debtor actually becomes insolvent, as determined by the judge, and often with a further back-dating of 10 days or more, so that there is no upper limit. Here and there, there is a maximum period of back-dating (sometimes only for some transactions, e.g. non-gifts) – six months in Belgium and Luxembourg, 18 months in France. Pro-creditor countries in this group, such as Norway and Switzerland, generally fix an upper limit. But there is a bewildering variety of periods.

The United States has a basic 90-day period (lengthened by state statutes) whereas six months is the international norm for the ordinary non-gift non-fraudulent preference.

Insiders and connected persons

6–5   The preference rules are frequently tougher for insiders. Older statutes have often stigmatised transfers to spouses and other relations. More modern versions extend the concept of insiders to co-directors, controlling shareholders or commonly-controlled corporations or affiliates. The reason for the tougher rules for insiders is that manipulation by those in control is more likely (they are more likely to have advance knowledge of the debtor's demise), that the temptation to prefer themselves is greater and that insiders should be subordinate to external creditors.

The trends are: (1) a longer suspect period; (2) reversal of the onus of proof, e.g. as to insolvency or of creditor-awareness of the insolvency; and (3) insolvency at the time of the transaction may not be an essential element (e.g. in England for floating charges granted to connected persons).

In the context of groups of companies, the insider doctrine affects, for example, security granted to a parent by a subsidiary, asset-stripping, shuffling assets around the group at an undervalue, the payment by a group company of an inter-company debt during the suspect period and guarantees by an affiliate or a director.

Composition proceedings

Apart from the Pauliana (which can apply outside formal insolvency pro- 6-6
ceedings), always the preference doctrines apply to final bankruptcy proceedings or insolvent liquidations. As to whether they apply to composition or rehabilitation proceedings, see para 11-36.

Where the preference rules do not apply on a composition or rehabilitation proceeding, but the composition fails, e.g. because the debtor does not comply with his reduced obligations, and the debtor is bankrupted instead, it is sometimes the case that the suspect period is calculated up to the application for or promulgation of the composition as opposed to the subsequent bankruptcy. The purpose of this is to maintain the suspect period up to the commencement of insolvency proceedings, albeit of a compository sort, e.g. in Belgium, Denmark and Luxembourg.

Defences

Summary

The defences available to the preferred creditor are influenced primarily by: 6-7
(a) the pro-creditor or pro-debtor orientation of the bankruptcy laws, ie the policy of protecting creditors and enhancing the predictability of transactions as against the policy of enlarging the debtor's estate and protecting him and his creditors or, more commonly, priority creditors, such as taxes and employees; (b) the culpability of the preference, e.g. intentional preferences and gifts enjoy less favour than ordinary course of business payments; and (c) the proximity of the transaction to the opening of the insolvency proceedings.

The prime dividing line between jurisdictions, ranking in importance far ahead of such matters as what is deemed preferential and the length of the suspect period, is the availability of creditor defences, even though objectively the creditor has improved his position in the suspect period to the detriment of other creditors.

The two main defences internationally are as follows:

1. The debtor did not intend to prefer.

2. The creditor did not know that the debtor was insolvent.

Of course, there are other defences in particular situations, such as the frequent requirement for creditor collusion in the case of fraudulent transfers within the Pauliana, and the protection of ordinary course of business payments. But the above two are the fundamental protections and may now be examined in turn.

Preferential intent

6–8 A characteristic of England and many English-based jurisdictions is the moral culpability or wrongful intent of the debtor – he must have intended to prefer the creditor. In England, since 1986 the intent need be only one of the motives influencing the transaction, but in many other English-based countries it must still be the dominant motive. This intent requirement does not apply to gifts or transactions at an undervalue where preferential intent is presumed. Creditor knowledge of the debtor's preferential intent is irrelevant. These countries belong to the subjective school.

Classification of "intent"jurisdictions Apart from the Pauline action (deliberate prejudicial intent by the debtor, usually with creditor collusion) and apart from gifts, the "intent" doctrine applies, as mentioned, in **England** and many (but not all) English-influenced countries. In **Austria**, in the case of the grant of security or payments by the debtor, no debtor preferential intent need be shown if the creditor was not entitled to the security or payments or not in that form, but in other cases debtor intent is necessary when the security or payment is to non-insiders: there is only a preference if the transferor was aware or should have been aware of the intent of the bankrupt to prefer: BA s 30(3).

In **Switzerland** creditor collusion is also required except in the case of (1) gifts, (2) pledges for pre-existing debt otherwise than pursuant to obligation to do so, (3) abnormal payments and (4) prepayments. In the last three cases, the transactions are protected if the beneficiary proves he was unaware of the insolvency. Hence Switzerland appears highly protective of creditors in this respect. **Spain** requires intent in some cases: see Art 881.

Apart from the Pauliana, the intent doctrine does not apply in the following countries and is usually (but not always) replaced by a requirement that the creditor knew of the debtor's insolvency: these countries may be classed as the objective school:

- Australia
- Denmark
- Italy
- Japan
- Korea (probably)
- Netherlands
- Norway
- South Africa and probably related countries, like Botswana, Lesotho and Zimbabwe
- Sweden
- Traditional French group (e.g. Belgium, France, Greece, Luxembourg, Egypt, former French colonies and many Latin American countries)
- United States (where even creditor knowledge of the insolvency is not a defence)

Advantages and disadvantages of intent doctrine The advantage of the   6–9
intent test is that it can be used by courts to validate transactions so as to
protect creditors. It also helps protect ordinary course of business transactions, security for pre-existing debt (*Re MC Bacon Ltd* [1990] BCLC
324), the correction of errors in the original void security (*Re Tweedale*
[1892] 2 QB 216), even discriminatory payments where the motives of the
debtor may simply have been to do a deal or to finance the business or to
keep the business going or to secure further supplies or otherwise to benefit
himself: see *Re FLE Holdings Ltd* [1967] 3 All ER 553. It has also validated
security for pre-existing debt if there was an obligation to grant it: the
debtor intends to perform his obligations, not to prefer. Effectively the
"intent" test, regardless of its logic, is a leading creditor protection.

But a disposition made where the motive is to favour a creditor who is
himself in difficulties or to whom the debtor feels he owes a moral obligation or where the motive is to favour all creditors except a hated creditor
is with intent to prefer in England: there is a deliberate intention to discriminate and the fact that one creditor is regarded as more deserving than
another is immaterial: *Re Fletcher* (1891) 9 Mor 8.

The disadvantages are that the motives of the debtor are irrelevant to
other creditors who are actually prejudiced, that proof is often difficult, and
that the preferred creditor cannot necessarily know the debtor's subjective
state of mind so that the doctrine is unpredictable. These disadvantages can
lead to a requirement for creditor collusion or for notice to the creditor of
the preferential intent, but this is not a requirement in England. But for the
above reasons, the intent doctrine has been abandoned in the US and in
Australia for some of the preference tests. The net effect is greatly to
increase creditor exposure to the avoidance of transactions. The argument

therefore is not whether the debtor's intent is logically relevant, but whether the preference doctrine should be broad or narrow.

In the English-based jurisdictions there are numerous cases on the intent doctrine, all of which turn on the particular facts of the cases.

6–10　　**Pressure negates intent** A leading feature of the intent doctrine is that a disposition which is not voluntary but is made under pressure is not made with intent to prefer but with intent to escape the pressure.

There are many English cases on this point, but just as there are cases where the threat of legal proceedings was sufficient, so also are there many cases where creditor pressure did not negative intent. The general trend seems to be that mere pressure is not enough to negative intent but is enough if coupled with some other motive, such as the debtor's expectation of maintaining financial or commercial relationships with the creditor or where the debtor seeks to protect himself from a criminal prosecution. The courts do not encourage creditor bullying.

> In *Re Ramsay* [1913] 2 KB 80, the creditor threatened to "make it hot" for the debtor unless he was paid. The debtor returned goods to cover debts due and also those not yet due. *Held*: fraudulent preference.
>
> Compare *Re Wilkinson* [1864] 1 Morr 65. A judgment creditor threatened the debtor with execution. The debtor gave the creditor security. The creditor agreed to pay off the debtor's existing mortgage and to pay arrears of rent. *Held*: not a fraudulent preference. The creditor gave something in return.
>
> In *Re Wrigley* [1875] LR 20 Eq 763, a creditor pressurised an insolvent debtor into buying goods from others on credit and then using the proceeds of sale to pay the creditor, instead of the supplier. *Held*: notwithstanding the pressure, the transaction was fraudulent in its inception.

6–11　　**Protection of debtor against misfeasance negates intent** A disposition which the debtor makes to protect himself against possible proceedings for a misfeasance or wrongdoing or which he makes out of shame to repair an evil deed is not made with preferential intent. Without an "intent" doctrine, the creditors of the debtor would win as against the victims of the wrongdoing. This principle has been applied where a person repays moneys which he has misapplied, e.g. *Sharp v Jackson* [1899] AC 427 (a solicitor misapplied trust moneys), *Re Lake* [1901] 1 KB 710, CA (trustee misapplied trust moneys); contrast *Re Cutts* [1956] 2 All ER 537.

6–12　　**Onus of proof** The onus in the traditional English jurisdictions is on the party seeking to avoid the transfer to show that there was intent to prefer. The effect therefore is an initial presumption in favour of the validity of the disposition. This proof is somewhat difficult because the bankrupt himself will often be disinclined to admit an intention to prefer since this will disfavour the creditor and will potentially expose the bankrupt to penalties. In such a case the court may, in view of the circumstantial evidence, be drawn to disbelieving the bankrupt: *Re M Kushler Ltd* [1943] Ch 248, CA.

Creditor ignorance of the insolvency

Jurisdictions inclined to favour the predictability of transactions give the creditor a defence if he did not know of the insolvency – this may be knowledge of a stoppage of payments, or of balance-sheet insolvency, or of the commencement of proceedings by the filing of a petition.   6–13

The countries which espouse the "creditor knowledge" rule are in the "objective" school, as opposed to those who require debtor intent to prefer – the subjective school described above.

The objective school generally excludes the countries listed above as requiring debtor intent, e.g. England and the traditional English countries, and includes the following states:

- Franco-Latin countries
- Italy
- Japan
- Korea (probably)
- Netherlands, where the test is commonly that the creditor knew that the act prejudiced creditors. The satisfaction of a material obligation is preferential if the satisfaction is made pursuant to consultation between the debtor and the creditor with a view to a preference.

In the **United States,** the test of a preference is wholly objective (apart from fraudulent conveyances) and creditor knowledge of the debtor's financial state is irrelevant.   6–14

The advantage of the awareness rule is that, if the awareness is actual and obvious awareness, creditors know where they are, ie that further dealings with the debtor may be vulnerable. The disadvantage is that the effect of the rule is that, once creditors know of the debtor's embarrassment, his further dealings are frozen and he is no longer in a position to trade out of his difficulties. He has little chance of recovery. This is not because of creditor disincentive to carry out transactions which may be set aside (creditors prefer a potentially voidable payment to no payment at all), but because the debtor and his controllers may be exposed to penalties if they do prefer creditors. In practice, many attempts to save major groups in difficulties, e.g. by a private bank restructuring exercise, are carried out at a time when the bank and other creditors are fully aware of the debtor's financial state in which even the sole defence of creditor's lack of knowledge of the insolvency is of no assistance. The English-based "intent" doctrine tends to avoid this diffi-culty. Hence an "intent" doctrine favours a policy of helping debtors to sur-vive, but a pure "awareness" doctrine is less effective to this end.

From the point of view of the disappointed creditors, it is irrelevant to them that a particular creditor did not know of the insolvency if he was in fact preferred and so theoretical logic would point to the elimination of the knowledge defence. But against this logic is the wider policy of whether or not to confer predictability on transactions and whether or not to back-date the insolvency to some date prior to the actual formal commence-ment.

The state of insolvency may be inferred. Thus in Belgium the creditor's knowledge that the debtor is insolvent will be inferred where, for example, the creditor has issued proceedings asking for the debtor to be declared bankrupt, or a creditor has refused to grant further credit to the debtor, or a creditor has made advances to the debtor to help him overcome a liquidity crisis.

Avoidance and recapture

Avoidance procedure

6–15   Commonly the transactions may be either automatically void or merely voidable. The importance of the distinction is that, where a transaction is only voidable, this may allow the court to exercise a discretion.

Whether the avoidance is initiated by the insolvency administrator or a committee of creditors or is supervised by the court is a procedural matter for which there are many solutions. But, except for the Paulian action, the recovery is usually an asset of the estate available to all creditors.

Recapture

6–16   The basic principle of the recapture is to put the parties in the position they would have been in if the transaction had not occurred and tends to follow the broadly traditional pattern of avoidance procedures in other contexts, e.g. the restoration of a party induced into a contract by misrepresentation or in the case of a contract collapsing by frustration or *force majeure*. In view of the complexity of the circumstances, some countries, including England and the US, give the court broad discretions as to manner of recov-ery (though, in the case of England, the statute sets out a range of specific options without prejudice to the generality of the discretion), while others, like Norway, attempt some specific rules: Debt Recovery Act 1984 ss 5–11, 5–12.

Broadly one may expect that the recapture will involve the repayment of cash payments, the return of gifts or other property or cash in lieu (especially if it would be overburdensome to require the re-transfer of goods, securities or other property already abroad or readily available elsewhere in the market or where the transfer was at an undervalue but not wholly a gift), or the release of preferential security. In the United States, BC 1978 s 550 allows either recovery in specie or money's worth in damages, at the court's option. The questions of accounting for income or interest and improvements, and the time of valuation (time of transfer or time of recovery action – the transferee may have sold for less) must be dealt with. There are usually time limits on the recovery actions ranging from one year (Austria) upwards.

Revival of guarantees

If the debtor paid off a guaranteed debt in order to prefer the guarantors, 6–17 the paid creditor may have released the guarantee. If the creditor is obliged to restore the amount paid, the debt owing to him springs up again – but with the guarantee gone. One solution is to treat the guarantor as the creditor who is preferred – he is a creditor because he has a contingent right of reimbursement against the debtor – and to order him to repay the estate. The other more logical solution is to cause the creditor to disgorge and to resurrect the guarantee so that the creditor is in the same position he was before, e.g. if the guarantor is bankrupt or the guarantor is prevented from competing with the creditor. In any event, in England the insolvency statute allows the court to order a revival of the guarantee and any security for the guarantee as well as security granted to the creditor for the debt which was paid off: IA 1986 s 241. Where this is in question, the beneficiary of the guarantor should expressly condition the release of the guarantee on the validity of the payment by the principal debtor and many guarantees contain an express provision to this effect. If the guarantee contained an expiry date for demands, that expiry date may have passed when the guarantee resurrects. Whether the court can extend the expiry date depends upon its powers to reform the original transaction.

This issue also presents itself where the subsequent holder of a negotiable instrument has to repay a payment made to him: he has lost his rights against previous holders on the instrument by virtue of the initial preferential payment. This is dealt with by specific statutory provisions in traditional French jurisdictions: see para 5–9.

Revival of security

6–18   A similar problem arises where a secured creditor is paid off preferentially and releases his security. The English courts are authorised to reinstate the security on recovery of the preferential payment by the debtor's estate. Security documents often contain a provision that the security-holder can retain the security for the applicable preference periods despite a redemption of the debt, but this may conflict with a rule that the debtor is entitled to have his security back once he pays the secured debt. One possible solution is to provide that the security covers debts resurrected on an invalidation of a payment as a preference and to require the debtor to show at the time of the payment that the payment is not preferential. There are obvious practical problems. The saving for many of these situations is that, as has been shown, the payment off of a fully secured creditor is not generally in itself preferential because there is no improvement in position.

Protection of third parties

6–19   Generally transferees from the preferred party are protected if they acted in good faith for value and without notice of the preference: this is so in the United States, England and probably in most jurisdictions which have thought about the matter.

   Thus in England no avoidance order can be made against a person (other than the immediate transferee who is preferred) who acquires an interest in the property in good faith, for value and without notice of the fact that the transaction would be a preference if the company were to go into insolvent liquidation or become subject to an administration order, ie notice of insolvency and of preferential intent: see IA 1986 s 241. As to the US, see BC 1978 s 550.

Security over after-acquired assets

6–20   Where security validly extends to after-acquired assets, such as an English-based floating charge covering all present and future assets, the asset recovered by the estate may fall within the clutch of the charge in favour of the secured creditor. The objection to this is that the secured creditor is effectively improving his security after the insolvency which ought to be the cut-off date. The policy in favour is that the holder of a general business charge ought to have everything so that the business can be sold as a whole and that the right to possessory management through a receiver must include future income produced by the assets and should also include assets which would have been included in the charge but for the preferential transfer by the creditor: the secured creditor should not be deprived of his rightful security and the unsecured creditors should not receive a windfall as a result of the wrongful act of the debtor.

Norway comes down in favour of the secured creditor as does Sweden: see the Swedish Supreme Court *Minitube case* (NJA 1982, p 900), which gave the holder of a Swedish floating charge the benefit of the recovered asset. England however took a contrary view in *Re Yagerphone Ltd* [1935] Ch 392.

Preferred transferee insolvent

Where a preferred transferee obliged to repay the estate fails to do so, he   6–21
ought not to be entitled to dividends on any debt owed to him by the debtor to the extent he fails to repay. In England, the courts are likely to apply the doctrine of retainer whereby, if a person is liable to contribute to a fund and if he is also entitled to a share of the fund, then the administrator of the fund (the insolvency representative) can retain that person's share to cover the unpaid contribution. The manner of calculating the retainer is detailed, but broadly the calculation has a similar result as if the administrator had a charge over the share to secure the contribution. By the British IA 1986, the court may provide for the extent to which a person refunding a preference is to be entitled to prove in the insolvency (see ss 240, 342). This may be taken as a statutory recognition of the rule of retainer.

Set-off against repayment claim

It seems to be generally the case that where an insolvent party must return to   6–22
the estate a preference or a fraudulent transfer, then he must pay the refund or the liability without set-off of either the debt paid by the preference or another debt owed by the insolvent to the creditor. The question can only arise in those jurisdictions which permit insolvency set-off. If the position were otherwise, the purpose of the recovery of property of the estate and the policies against preferential transfers would be vitiated. Property for turn-over is property of the bankrupt estate not liable to be consumed by set-off.

This is the position in England (subject to some refinement – see Wood, *English & International Set-off* (1989) paras 7–262 et seq) and also generally in the United States: see, for example *US v Roth*, 164 Fd 575 (CA2).

If the return of the preferential payment results in the preferred debt springing up again, this claim may become eligible for set-off as if it had never been paid: see, for example, the US BC 1978 s 507(7) and the English case of *Re Washington Diamond Mining Co* [1893] 3 Ch 95, 111, CA.

The point may be illustrated by examples:

> A debtor makes a gift of 100 to a donee. The gift is avoided so that donee must repay 100 to the estate. The estate owes the donee another debt of 120. No set-off. The 100 belongs to the estate and is not mutual with the 120. If there were a set-off, then debtors could safely make preferential gifts to creditors who would be protected by a set-off. *Lister v Hooson* [1908] 1 KB 174, CA (England); *Re Hermann* (1916) SRNSW 246 (New South Wales).

> A debtor repays a loan of 100 to a creditor. The repayment is avoided so that the creditor must repay 100 to the estate. The result is that the creditor is entitled to claim the loan in the insolvency. The creditor owes another debt of 120 to the estate. Set-off permitted. The creditor would have been entitled to the set-off if he had not been preferred and other creditors are not prejudiced. There is no point in ordering the refund of the loan. See the English cases of *Re Washington Diamond Mining Co* [1893] 3 Ch 95, 111, CA, as explained in *Re BP Fowler Ltd* [1938] Ch 113.

Deterrence and penalties

6–23   The penalty suffered by transferees who have been preferred is that they are liable to return the property or its equivalent. This may not be a great deterrence in some cases, because the hope of retention of an asset may be better than no asset at all. This is a view which banks may take when insisting on security for pre-existing debt.

Nevertheless it is not generally considered appropriate to penalise transferees further, except in the case of clear fraudulent collusion involving actual dishonesty. The business of bankruptcy law is not the punishment of creditors nor would the criminalisation of creditor conduct be generally acceptable: society has more usually tended to punish the defaulter than his hapless creditors.

It is otherwise with the debtor who confers the preference. Everywhere it is thought that dishonest fraudulent transfers and concealments of assets will meet with bankruptcy penalties. Thus in Italy preferential payments to creditors with intent to favour them are within the group of bankruptcy offences entailing imprisonment from three to 10 years. But ordinary preferences, not involving true fraud or deceit, merit a range of sanctions. It is of the essence of criminal penalties that the criminal must have criminal intent or *mens rea* and this is generally true of the bankruptcy penalties. How the courts interpret this in practice in relation to transfers deemed preferential, e.g. security for pre-existing debt, where the debtor acted honestly or under pressure, is a matter for investigation: criminalisation without *mens rea* would reveal an intense hostility to preferential transfers and a vestige of the old idea that debtors ought to be punished.

In England a director participating in a corporate preference may be liable for misfeasance proceedings and the conduct is a factor to be taken into account in disqualification proceedings under the Company Directors Disqualification Act 1986. Paying one creditor preferentially out of moneys received is not criminal fraud except in unusual circumstances: *Re EB Tractors Ltd* [1987] PCC 313.

CHAPTER 7

SELECTED PREFERENCE LAWS

7–1   The selection in this chapter is intended to show both the similarity and variety of approach by reference to representative countries. For a summary of English law and the law which applies, or is likely to apply, in most English-based jurisdictions (around 80 states), see para 4–7 *et seq*. Australia, Canada and New Zealand are distinctive. For the United States, see para 4–14 *et seq*. A large proportion of Franco-Latin states (probably about 75 states) are, or are likely to be, based on the original French provisions – see under Belgium (although usually the suspect periods are longer than the six-month Belgian period). France is now different. For Franco-Latin states, see para 4–12 *et seq*. Germany is not included, pending the new bankruptcy act due to come into force at the end of the 1990s. All provisions are summarised and not verbatim, unless in quotation marks.

Argentina

7–2   The following acts of the debtor within one year from the date the judge determines the debtor became insolvent are invalid: (1) gifts; (2) prepayments of debts falling due on or after the date of declaration of bankruptcy; (3) payments in kind; (4) mortgages, liens granted to secure existing unsecured debts.

Other alienations by the debtor may also be declared invalid, if the disposition was made during the suspect period and if the beneficiary of the alienation was aware of the insolvency of the debtor. Law No 19551 of April 4 1972 as amended. [*Source*: *Digest of Commercial Laws of the World*, Dobbs Ferry.]

Belarus

7–3   Transfers in year prior to bankruptcy order or submission of insolvency application (for rehabilitation) (1) intended to conceal property or avoid payment of debts, or (2) debtor received considerably less than economically justified price of the property, or (3) debtor was insolvent (not defined). Trustee initiates avoidance which is ordered by court. Seems unclear whether suspect period of one year applies to (2) and (3). Art 28 of the Law of Economic Insolvency and Bankruptcy 1991. [*Source*: Translation by Carol Patterson.]

Belgium

BA 1851 Maximum suspect period of six months. Court orders nullity. By 7-4 Art 445, the following are null and void if entered into by the debtor since the time determined by the court as being that of insolvency (*cessation des paiements*) or during the ten days preceding such time: (1) gifts and transactions at a significant undervalue; (2) payments in cash, transfer, sale, set-off or otherwise in respect of unmatured debts; and for matured debts, all payments made otherwise than in cash or by negotiable instruments; and (3) security (including judicial land charges) for pre-existing debt. The good faith of the creditor, or the fact that it did not know of the insolvency of its debtor, are immaterial for Art 445.

Art 446 renders voidable all payments made by the debtor in respect of due debts and all other onerous acts (*actes a titres onereux*) made by him after the date of cessation of payments and before the opening judgment, if the persons who benefited from a transfer by the debtor or entered into a transaction with him knew of the cessation of payments. Case law decides that the creditor must have actual notice of the fact that the debtor has ceased its payments and fulfils the conditions for bankruptcy. The onus of proof is on the receiver.

By Art 448, all fraudulent acts or payments are void, whatever their date and regardless of insolvency. Art 448 is an application of the Paulian action in CC Art 1167. The Paulian action requires fraud of the debtor, the collusion of the creditor and prejudice to creditors.

If a payment or a transaction is nullified under the above, the estate must be placed in the same situation as if it were not concluded. The creditor must reimburse the payment or give back the goods received, but, where a whole transaction is nullified, the estate must compensate the creditor for any benefits received under the nullified transaction.

If the benefits received under the nullified transaction are still in the bankrupt estate (e.g. the object of a sale) the creditor ranks in priority to ordinary unsecured creditors. If the benefits cannot be identified (e.g. the price of a sale), case law holds that the creditor ranks pari passu with ordinary unsecured creditors.

The rules do not apply to the *concordat judiciaire* or the *sursis de paiement*, but Art 445 (not Art 446) applies if a *concordat* is cancelled; the suspect period dates back from the *concordat*. The rules of the Paulian action

(CC Art 1167) apply to composition proceedings. [*Source*: paper submitted by Belgian law firm.]

Brazil

7–5 The following acts are voidable whether or not performed with knowledge of the financial condition of the debtor or with intent to defraud the creditors: (1) payment of unmatured debts within the suspect period (usually 60 days prior to petition); (2) satisfaction of matured debts within the suspect period by any means other than as provided in the contract; (3) execution by a merchant of mortgages or other real security within the suspect period as security for debts contracted prior to that period; (4) gifts by a merchant made within two years preceding the adjudication (other than small gifts); (5) renunciation of a devise, legacy or usufruct within two years preceding the adjudication; (6) restitution or delivery of dower before the time stipulated in the antenuptial contract; (7) registration of mortgages, liens or transfers inter vivos effected after sequestration of the bankrupt's property or after adjudication; (8) sale or transfer of business without obtaining consent of creditors; and (9) any act performed by the debtor with the intention of prejudicing his creditors, provided there was also fraud on the part of the other party. [*Source*: Martindale-Hubbell Law Digest 1991.]

Czech Republic; Slovak Republic

7–6 **Bankruptcy and Composition Act No 328 1991, as amended, s 15** Creditor can ask court to avoid against that creditor any juridical act by debtor which curtails satisfaction of the creditor's enforceable claims. Creditor may contest juridical acts of debtor in previous three years (note long suspect period) intended to prejudice creditor's rights, if this intention was known to the other party (knowledge not being necessary in the case of persons close to the debtor), but not if the other party, despite exercising due care, could not have learned of the debtor's deliberate intention to prejudice the creditor's rights. The right to contest is asserted against the person who benefited from the debtor's act. Successful creditor is entitled to satisfaction out of assets withdrawn from debtor's estate by the contested act or, if this is impracticable, to compensation from the person benefited. Right to attack transactions is given to administrator or a creditor, but proceeds must be paid into the estate. No set-off of disgorge amount against transferee's original claim.

France

The Bankruptcy Act of 1985 distinguishes between transactions in the sus-   7–7
pect period which are automatically null and void (*nullité de droit*) and
those which are voidable only (*nullité facultative*).

Art 107 (automatically void):

> "The following transactions, if entered into by the debtor since the date
> of cessation of payments, are void:
>
> (1) All gratuitous acts which operate to transfer real or personal
> property.
>
> (2) Any bilateral contract under which the obligations of the debtor
> significantly exceed those of the other party.
>
> (3) Any payment made in whatever way, for debts which had not
> fallen due at the date of payment.
>
> (4) Any payment for due debts, made in a form other than in cash,
> securities, bank transfer, assignment of debts under the Act. No.
> 81–1 dated 2nd January, 1981 facilitating the credit for com-
> panies or any other mode of payment commonly used in busi-
> ness relationships.
>
> (5) Any deposit and pledge of amounts of money made pursuant to
> articles 567 of the Civil Procedure Code and 2075–1 of the Civil
> Code, in the absence of a final judicial decision.
>
> (6) Any contractual mortgage, judicial mortgage and spouses legal
> mortgage and any pledge on the debtor's assets made in respect
> of debts incurred previously.
>
> (7) Any privilege registered pursuant to articles 53 and 54 of the
> Code of Civil Procedure unless such registration was made prior
> to the date of cessation of payments.
>
> Further, the tribunal may declare void unilateral acts referred to in (1)
> above and which were made within the 6 months preceding the date of
> cessation of payment."

The suspect period is fixed by the tribunal and cannot usually exceed 18
months. An Art 107 transaction is a preference even though the creditor did
not have notice of the insolvency.

Art 108 (voidable, not automatically void):

> "Payments in respect of due debts made after the date of cessation of

payments and onerous acts performed after that date are voidable if the persons dealing with the debtor were aware of the cessation of payments."

Paulian action (CC Art 1167):

"[The creditors] may also, acting in their own name, challenge the fraudulent acts made by the debtor to their detriment."

Italy

7–8   **BA 1942 Art 67** (applies also to *liquidazione coatta amministrativa* – BA Art 203): Void transactions: unless the other party proves that he had no knowledge of the state of insolvency of the debtor, the following are revoked:

1. Transactions at a significant undervalue within the two years prior to insolvency declaration.

2. The payment of accrued monetary debts otherwise than in money or other normal means of payment if made within the two years prior to insolvency declaration.

3. Pledges, antichreses and voluntary mortgages created within the two years prior to insolvency declaration to secure pre-existing debts which are not due and payable.

4. Pledges, antichreses, judicial or voluntary mortgages made within the year prior to the date of insolvency declaration as security for debts which are due and payable.

Payments of debts which are due and payable, transactions for value and those creating a preferential right in consideration of debts arising simultaneously which are made within one year prior to the declaration of insolvency are revoked if the trustee proves that the other party knew of the insolvency of the insolvent party. The creditor must have actual notice of the suspension of payments. Subject to special laws, Art 67 does not apply to Bank of Italy, to other institutions authorised to grant credit facilities secured by pledge (but limited to those transactions) or to building societies.

Paulian action Independently of an insolvency proceeding, creditor may request a court to avoid any transaction made by debtor, if the transaction jeopardises his claims against the same debtor: CC Art 2901. The action is barred after five years from the date of the transaction: Art 2903. Both debtor and third party creditor who dealt with him must be actually aware of prejudice to the creditor's claim: Art 2901. Burden of proof is on the creditor.

If a transaction is nullified or avoided, the bankrupt estate must compensate the creditor concerned for any benefits received under the nullified transaction. Claim of the creditor ranks pari passu with ordinary unsecured creditors: see BA Art 71. Third party creditor may not set off his claim against debts due to the bankrupt as a result of the revocation.

Above preference rules do not apply to *concordato preventivo* or to the *amministrazione straodinaria.*

Japan

BL (Law No 71, April 25, 1922, as amended) Arts 72–86:   7–9

1. Any act done by the bankrupt with the knowledge that it would prejudice creditors in bankruptcy.

2. Any act related to creating security or discharging obligations of the bankrupt, or any other act prejudicial to creditors in bankruptcy, done by the bankrupt after the suspension of payments or filing of the petition for bankruptcy if the creditor benefiting from the act knew at the time of the act that there had been a suspension of payment or that the petition for bankruptcy had been filed.

3. Any of the acts mentioned under the preceding item, where the beneficiary creditor is related to the bankrupt or a person who lives with the bankrupt.

4. Any act related to creating security or discharging obligations of the bankrupt within thirty days before suspension of payment or filing of the petition for bankruptcy, which does not arise pursuant to the bankrupt's legal obligations existing at the time of the act or which does not arise pursuant to the bankrupt's legal obligations existing at the time of the act with respect to its time or method.

5. Any gratuitous act, or non-gratuitous act which is nevertheless deemed to be the same as a gratuitous act, done by the bankrupt after suspension of payment or filing of the petition for bankruptcy, or within six months prior thereto.

If the creditor benefited by the acts mentioned under items 1 and 4 did not know at the time of the acts that the acts would prejudice creditors in bankruptcy, these acts shall not be regarded as preferences.

If the creditor benefited by the acts mentioned under the items 2, 3 and 4 did not know at the time of the acts that there had been suspension of payment or that petition for bankruptcy had been filed, these acts are not preferences.

The acts mentioned in item 5 are preferences whether or not the creditor benefited by the acts knew at the time of the acts that the acts would prejudice creditors in bankruptcy or that there had been suspension of payment or that petition for bankruptcy had been filed.

Only the administrator has the right to challenge preferences: BL s 76. He must bring action within two years from the opening of the bankruptcy proceedings. The fraudulent transaction is not void, but only invalid *vis-a-vis* other creditors. The administrator may request the return to the bankrupt's estate of any property sold, given away or surrendered by the fraudulent transaction or, if this is not possible, appropriate compensation.

If a transaction is set aside, the bankrupt estate must compensate the creditor concerned for any benefits received under the nullified transaction. The creditor's claim ranks in priority to other unsecured creditors (BL s 78(1)) but only to the extent of such benefits.

The Corporate Reorganisation Law of 1952 (as amended) provides for fraudulent preferences in the same way as BL: Art 78.

Netherlands

BA 1897 as amended (summary only) Art 42

7–10　1.　The trustee may avoid transactions performed by the debtor without consideration which he knew or should have known at that time would prejudice creditors. CC Art 50.2 does not apply.

2.　A transaction, other than for no consideration, may only be avoided on the grounds of prejudice to the creditors if the party dealing with the bankrupt also knew or should have known that it would prejudice the creditors.

Art 43 If the transaction prejudicing creditors was performed within one year prior to the declaration of bankruptcy and if the debtor was not already legally committed to the transaction before the beginning of this period, the knowledge referred to in Art 42.1 is presumed to exist on both sides in the absence of proof to the contrary:

1.　in the case of contracts in which the value of the debtor's obligations considerably exceeds the value of the other party's obligation;

2.　in the case of transactions constituting payment of, or security for, a debt which is not yet payable;

3.   in the case of transactions performed by a debtor with or as against certain relatives, insiders and affiliates.

Art 45 In the event of prejudice to the creditors caused by a transaction for no consideration performed by the debtor within one year before the declaration of bankruptcy it is presumed that he performed the transaction with the knowledge that it would prejudice the creditors.

Art 47 Payment by the debtor of a claim which has accrued due may only be avoided if it is proved either that the person receiving the payment knew that the bankruptcy of the debtor had already been applied for or that the payment was the result of negotiations between the debtor and the creditor with the intention of preferring that creditor over other creditors.

Art 48

1.   By virtue of the previous article no reimbursement may be claimed from a person who, as holder of a negotiable instrument made out to order or bearer, was obliged to accept the payment in view of his legal relationship with former holders.

2.   In such event the party in whose favour the negotiable instrument was issued is obliged to reimburse the amount paid by the debtor to the bankruptcy estate if it is proved either that at the time the negotiable instrument was issued he had the knowledge referred to in the previous article or that the negotiable instrument was issued as a result of the negotiations referred to in that article.

Art 49 Legal proceedings based on Arts 42 to 48 are commenced by the trustee. Nevertheless the creditors are able to dispute the admission of a claim on grounds derived from these provisions.

Art 51

1.   Assets removed from the property of the debtor due to an illegitimate act must be returned to the trustee by the persons who are parties to the transaction which has been avoided with due regard to CC s 2, Title 4, Bk 6.

2.   Rights which have been acquired by third parties in good faith against payment will be honoured. Assets obtained by a third party in good faith for nothing will not be claimed back, in so far as the third party

proves that at the time of the declaration of bankruptcy he had not benefited as a result of the transaction.

3. Assets received by the debtor under a transaction which has been avoided, or the value thereof, will be returned by the trustee to the extent that this benefits the bankruptcy estate. The person who is a party to the transaction which has been avoided may file a claim for the deficit as an unsecured creditor.

Peru

7–11   Alienations without consideration by an insolvent debtor or which cause a debtor to become insolvent may be annulled by his creditors. Alienations for a consideration made by an insolvent may likewise be annulled if his insolvency was notorious or should have been known by the other party. The following are invalid with respect to creditors of a bankrupt: (a) acts and contracts after the bankruptcy declaration; (b) liens and alienations effected within six months before bankruptcy declaration, except liens to secure loans of Banco Industrial del Peru and alienations resulting from these liens; (c) gratuitous acts and contracts within six months before cessation of payments; (d) certain conveyances of real property, mortgages, etc, made within 60 days before bankruptcy; (e) following acts effected within 10 days before cessation of payments: (1) payments of unmatured debts; (2) payments of matured debts in a manner other than that provided by the contract.

However, third persons who acquired real estate in good faith from debtor are protected.

CC 195–229; Decree 7566 of 1932 Arts 68–78 and Law 16267 of October 20, 1966. [*Source*: Martindale-Hubbell Law Digest 1991.]

Russia

7–12   **Law of Bankruptcy of Enterprises 1992** The liquidator may dispute the debtor's transactions executed within six months prior to the commencement of the winding up proceedings in the court. The arbitration court can deem invalid any actions executed by the debtor or on its behalf if: (1) within six months prior to the commencement of the winding up proceedings, an enterprise, de facto bankrupt, satisfies obligations to individual creditors; or (2) regardless of the six-month limit, if such actions were undertaken with an intention to cause damage/losses to other creditors and the creditors for whose benefit the actions mentioned were undertaken were aware of this fact. Transactions intended to satisfy obligations to individual creditors will be deemed invalid if the date of settlement falls within the period in which the enterprise was de facto bankrupt and the parties were aware of its actual position.

Creditors are obliged to return all assets received, or, if this is not possible, pay an equivalent value in cash to the liquidator.

Spain

Commercial Code of 1985

Art 879 Payments of unmatured debts (maturing after the judicial bank-   7–13
ruptcy declaration) within 15 days before the judicial bankruptcy declaration.

Art 880 The following transactions are deemed to be void if within 30 days before the declaration: (1) transfers of real estate without consideration; (2) gifts in favour of daughters of the debtor of assets belonging to the debtor; (3) transfers of rights to and title in real estate to settle debts that have not matured at the time of the declaration; (4) creation of voluntary mortgages in respect of debts not previously secured; loans and purchases of merchandise when the delivery of the moneys and goods have not taken place under a notarised and witnessed agreement; (5) gifts made after the last balance sheet of the debtor revealed that the debtor's liabilities exceeded his assets.

Art 881 Creditors can obtain a declaration that transactions are void if they show that the debtor acted with a fraudulent intention in relation to: (1) sales of real estate performed within one month before the bankruptcy declaration; (2) gifts in favour of daughters of the debtor with assets belonging to the husband/wife community ("*sociedad conyugal*") or any transfer of those assets without consideration, within one month before the declaration; (3) gifts and acknowledgements of debts by trader in favour of his/her spouse within six months before the declaration, provided that they were not real property already belonging to or possessed by the other spouse; (4) any debt created or acknowledgement of loan made within six months before the declaration, without the document having been executed in front of a notary public, or, if under a private instrument, were not properly recorded in the books of the parties; (5) any contract or obligation entered into within 10 days before the declaration.

Art 883 (Pauline action) Any donation made or contract entered into within two years before the declaration can be challenged by the creditors, if any suspicion of fraud or attempt to defraud the creditors can be proved.

Sweden

7–14 **BA Chapter 4** Significant tightening up in 1975 amendments.

Section 2 "The limit date [Fristdag] is the date when the bankruptcy petition was lodged with the Court (Tingsrätten). If a trustee has been appointed pursuant to the Law on Compositions (Ackordslagen 1970: 847) the limit date is instead the date when the application for appointment was lodged, provided a bankruptcy petition is lodged within three weeks of the appointment of the administrator being revoked or, when composition proceedings have ensued, when the scheme of arrangement has been decided upon."

Section 5 [Pauline action]:

"A transaction whereby a creditor has been improperly preferred to others or whereby a part of the debtor's property has been placed out of reach of the creditors or the debtor's debts have increased is voidable if the debtor was or, as a result of the transaction, by itself or in conjunction with other circumstances, became insolvent and the other party knew or ought to have known that the debtor was insolvent and circumstances rendering the transaction improper. A person connected with the insolvent debtor shall be deemed to have such knowledge described above unless it is shown that it was (on a balance of probabilities) improbable that he had or should have had such knowledge.

If the transaction took place more than five years before the limit date it may only be voidable if it was with a connected person."

Section 6 A gift is voidable if completed [i.e. has become effective against the donor's creditors] within six months of the limit date. Insolvency is irrelevant. A gift is voidable if completed within one year of the limit date, or if made to a connected person within three years of the limit date unless it is shown that the debtor remained solvent ["he retains sufficient assets to clearly cover his debts"] following the making of the gift. This also applies to purchases, exchanges and other agreements if the disparity between the consideration of each side is such that it is apparent that the agreement is partially in the nature of a gift.

Section 8 Unreasonable remuneration paid within six months of the limit date. Extensions similar to s 6 circumstances.

Section 10

"Payment of a debt made within three months of the limit date and made by an unusual method of payment, in advance or in an amount which causes the debtor's financial situation to deteriorate considerably is voidable unless in the circumstances the method of payment can nevertheless be deemed ordinary. If the payment was made to a person connected with the debtor and made within two years of the limit date, it is voidable unless it is shown that the debtor neither was, nor became insolvent as a result of the payment.

The above applies also where set-off has taken place, if the creditor according to chapter 5 ss 15 or 16 would not have been entitled to set-off on the debtor's insolvency."

Section 11

7–15

"Payment on a bill of exchange or on a cheque is voidable in the circumstances contemplated in Section 10 above only insofar as the person who accepted payment could have refused to do so without losing the right to payment on the bill of exchange or the cheque from another.

If recovery of a payment is prohibited as the result of the application of the above paragraph, it is the duty of the person who would ultimately have borne the loss if the payment had remained outstanding to pay compensation on the same conditions as would have applied in an action to recover (a voidable payment), if the payment had been made to him as a creditor."

Section 12:

"Security given by the debtor within three months of the limit date is voidable unless it was a condition [of the transaction] at the time the debt was incurred or it was given without delay following the creation of the debt. If the security was given to a connected person within two years of the limit date it is voidable in the above given circumstances unless it is shown that the debtor neither was nor became insolvent as a result of the measure.

The giving of a security includes other measures taken by the debtor or his creditor which are intended to secure the rights of the creditor.

When the security requires registration the delay referred to above is deemed to have been established if application for registration has not been made before the first (available) date for registering an entry two weeks after the creation of the debt."

This applies, e.g. to Swedish floating charges.

Section 13:

"A preference or payment obtained by a creditor through execution levied on the debtor's property is voidable where the preference arose within three months of the limit date. Where the execution occurred in favour of a connected person the payment or preference acquired is also voidable if the preference arose within two years of the limit date and it is not shown that the debtor neither was, nor became insolvent as a result.

A preference arising by virtue of a security for payment ('*Betalnings-säkring*') is voidable if it arose within three months of the limit date."

Recovery proceedings must be instituted within one year of judicial declaration of bankruptcy, or, if later, within six months of awareness. Longer periods for preferences of connected persons. Creditors may institute action if trustee fails to do so.

Switzerland

7–16   Federal Debt Collection and Bankruptcy Act of 1889 (*Bundesgesetz über Schuldbetreibung und Konkurs vom April 11, 1889 – SchKG.*)

Section 285

1.   A fraudulent preference action aims to invoke the nullity of the legal acts mentioned in sections 286 to 288.

2.   The action can be brought by:

   (1)   every creditor who received a preliminary (s 115 (2)) or a definitive certificate of losses (ss 115(1) and ss 149, 265);

   (2)   the bankruptcy administration or, pursuant to ss 260 and 269 (3), every creditor of the bankrupt's estate.

Section 286 ("*Schenkungsanfechtung*")

1.   With the exception of normal occasional presents (ZGB 527 No. 3, 632) the nullity can be invoked of all gifts and gratuitous disposals which have been undertaken by the debtor within the last six months before the distraint (ss 89, 112 (1)) or the opening of the bankruptcy proceedings.

2. Treated equivalently to gifts are:

(1) agreements under which the debtor has received consideration which is disproportionate to his obligation;

(2) agreements under which the debtor has acquired for himself or a third party a life annuity (OR 516) or a usufruct (ZBG 746).

The motives of the parties are irrelevant, as is insolvency at the time of the transaction. The test of undervalue is objective and it is immaterial that the parties did not know of the undervalue.

Section 287 (*"Überschuldung"*)

1. Furthermore, the nullity can be invoked of the following legal acts provided that the debtor has undertaken these within the last six months before the distraint (s 89, 112 paragraph 1) or the opening of the bankruptcy proceedings (s 175) and at the time of the undertaking was already insolvent:

(1) the creation of a pledge (s 27) for pre-existing debt, which the debtor was not bound to grant under a prior agreement;
(2) the discharge of monetary debts in another way than by means of cash or other usual manner of payment;
(3) payment of a debt not yet due.

2. Nevertheless, nullification on the basis of the above is not permissible if the beneficiary proves that he was not aware of the insolvency of the debtor.

Section 288 (*"Absichtsanfechtung"*) Pauline action

Nullity can be invoked of all legal acts (without regard to the moment of the undertaking (s 292), which the debtor undertook with the "intent to prejudice his creditors or to give preferential treatment to one creditor to the detriment of the other, provided the intent was recognisable to the other party".

The action must be brought within five years from the date of the challenged transaction, s 292 of the Code. The transaction is not void, but only invalid vis-a–vis the creditors: s 291 of the Code. The administrator may request the return to the bankrupt's estate of any property sold, given away or surrendered by the transaction. If this is not possible, compensation in kind must be made for its value.

There are specific rules for preferences for composition proceedings relating to banks.

Ukraine

7–17   **Bankruptcy Law 1992 Art 15** On application of debtor, administrator or creditor, court may: (1) avoid any sale (transfer) of debtor's property effected three months before order made in favour of those having an interest in the debtor (insiders—not defined); (2) avoid any sale (transfer) of property or any obligation incurred by the debtor within one year before order if:

(a) the intention of the sale (transfer) or incurrence of the obligation was to hide the assets or to avoid payment of the debtor's liabilities, or

(b) the debtor received substantially less than the reasonable value of the asset, or

(c) the debtor was insolvent in fact on the date of the transfer or incurrence of the obligation or became insolvent as a result of the same.

There is no express exception for ordinary course of business payments. Unclear if security for new money in the suspect period is voidable. Debtor need not be insolvent in the case of intentionally fraudulent transfers and transactions at an undervalue within (a) or (b). [*Source*: Translation of BL 1992 by Carol Patterson.]

CHAPTER 8

VEIL OF INCORPORATION: INTRODUCTION AND DIRECTOR LIABILITY

Introduction

Candidates for personal liability

One of the fundamental decisions jurisdictions have to make is whether to honour the veil of incorporation. The test is whether the law visits personal liability on persons other than the company when it is insolvent. 8–1

The main candidates for personal liability are:

(a) the directors and officers, whether de jure or de facto,

(b) shareholders, including parent companies,

(c) other group companies, i.e. siblings or brother-sister corporations under common ownership,

(d) financing banks (especially in the context of work-outs or security enforcement),

(e) regulators.

Policies

The main attitudes which are likely to influence the transfer of responsibility for the insolvency to persons other than the company and thereby to lead to the dishonour of the veil of incorporation are: 8–2

1. The desire to prevent abuse of the corporate form. The prioritisation of an anti-fraud policy can result in an effective criminalisation of commercial law since the financial sanction tends to be massive, even though not accompanied by a criminal taint. The real question is how punitive commercial law should be and the degree to which the society is content to absorb abuse in the interests of some higher business objective.

2. The intensity of big pocket liability, i.e. finding another pocket to pay, preferably a deep one. The big pocket may be a regulator, a shareholder, a group company or a financing bank. Directors are not usually big enough pockets. The essence of the big pocket liability is that it imposes liability on a bystander who is not primarily responsible, but who happens to be able to pay the victim and who was sufficiently involved for a case to be made out against him.

3. The desire to stop a business before it is too late. This policy shows itself in a greater readiness to fix personal liability on directors (to encourage them to apply early for bankruptcy) and in rules for the mandatory presentation of insolvency petitions if the company becomes balance sheet insolvent (as opposed to being unable to pay current debts) or loses half its capital. The theory is that creditors would be protected if business is halted before the wave of debt engulfs the assets. The opposing view is that attempts to compel an early stoppage can prevent companies from trading out of their difficulties or carrying out a private work-out, and may instead force them into formal insolvency proceedings, which almost invariably have a cataclysmic effect on values, even if they are survival proceedings.

8–3   A company is a mark in a registrar's book. It is invisible, intangible and exists only in the contemplation of the law. But this fiction, this artificial creation of legal personality, secured two great conveniences – the first as a protection against insolvency and the second as a business convenience. From the point of view of the second of these, business convenience, the clothing of companies with legal personality was to enable the business to raise capital through shares, to avoid the transfers and revesting of assets which would otherwise be required on a change of individual participants, to facilitate the transfer of shares in the business without a transfer of a share of the underlying assets, to give the capital providers an equity interest in a business which they do not manage, and to enable them to transfer their interests and to establish a body which could sue and be sued without joining all the participants.

But these administrative advantages are largely mechanical and procedural and are far outweighed by the advantage that the insolvency of the business is not visited upon the owners and managers. Under the classical scheme the owners are liable on insolvency only up to the amount unpaid on their shares. The managers are not intended to be liable since they are purely agents of the legal person. The company is therefore seen as an encouragement to business enterprise and risk-taking.

There is no question that this has been fundamentally beneficial in the industrialised economies beyond peradventure. There can be no doubt that the development of large enterprises would have been paralysed if the owners or directors were personally liable for their debts. Nobody would then have been willing to invest capital on those terms and nobody would have bought shares on the stock exchanges, nor would anyone, other than the brave or foolhardy, have been willing to come forward to manage risky operations.

But the pressures to impose liability on someone other than the corpor-   8–4
ation itself have often become irresistible. The walls of the citadel have been breached. In the United States, the attacks have come mainly from case law, though some flow from the statute-makers in specific areas, notably in relation to environmental pollution and to the liabilities of the management of banks and thrifts. In many other countries the erosion has come from statute, mainly intended to impose liabilities on directors as the prime actors.

The visiting of liability on directors and shareholders should be distinguished. Directors become liable because they are responsible for conducting the business and are entrusted with its proper management in the interests of shareholders and creditors. Their duties are a development of ordinary agency duties which arise wherever one person is entrusted by others with power to affect the economic position of the principal.

Shareholders only incur liability under this head when they adopt the mantle of management by clothing themselves as managers. Shareholder liability tends to arise in the context of groups of companies which are run as a single enterprise and also in the context of close or private or small companies where the management and the shareholders are the same, particularly the family business. No case has been found where a public shareholder of a listed company has been held responsible for the liabilities of the company. Except in the most extraordinary circumstances, such a liability would instantly put an end to the investment by the public in large commercial and industrial undertakings.

Private and public companies

The ordinary company in most developed jurisdictions is either a private   8–5
company or a public company. The usual differences spring from the fact that public companies can invite subscriptions for their shares and debentures from the public and hence they are subject to stricter rules for safeguarding the interests of public shareholders and creditors. The differences typically arise in eight main areas:

1.   Restrictions on issue of the company's securities to the public

2.   No minimum number of members

3. Limited transferability of shares

4. Lesser maintenance of share capital, e.g. initial minimum capital, redemption of shares out of capital is subject to a solvency test, no legal reserves, relaxed valuation requirements for contributions of assets in kind and the like

5. Reduced size and composition of the directorate (e.g. no two-tier boards or employee representatives)

6. Less financial disclosure, notably audited accounts, publicisation, and degree of information

7. Reduced corporate formalities

8. No necessity for shareholder approval of major transactions

8–6   In English-based countries, the usual division is between the private and public company. This is no longer true of Britain but is broadly true of the Republic of Ireland, Australia, New Zealand, Israel, South Africa and numerous former British territories such as India, Pakistan, African countries and the island states such as Hong Kong. The company law of Malta is based on British company law. In such countries as Australia and South Africa, these private companies are called proprietary companies.

In the French-based and Latin countries, the usual division is between the *société anonyme* and the *société à responsabilité limitée*. The typical Latin American corresponding companies are the *sociedad anónima* (Argentina, Brazil, Chile, Colombia, Mexico) and the *sociedad de responsabilidad limitada*. This is true also of Spain. In Italy the two forms are the *società per azioni* and the *società a responsabilità limitata*.

In Germany, Austria and Switzerland the division is between the *Aktiengesellschaft* and the *Gesellschaft mit beschränkter Haftung*. The Hungarian Business Corporations Act 1988 is based on Swiss and German models and similarly divides companies. In Denmark the public company is the *aktiegeselskab* and the private company, the *anpartsselskab*. Netherlands companies are divided into *Naamlose Venootschap* and the *Besloten Venootschap*. In Scandinavia the typical pattern is the unitary company covering both large companies and small family companies, e.g. the Swedish *Aktiebolag*, the Norwegian *Aksjeselskab* and the Finnish *Øsakeyhtiö*.

In the Far East, the joint stock company in Japan is the *Kabushiki Kaisha* and the limited corporation the *Yugen Kaisha*. Korea is similar.

Greece has the *Anonymos Eteria* for public companies and *Eteria Periorismenis Efthinis* for private companies. Turkey has a single form of company. Saudi Arabia has a joint stock company and a limited liability company.

Scale of jurisdictions

It would be possible to scale jurisdictions according to whether they honour   8–7
the veil of incorporation on insolvency but this would require huge comparative research.

Those high on the scale would be intensely loyal to incorporation and require creditors of an insolvent company to look only to the assets of that company and not to some third party. Those lowest on the scale would be intensely suspicious of incorporation and regard the corporate form more as an administrative convenience and not as a protection against insolvency. Purely impressionistically, one suspects that South Africa, Switzerland and Germany have a strong veil, while France and perhaps Belgium and Spain have a weak veil, with countries like England, Australia, Japan, Scandinavian countries, Netherlands, Ireland, Austria, the United States and Italy ranging from a fairly strong to a fairly weak veil.

Extensive search would be required to substantiate the scale and even then it would be essential to compare case law (the individual facts are crucial) and the actual practical application of legal rules. One could only show rough trends.

The scale would be based on weightings. The prime weighting should be given to the risk of liability being imposed on persons other than the company, mainly directors and shareholders. Other subsidiary factors – which tend to be merely indicative of attitude but are not paramount in terms of legal risk or economic importance – would include rules as to the maintenance of capital (especially financial assistance for the purchase of own shares, redemption of capital, special reserves, and the action to be taken on loss of capital); conclusivity of corporate formation (economically unimportant since in practice companies are easy to form in most jurisdictions); and the minimum number of shareholders (also unimportant in practice and influenced by attitudes to the family enterprise sector and the convenient availability of the corporate privilege).

The US is difficult to characterise. Although bankruptcy law is federal, corporation law is not and there are state variations. There is no concept of wrongful trading imposing liability on directors, but on the other hand the concepts of tort liability, of stripping the veil, of equitable subordination and of lender liability appear to be quite potent in comparative terms, but this may be because plaintiff-orientated rules encourage litigation, e.g. contingent fees, no liability of the loser for costs, the jury trial treble or punitive damages, and class actions.

Director's personal liability for debts of insolvent companies

Summary of heads of liability

8–8   Internationally, there are broadly six regimes for director liability:

1.   Fraudulent trading

2.   Wrongful trading

3.   Duties to act when the company is insolvent or has lost most of its capital

4.   Negligent management

5.   Breach of company law or securities regulation

6.   Miscellaneous liabilities, including tort and breach of general statute

These are examined in turn.

Fraudulent trading

8–9   Fraudulent trading is the intentional or reckless (Nelsonian) incurring of debts while the company is insolvent which the company has no hope of being able to pay. It was introduced in England by the Companies Act 1929 (preserved by the Insolvency Act 1986 ss 213 and 215), and is general in the English-based jurisdictions e.g. New Zealand; Hong Kong; Singapore and other island states; Jersey (Companies (Jersey) Law 1991); the former English colonies in Africa; and also in South Africa: see the South African Companies Act 1973 s 424. For some reason, common law Canada escaped. Australia did not, but has taken its own (tough) line.

English-based case law on fraudulent trading is sparse since directors were protected by the "silver lining" or "sunshine" test or by the test of the "light at the end of the tunnel" (which is not a freight train coming the other way). Very few cases have been successful.

In the oft-quoted unreported 1960 case of *Re White & Osmond (Parkstone) Ltd*, Buckley J said:

> "There is nothing wrong in the fact that directors incur credit at a time when, to their knowledge, the company is not able to meet all its liabilities as they fall due. What is manifestly wrong is if directors allow a company to incur credit at a time when the business is being carried on in such circumstances that it is clear the company will never be able to satisfy the creditors. However, there is nothing to say that directors who genuinely believe that the clouds will roll away and the sunshine of prosperity will shine upon them again and disperse

the fog of their depression are not entitled to incur credit to help them get over the bad times."

It appears that only three successful proceedings were brought under the fraudulent trading provision and its precursors in England.

An example is the South African case of *Orkin Bros Ltd v Bell*, 1921 TPD 92 where it was held that there was an implied representation when the directors of limited companies ordered goods from a merchant that they believed the company would probably be able to pay, and if they know that there is no likelihood of payment and no means of payment they commit a fraud. See also *Brenes & Co v Downie*, 1914 SC 97; *Ruto Flour Mills (Pty) Ltd v Moriates*, 1957 (3) SC 113 (T).

8–10 In countries like the Netherlands and Denmark, there is no statutory codification of fraudulent trading but it would appear that a similar result is reached by case law. Thus in Denmark and Norway the directors may be liable if the company fraudulently orders goods on credit when there is no hope of the company being able to pay for them. But few actions have succeeded.

> In the decision of the Danish Supreme Court, UfR 1977, p 274, a department store in Copenhagen was in financial difficulties. The officers of the company decided that the corporation should file for bankruptcy. On the very same day a supplier delivered goods on credit and thus suffered a loss due to the bankruptcy. The supplier sued the board of directors. *Held*: the directors were not liable to the supplier. Although the possibility of carrying on the business at the time of the delivery was severely limited, the bankruptcy was not completely unavoidable.

In the Netherlands case law has used CC Art 6:162, which contains a general provision for tort liability, to render a managing director liable if he entered into a contract on behalf of the corporation and if he knew at the time of the contract or had reason to know that the corporation would not within a reasonable period of time be able to fulfil its obligations and would not have assets for the creditor: Supreme Court, October 6, 1989, NJ 1990, 286. The burden of proof rests on the prejudiced creditor.

Fraudulent trading is not generally found in the US, but it seems there is case law on the lines of the above in New York.

Wrongful trading

8–11 Wrongful trading is the incurring of debts which the director should reasonably have known the company would not be able to pay: the test is objective rather than subjective and erodes the "silver lining" and "light at the end of the tunnel" defences. There is an objective reasonableness test. The personal liability is accompanied by disqualification rules.

Three of the chief proponents of this approach are England, the Republic of Ireland and Australia, but not Canada or the United States, nor the numerous English-based states which remain in the traditional English mould of the Companies Acts of 1929 and 1948.

8–12　　In **Britain**, ss 214 and 215 of the British Insolvency Act 1986 establish the personal liability of directors if the company has gone into insolvent liquidation and the director liable "knew or ought to have concluded that there was no reasonable prospect that the company would avoid going into insolvent liquidation" (there is no time period). The director has the deemed competence of a "reasonably diligent person" having (a) the general knowledge, skill and experience reasonably expected of his function (contrast a finance director with a technical, sales, personnel director or a non-executive director) and (b) the general knowledge, skill and experience he actually has.

The test is objective but serious negligence on a balance of probabilities is enough: moral blame or intention to defraud creditors is irrelevant. The object is to encourage directors to take action at an earlier stage. The director is credited with knowledge which he may not in fact have had.

The director has a defence if he took "every step with a view to minimising the potential loss to the company's creditors he ought to have taken". The practical steps might include calling a board meeting, commissioning auditors to report, seeking advice of insolvency experts and taking other steps to improve the company's position e.g. reducing overheads or disposing of loss-making businesses. In a hopeless case, the directors must call a halt to trading. Contrary to the legislative intentions, practitioners sometimes stand the test on its head on the ground that creditors are better protected if the company trades on – which shows how even the legislative wand is sometimes powerless to stem indelible legal tradition, i.e. that forcing directors into a formal proceeding is not usually the best way to save the business for the benefit of creditors.

If a director is guilty of wrongful trading, the court may order him to make such contribution to the company's assets in a winding up as the court thinks proper.

> In the English case of *Re Produce Marketing Consortium Ltd* [1989] 5 BCC 569, a company's liabilities exceeded its assets in 1984, as shown in its audited accounts. The directors continued to trade until 1987 when the company went into liquidation, even though they had known for at least a year that liquidation was inevitable. They took no substantial steps to correct the irreversible decline or to halt trading, nor did they attempt to obtain up-to-date financial information. The deficit was £320,000. *Held*: the senior director should

personally contribute £50,000 and the junior director £25,000. See also *Re Purpoint* [1991] BCC 121; *Re DKG Contractors Ltd* [1990] BCC 903.

Directors guilty of wrongful trading (and other breaches of company law) can be disqualified under the Company Directors Disqualification Act 1986 for a minimum period of two years and a maximum period of 15 years. Guidelines were laid down by the Court of Appeal in *Re Sevenoaks Stationers (Retail) Ltd* [1991] Ch 164, CA. There have been many disqualifications.

The test introduced in **Ireland** by s 138 of the Irish Companies (Amend-   8–13 ment) Act 1990 is similar. There is an analogous provision in the **Australian** Corporate Law Reform Act of 1993.

In **New Zealand,** s 321(a) of the Companies Act 1955 also imports an objective standard by providing that an officer of the company may be liable for debts of the company if he was knowingly a party to the contracting of a debt by the company and did not at the time honestly believe on reasonable grounds that the company would be able to pay the debt when it fell due. The provision was introduced in 1980. Previously liability arose only in relation to reckless or fraudulent trading.

Director's duty to petition for insolvency or call shareholders' meeting

Although the codification of director liability in the form of fraudulent or   8–14 wrongful trading appears to be a feature only of the English-based jurisdictions, the concept seems to be paralleled in numerous other jurisdictions by two provisions:

1. A duty on directors to petition for insolvency.

2. A duty on directors to call a shareholders' meeting if there has been a serious loss of capital.

Duty to petition for insolvency

The managers of a company may be obliged to petition for insolvency if the   8–15 company is actually insolvent – for which purpose balance sheet insolvency is often enough (as opposed to liability to pay debts as they fall due). This provision is common in Napoleonic countries. Thus in France the debtor must file within 15 days of the cessation of payments: Law of January 25, 1985, Art 3(2). But is not limited to them. It is, for example, found in the new Hungarian insolvency legislation. It is not found in the English-based group.

Duty to call shareholders' meeting on serious loss of capital

8–16　It is more commonly provided that the directors must call a shareholders' meeting if more than one-half of the capital is lost. The objective of this duty is no doubt to restore the situation before it is too late, but it is not uninteresting to enquire whether this is realistic or sensible.

In any event the requirement appears in all EU countries as a result of Art 17 of the EU Second Company Law Directive, but its implementation in the member states is very different. In the hard line states, like Belgium (adopting an attitude which is also followed by Sweden), a failure by the directors to call the meeting results in civil liability and, if proposals are not forthcoming to restore the capital of the company, the liquidation of the company must be applied for. In soft line countries, such as the United Kingdom, the duty is merely to call a meeting to consider the situation: there is a criminal penalty but no civil remedy is expressly provided for.

The idea of calling a shareholders meeting to decide on an "either/or" basis of capital restoration or liquidation is a concept found in many other countries e.g. in Latin America, in Switzerland, Finland and in Saudi Arabia but is not favoured by the English-based countries and (it is believed) it is not found in the United States or common law Canada.

8–17　Comparative examples of these provisions may be given.

Argentina Where 50 per cent of the capital of a SA has been lost, the directors are required to report the fact to the Court of Commerce and to publish a statement to that effect. Where 75 per cent of the company's capital has been lost, the company is deemed to be dissolved and the directors are made jointly and severally liable to third persons for all the obligations which the directors have contracted since the existence of the deficit came or should have come to their knowledge.

Belgium It is the duty of the management of a company in financial difficulties to notify the court within three days of the time that the company has suspended payment. Failure to do this may involve the management in criminal liability and, although this time limit is not strictly enforced by the court, the requirement frequently deters attempts to arrive at informal reorganisations. Further, when losses have made the net assets decrease below one-half of the share capital, a general meeting must be convened to deliberate and decide upon the possible winding up of the company. The board of directors is required to justify its conduct and to submit a special report to this effect. This obligation on the directors forms part of their general duty to provide information when a company is in financial distress. There is a similar duty when the net assets have fallen to less than a quarter of the share capital. The management must convene a general meeting of shareholders. If this obligation is ignored or neglected, any damage to third parties arising out of the financial demise of the company will refutably be presumed to have been caused by the failure to call the meeting.

Colombia Directors must convene a shareholders' meeting if the net worth of a SA is reduced below 50 per cent of subscribed capital. The meeting must restore net worth in six months or dissolve the company.

Denmark Companies legislation introduced provisions concerning serious loss of capital in 1982 pursuant to a European Directive. As to public companies, Art 69 of the Public Companies Act places a duty on the board to convene an extraordinary general meeting of the company if the net assets are less than half the amount of the company's paid-up share capital. The meeting must be convened within six months after such a loss has actually occurred. The board is thus under a continuing obligation to supervise the capital position of the company and may not await the results of the financial year. At the extraordinary general meeting, the board must make a statement concerning the financial position of the company and the board is required to submit a proposal concerning the measures which should be taken to deal with the situation or a proposal for the winding up of the company. Defaulting directors are criminally liable but the Act does not stipulate for any civil consequences.

Finland If the board discovers that the company's capital is less than one-third of share capital, the board must as soon as possible convene a general meeting of shareholders to consider liquidation of the company. Unless a balance sheet adopted at the annual general meeting during the next fiscal year shows that equity capital amounts to not less than half of the share capital, the board must, if the general meeting does not resolve to liquidate the company, apply to the court to order liquidation.   8–18

France If the assets of a SA fall below one-half of registered capital, a shareholders' meeting must be called within four months following the approval of the accounts showing the loss for the board to decide whether to dissolve the company. Within two years after the end of the fiscal year during which the loss occurred, the SA must reduce its capital by at least the amount of the loss or restore its net assets to at least one half of registered capital: Law of January 6, 1969.

Sweden Chapter 13 of the Companies Act of 1975 s 13.2 requires the board of a limited liability company to draw up a balance sheet for liquidation purposes as soon as there is reason to suppose that the company's equity has fallen below half of the registered share capital. If the balance sheet shows that equity is less than half the capital, the board must refer the question at the earliest opportunity to a shareholders' meeting to decide whether the company should be wound up. Unless the shareholders' meeting is held within eight months and unless the meeting adopts a balance sheet showing a restored share capital, the board must lodge a petition for liquidation. If the directors do not carry out their duties, they are jointly and severally liable for the obligations of a company together with others who act on behalf of the company in knowledge of the failure. A director has a defence if he can show that the failure was not due to negligence on his part but the onus is on him. A shareholder may also be jointly and severally liable for the company's obligations if, at the time a duty to wind up the company arises, he participates in a decision to continue the business of the company while being aware that the duty exists.

Switzerland By CO Art 725 if the last annual balance sheet shows that one-half of the share capital of statutory reserves has been lost, the board must immediately convene a general meeting and request measures for the reorganisation of the company. If there are reasonable grounds for believing that the company might be insolvent, the board must prepare an interim balance sheet and submit it to the auditor. If this balance sheet shows that the company's liabilities exceed its assets, either on the basis of going concern values or liquidation values, the board must notify the court. However the court need not be notified if creditors representing an amount equal to the shortfall agree to subordinate their claims to all other creditors.

Saudi Arabia If a joint stock company or a limited liability company (corresponding to public and private companies respectively) loses more than three-quarters of its capital, the directors must convene a meeting to decide whether to dissolve the company or to continue it and in either case public notice must be given indicating the action taken: Saudi Regulations for Companies.

United Kingdom The Companies Act 1985 s 142 provides that, where the net assets of a public company are half or less of the amount of the company's called up share capital, the directors of the company must duly convene an extraordinary general meeting of the company to consider whether any, and if so, what, measures should be taken to deal with the situation. There is no provision insisting that the company must be wound up if the capital is not restored. A meeting must be convened less than 28 days after the earliest day on which a director learns of the fact, to take place at a date not later than 56 days after that date. Defaulting directors who knowingly and wilfully authorise a default are liable to criminal conviction, but there is no civil liability. The UK provision hence shows a policy in favour of encouraging the workout and not needlessly putting the company into a mandatory liquidation when it could be saved by private means.

Negligent management

Business judgment rule The "business judgment rule" seeks to protect and 8–19 promote the full and free exercise of the directors' managerial power by insulating all decisions from judicial review and shielding directors from liability for those decisions, even if they subsequently turn out to be mistaken and lead to insolvency. All that is required is that the directors acted honestly with a view to what they thought were the best interests of the company and with a minimum standard of competence. It seems that this general principle is espoused, more or less, by England and many English-based jurisdictions, including Australia, by Canada and the United States, by Finland, Norway and Sweden, by Austria, Germany, the Netherlands and Switzerland, and probably by Japan. However the business judgment rule gives less protection to directors in Belgium, Luxembourg and perhaps Spain, and very limited protection, it seems, in France but the case law would have to be meticulously compared to justify this impression.

If a jurisdiction imposes liability for commercial mistakes, then almost invariably directors will be liable on insolvency since most insolvencies can be said to be attributable to some business misjudgement or lack of supervision, as opposed to a cataclysmic external event which nobody could have foreseen or guarded against by insurance at a reasonable commercial rate.

Experience has shown that in countries which espouse this test, notably France, the insolvency of companies is followed routinely by the imposition of responsibility on directors and their personal bankruptcy.

Apart from the erosion of the corporate protection, two aspects of this approach are; first, that the hindsight rule can take over – it is often easy to pin-point the mistake after the event when it would not have been obvious in the usually hectic environment in which the decision was made; and, secondly, that the court is invited to make the sort of commercial judgement which it is not appropriate for it to make except in the case of obvious gross culpability.

The class of negligence which is relevant here is not negligent breach of a 8–20 specific requirement of company law, e.g. paying dividends out of capital, but rather a business error, e.g. borrowing beyond the capacity of the company to repay, committing the company to risky business ventures, inadequate budgeting, inadequate financial monitoring or supervision, inadequate insurance, unfunded capital investments, excessive dividends, excessive executive remuneration having regard to the future financial needs of the company, or imprudent investment in a high risk security. Many of the cases render a director liable because he failed to supervise a co-director or manager. This may be because failures of detection are obvious when the villainy is discovered, but difficult if it is unsuspected.

In small or close companies the directors will often be the same as the shareholders. But in large companies the management will inevitably be tiered between those who have overall management of policy and strategy – the board of directors, with or without a supervisory board or non-executive directors – and those who have executive functions without being on the board, such as the chief sales, finance, secretarial, marketing or personnel executives or officers. In practice, the task of a board of a large company is to lay down matters of strategy, e.g. what products to make, what markets to go into, whether to approve large capital investments, budgets, financial commitments and to supervise executive management, i.e. to see whether it is performing its functions and providing adequate information and reports. It is the task of the executives to implement the policy. Hence the management of large companies are purely supervisory, while the management of small companies are invariably executive.

It is probably true that director liability is most often found in relation to close or private companies but not large public companies, except in the case of banks, insurance companies and the like where the public responsibility and the public indignation at insolvency is at its most intense. This at least appears to be the experience in the United States and Britain.

8–21   **Belgium** The liability for negligent management springs from the Commercial Code Art 62.1 which provides that those concerned are liable to the company for any losses arising if the managers manage the company negligently. In addition under Art 62.2, they are jointly and severally liable to the company and to third parties for any losses resulting from breaches of company law or the company's articles of incorporation. Finally under Art 63.3 managers may be personally liable for all or part of the company's debts if the company is declared bankrupt and the manager committed a fundamental error verging on gross negligence, and the error has contributed to the insolvency of the company.

France Liability for negligence arises under Art 180 of BA 1985 and is imposed for mismanagement (*faute de gestion*). The action is known as the "*action en comblement de passif*". There is a long history in France of personal liability on directors stemming back to 1935 and before, but there was a slight retreat in 1985. Previously under the 1967 insolvency legislation, directors were automatically liable unless they could prove to the contrary, but the onus of proof was changed in 1985.

Luxembourg The liability arises under Art 59 of the Company Law of August 10, 1915 for failure to execute properly the mandate which has been conferred on directors.

Spain The concept of negligent liability was introduced in the Companies Act of 1989 (Royal Legislative Decree 1564/1989, s 133). This probably appeared as a result of a rush of enthusiasm for the European Community. The draft EC Fifth Company Law directive proposed a high level of fault but has not been adopted because of member state resistance. Nevertheless, Spain adopted it.

It may be that the tough standard also appears in s 146.2 of the **Italian** Bankruptcy Act of 1942: an action may be instigated against directors for having negligently or wilfully caused damage to the company or having dissipated its assets to the detriment of its creditors. But one would have to study the cases.

Of course it is possible to find statutory provisions or common law statements in many of the major jurisdictions which impose liability for negligence. However it is essential to see how the rule of law is in fact applied: this requires a close comparative examination of the facts. It would be interesting to see whether there is greater international convergence in the case law than the divergence in statutory provision would indicate.

England Misfeasance actions may be brought against directors under IA   **8–22**
1986 s 212, but case law has held that negligence is not enough: see for example *Re Johnson & Co (Builders) Limited* [1953] Ch 634. The business judgement rule, which is a feature of perhaps the majority of the commercial states, prevails. Probably the most notorious case is *Re Cardiff Savings Bank* [1892] 2 Ch 100, where a director who was appointed to the board of the Cardiff Savings Bank at the age of six months and who attended only one board meeting in 38 years, was held not to be liable in negligence for a mismanagement that had occurred.

On the other hand the English attitude is now tougher:

> In *Dorchester Finance Co Ltd v Stebbing* [1989] BCLC 498, the company claimed against an executive and a non-executive director, both of whom were chartered accountants, and against another non-executive director who had considerable accountancy experience. The two non-executive directors had not attended board meetings, had shown no interest in the company's affairs, relied on the active full-time director and the auditor, and often used to sign cheques in blank to be countersigned later by the active director. *Held*: all three were liable in damages for the negligence and misappropriation of the active partner even though the two non-executive directors acted in good faith throughout. A director must act in good faith and in the interests of the company, he must display such skill as may reasonably be expected of a person with his knowledge

and experience, and he must at all times take such care as a prudent man would take on his own behalf. No distinction was to be drawn between executive and non-executive directors in this regard.

In *Re D'Jan of London Ltd* [1993] BCC 646, a director of a company owned by himself and his wife signed a fire insurance proposal form in which he responded negatively to the question whether he had ever been a director of a company which had gone into liquidation. This was incorrect. A fire occurred at the company's premises and the insurers repudiated liability. The company went into insolvent liquidation. The director had not completed the form himself, but had signed it without reading it in the expectation that his insurance broker would have completed it correctly. *Held* that the director had been negligent. Even though he held 99 shares, he had not specifically mandated the error. It made no difference that the company was solvent and prosperous when the negligent act occurred. However the court had power under s 727 of the Companies Act 1985 to relieve a director wholly or in part from liability for breaches of duty if the court considered that he had acted honestly and reasonably and ought fairly to be excused. In this case the director was excused from some, but not all, of the liability which he would otherwise have incurred. See also *Norman v Theodore Goddard* [1991] BCLC 1028.

8–23   The classic statement of supervisory responsibility of directors and collective responsibility in England was an insurance company case which runs parallel to the numerous insurance company cases in the United States where directors have been held liable for inadequate supervision of a defaulting director.

In *Re City Equitable Fire Insurance Co Ltd* [1925] Ch 407, the managing director of an insurance company had been given a free hand by his colleagues. He had concealed the fraud by showing items in the balance sheet as "loans at call" and "cash in hand", but the other directors never enquired about these items. In fact they were loans mainly to himself, and the cash included a large sum to a firm of stockbrokers of which the managing director was a partner. The auditors failed to ask to see the various treasury bonds appearing in the balance sheet and other directors left the managing of the company's affairs to the chairman. *Held*: a director is, in the absence of grounds for suspicion, justified in trusting an official to whom duties are delegated by the constitution of the company to perform the duties honestly. But the degree of attention was grossly inadequate and the co-directors were liable in negligence.

A leading Australian case is *Walker v Wimbourne* (1976) 50 ALJR 446: a company which was insolvent made an intra-group loan to another insolvent company, paid salaries and made an intra-group payment for work which had never been done. *Held*: once a company is insolvent, the directors must take account of the interests of creditors as well as shareholders. The directors were liable for misfeasance. The company need not necessarily be insolvent at the time: see *Ring v Sutton* (1980–81) 5 ACLR 546 where a loan at less than market rates was held to be detrimental to the creditors' interests even though it had been entered into when the company was solvent. For a case where the liquidator did not succeed, see *Nicholson v Permakraft (NZ) Ltd* (1985) 1 NZLR 242.

In *AWA Ltd v Daniels* (1992) 7 ACSR 759 (Supreme Court of New South Wales) a listed Australian company had lost about A\$50m on speculation in foreign exchange operations. The company sued the auditors for negligence. The auditors claimed that the company was guilty of contributory negligence and brought claims for a contribution against the chairman and chief executive and other non-executive directors of the company. The auditors had brought the defects to the attention of the chairman but neither the chairman nor the management had brought them to the attention of the board as a whole. *Held*: the auditors had been negligent in not advising the board, but the company, through the actions of its senior management, including the chairman and chief executive, was found to have contributed to its own losses.

Subsequent legislation in Australia introduced a standard of care for directors of Australian companies by requiring a director, in the exercise of his duties, to exercise the degree of care and diligence that a reasonable person "in a like position" in a corporation would exercise in the corporation's circumstances. Directors in breach are liable to a civil penalty regime. The *AWA Ltd* case seems extreme.

Canada Companies legislation (which is both provincial and federal) usually imposes a duty on directors to exercise the care, diligence and skill that a reasonably prudent person would exercise in comparable circumstances: see the Federal Canada Business Corporations Act. It would appear that the business judgement rule applies and that the threshold of competence is not particularly high. 8–24

United States Here also it appears that the decisions of the board of directors will be protected by the business judgement rule, i.e. the presumption that, in making business decisions, a director satisfies his fiduciary duties by acting on an informed basis, in good faith, and in the honest belief that the action taken was in the best interests of the corporation.

Most of the US cases have concerned banks or insurance companies where either the directors themselves were guilty of gross negligence or failed to supervise properly so that a fraud by a bank officer went undiscovered. In the case of industrial companies, there do not seem to have been a very large number of cases. The American Law Institute reported in 1985 that since the turn of the century there had been about 30 appellant decisions which found fault in the director duty of care. A sample list is to be found in Norwood P Beveridge "The Corporate Director's Duty of Care: Riddles Wisely Expounded", *24 Suffolk University Law Review*, 923, 947, n129. The number of industrial cases does not seem high for such a large economy.

Some of the more recent cases have involved derivative shareholder actions to block management buy-outs at an alleged undervalue and defensive tactics in the context of tender offers. Following the very large number of bank and thrift failures in the United States in the 1980s, the Financial Institutions, Reform, Recovery and Enforcement Act of 1989 provided for actions to be brought against directors of insured depository institutions for gross negligence and also against accountants, lawyers and other professionals who were involved. Several hundred suits were brought by the Federal Deposit Insurance Corporation.

8–25   **Japan** A Japanese case is of interest:

> In a decision of the Supreme Court on April 15, 1966 (20 Minshu 660), a representative director of a company issued a promissory note to a lender to the company to ensure the payment of a loan. The representative director intended that the proceeds of the loan would be used to expand the business of the company. He carelessly believed, in spite of insufficient research, that the incremental profit from the expanded business would be sufficient to repay the loan. The company failed in the expansion of its business and went bankrupt. *Held*: the investment, which eventually caused the bankruptcy of the company, was a reckless way to manage a company and the director was personally liable for gross negligence in connection with the issue of the promissory note.

There are statutory provisions imposing diligence duties on directors in, for example, **Japan,** the **Netherlands, Norway, Portugal, Switzerland** and **Sweden.** More research is needed to see how they are applied.

8–26   A number of statutory formulations may be cited.

Bermuda The Companies Act 1981 s 97(1) requires a director to act honestly and in good faith with a view to the best interests of the company and to exercise the care, diligence and skill that a reasonably prudent person would exercise in comparable circumstances.

Denmark Sections 140 and 141 of the Act on Public Companies and s 110 of the Act on Limited Companies impose liability on officers and auditors for negligence or fraudulent behaviour. This usually arises when the officers continue the business of the company regardless of continuing deficits, although successful suits are rare.

Germany Cases where a director has been responsible for the company's debts are rare. Personal liability may arise if there has been criminal activity with intent to defraud creditors. The standard of care is that of a "well organised and conscientious manager" (see s 93(1) Aktiengesetz) or a "well organised businessman": s 43(1) of the GmbH Act.

Italy By s 146(2) of BA 1942 the *curatore* may bring an action for damages against directors and others for negligence or wilful damage to the company or for having dissipated its assets to the detriment of creditors.

Japan ComC Arts 254–3 places upon directors an obligation to obey all laws and ordinances applicable to them, the Articles of Incorporation, and Resolutions adopted at shareholders' meetings and to perform their duties faithfully on behalf of the corporation. It is believed that the business judgment rule applies.

Netherlands Art 2.9 of Book 2 of the Civil Code provides that each managing director is obliged to perform his duties properly but case law establishes that only serious negligence will render him liable: Supreme Court, February 4, 1983, NJ 1983, 543. A typical case would be completely inadequate supervision.

Norway Both the Joint Stock Companies Act and the Companies Act have provisions on liability for officers of a company for damages intentionally or negligently caused by them during the conduct of their officership of the company. Findings of mismanagement are rare.

Portugal The managers and directors of a company may be liable to creditors if, due to their fault or negligence, the company's assets are insufficient to cover liabilities, e.g. if they have misapplied or given away assets to the detriment of creditors: see Art 78.1 of CCC.

Switzerland Personal liability may lie against officers for intentional or negligent breach of duty in relation to various legal entities: see CO Arts 754, 764, 827, 916. It is believed that actions are unusual.

Director's liability for breach of company law

It is universally the case that directors are liable for specific breaches of company law or violations of the constitution of the company.   8–27

Examples are: paying dividends out of capital while the company is insolvent; unlawfully redeeming shares or procuring that the company gives financial assistance in connection with the purchase of its own shares; ultra vires transactions; self-dealing transactions; fraudulent transfers in breach of the Pauliana and its derivatives; failure to keep proper books of accounts; negligent errors in financial statements; and the omnipresent prospectus liability. As to self-dealing, a director acts in conflict of interest where he uses his position to make a personal profit. Those in charge of the assets of others should not take them for themselves. The doctrine is also insolvency-related because the temptation to use the business for personal profits can lead to a dangerous and infected depletion of assets, poor business decisions resulting from a polluted judgement, a weakening of the ability of a company to pay, and hence the quickening of insolvency. The classic example is insider lending by directors of a bank to entities in which they have an interest – historically one of the commonest causes of bank failures in the United States. Other examples are secret commissions paid by the company on company contracts, the diversion of orders to other director controlled companies and the diversion of profitable opportunities, the granting of credit or guarantees by the company for the benefit of directors, the use of information acquired as a director for personal profit, such as inventions, long term employment contracts, excessive payments for loss of office and excessive remuneration.

There is a wealth of case law in all senior jurisdictions on these matters and the principles are so firmly established and generally known that it is not necessary to go into detail. In addition, company law in various jurisdictions has introduced specific controls on such matters as loans to directors and disclosure of directors' interests in shares and debentures, their remuneration, directors' employment contracts and transactions with directors. The detail is substantial but the import simple. France is particularly draconian: by BA 1985 Art 182, the court may extend bankruptcy proceedings to any de jure or de facto officer who, amongst under things, under the veil of the legal entity carried out business transactions or used corporate assets as his own or continued the operation of the legal entity in order to further his own interests, even though the continuation could only cause the bankruptcy of the legal entity, or used corporate assets or credit for his personal benefit.

8–28　**Financial statements** As to financial statements, as a general proposition, company law requires that proper accounting records are kept, specifies the contents and format of the accounts, provides for their presentation to members and their publication and lists the items which must be reported on. The main question is the degree of due diligence that directors must exercise and the extent to which they can rely on the auditors. If the auditors themselves are sued, they may seek a contribution from the directors.

In the Scottish case of *Andrew Oliver and Sons Ltd v Douglas* (1982) SLT 222, the court accepted the possibility of a contribution claim where the directors had negligently supplied the auditors with inaccurate information which was then relied on by a third party.

In the Australian case of *AWA Ltd v Daniels* (1992) 7 ACSR 759 (New South Wales Supreme Court), it was held that auditors should have informed the whole board, and not just the chairman and chief executive, of various defects in a speculative foreign exchange programme being carried out by executives. It was held that the company had shown contributory negligence. An extreme decision.

In a decision of the Danish Supreme Court (U 1982.595) a financial statement included uninvoiced profits on work in progress contrary to the conduct of an audit. The statement did not, but should have, shown a deficit. *Held*: the creditor who suffered a loss on deliveries, which had taken place after the financial statements had been made public, was awarded damages against the officers of the company and the auditor.

There appear to be different emphases on the degree of liability, but the topic is too large to embark on an international comparison.

Ratification by shareholders The ability of the shareholders of the company   8–29
to whitewash violations by the directors varies. Many commercial jurisdictions entrench certain mandatory rules and provide at least minimal minority protection against other overweening breaches, especially in the area of self-dealing, and prohibit the whitewash if the company is insolvent – since creditors now have an interest. The general trend is to permit companies to indemnify the directors, although this is useless from the point of view of directors at the very time when they are most likely to need it (when the company is insolvent). Perhaps there is less harmony on whether the company can pay for director insurance. But D&O insurance may be limited or expensive. The company can do so (usually) in the US, in the Netherlands and in England: Companies Act 1985 s 310(3), as amended in 1989.

Director's liability for preferential claims

In most jurisdictions, preferential debts, such as taxes and employee wages,   8–30
are priority claims in the insolvency which are paid before general unsecured claims. Nevertheless, so great is the policy pressure to ensure that these claims are paid, that in some countries personal liability may result. For example, directors are personally liable for certain taxes in Canada (failure to withhold and remit taxes on dividends and wages), Greece (income tax), Netherlands (income tax, VAT, social security, pension contributions under the Second Abuse Act of 1987, subject to defences), Norway (taxes and social security contributions), Portugal (unpaid taxes and debts due to the state) and Sweden (non-deduction of taxes from employee wages, social

charges on employee remuneration and VAT if wilful or grossly negligent). As to unpaid employee remuneration, personal liability on directors for this appears to be rare. Canada seems to be an exception. Under the Federal Canada Business Corporations Act directors are liable to employees of the corporation for up to six months' wages (and under the common law 12 months' vocation pay) for services performed during their term of office. Ontario's Employment Standards Act imposes a similar liability.

Director's tort and environment liability

8–31   Personal liability for tort appears more common. In England directors are personally liable for torts if they actively participated in the tort or authorised it. For example:

> In *Mancetter Developments Ltd v Garmanson Ltd* [1986] 1 All ER 499, on giving up possession of leased premises by the company, the company's employees, on a director's instructions, removed certain pipes and fans, leaving holes in the outside walls. Weather damaged the building through the holes left by the removal of the fixtures. *Held*: the director was personally liable to the owner of the premises. He had procured the commission of the tort by the company by instructing the employees to remove the fixtures.

> In *Thomas Saunders Partnership v Harvey, The Times*, May 10, 1989, a director of a supplier of flooring confirmed to architects that the flooring complied with certain specifications. The architects claimed for losses, but the supplier had gone into liquidation and they therefore claimed against the director personally. *Held*: the director was personally liable because he knew that the statement was untrue. But the court also said that he would have been liable if he had negligently made the statement.

But general tort liability in England is relatively limited, especially for economic torts.

The other prime example of tort liability is the personal liability of directors for environmental pollution which is appearing in European countries and is particularly potent in the United States and Canada.

De facto directors

8–32   A director may incur the liabilities of a director, even though he has not been formally appointed as a director, by virtue of the management control which he exercises. It is generally the case that these interlopers or usurpers are subject to the liabilities of directors, just as if they had been properly appointed and it seems correct in principle that the duties of a director should not be evaded by the use of a different title or by reason of failure to comply with the legal technicalities of his appointment. This will catch real controlling spirits behind the board, but the question does arise as to whether the big pocket principle intervenes so as to catch shareholders or banks interfering in the management of the company in financial difficulties by virtue of their bargaining power.

In many jurisdictions the de facto director has been recognised formally by statute. Thus the British Companies Act 1985 s 741(1) defines a director to include shadow directors, namely any person in accordance with whose directions or instructions the directors of a company are accustomed to act. This expressly excludes professional advisers and it is further provided that a company is not to be deemed to be a shadow director of any of its subsidiaries by reason only that the subsidiaries' directors are accustomed to act in accordance with the directions or instructions of the parent or holding company. In Belgium, the management for the purposes of liability includes the management or executives as well as the directors. In Switzerland, liability depends upon the functions management actually performs.

In France, a decision of the Paris Court of Appeal, March 17, 1978, extended the personal liability for a bankrupt party to any individual or legal entity which assumes the same functions and powers as a de jure officer and in fact independently exercises a management activity.

In the English case of Re A Company (No 005009 of 1987) (1988) 4 BCC 424, it was held that a company's bank which commissioned a financial report into the company's affairs and then took steps to ensure implementation of the report's recommendations could be a shadow director of the company. In Re Tasbian Ltd (No 3) [1991] BCLC 792, the Court of Appeal held that there was an arguable case that a management consultant who had been appointed a company doctor to advise and assist in the recovery of a company in financial difficulties was a shadow director.

In the Australian case of 3M Australia Pty Ltd v Kemish (1986) 4 ACLC 185, a company's accountant, who was an external consultant, became involved in the affairs of the company so as virtually to become its financial controller. He placed orders with suppliers for the provision of goods which were subsequently sold to the company and applied the profits of sale to the payment of other debts. The company failed to pay the supplier and became insolvent. Held: the accountant was personally liable for the cost of the goods.

CHAPTER 9

VEIL OF INCORPORATION: SHAREHOLDER AND LENDER LIABILITY

Shareholder liability

Generally

9–1　There appears to be much greater international consensus on the personal liability of shareholders for the debts of a company.

The usual position is that the shareholders are not liable for the debts of the company beyond the unpaid amount on their shares. This is so even in the case of groups and small family companies.

> In *Salomon v Salomon & Co Ltd* [1897] AC 22, HL, Salomon converted a shoe manufacturing business into a company, and received in exchange shares, cash and debentures secured on all the assets. Subsequently the company failed and the unsecured creditors contested the validity of Salomon's debenture, which gave him priority, and of the company itself. *Held*: the veil of incorporation must be honoured. Lord Macnaghten stated at 51 that, on incorporation, the company became a legal entity distinct from the members or shareholders: "it may be that after incorporation the business is precisely the same as it was before, and the same persons are managers, and the same hands receive the profits, the company is not in law the agent of the subscribers or trustee for them. Nor are the subscribers as members liable, in any shape or form, except to the extent and in the manner provided by the Act."

This leading English House of Lords case has always been the bedrock of company law in English-based jurisdictions.

The classic American statement of the lifting of the veil is by Cardozo J in *Berkey v Third Ave Ry*, 244 NY 84, 155 NE 58 (1926) where he said:

> "The whole problem of the relation between parent and subsidiary corporations is one that is still enveloped in the mists of metaphor. Metaphors in law are to be narrowly watched, for starting as devices to liberate thought, they end often by enslaving it. We say at times that the corporate entity will be ignored when the parent corporation operates a business through a subsidiary which is

characterised as an 'alias' or a 'dummy'. All this is well enough if the pictures-queness of the epithets does not lead us to forget that the essential term to be defined is the act of operation. Dominion may be so complete, interference so obtrusive, that by general rules of agency the parent will be a principal and the subsidiary an agent. Where control is less than this, we are remitted to the tests of honesty and justice."

For a detailed review of US law, see Blumberg, *The Law of Corporate Groups*, 3 vols (1983–87, Little, Brown & Co).

Uniformly, there are exceptions where the minimum membership is not maintained, where the company is used as a cloak for fraud, e.g. to siphon away assets (see para 5–31), or where a company is set up to evade a restrictive covenant (there are English and Swiss decisions on this point). **9–2**

The notional stripping of the veil in special cases, such as expropriation, judicial jurisdiction and trading with the enemy, are not true instances of dishonouring the veil of incorporation in our sense.

There are also various cases where a shareholder may be liable to return assets to the company following on a breach of duty by the directors in which the shareholder participated. An example is where shareholders unlawfully receive share capital ahead of creditors in breach of maintenance of capital rules, where a shareholder receives a dividend when the company was not entitled to pay a dividend because it was insolvent, where a shareholder is liable to disgorge assets or profits to the company as a result of a director self-dealing transaction, or where the shareholder must turn over to the company a fraudulent preference made by the company in his favour. These also are not strictly cases of lifting the veil of incorporation.

However there are some important exceptions to the general tendency not to impose liabilities on shareholders. These are mainly as follows:

- commingling, notably in the context of groups and family companies;
- group liability for tax;
- US equitable subordination;
- consolidation on insolvency.

Commingling, undercapitalisation and informalities

There have been a series of mainly US cases which have imposed group or shareholder liability in the case of extreme commingling. The chief factors pointing to liability in the US, particularly in the case of groups, have been common directors or employees, consolidated accounts, financial or economic dependence on the shareholder, holding out, inadequate capital, **9–3** non-observance of corporate formalities, intrusive management control by a shareholder, participation in ultra vires transactions, participation in fraudulent disposals, self-dealing, and breach of obligations as a shareholder. Examples are as follows:

> In the US Supreme Court decision of *Consolidated Rock Products v DuBois*, 312 US 510 (1941), a parent and two subsidiaries were in the rock and gravel business. The affairs of the three corporations were united under an operating agreement under which the management, operation and financing of the business of the subsidiaries was undertaken by the parent. The corporations became subject to insolvent reorganisation proceedings. *Held*: the parent was liable for the debts of the subsidiaries. The parent dominated their management and commingled assets, and the subsidiaries had failed in the main to observe corporate formalities.

> In *Henderson v Rounds & Porter Lumber Co*, 99 F Supp 376 (WDR Ark 1951), shareholders manipulated the company's affairs to their own advantage. The company had been compelled to sell lumber and flooring to the shareholders below cost. The parent was the only secured creditor with a mortgage on the debtor's fixed assets. *Held*: the shareholders were responsible for losses caused to the company. The veil of incorporation should be pierced. The court said that the corporation was a mere agency or department for the advancement of the parent's own interest.

> In *Re Typhoon Industries Inc*, 6 Bankr 886 (Bankr EDNY 1980), a bankruptcy court imposed liability on one affiliate for the tax liabilities of three sister companies which had been dissolved. The corporations had functioned as a "single-unit" under the common management of the sole shareholder and had shared the same office with the same telephone. The debtor paid all major expenses and approved all contracts for its affiliates, deposited their sales proceeds into a bank account, appropriated all cash surpluses, and described the affiliates as its divisions on its letterhead. The court said that the affiliates were "mere instrumentalities and alter egos" and that it would be inequitable to allow the debtor to escape the affiliate's capital tax liability.

9–4   In a review carried out by Robert B Thompson, "Piercing the Corporate Veil: An Empirical Study", 76 *Cornell Law Review* 1036 (1991), some 600 US piercing cases were subjected to a statistical analysis. Some of the conclusions from this survey were: first, piercing of the corporate veil is limited to close corporations and corporate groups, never in the case of publicly held corporations. Secondly, there did not appear to be a trend to a greater piercing. Thirdly, the statistical differences between states did not seem statistically significant, with California perhaps in the lead. The fewer the shareholders, the more likely the piercing, with greater piercing occurring in the case of a one-man company. Surprisingly, courts have pierced more in the case of contract than in the case of tort, contrary to the repeated assumption that tort liability is more likely because the tort victim is an involuntary creditor. The courts always pierce where they find misrepresentation.

The reasons given for piercing included: (1) undercapitalisation; 9–5 (2) informalities (matters relating to meetings or records and the like); (3) "overlaps" including overlap in meetings, directors, business activity, owners, management, bank accounts, control of employees, books, contracts, insurance policies, advertising, corporate acts, officers, assets, records, tax returns, stationery, employees, retirement plans and the like; (4) misrepresentation as to the company's assets and financial condition and misrepresentation as to the party responsible for payment; (5) shareholder domination, such as shareholders paying corporate expenses or continuing losses or paying salaries of corporate employees or guaranteeing corporate debts or owning all of the stock of the corporation or treating the corporation as a department or the corporation engaging in no independent action; (6) intertwining and lack of substantive separation (commingling of funds or siphoning of corporate funds, the shareholder treating corporate assets as his own and the like); and (7) general terms such as "alter ego" and "instrumentality". The survey showed a very high degree of piercing in the case of "instrumentality", "alter ego" or "dummy" and in the case of misrepresentation as well as in the case of intertwining or lack of substantive separation. Undercapitalisation and failure to follow corporate formalities were lower on the list, as were domination and control. The various types of overlap were even lower.

Failure to observe corporate formalities has often been criticised as an inadequate reason for making shareholders liable since the absence of corporate formalities is irrelevant to liability; the imposition of the liability on this ground may merely be to emphasise that a company's accounts and records are essential to establish who is liable to whom.

Similarly, undercapitalisation, i.e. that a company is inadequately capitalised in relation to the risk that it is likely to undergo and its likely economic needs, is an extremely vague test because, if pursued to its ultimate conclusion, the veil of incorporation will never be protective against insolvency since the fact that a creditor of the company has suffered loss must mean that it has inadequate capital. If that is not the rule, then the court is left with a commercial judgment of what is adequate capital in relation to the risks likely to be encountered.

Common ownership of shares, common directors or common employees 9–6 or consolidated accounts or tax returns also seem unconvincing, as do ideas of dependence on business or finance, or division of the business into component parts or common headquarters services. Customer dependence is not unusual in commercial life, nor is the division of a business into its component parts illegitimate, e.g. financing subsidiaries for bond issues, nominee companies for holdings of securities, captive insurance companies, a company holding the property lease, or a marketing or manufacturing or advertising company. It would not seem illegitimate that companies have common legal, pension, insurance or payroll control services or that the parent is responsible for computers or general administrative support or for providing premises. The fact that a company contracts out its services should not on its own render that company liable for the engagements of the company assuming those services. Nor should the centralisation of group bank accounts be a test provided that clear delineations are made in the books; this might well be to reduce interest costs. It is different in the case of self-dealing transactions where a shareholder usurps corporate opportunities, uses the company's inventions without paying for them, demands excessive service fees or excessive prices for sales, or procures the subsidiary to give guarantees which are not in its interest, or arranges for the subsidiary to improve the property of the parent without payment, or procures the subsidiary to lease property to the parent or another group company interest-free, or drains cash from the parent in terms of excessive dividends or remuneration or loans, or uses assets of the subsidiary to repay parent loans.

Undercapitalisation as a test is also found outside the US. In Belgium, Art 25 of the Companies Act provides that, where a company is declared bankrupt within three years following its incorporation and where the registered share capital at the time of incorporation was manifestly insufficient for the normal exercise of the intended activities of that company for a period of at least two years, the incorporators are jointly and severally liable in respect of any obligations of the company to the extent determined by the court.

Shareholders as de facto directors

9–7   There is a common rule that shadow or de facto directors are liable in the same way as directors e.g. a shareholder who intrusively intervenes in management. There appear to be few international cases imposing this liability on shareholders in the major jurisdictions outside the United States.

> In *Re Hydrodan (Corby) Ltd*, December 17, 1994, the company was a subsidiary of a public company and went into liquidation. *Held*: the parent company was a shadow director of the subsidiary, but the directors of the parent were not shadow directors of the subsidiary. The holding company gave instructions and directions to the directors of the subsidiary, but the directors of the holding company did not personally give those instructions but only as representatives of the holding company.

Group liability

Germany The German Joint Stock Companies Act 1965, applicable to pub-   **9–8** lic stock companies, provides for integrated groups (imposing liability on the holding company for the obligations of subsidiaries), for control contract groups (where there is a control contract imposing liability on the controlling company to make good any deficit in the controlled company's accounts if the controlled company is instructed to take any action which is not in its own or the group's interest) and "de facto" groups where there is a relationship of dependence. The European Ninth Draft Company Law directive proposed a reform of member state company law along the lines of the German law of integration but this proposal did not meet with general approval, no doubt on the ground that business in Europe placed a greater value on the insulation of subsidiaries as opposed to the advantages of group consolidation.

Hungary If the equivalent of a public company (Rt) holds more than three quarters of the shares of another Rt, the controlling Rt will be liable for all the debts of the controlled Rt: Business Corporations Act 1988, as amended. This does not apply to other corporations.

England The view that shareholders may be liable for ratifying a breach of   **9–9** duty by the directors was resolutely rejected in the case of *Multinational Gas & Petrochemical Co v Multinational Gas & Petrochemical Services* [1983] 3 WLR 492, CA. In the absence of fraud or misfeasance, if the creditors, through the liquidator, could sue the shareholders for negligence in ratifying the acts of the directors, then the concept of limited liability arising from incorporation would be meaningless.

Austria Case law in Austria has imposed liability on state-owned banks which continue to extend loans to insolvent subsidiaries, thereby creating the impression that those subsidiaries were still solvent. These cases are probably explicable on the grounds that the debtor's management was liable for fraudulently incurring credit, and the bank, as the owner, was liable on account of its participation in the management. The sole bank stockholder not only materially influenced the management's formulation of its objectives, but also itself negligently consented to the obstruction of a necessary bankruptcy which would inevitably follow and was thus a contributory accomplice to the negligent offence against the bankruptcy law. See the decision of the Austrian Supreme Court of July 14, 1986, 10b 57/86 Jbl 1986 713; WBl 1988 129.

> In an Austrian case decided by the Supreme Court, 60b 656/91, December 10, 1992, a property construction company was hopelessly insolvent for some

years, but nevertheless contracted new debt with suppliers and the like. Notwithstanding that they knew of the insolvency, the three shareholders, each holding one-third of the shares, voted at shareholders' meetings to continue the company. The company finally went into bankruptcy. *Held*: the company contracted new credit at a time when there was no prospect of paying the debts and when it should have been put into bankruptcy. The duty to apply for bankruptcy applied to the managers of the company, but the shareholders voted in favour of not applying for bankruptcy and therefore confirmed the management's attitude. The shareholders were personally liable.

9–10 **Sweden** A similar idea to the Austrian position is evidenced in Sweden, which has stringent duties in Chapter 13 of the Companies Act of 1975 s 13.2, requiring the board of a company to call a shareholders' meeting if the company has lost more than half its capital. Shareholders who participate in a decision to continue the business where the company should have been wound up are jointly and severally liable to those suffering loss from the decision.

New Zealand The Companies Amendment Act 1980 allows the court to impose liability upon a related company for the debts of the company being wound-up whenever the court is "satisfied that it is just and equitable to do so". In exercising this authority, the court is required to be guided by certain guidelines e.g. the extent to which the related company took part in the management of the company being wound up, the conduct of the related company towards the creditors of the company being wound up, the extent to which the circumstances giving rise to the winding up of the company are attributable to the actions of the related company and such other matters as the court thinks fit. But mere inter-relatedness is not enough.

Group liability for tax

9–11 There appears to be a higher incidence of the imposition of tax liabilities on group companies than tort or a contract liability: there are a number of cases in England, e.g. *Firestone Tyre and Rubber Co Ltd v Llewellyn* [1956] 1 All ER 193, HL.

US equitable subordination

9–12 US equitable subordination seems to be a peculiarly US doctrine, although it exists in isolated pockets elsewhere. Under this doctrine, a creditor is not permitted to prove his claim until all other creditors have been satisfied. His claim is not altogether disallowed but rather it is made junior to other creditors and in effect this generally results in the subordinated creditor receiving nothing at all.

Its popularity in the United States seems to spring from the fact that equitable subordination is a halfway house: subordination does not impose personal liability on the shareholder but rather diminishes or nullifies the value of the shareholder's asset. The loss of the claim is less draconian then the direct imposition of liability. Hence the misconduct needed to justify subordination is often less delinquent then that needed to justify direct action by a creditor or the insolvency representative against a shareholder.

The doctrine was originally introduced to protect public creditors and public preferred stockholders of the subsidiary against a competing claim by the dominant parent, ie to protect public investors against an insider claim.

> In *Taylor v Standard Gas & Electric Co*, 306 US 307 (1939) (S Ct), Deep Rock was a subsidiary of Standard. Deep Rock's common shares were wholly-owned by Standard, but the public owned most of the preferred stock and also debt securities of Deep Rock. Deep Rock owed Standard nearly $10 million for loans, inter-company transactions, declared but unpaid dividends, management fees and the like. Deep Rock went into insolvency reorganisation proceedings. *Held*: Standard's claim should be subordinated to Deep Rock's external creditors and to the preferred stockholders. The reasons were (1) Deep Rock was undercapitalised in relation to its business and had to be financed by loans from the parent including for the payment of dividends on the public preferred stock (although Deep Rock had very substantial share capital); (2) Standard controlled the management of Deep Rock (not unusual in controlled companies); and (3) some evidence of manipulation of inter-company transactions to the detriment of Deep Rock, e.g. dividends declared at times of cash shortage to satisfy the external stockholders and paid out of loans from Standard, high rates of interest and alleged excessive rentals payable to Standard on an oil cracking plant leased to Deep Rock. Effectively the court was subordinating the insider entirely to the public and in the practical result disallowed the parent's claim by treating it as junior equity. The decision was not based on piercing the veil or instrumentality but on fairness.

> In *Pepper v Litton*, 308 US 295 (1939) (S Ct), the controlling shareholder of a one-man insolvent corporation claimed allegedly excessive salaries for five years. *Held*: the claim was a serious misappropriation of the assets of the company in the circumstances and should be subordinated. On the facts many jurisdictions might well have disallowed the claim and the importance of the case lies in its restatement of the subordination principle.

Often the emphasis has been on the protection of public investors. Hence subordination of the parent's debt to minority public shareholders in the subsidiary has been upheld, so that the parent's claim is treated as junior to outside equity, not just outside debt: see, for example, *Boyum v Johnson*,

127 F 2d 491 (8th Cir 1942). This effectively amounts to cancelling the parent's claim altogether.

9–13   The main features have been (although usually a combination is required):

1. The first is inadequate capitalisation in relation to needs where the parent's loans are really equity, e.g. because there is no real expectation of repayment or where the subsidiary has to borrow from the parent to pay its way, and inability to borrow externally. Ratios have differed from 9:1 to 80:1. Borrowing where the subsidiary is in extremis to keep the business going have often been subordinated and often not. The problem is, what is adequate capital?

2. The second is wrongful management going beyond more negligent business judgement. This factor is present in most of the cases, but it involves the court in determining, e.g. market values and fair rates of interest and overall commercial fairness. Inequitable conduct towards the subsidiary have included mainly:

    (a) Operating the subsidiary without a profit objective, e.g. where plant is operated for the parent's benefit without profit to the subsidiary so that creditors of the subsidiary suffer: *International Tel & Tel Corp v Holton*, 247 F 2d 178 (4th Cir 1957); *Gannet Co v Larry*, 221 F 2d 269 (2d Cir 1955).

    (b) A dividend policy of the subsidiary which is for the parent's benefit even though there is no breach of dividend law in that dividends are paid out of profits and while the company is solvent. The basis is that dividends deplete the assets available to creditors. Usually, the dividends have been a factor in the subordination where the subsidiary, though entitled to pay them, does not have the cash and the dividend is financed by a loan from the parent. It is irrelevant that the dividend payment did not cause direct loss: the advance is subordinated.

    In *Re Tri-State Building Materials Co*, 279 F Supp 1020 DSD (1968), a parent lent $140,000 to a subsidiary which used the advance to pay a dividend to the parent. The companies were on the verge of bankruptcy. *Held*: the advance for the dividend should be subordinated.

    (c) Spoliation of the subsidiary, such as compound interest at high rates on the parent's advances, stripping assets at an undervalue, commingling of assets, excessive salary claims for common directors of the parent, diverting high-risk business to the subsidiary, using the subsidiary's assets for security for parent borrowings, as well as breaches of corporate law which everywhere lead to recovery, e.g. unlawful redemption of share capital or issuance of stock for less than fair consideration.

(d) Inequitable conduct favouring the parent, such as where the parent secures its claims against the subsidiary, so that outside unsecured creditors do not get paid. Surprisingly, public recordation of the parent's lien has not prevented a creditor from claiming subordination: see, e.g. *Arnold v Phillips*, 117 F 2d 497, 501 (5th Cir).

(e) Conduct justifying piercing of the veil, e.g. disregard of corporate formalities (even though this does not cause the loss), commingling of assets, and economic integration of the operations of the parent and the subsidiary so that the subsidiary is in a position of dependence.

Subordination can result in penalising innocent creditors. For example, if   9–14
the parent company's debt is subordinated to innocent creditors of the subsidiary, the innocent creditors of the parent lose an asset. This will particularly be the case where the parent's debt is subordinated to outside shareholders of the subsidiary. This has not prevented subordination, as the *Deep Rock* case showed.

Another example arises where a parent has pledged stock of its subsidiary to creditors of the parent. If the parent is subordinated to rank after the stock, the creditors of the parent are injured. But this has not prevented subordination.

> In *Re Inland Gas Corp*, 187 F 2d 813 (6th Cir 1951), the subsidiary had external public shareholdings. The parent pledged its majority shareholdings in the subsidiary to secure public notes issued by the parent. The parent had an unsecured claim on the subsidiary. The subsidiary becomes subject to insolvent reorganisation proceedings. *Held*: the parent's claim on the subsidiary was subordinated to the stock of the subsidiary (thereby protecting its noteholders but not the parent's other unsecured creditors). It was not subordinated to the public stockholders in the subsidiary.

Note that in Germany there are statutory provisions for the subordina-   9–15
tion of shareholder loans made at a time when the shareholder should have injected equity: see s 32A and B of the GmbH Law.

Equitable subordination does not apply in Canada.

> In *AEVO Co v Macleod & Co* (1991) 4 OR (3d) 368, a trustee in bankruptcy argued that the rights of AEVO, which was a secured creditor of the bankrupt, should be subordinated on equitable grounds to the claims of the unsecured creditors of the bankrupt. The trustee said that through AEVO's control of the operations of the bankrupt, AEVO allowed and encouraged the bankrupt to continue operations and incur debts to creditors which it knew, or ought to

have known, would not be paid, in order to ensure that AEVO would achieve the maximum possible recovery under its security. *Held*: equitable subordination does not apply in Canada. If it did, this "would create chaos". In any event, subordination would not have been applied on the facts, even if the US principles were applicable.

Consolidation on insolvency

9–16　Provisions whereby a court can order the assets and liabilities of a group of companies to be consolidated if they are insolvent and their affairs are hopelessly commingled appear to be common, and not unreasonable if cautiously applied.

This is an extreme measure because it results in a fusion of the assets and liabilities and may be prejudicial to the creditors of one of the companies. For example, creditors of an asset-rich company would have their assets diminished by the load of creditors on a low-asset company. Fusion or loss of corporate personality results in elimination of all inter-company claims and guarantees, elimination of contracts between shareholders and the company, the collapse of leases of land or equipment by the shareholders to the company, and theoretically the establishment of set-off mutuality between parent and subsidiary with regard to an outside creditor. Fraudulent transfers and self-dealing transactions between the companies would be ignored. The combined creditors vote on reorganisation plans.

It seems to be generally true that this form of consolidation is only reluctantly ordered by the courts in those countries where it is possible. The rationale usually is that the affairs of the various companies have been inextricably inter-mingled and there are no records to evidence them so that the expense or impossibility of reconstructing the books and the transactions would lead to such delay and so consume the assets as to be severely prejudicial to the creditors – more prejudicial than the consolidation itself. Consolidation may be partial.

In the United States substantive consolidation or pooling of assets of group companies rests on judicial authority, not on statute or any bankruptcy rule other than the general equity power in BC 1978, s 105: see, for example, the foundation case of *Chemical Bank NY Trust Co v Kheel*, 369 F2d 845 (2d Cir 1966). This case involved eight shipping corporations all controlled by a single individual which were operated as a single unit, with little or no attention to corporate formalities.

The leading cases on substantive consolidation in the US include *Stone v Eacho*, 127 F 2d 284 (4th Cir 1942); *Soviero v Franklin National Bank*, 328 F 2d 446 (2d Cir 1964); *Re Flora Mir Candy Corp*, 432 F 2d 1060 (2d Cir 1970); *Re Continental Vending Machine Corp*, 517 F 2d 997 (2d Cir 1975), *cert denied*,

424 US 913 (1976); *Re Gulfco Investment Corp*, 593 F 2d 921 (10th Cir 1979); *Re Augie/Restivo Baking Co*, 860 F 2d 515 (2d Cir 1988).

In England the liquidation of associated companies can be consolidated under IA 1986 ss 165 and 167 which give the liquidator power to effect compromises with the appropriate sanctions. In New Zealand the Companies Act 1955 s 315B, introduced in 1980, provides for the pooling of assets of related companies if it is just and equitable to do so.

Lender liability

The imposition of liability on lenders (or regulators) for the debts of a com- 9–17
pany is primarily based on big pocket views and is the least attractive of all the theories for dishonouring the veil of incorporation.

There appear to be a number of basic approaches, of which two may be mentioned – interference in management and abusive support. The heads of lender liability generally are summarised at para 21–1 *et seq*.

Interference in management

Under this theory the bank is liable because, in the course of a workout or in 9–18
enforcing its security, it intrusively interfered in management and hence became a de facto director responsible for creditor losses. Notwithstanding that in many jurisdictions, e.g. England and France, a de facto director is treated as incurring all the liabilities of a de jure director (otherwise directors could escape liability merely by calling themselves by another name), the real test is the readiness with which the courts *in practice* find another victim to pay the debts. There are no English cases where liability was imposed on a bank and it is probably the case that only the most excessive and unconscionable conduct by a bank would result in lender liability. The accent in England is on borrower liability, not lender liability.

There have been a few well publicised cases in the United States but in at least some of them it appears that the bank's conduct was indeed excessive. Note that in most cases the lender has not been made personably liable; rather his claim has been subordinated so that usually it is lost.

> In *Re TE Mercer Trucking Co*, 18 Bankr 176 (Bankr ND Tex 1981), the lender had joint control of the bank account, representation on the board, veto power over day-to-day decisions, fixed the salaries of directors and officers and had the right to require the disposal of assets. *Held*: the lender's rights went beyond legitimate supervision of the business by a creditor and the lender should be subordinated.

> In *Re American Lumber Co*, 5 Bankr 470 (D Minn 1980), the bank completely controlled management, cut officer's salaries, compelled the liquidation of assets, terminated employees, restricted payments to other creditors, and was the sole signatory on the debtor's bank account. *Held*: the bank should be subordinated.

A clause giving the bank the right to approve management was held to be a proper protection of a lender in *Parsons Steel Inc v first Alabama Bank of Montgomery*, NA 679 F 2d 242 (11th Cir 1982).

It has also been held in the US that the mere enforcement of a lender's rights, or a threat to do so, is not control or dominance.

> In *Re WT Grant*, 699 F 2d 599 (2d Cir 1983), the court stated "a creditor is under no fiduciary obligation to its debtor or to other creditors in the enforcement of its claim . . . [T]here is generally no objection to a creditor using his bargaining position, including his ability to refuse to make further loans needed by the debtor, to improve the status of his existing claim."

> However, in *State National Bank of El Paso v Farah Manufacturing Co*, 678 SW 2d 661 (Tex CA 1984) institutional lenders collected $22 million under a loan agreement by interfering in Farah's management. *Held*: the lenders had caused losses to Farah and were liable for $18 million.

9–19   But lender liability based on control has been found elsewhere. Thus in the Canadian case of *Canadian General Electric Co Ltd v Bank of British Columbia* (1983) 52 CBR(NS) 1 (Alta CA) a lender was found, through the actions of its monitor, to have taken over management of the business and was therefore liable to suppliers. But in Finland the Supreme Court (KKO 1968–II–66) found that it was in order for a customer company to transfer the decision-making power in the company to the bank in return for an extension of the repayment deadline for the bank loan.

It is understood that the present trend in many US jurisdictions is away from the more expansive notions of lender liability which featured in the past two decades, e.g. liability for "arbitrarily" cutting off credit. See para 21–1 *et seq*.

The Swiss Federal Supreme Court has established that wherever the lender controls the borrower's management, the lender may be liable to the borrower's shareholders and creditors in the same way as the directors themselves.

> In the *Zumbrunn* case decided by the Swiss Federal Supreme Court (BGE 107 II 349), Zumbrunn was a majority shareholder of Zumbrunn AG, and two subsidiaries of Swiss Bank Corporation were minority shareholders. The SBC subsidiaries were engaged as "advisers" of Zumbrunn AG which paid them an annual fee. The subsidiaries also had the right to appoint representatives who were allowed to participate in the meetings of Zumbrunn AG's board but were

not formally elected to the board. The bank was banker to Zumbrunn AG and Zumbrunn had assigned its accounts receivable to the bank as security for outstanding credits. Zumbrunn AG went into bankruptcy. Under CO Art 754 all persons entrusted with the administration, management or audit of a company are liable to the company and to the individual shareholders and creditors of the company for any damage which they intentionally or negligently cause by failure in the discharge of their duties. *Held*: the bank, through its representatives, controlled the company and hence those representatives were liable for damages caused to the company's creditors on the basis of Art 754. They actually directed the company and it was immaterial that they were not formally elected as board members.

Abusive support of insolvent company

The abusive support of insolvent companies seems to be a mainly French   9–20
doctrine but it has appeared elsewhere. The most noticeable example is in those countries which by case law have allowed the development of a quasi-universal business charge which, however, is not publicly registered. This is the Germanic fiduciary transfer which appears in Germany, the Netherlands and, to a lesser extent, in Switzerland and Japan. The effect is that creditors may be prejudiced by the false appearance of wealth. Banks have been penalised where they allowed the company to incur credit with a view to the acquisition of assets which the bank then immediately sought to snatch away. See para 21–10.

CHAPTER 10

JUDICIAL RESCUE PROCEEDINGS: INTRODUCTION

Introduction

Rescue proceedings and private restructurings

10–1   A feature of modern insolvency law is the adoption of corporate rescue proceedings designed to resuscitate debtor companies in distress.

The alternative is a private consensual debt restructuring (work-out) agreed between creditors, or more usually by bank creditors. The pros and cons of formal rehabilitation proceedings compared to work-outs are summarised at para 18–2 *et seq*. The main advantages of formal proceedings are a statutory freeze on individual creditor enforcements and a power to bind dissentient creditors. The main disadvantages are that the public declaration of insolvency normally devastates a business, that the freeze can prejudice creditor protections and that formal proceedings are costly. Formal rehabilitation proceedings have a low rate of success – often around a mere 10 per cent of those initiated. An essential question for countries is whether to encourage the private restructuring – in which event the formal proceeding must be discouraged – or whether to opt for a formal proceeding – in which event the private restructuring is more difficult because the debtor will inevitably choose to pre-empt its creditors by forcing them into a formal proceeding. Many experienced practitioners in this field agree that the private restructuring is much faster, safer and cheaper than a formal proceeding and that a formal proceeding is a last resort to be used only if there is absolutely no alternative.

The emphasis in these chapters is on large corporations and not small one-man or family companies, which are not commonly prime actors in international finance. One may therefore dispense with debate over the economic requirements of small businesses and the protection of consumers, while recognising that they too may become the victims of debt and seek survival.

Short history of rehabilitations

Rehabilitation statutes have been promoted for different reasons, e.g.   10–2
protection of public investors, protection of employees, protection of big
businesses (often identified with employee or state interests), protection of
small businesses or the protection of particular enterprises deemed to be of
national importance. But almost invariably the impetus has come from an
economic recession which has led to political pressure to rescue economic
enterprise and to succour those who were the victims.

The history is excellently portrayed in Dr Jan Dalhuisen's path-breaking
study *International Insolvency & Bankruptcy* (1982), on which the early
part of the following summary is largely based. The classical Romans
contemplated a partial release (*remissio*) and the later delay in payment
(*dilatio*), in addition to an inchoate bankruptcy involving pooling of assets
amongst a plurality of creditors, then known as the *distractio bonorum,* or
assignment for the benefit of creditors, the *cessio bonorum*. These were res-
tated by the Emperor Justinian in his Digest and Codes between 529 and
534 AD, which were restudied in Western Europe from the eleventh century. The *dilatio* appears in the Constitutio Gratiani (367–383 AD) and was
largely regarded as a favour available only to bona fide debtors who could
prove force majeure – a concept which survives in the older Franco-Latin
codes. The debtor had to offer sufficient security for eventual payment in
full.

The *remissio* and *dilatio* were developed in Italy in the fifteenth century
(Naples, Florence) and in Spain since the thirteenth century in the *Ley de
Las Siete Partidas*. The Italian example spread mainly to French rural fairs,
notably at Champagne and Brie, and was subsequently developed in the
Règlements de Lyon of 1667 and the remarkable *Ordonnance de Commerce* of 1673 which applied to all France and which was the basis of the
French bankruptcy law of 1807. Dutch cities adopted compositions in the
seventeenth century, with a more hesitant acceptance in the German cities
and states. Parallel to these developments were the delays granted by public
authorities for taxes, which were not really compositions.

The composition appeared in Scotland in BA 1772 and more convinc-
ingly in BA 1793. But the English were very resistant to composition and,
despite some flirtation with the idea in the seventeenth century, grudgingly
allowed a composition in the mid 1820s which required an impossibly high
majority and did not bind a minority or provide a discharge.

The next step was the French bankruptcy law in Book III of the Commer-   10–3
cial Code of 1807. Napoleon did not approve of bankruptcy and composition was not encouraged, but the law was liberalised in 1838 and again in
1889. Preventive compositions appeared in many European countries

towards the end of the nineteenth century. In England preventive compositions proper date from BA 1869. The US did not have federal bankruptcy laws for much of the nineteenth century, except episodically in response to economic crises: there was federal bankruptcy legislation in 1800–1803 resulting from land speculation, 1841–43 resulting from the 1837 depression, and 1867–78, initiated by the dislocation following the Civil War. The 1867 law introduced a composition, subsequently improved in 1874. The void in between was filled by various state proceedings. The Bankruptcy Act of 1898 contained a modest composition procedure.

But it was the miseries of the Great Depression of the 1930s which led to a new wave of rehabilitation statutes. The new factors which fuelled this development were the presence of large corporations which were unquestionably now the main vehicles of enterprise and which were financed by public shareholders and public debt, especially in the United States and Britain. The plight of the investing public aroused intense resentments.

In the United States, compositions were strengthened in 1933 and 1934 and developed in the Chandler Act of 1938 which allowed reorganisations in a new Chapter XI and in a complicated Chapter X, which allowed secured creditors to be stayed and obliged them to turn over their collateral to the trustee, subject to adequate protection, and which allowed the court to authorise certificates of indebtedness with priority over unsecured debt and (subject to protection) secured debt. These ideas were later taken up in the 1978 Chapter 11.

By contrast, the British did not react by the adoption of any far-reaching corporate reorganisation, preferring instead the out-of-court work-out or the privately-run floating charge receivership as a vehicle of orderly reconstruction. The Dutch made only slight amendments to their *surséance* (judicial extension) protection in 1935, and the Belgian reorganisation lasted only between 1934 and 1937. Germany introduced the *Vergleichsordnung* in 1935, but the entry requirements were so high that it was little used.

The French response, apart from short-lived special laws, was primarily a toughening-up of the attack on directors of failed enterprises in decrees of August 8, 1935, which was a resurgence perhaps of the repressive views of Napoleon towards debtors.

Hence, prior to the 1960s, the composition and rehabilitation laws were very cautious, except in the United States.

10–4   The next wave was fomented not so much by recession, although this was a feature, but by employee-orientated policies of socialist governments. The clearest expression of this was the French law 67–563 of July 13, 1967. This completely overhauled French bankruptcy law and expanded the *règlement judiciare* as a vehicle for a reorganisation. This was the first such procedure of its kind in Europe and was extended in the Decree-Law of January 25, 1985. Meanwhile in 1979 Italy brought in the *amministrazione straordinaria* for large enterprises which dispensed with the courts and put the politicians in charge. Both the French and Italian legislation was avowedly to save jobs.

Meanwhile the Unites States enacted the celebrated Chapter 11 in the Bankruptcy Code of 1978 and the British their conservative administration in the Insolvency Act 1986. Ireland followed in 1990 and Australia in 1992.

Japan, unimpressed by all this, sat tight.

In Central and Eastern Europe, the situation at the turn of the 1990s was very different. Many of these countries had devastated state enterprises which were insolvent. Privatisation required bankruptcy laws. Some countries in Central Europe resurrected more or less what they had in the 1930s which involved traditional European compositions. Others brought in new laws with very broad and well-meaning provisions for corporate reorganisation.

The real history of the success or otherwise of judicial compositions, as opposed to private settlements, remains to be written. All that one can say is that the experience of recent corporate rehabilitation tends to show that the suitability of judicial proceedings for debt restructuring is not as great as is commonly supposed. What is now needed is a careful study to show whether or not this judgment is justified by the international experience.

Classification of proceedings

One may in outline classify the various forms of present-day proceedings 10–5 into the following groups:

– Voluntary compositions

– Traditional compositions and moratoriums

– Corporate rehabilitation proceedings

The first two are little used in those countries which have them and hence it is mainly the corporate rehabilitation proceedings which are of interest. Nevertheless, the first two groups may briefly be described prior to a more detailed review of corporate rehabilitations.

Voluntary compositions

These are compositions which are either voluntary or operate without the benefit of a freeze on legal proceedings by creditors. They include corporate schemes of arrangement and individual deeds of arrangement with creditors in England and other English-based countries, such as Australia, Singapore and New Zealand. The English-based schemes of arrangement under companies legislation (in Britain now under s 425 of the Companies Act 1985) do not impose an initial freeze on proceedings and so are virtually ineffective as an insolvency proceeding (although sometimes they can be implemented behind the curtain of bankruptcy or rehabilitation proceedings, as in the case of the English administration). Other compositions are ineffective because they require unanimous creditor approval (Swedish *ackord*).

Traditional compositions and moratoriums

10–6   **Preventive composition proceedings** These are widespread and are usually little used or rarely successful. One reason for this in some countries is that the composition must offer a minimum immediate payment to creditors. It is generally found that the debtor's position is hopeless and the threshold payment unattainable. This is the case, for example, in Austria, Brazil, Denmark, Italy, Norway and Sweden. The thresholds vary from 25 per cent to 40 per cent for immediate payments with, sometimes, a sliding scale upwards for delayed payments. The debtor is generally in no position to make any payments at all, let alone payments of that order – which far exceed the normal dividends on a liquidation (zero to 20 per cent in the usual case). Alternatively, as in Belgium and Luxembourg, the debtor must show that his insolvency resulted from misfortune and not mismanagement – something which only courts which are exceptionally sympathetic to debtors find convincing.

The usual pattern is that a petition for composition stays creditor executions and bankruptcy petitions, but does not freeze the rights of preferential creditors or secured creditors, nor does it prejudice title finance, set-off, contract cancellations or lease forfeitures: hence the debtor loses assets which might otherwise be used in the rehabilitation process. In other words, the procedures are primarily distributive in an order which reflects the bankruptcy hierarchy and are intended to result in a writing-down of debt or a sale so that the debtor can start again.

Although the debtor's management often remains in possession, any transaction of significance usually has to be approved by a supervisor or by a creditor committee.

The debtor presents his composition plan, usually in consultation with a creditors committee or a supervisor, and the plan is voted on by unsecured creditors. The majorities vary from 50 per cent to 80 per cent or more and sometimes the majorities required increase according to the degree that debts are written down, e.g. Norway. The composition must generally be approved by the court to give it judicial force and to bind dissentient creditors. Normally this homologation is conditional on equality of treatment between unsecured creditors of the same rank and the prior payment in full of preferential creditors (such as taxes and employees), although here and there the rules recognise the fact that it may be desirable to pay off small creditors in full.

These compositions may be preventive in that they precede bankruptcy as an alternative to bankruptcy or they may be suspensive by suspending bankruptcy proceedings which have already begun.

Moratoriums These are often limited in time. Some are short breathing-spaces, e.g. the 1982 Austrian preliminary procedure – five weeks – which stays the enforcement of security, and the Danish suspension of payments (up to 12 months). Others are much longer, e.g. the Belgian and Luxembourg *sursis de paiement* – three years; the Dutch *surséance van betaling* – three years; and the Italian *amministrazione controllata* – two years.   10–7

Country examples

Examples of preventive compositions and moratoriums are: 10–8

– In **Austria**, a judicial composition proceeding (*Ausgleich*): minimum dividend to unsecured and unprivileged creditors of 40 per cent.

– In **Belgium**, a court composition (*concordat judiciaire*). But the debtor must show that his insolvency resulted from misfortune and has not been contributed to by his own mismanagement or misconduct. Bankruptcy and execution proceedings are stayed. The **Belgian** *sursis de paiement* is little used because of the onerous opening requirements. There must be an expectation that debts can be paid in full and the procedure requires the approval of 50 per cent of the creditors. The maximum period of delay is three years (normally 12 months with the possibility of two extensions of 12 months each). The **Luxembourg** *sursis* is similar.

– In **Brazil**, a preventive *concordata* available before bankruptcy. The debtor must offer 50 per cent of claims immediately with rising percentages for delayed payment culminating in 100 per cent for payments after 24 months. Execution proceedings are stayed. A bankrupt may also propose a suspensive composition during bankruptcy proceedings but must offer 35 per cent immediate payment or 50 per cent if not immediate, with payment in full being made in two years. This is typical of the Latin American pattern.

– In **Denmark**, a preventive composition under BA 1977 – the *tvangs-*

akkord, available before or during a bankruptcy. Forty per cent of unsecured creditors must be willing to support the debtor's proposals. The Danish suspension of payments (*betalingstandsning*) under BA 1977 lasts initially for three months with the possibility of extensions for up to 12 months in all. The court will usually enter a stay on execution proceedings. Post-commencement interest is deferred in the case of subsequent bankruptcy proceedings. The debtor remains in possession but may not perform essential transactions without the consent of the supervisor. Most suspensions end in bankruptcy.

10–9 — In **Germany**, a judicial composition – *Vergleich*, dating from 1935 – and a composition procedure within bankruptcy – the *Zwangsvergleich*. The procedure has high opening requirements, e.g. 35 per cent payment within one year, or 40 per cent within 18 months or over 40 per cent if more than 18 months. On court order, execution proceedings are suspended provisionally. There are high voting majorities for the composition. Secured creditors and creditors with a set-off are not affected by the *Vergleich*. A new German bankruptcy law was enacted in 1994 to come into force in 1999.

— In **England**, under IA 1986 the directors of a company may propose a voluntary arrangement with creditors which is voted on by creditors and shareholders. The business is carried on under the supervision of an insolvency practitioner. The proposal does not stay execution proceedings or freeze the enforcement of security, but it can be initiated by the insolvency administrator after the making of an administration or winding-up order which does stay proceedings, security enforcement, some title finance repossessions, but not set-off.

— In **Italy**, the judicial composition (*concordato preventivo*) under BA 1942. The debtor must provide adequate security or personal guarantees for all preferred claims and 40 per cent of common claims. Execution proceedings are stayed. Interest ceases to run. Set-off and security are not affected. The debtor retains the administration of his assets under the supervision of the judicial commissioner but transactions outside the ordinary course require the court's consent. Italy also has an *amministrazione controllata* under BA 1942 for debtors with liquidity problems but no deficiency of assets. The maximum moratorium is 24 months and the business must at the end of that time show that it is able to meet its obligations. Contrast the potent three-year extraordinary administration (*amministrazione straordinaria* – 1979) discussed below.

— In **Luxembourg**, a controlled management (*gestion controllé*) which is available unless the debtor's financial position is hopeless. All legal proceedings are stayed. There is also a preventive composition (*concordat* *préventif a la faillite*) which is rarely successful, largely because the debtor must show that he became insolvent through misfortune rather than fraud or negligence. Secured creditors are not affected. As to the Luxembourg *sursis de paiement*, see under Belgium above.

— In the **Netherlands**, a judicial composition – the *akkoord*. Secured and **10–10** preferential creditors are not affected. The Dutch judicial moratorium (*surséance van betaling*) is rarely successful since it is an opening requirement that the debtor affirms that all creditor claims can eventually be satisfied. Secured creditors are not affected. Execution and bankruptcy proceedings are stayed. The procedure lasts a maximum of three years.

— In **Norway**, the insolvency legislation is found in two Acts, the Debt Reorganisation and Bankruptcy Act 1984 and the Act on Creditors Access to Assets 1984. This legislation was designed to modernise Norwegian insolvency law, but remains in the classical mould. The debt reorganisation procedure is instituted by the debtor who must show that he is insolvent but that it is not unlikely that he will obtain a composition with his creditors. The debtor prepares the composition proposal in conjunction with a creditors committee and auditors: the proposal must pay 25 per cent of unsecured claims. Initially at least 40 per cent of creditors must approve the composition. The first phase is idiosyncratic in that it is non-public and the debtor outwardly remains fully authorised to transact business with third parties but the debtor in effect loses control of the business to the debt committee: the debtor cannot incur new debt, grant security or sell or rent real property or any asset of significance without the approval of the supervisory committee. In effect therefore the debtor is restricted to minor cash transactions. If the required sliding scale of majority creditors approve, the composition becomes binding on dissentient creditors.

— In **Sweden**, the *ackord* (which is a little used court composition requiring the agreement of all creditors), and a public composition (*offentligt ackord*) similar to preventive compositions on the European model. Creditors must receive 25 per cent of their claims within 12 months. Secured and preferential creditors are not affected. A minimum of 40 per cent of unsecured unpreferential creditors must support the proposal. Creditor executions and bankruptcy petitions are stayed.

CHAPTER 11

CORPORATE REHABILITATION
PROCEEDINGS: ENGLAND, FRANCE,
JAPAN, UNITED STATES

General

11–1   Modern forms of corporate rehabilitation impose a freeze on creditor proceedings and also significantly impinge on creditor rights. The rationale of
the disturbance of creditor rights is that the rights are merely delayed and
are reinstated if the rescue is successful so that the creditors, it is said, lose
nothing. However, these rescue proceedings have had a very low rate of success, e.g. 10 per cent, so that this rationale appears to be more difficult to
justify.

They include:

Mild proceedings, such as:

- In **Australia** the voluntary administration and deed of company arrangement under the Corporate Law Reform Act 1992

- In **Britain,** an administration under IA 1986

- In the **Republic of Ireland,** an examinership under the Companies
  (Amendment) Act 1990

- In **Japan,** the Corporate Rehabilitation Law of 1952, based on the
  pre–1978 US Bankruptcy Act of 1898 Chapter X as amended and intro-
  duced at the suggestion of the Occupation authorities. The Bankruptcy
  Law of 1923 was based on German ideas. See Brooke Schumm III
  "Comparison of Japanese and American Bankruptcy Law", *Michigan
  Year Book of International Legal Studies*, 291 (1988).

- In **Singapore,** the judicial management introduced by the Companies
  (Amendment) Act 1987 and largely based on the British administration
  under IA 1986, but limited to 180 days. As in Britain, floating chargees
  have blocking powers.

- In **Spain,** the suspension of payments under the Suspension of Payments
  Act of 1922

Tough proceedings, such as: 11–2

- In **Canada,** the commercial reorganisation under the Bankruptcy and Insolvency Act 1992 and the older but tougher Companies' Creditors Arrangement Act dating from the 1930s. Both are federal.

- In **France** the *redressement judiciaire* under the Law of January 25, 1985

- In **Italy,** the extraordinary administration of 1979 (*amministrazione straordinaria*), a dirigist statute, dispensing with the rule of law

- In **New Zealand,** the statutory management under the Corporations (Investigation and Management Act) 1989

- In the **United States,** Chapter 11 of the Bankruptcy Code of 1978 which is a federal statute

Key issues

The law may choose to encourage a formal proceeding by enlarging the   11–3 debtor's control of the business and by major inroads on creditor rights, in which event the proceeding is pro-debtor. The key indicators of whether the rescue proceedings are pro-creditor or pro-debtor include:

- **Ease of entry** Entry is encouraged if there need be no proof of actual or potential insolvency, no court approval of the opening (cost and delay), no proof of likelihood of success, and a unilateral application by the debtor.

- **Debtor incentives to commence proceedings** These include: avoidance of personal liability for wrongful trading or negligent trading or for failing to petition when insolvent; right of management to remain in charge.

- **Freeze on executions and liquidation petitions** These are universal.

- **Impact on security** For example, stay on enforcement; use of secured assets or their income by administrator; period of freeze; substitution of security by the administrator; stretching of secured debt by creditor voting; priming of security by the administration costs or super-priority moratorium loans; exclusion of after-acquired property from the security; and extent of carve-outs from the freeze.

- **Impact on title finance** For example, retention of title, factoring, sale and repurchase, finance leasing, hire purchase, sale and repurchase. The same considerations apply as for security.

- **Impact on insolvency set-off and netting**

— **Impact on contract rescissions and lease forfeitures** For example, stays on these rights

— **Disclaimer and abandonment powers** by the administrator for contracts, leases and onerous property

— **Avoidance of pre-commencement preferences** so as to increase the debtor's property

— **Ability to replace the management** and extent of the supervisory powers of the court, creditors' committees and the insolvency administrator

— **Financing of the rescue** For example, by super-priority loans, by the use of secured property, and by prioritising administration costs and contracts

— **Scope of the rehabilitation plan** For example, debtor's power to initiate; time limits for submission of a plan; limits on debt write-downs or debt/equity conversions; compulsory sales by the administrator binding lessors and contracting parties; power to bind creditors with security, asset protection in the form of title finance or set-off; protection of unfairly prejudiced creditors; voting majorities; power to bind unnotified creditors; disclosure of the debtor's position; priority creditors; excluded creditors (e.g. foreign taxes, tort); shareholder involvement; court approval; compulsory currency conversions into local currency; stopping of post-order interest and rentals.

— **Jurisdictional reach** For example, foreign companies with local assets; application to public interest businesses, e.g. banks, insurance companies, and savings institutions

11–4   In practice, the crucial features in terms of economic impact are:

— freezes on set-off, netting, and contract cancellations;

— freezes on the enforcement of security and interferences in the security, e.g. by super-super-priority loans;

— right of the debtor's management to stay in possession and initiate a plan.

Everybody recognises that there must be a stay on piecemeal creditor executions by unsecured creditors and on liquidation petitions.

Probably the most important factor in a successful reorganisation is the ability to raise fresh money to keep the business going. Almost invariably, this will require the priming of existing creditors by giving priority to the new finance and some jurisdictions have been tempted to take away existing creditors' asset protection, e.g. security, to ensure the availability of fresh capital. Both can result in a worsening of the position of creditors if the procedure fails.

This chapter discusses some of the main issues and compares the approach in Britain, the US, France and Japan. There follows in the next chapter a summary of rehabilitations in Australia, Canada, Italy, New Zealand, Spain and countries in Central and Eastern Europe.

Eligible debtors

Generally These rehabilitation proceedings apply mainly to ordinary cor-   **11–5** porations. Jurisdictions differ in whether they apply to: foreign corporations having a local place of business (US, France but usually not Britain); banks, insurance companies and other public interest businesses (Britain, but special regimes in the US); and individuals (the US, but not England).

The difficulty with the adoption of a wide jurisdictional reach to foreign corporations which have local assets is that corporate rehabilitation proceedings are more destructive of creditor rights than bankruptcies in the interests of preserving the business and hence are likely to lead to the risk of more intense and disruptive international collisions. These collisions are accentuated if there are parallel proceedings – rescue in the home country but final bankruptcy abroad so that the proceedings have conflicting objectives.

As regards banks, insurance companies and the like, some jurisdictions have opted for a special regime, having regard to the special sensitivities of these businesses and the need to protect public confidence and the rights of retail creditors.

The **British administration** under IA 1986 applies only to British incorporated companies, including banks (subject to modifications in the Banks (Administration Proceedings) Order 1989 (SI 1989 No 1276)) but not including (a) insurance companies, (b) individuals or partnerships and (c) foreign incorporated companies. However an administration has been ordered in respect of a foreign company under the special provisions of IA 1986 s 426 relating to insolvency co-operation with designated countries: see *Re Sunar Hausenman Inc* (1989) unreported; *Re Dallhold* [1992] BCC 994. There has been subsequent case law which does not resolve the issue, but the better view is that, apart from companies in s 426 countries, the procedure does not apply to foreign companies.

The **US Chapter 11** applies to most business enterprises, corporate or   **11–6** unincorporate, except stockbrokers, commodities brokers, insurance companies and banks and various other financial institutions. Individuals with substantial personal liabilities above prescribed thresholds can file. A foreign person who resides or has a domicile, place of business or property in the United States can file: see BC 1978 s 109 as amended in 1984. Unlike other rehabilitation laws, it is not necessary to show insolvency or feasibility: a solvent corporation can file. There are obviously much tougher standards for involuntary petitions, including who can file and proof of non-payment of undisputed debts as they fall due: BC 1978 s 303. A loan agreement prohibition on filing is void: see for example *Re Tru Block Concrete Products, Inc*, 72 Bankr 486, 10 BCD, 106 (Bankr SD Cal 1983).

The **French** *redressement judiciaire* applies to individual merchants, craftsmen and farmers (but not other private individuals and not professionals) and to all legal entities subject to private law, including state-owned banks and insurance companies (not public law entities, local or regional authorities or universities). See 1985 Law Art 2. Jurisdiction exists over debtors having a domicile or head office or principal place of business in France and has been assumed where the debtor has assets in France or has conducted business there.

The **Japanese corporate reorganisation** applies only to publicly-held limited companies (*kabushiki-kaisha*) but is effective only with respect to the company's properties existing in Japan: CRL Art 4. Various compositions are available to other debtors. Reciprocally, reorganisation proceedings commenced in a foreign country are not effective with respect to properties situated in Japan: Art 4.2. For this purpose obligations of which demand can be made by way of judicial proceedings under the Code of Civil Procedure are deemed to be situate in Japan, e.g. deposits with Japanese banks. Note that Japan espouses the Germanic jurisdictional rule whereby the location of assets in Japan grounds jurisdiction over the owner of the assets, irrespective of whether the claim concerns those assets. Subject to these limitations, foreign companies are subject to the jurisdiction to order a reorganisation at the principal place of business in Japan: CRL Art 6.

Grounds for petition and ease of entry

11–7   **General** The key issue here is the ease of entry into the proceedings – ease of entry prioritises the formal proceedings over private work-outs. Factors are:

- whether the debtor must show actual insolvency or the likelihood of insolvency, whether he is not required to prove insolvency at all, and whether insolvency is a balance sheet test or a liquidity test or both. If the objective of early rehabilitation is to be achieved before it is too late, the debtor should not be required to show actual insolvency, but rather the probability of an impending insolvency;

- whether the debtor must show that survival is feasible so as to avoid abuse of the process;

– whether entry is by court order or by unilateral initiation by the debtor (Australia, but not Britain or the US). Judicial approval increases cost but controls abuse and discourages an over-easy entry with a view to promoting a work-out, i.e. the proceeding is a last resort.

The British administration has high entry requirements. A petition is available (a) if the company is unable or *likely to become* unable to pay its debts (which is defined to include both a cash-flow and a balance-sheet test of negative net assets under IA 1986 s 123) *and* (b) if the administration is likely to achieve survival of the company as a going concern or a more advantageous realisation than on winding up or the approval of a voluntary arrangement (a composition with creditors) or a court-approved scheme of arrangement (involving court confirmation of a restructuring following creditor and shareholder voting – rarely used in this context): IA 1986 s 8.

Hence an administration cannot be used to upset creditor rights unless there is a likelihood of an insolvency and unless (usually) feasibility is shown. There must be a "real prospect" of achieving the statutory purpose, but the threshold of probability is modest: *Re Harris Simons Construction Ltd* [1989] 1 WLR 368. The court has a wide discretion and considers, for example, the impact on secured creditors, the fact that preferential creditors would be preferred on winding-up but not administration, and that a liquidator has wider powers of investigation, e.g. for fraud, than an administrator: see *Re Imperial Motors (UK) Ltd* (1989) 5 BCC 214; *Re Consumer and Industrial Press Ltd* (1988) 4 BCC 68. Generally the initial order is limited to three months, but can be extended in the discretion of the court and there is no mandatory maximum. The company, the directors, and a creditor can apply – but not a shareholder (unlike a winding-up). Certain regulatory authorities can apply, e.g. in relation to banks and investment businesses. In urgent cases, e.g. in relation to banks, the application can be made *ex parte* in camera: *Re Chancery plc* [1991] BCC 171. The supporting documents needed to justify feasibility increase the cost, e.g. a non-compulsory, but in practice essential, report by the insolvency practitioner: see IR 1986, r 2.2. The petition can be blocked by the holder of security over substantially all the assets of the company which includes a floating charge: para 11–16.

The **US Chapter 11** does not require proof of insolvency in the case of a   **11–8** voluntary filing. As a result major corporations with substantial net worth have filed, e.g. to mitigate enormous tort claims (asbestos, other toxic injuries), to maintain order while negotiating a treble damages claim (Texaco Inc – $11 billion judgment), or to renegotiate union agreements with employees or to counter a strike (Eastern Airlines).

In **France** the ground for instituting the *redressement* is cessation of payments, defined as inability to meet current liabilities with available (current) assets, not a balance sheet test. A simplified procedure applies to small businesses (50 persons or FF20m of turnover). All debtors start in the *redressement*, but this may quickly be converted into a judicial liquidation. In Anglo-American schemes, there is no duty to go through the rehabilitation first, and indeed in France it has been found that the initial observation period is inconvenient, since more than 90 per cent of the cases go into final liquidation. The proceedings are filed by the debtor, a creditor, the court, the public prosecutor or the employees: 1985 Law Art 4. The debtor must file within 15 days of the cessation of payments: 1985 Law Art 3(2). Feasibility is irrelevant at this point.

11–9   The grounds for an application for a **Japanese corporate reorganisation** are that the company is unable to pay its debts when due without materially impeding the continuance of its business or where facts comprising causes of bankruptcy are likely to take place with respect to the company: CRL Art 30. The company applies, but in the latter case creditors holding 10 per cent of the capital may apply, as may shareholders holding 10 per cent of the issued shares. The court must dismiss the application if (amongst other things) there is no prospect of rehabilitation or if the principal purpose is to avoid payment of tax liabilities. Substantial financial information is required to substantiate the application – much more than in the US. In Tokyo, pre-case meetings with court officials to decide whether the application is appropriate are common, but not apparently in Osaka.

In the case of judicial management in **South Africa**, introduced in 1926 (and copied by Australia in 1961 with an "official management"), the courts have required the debtor to make out a very clear case for an order if it is to keep the company's unpaid creditors out of their money for a long time, e.g. *Tenowicz v Tenny Investments*, 1979 (2) SA 680.

Debtor incentives to commence proceedings

11–10   If the law imposes penalties on management if they fail to commence proceedings, it is more difficult to achieve a private work-out. In **Britain** the personal liability of directors for wrongful trading cannot be invoked if they file for an administration, so that this is an incentive to directors to file. For penalties in other countries, e.g. for fraudulent or wrongful trading, or failure to petition if the company is insolvent or has lost half its capital, see chapter 8. These factors do not appear to apply in the United States or Canada, although one suspects that everywhere, if the management incur a debt which they know has no chance of being paid, they will be liable for ordinary fraud under the law of nature.

Stay on legal proceedings

The order (and usually the petition itself) generally operates as a stay on **11–11** legal proceedings and bankruptcy petitions by creditors without the consent of the court, including a stay on enforcement by attachments, executions and the like. This applies to a British administration, the US Chapter 11, the French *redressement* (except employees – 1985 Law Art 124), the Japanese reorganisation (in the discretion of the court on petition but automatically on the order – CRL Art 67) and is probably universal. The stay on creditor attachments and liquidation petitions is a minimum so that the debtor has a breathing-space while an orderly rehabilitation or sale can be arranged.

The position as to whether the stay catches proceedings (as well as executions), licence revocation and administration proceedings varies. A permit could be essential to the debtor's business. In the US, case law has held that cancellation of governmental building permits and liquor licences are stayed under BC 1978 s 362(a). The invocation of the stay on proceedings against a debtor who is one of a number of defendants and its impact on the litigation has occasioned much US case law, notably in the Johns-Manville asbestosis litigation in the 1980s. Similarly, US courts have been perplexed by the impact of the stay on environmental clean-up orders from environmental agencies, especially where the debtor might have used the blocking Chapter 11 because of the clean-up expense. The cases demonstrate the almost over-powering pressure to carve-out some exception to favour an intense public policy; one cannot go into the case law, except to remark that generally public health and safety has won the day.

The stay does not prevent third parties from recovering property held in trust for them by the debtor since this is not property of the bankrupt (although technically a consent may be required).

In the US, violations of the stay result in contempt of court fines and damages, but only if wilful. This applies to all violations, e.g. the stay on security enforcement.

Security interests

General Jurisdictions fall into four main groups as regards their attitude to **11–12** security as a protection against insolvency – (1) those very sympathetic to security (e.g. English-based countries, Sweden); (2) those fairly sympathetic (e.g. Germany, Netherlands, Japan, Switzerland, United States), (3) those quite hostile (e.g. Belgium, most Latin American countries, Spain) and (4) those very hostile (e.g. Austria, France, Italy). These attitudes tend to be reflected in rehabilitation statutes in that the sympathetic jurisdictions surrender the benefits of security more grudgingly, while those initially hostile to security have in any event subordinated the role of security as a creditor-protection and therefore lose little by subordinating it further on rehabilitation.

If there is a **stay on the enforcement** of security, the main points to be considered are the period of the stay and whether the stay is limited to assets essential to the continuing business which are idiosyncratic (not securities, cash or ordinary commodities). The alleged object of the stay is to keep the business together while the rehabilitation is allowed to work, e.g. by preventing the mortgagee sale of the main factory, computer equipment, or an essential patent or unfinished inventory. But the effect of excessive interference in the security is to deprive the creditor of the benefit of the security: the whole purpose of security is that it should be available on the insolvency of the debtor and therefore, if the jurisdiction destroys the security when it is most needed, the value and utility of security itself is demoted. Accordingly jurisdictions have to decide whether they desire the advantages of security or whether they prefer the draconian rehabilitation procedure, although middle courses are possible, e.g. a stay on enforcement for a limited period.

The stay causes problems for perishable assets; volatile assets, such as securities, commodities and foreign currency deposits, especially margin collateral for market dealings; ships, aircraft and other assets which are in need of special protection or which could attract an "assets" bankruptcy jurisdiction just because they happen to be there or which can be spirited away to avoid a surprise attachment; liens covering small assets not essential to the business; income-earning assets if the debtor can use the income e.g., rent from land and equipment leases, dividends and interest on securities, recoveries on receivables, royalties and intellectual property rights (the income may have been essential to service the creditors' interest); and possessory pledges and liens since the security is lost if possession must be surrendered.

11–13   Other factors are: (1) a stay results in the erosion of security if it falls in value or if interest continues to pile up – the period of the stay is germane; (2) whether the debtor can use the secured assets for the purpose of the continuing business and the powers which the creditor has to preserve the asset; (3) whether the debtor can substitute alternative secured assets in order to retain some essential asset; (4) whether a plan can bind dissentient secured creditors to an extension of the maturity of the debt or a reduction in amounts or a change of currency; (5) whether the security is primed by the costs of the administration (liabilities incurred in continuing the business, super-priority loans, employees, taxes) so that the creditor's security is eroded and its value highly unpredictable; (6) whether security expressed to cover after-acquired property such as a floating charge over all present and future assets or an aircraft mortgage over engines subsequently replaced, can catch assets acquired by the debtor post-commencement; (7) the degree of protection given to secured creditors against unfair prejudice; (8) whether cash collateral can be taken away in the interests of financing the business; and (9) whether post-commencement interest continues to run and can be added to the secured debt. A common problem is whether a creditor who has security over investments or receivables violates a stay if he receives payment on the assets from the third party and applies it to the secured debt: this would be a violation of the US stay in BC 1978 s 362.

Plainly, there can be many degrees of interference, ranging from a short freeze on enforcement to total expropriation.

English administration In an English administration, the petition stays the   **11–14** enforcement of security without administrator consent or court leave: IA 1986 ss 10 and 11. There is no time limit, although in practice the position is contained by court guidelines which support secured creditors. This freeze applies not only to mortgages and the like but also mortgages of ships and aircraft, liens and (probably) the collection by the secured creditor of assigned receivables. These liens include unpaid vendor liens, probably possessory liens (including liens on cheques being collected) and the statutory rights of an airport to detain aircraft leased to the debtor for unpaid airport charges: *Re Paramount Airways Ltd* [1990] BCC 130.

The courts have signalled adherence to the traditional English support of security and title finance by stating that an administrator should normally give consent to enforcement and repossession, unless substantially greater loss would be caused to others, since an administration for the benefit of unsecured creditors should not be carried on at the expense of those with proprietary rights: the guidelines were laid down by the Court of Appeal in the landmark decision of *Re Atlantic Computer Systems plc* [1990] BCC 859. Leave to enforce was refused in *Re Meesan Investments Ltd* [1988] 4 BCC 788 because the administrator had nearly completed a satisfactory sale.

The administrator can dispose of the property charged with the leave of   **11–15** the court, e.g. to obtain a more advantageous realisation. The object of this is to facilitate a sale of the business, or a segment of the business, as a whole and thereby to secure a better price: this might be prejudicial if, say, a creditor had a mortgage over the factory or over some essential intellectual property right. The secured creditor is entitled to the net proceeds plus a top-up for any shortfall below market value as determined by the court: IA 1986 s 15.

An administration does not suspend post-order interest and so this can continue to be covered by the security, although the forced stay causes extra interest to eat into the value of the security.

The secured creditor is not prevented from accelerating the secured debt by reason of the order and is not therefore relegated either to the original terms of the loan or to a moratorium on payments, nor can he be if a voluntary arrangement is instituted behind the protective curtain of the administration since voluntary arrangements cannot affect secured creditors.

The secured creditor is not bound to accept substitute security or alternative adequate protection so that his rights are more or less intact. Fixed security is not primed by ordinary preferential creditors or expenses of the administration. The court can sanction a lifting of the freeze in its discretion.

A secured creditor can make an "unfair prejudice" application to the court under IA 1986 s 27.

If the security is margin collateral or other security in an organised market, it may be exempt from the stay on security under the provisions of Part VII of the Companies Act 1989 applying to certain recognised investment exchanges and clearing houses, amongst others. These provisions recognised the paramount importance of protecting the integrity of markets.

11–16   But a remarkable feature of the English approach is that, in choosing whether to support the rights of the holder of a universal floating charge to manage the business through a receiver for his own benefit as against the rights of unsecured creditors on a rehabilitation, the English decided to support the holder of the floating charge. The reason for this is that the universal floating charge has been shown to be a highly effective method of saving a business when compared to other rescue proceedings and indeed the administration procedure was not modelled on the US Chapter 11, but rather on the equivalent for unsecured creditors of a floating charge receivership. The administration can be blocked by the holder of a floating charge who has security (fixed or floating) over "substantially the whole" of the assets of the company if he appoints an administrative receiver (broadly a private manager of the security) prior to the making of an administration order – the chargee must be notified of the petition for the administration to give him time to block: IA 1986 s 9. Five clear days are required, but this can be abridged: *Re A Company No 00175 of 1987* (1987) 3 BCC 124. The security must not be subject to avoidance. The theory is that it is not possible to have two persons managing the business of the company – the administrator and the chargee's receiver – the chargee's receiver takes precedence. As a result of this blocking power, banks and other creditors often take "featherweight floaters" over all the assets of a company which can be subordinated to other third party charges without losing their blocking vitality – so that the debtor is not restrained from raising fresh secured finance.

The holder of a floating charge is usually well-advised to block, although this is not necessarily so, e.g. because the chargee wishes to freeze liquidation petitions, but can control the administrator by virtue of the administrator's need for fresh funds from the chargee. But blocking is usually desirable because, if the security is a floating charge, it can more or less be wiped out on administration. See IA 1986 s 15.

In the case of a floating charge not used to block, the administrator can deal with the property charged as if it were not subject to the security (e.g. lease it, dispose of it, create prior charges over it to secure new loans) but, if the property is disposed of, the priority of the charge traces through to property directly or indirectly representing the charged property. Unlike fixed security, the administrator need not make up the sale proceeds to market value. The creditor is left with an "unfair prejudice" application under IA 1986 s 27. The administrator's contracts and expenses are a prior charge on the property so that the security is diminished if the administrator trades at a loss. The overall effect is that partial floating charges, e.g. over receivables or inventory or portfolios of securities, are virtually useless, because they cannot block unless accompanied by fixed charges so that substantially all the company's property is charged. This seems regrettable because partial floating charges were extremely useful. The English have therefore guillotined the partial floating charge but glorified the comprehensive charge. Whether a floating charge would extend to assets of the company acquired after the administration order is undecided.

The English stay on security is odd. This is because companies which borrow secured are usually small companies, property companies or single-project companies which give full fixed and floating charges over all their assets: hence the banks can defeat the administration and there would be no point in freezing the security. The effect therefore is to freeze isolated security, notably charges over investment securities or liens or over equipment where the need to realise quickly is more pressing, and the need to preserve the assets for the business less convincing. In the light of English financings, the stay therefore seems somewhat ideological. In practice, administrators have readily consented to realisations.

US Chapter 11 Under the US Chapter 11 the position is markedly different **11–17** and much more complicated. Initially the effect of the bankruptcy petition is to stay the enforcement of security without the consent of the court for "cause", e.g. that the debtor has no equity in the property. The creditor will usually satisfy the second test of "no necessity" if there is no reasonable possibility of a rehabilitation within a reasonable period, e.g. less than a year : see *US Association of Taxes v Timbers of Inwood Forest Associates Ltd*, 484 US 365 (1988) *and* the property is not necessary to an effective Chapter 11 organisation, or where the property is depreciating in value. See BC 1978 s 362(a)(4).

The security must not be capable of avoidance.

Rather than allowing relief from the stay, the court may order the creditor to be given adequate protection of its security interest , e.g. additional liens or cash payments to match the fall in value. The basic protection given to secured creditors is that they must receive indubitably adequate protection for their security.

11–18   The House Report indicated that the concept of adequate protection is derived from the Constitution's Fifth Amendment protection of property interests and from a policy that secured creditors should not be deprived of the benefit of their bargain, so that if the secured creditor does not get the exact collateral (because, like a factory, it is needed for the debtor's business), he must get the equivalent in value. Case law shows that the creditor has adequate protection if he is over-secured (to the extent of the cushion) or has a recoverable guarantee from a third party, but not usually if the guarantee is unsecured. The US Supreme Court established in the *Timbers* case above that, if the creditor is under-secured, the creditor is entitled to cash payments (or the equivalent) if his collateral is decreasing in value, that he is not entitled to compensation for loss of the ability to reinvest proceeds from a foreclosure, and that the creditor should be granted relief from the stay if the property is not necessary for an effective reorganisation which is feasible and in prospect.

The debtor in Chapter 11 can obtain permission to obtain credit that is secured by an equal or superior lien on the encumbered property if this is the only way credit can be obtained.

The debtor can use collateral for which purpose a distinction is made between cash and non-cash. Cash collateral includes cash, negotiable instruments, documents of title, securities, deposit accounts and the rents, income and proceeds of other collateral: s 363(a). Non-cash will therefore include, for example, inventory, machinery, equipment and real estate.

11–19   The debtor may also request emergency use of its cash collateral prior to a final hearing, subject to the likelihood of adequate protection being available on the final hearing in order to avoid a cessation of the business and to protect the value of the business: s 363(c)(2). Court approval is required for the use of cash or cash equivalents in which a creditor has a security interest. The debtor can use non-cash collateral without that approval in the ordinary course of business (s 363(c)(1)) but subject to "adequate protection", such as additional liens or cash replacements, in the absence of which the creditor may have grounds to apply for foreclosure. The object of using cash collateral is that the debtor needs cash to survive and would immediately collapse if, say, its cash balances at the bank were removed. Naturally any dissipation of the cash or securities would render security over these items quite useless. Generally the courts have recognised the importance of adequate protection; see, e.g. *Re CF Simonin's Sons Inc*, 28 Bankr 707, 10 BCD 343 (Bankr EDNC 1983); *Re Greenwood Building Supply Inc*, 23 Bankr 720, 7 CBC 2d 659, 9 BCD 907 (Bankr WD Mo 1982). For example, if the debtor can borrow 80 per cent of accounts receivables or inventory (which both turn into cash collateral as they are realised), that ratio must be maintained for fresh post-commencement advances which must be covered by replacement receivables and inventory, but there have been cases where this principle has not been honoured. There is case law on how to value the collateral – usually on the higher going concern basis: receivables and inventory generally collapse in value on a liquidation. There is also complex case law on whether a mortgagee of real estate is entitled to post-petition rents and hotel revenues: see *Butner v United States*, 440 US 48, 99 S Ct 914, 59 L Ed 2d 136 (1979). Generally rents can be protected under state law, but hotel revenues are usually treated as after-acquired property which belongs to the estate: the effect therefore is that the secured creditor loses the post-petition income from the hotels, e.g. *Re Sacramento Mansion Ltd*, 117 Bankr 592 (Banker D Col 1990).

If certain conditions are met, the debtor may sell encumbered property free of the lien so that the lien attaches to the proceeds of sale.

An undersecured creditor will not be entitled to adequate protection for time lost during which his enforcement rights are stayed.

BC 1978 s 507(b) provides that, to the extent that the trustee has given adequate protection to the interest of a holder of a claim under ss 362 (relief from automatic stay), 363 (relief from ability to trustee to use, sell or lease property of the debtor in which a third party has an interest) or 364 (super-priority security for post-petition loans which prime existing security) that proves to be inadequate (and such claims were secured on the property of the debtor), the secured creditor's claim has complete priority, including priority over administrative expenses, employees and taxes. The secured creditor's absolute priority is intended to be preserved.

Without court approval, a floating lien on accounts receivable, inventory **11–20** and the like will not extend to property acquired after the commencement of the case. The effect of BA 1978 s 552 is that a security interest cannot cover post-commencement property, but can cover the proceeds, product or rents which arise post-commencement out of pre-petition collateral, e.g. the sale of inventory. Thus the following have been held not to be caught by a security interest if received post-commencement : refund of state unemployment taxes; proceeds of crops planted after commencement; gate receipts from a car race-track; hotel room revenues; and the proceeds of sale of products made from materials purchased post-petition.

In *Re Cleary Brothers Construction Co*, 9 Bank 40, 1 CBC 2d 989 (Bankr SD Fla 1980), the trustee rented a crane to a third party. The crane was subject to a security interest in favour of a creditor. *Held*: the rents belonged to the debtor's estate and were not caught by the security interest. The creditor had not taken an assignment of the rents.

Contrast *Re Slab Fork Coal Co*, 784 F 2d 1188 (4th Cir 1986): the creditor had a security interest over a long term coal supply contract. The debtor continued to supply coal to the buyer post-petition. *Held*: the post-petition proceeds of sale belonged to the creditor since they were proceeds of pre-petition collateral.

Post-petition interest is not covered by the collateral if the creditor is undersecured: BC 1978 s 506(b). If he is over-secured, post-petition interest may accrue but may not be paid during the pendency of the case and the accrued interest becomes part of the secured creditor's claim to be treated under the plan.

11–21   As regards the plan, the general scheme is that secured creditors retain their liens to the extent of the allowed amounts of their claims (any unsecured portion being treated as an unsecured claim) and this is so even if the collateral is transferred to another entity. Each holder must at least receive deferred cash payments up to the allowed amount of the claim having a present value equal to the value of the collateral. Of course if the plan takes months or years to formulate, the secured creditor has to wait (asset erosion, interest pile-up). The security is valued on a projected use/going concern basis at the time of the plan: BC 1978 s 1111(b).

The secured creditor is not primed by administration expenses or preferential creditors except to the extent of the super-priority lien for debtor financing referred to above, which is subject to adequate protection.

There are special provisions in BC 1978 s 1110 applying to aircraft and to ships. The general effect of this section is that the holder of certain security interests in an aircraft operated under a Civil Aeronautics Board Certificate or a US flag vessel or a lessor or conditional vendor of such an aircraft or vessel can take possession unless the trustee, with the courts' approval, agrees to perform all future obligations and (generally) to cure past defaults. Hence there is an effective 60-day stay. Note that the protection does not avail foreign carriers or foreign ships so that a flag ship of a foreign entity can be subject to the general stay if the foreign entity becomes subject to a US Chapter 11.

11–22 **French *redressement*** In France security must be regarded as virtually worthless or at least highly unpredictable.

Initially, as in the case of England and the US, the proceeding operates as a stay on enforcement of security, unless the repossession is justified by the continuation of operations.

Post-order interest is not recoverable except for loans or deferred credits of one year or more.

But most crushingly the security is subject to post-order administration expenses and to bankruptcy preferential creditors – employees, taxes and the like. The administrator can, with judicial approval, raise new loans priming all security: 1985 Law Art 40. By Art 40(2) the order of ranking of post-opening creditors is: (1) certain wage claims; (2) legal expenses; (3) loans granted by credit establishments and claims resulting from the forced continuation of contracts pursuant to Art 37 (which nullifies cancellation, acceleration and forfeiture clauses in contracts arising by reason of the insolvency); (4) certain sums advanced in accordance with the Labour Code; and (5) all other claims according to their rank, including secured claims. Hence the secured creditor can never know what his security is worth.

Apart from this, the rights of the secured creditor depend upon whether   **11–23**
the security is a possessory pledge, a non-possessory security, or a mortgage of land and buildings. In all cases the court may order substitution of security if the plan provides for a continuation. If the plan provides for a general assignment to another entity, it is unclear if possessory pledges can go with it. In other cases the secured creditor receives the sale proceeds allocated by the court, subject to claims of higher rank.

Creditors cannot accelerate claims by reason of the proceedings (1985 Law Art 37) and further the secured debt may, as part of the plan approved by the court, be subject to a moratorium on debt service. Although the court cannot reduce the secured debt, the effect of a moratorium and the absence of post-proceeding interest have a similar effect. If the asset is sold, the proceeds receivable are discounted to reflect the fact that the particular creditor is achieving an advantage denied to other creditors.

If the enterprise goes into judicial liquidation, the secured creditors' rights of realisation revive.

There appear to be no special protections for aircraft or ships. But in the case of a liquidation, creditors with a retention of title clause and credit establishments to whom the debtor assigned professional debts (i.e. trade receivables) can enforce their rights and are not subject to the proceedings.

In the case of liquidation, security ranks as follows: **11–24**

1. employees have a super-priority over all security interests;

2. possessory pledgees and retention of title claimants have first priority over the property, subject only to employees;

3. post-opening creditors rank ahead of all security, except that in (2). These are as itemised above;

4. general real property security interests and then special real property security interests;

5. special personal property security interests, subject to (1) and (2) above, and to tax claims, and then general personal property security interests;

6. general personal property security interests in the order in CC Art 2101;

7. pre-opening unsecured creditors.

11–25 **Japanese reorganisation** Once the Japanese reorganisation has commenced, official auction sales and the enforcement of an enterprise hypothecation are suspended, as are the enforcement of tax claims (with a one-year extendable maximum for tax claims): CRL Art 37(1). But the court can lift the suspension: CRL Art 37(5). A pre-ruling suspension is available only if there is no "likelihood of inflicting unreasonable losses on the creditors": CRL Art 37(1). This may approximate to the English judicial hostility to stays on security.

By Art 123 interest on secured claims is limited to one year but this does not apply to debentures.

Apart from this, secured creditors form a separate voting class for the purposes of approval of the reorganisation plan and high majorities are required to postpone security rights (75 per cent) or to reduce security rights (80 per cent). If the secured creditors do not approve the plan as a class, then the court can nevertheless approve the plan, but only if the security is maintained over any asset to be transferred to a new company, or if the asset is sold, or if its fair price is paid to the security-holder, or if other "fair and equitable protection" is given to the holder.

Title finance

11–26 Title finance covers various forms of vendor or lessor finance, such as sale and repurchase, retention of title, debt factoring, financial leasing, sale and lease-back and hire purchase. It also covers ordinary land leases and true equipment leases.

The arguments for and against freezing rights of repossession are similar to those applying to security, e.g. the assets may be needed for continuance of the debtor's business but on the other hand the stay may detract from legitimate creditor rights. A choice therefore has to be made between encouraging title finance and encouraging rehabilitation proceedings. The real question is whether it is worth disturbing title finance if rescue proceedings have such a low rate of success.

If an asset which is leased to the debtor is sub-leased by him to a sub-lessor and if the head-lessor's rights of repossession are frozen, it would be inequitable if the debtor could retain the earnings on the sub-lease, but nevertheless decline to pay the head-rentals to the head-lessor whose repossession rights are frozen. One solution is for the creditor always to insist on a security assignment of sub-leases: although these may be subject to the freeze on security enforcement, the regime may accord the secured creditor better protection than if he had no hold at all on the sub-rentals.

The effect of an **English administration** is to apply approximately the   **11–27** same rules as apply to security to certain title finance transactions involving goods, namely hire purchase, chattel leases of more than three months, conditional sales and retention of title. Repossession is stayed, although there is no objection to an acceleration of debt or a cancellation, e.g. a lease termination. It is immaterial that the transaction was not a financing transaction, e.g. was an operating lease. There is no specific exception for aircraft or ships. The rights of a lessor of land and buildings to repossess can be stayed by an administration order: *Exchange Travel Agency v Triton Property Trust plc* [1991] BCC 341.

> In *Re Atlantic Computer Systems plc* [1990] BCC 859, CA, a company held computers on lease or hire purchase from financial institutions and leased them on sub-lease to operating lessees. The administrator wished to keep the sub-lease rentals, but to stop the head-lessors from repossessing or claiming the head rentals. *Held*: the lessors should usually be allowed to repossess. The court stressed that the administrator should normally consent to repossession since an administration for the benefit of unsecured creditors should not be conducted at the expense of those who have proprietary rights. Contrast *Re David Meek Access Ltd* [1993] BCC 175.

As regards the **US Chapter 11**, BC 1978 s 362(a)(3) prevents repossessions. Various forms of title finance are approximated to security interests, e.g. retention of title. Hence title finance can be disturbed, subject to the rules applicable to "adequate protection". There is an exception for certain US certificated aircraft and US vessels: para 11–16.

French *redressement* It would seem that the creditors concerned are subject   **11–28** to the regime applicable to all creditors – no repossession, no forfeiture, no acceleration and compulsory moratoriums on debt claims (but no compulsory remission), transfer of contracts to a transferee and subjection to post-order expenses. However a special regime applies to retention of title; provided certain documentary formalities are complied with, the seller is entitled to repossess if the goods are identifiable at the time of the opening of the proceedings (and not transferred or incorporated in another product and have not become attached to real property).

Set-off

11–29   **General** The object of preventing set-off on a rehabilitation is to preserve the cash available to the business, especially bank balances. On the other hand, the denial of set-off leads to the result that (a) the debtor takes but does not pay, and (b) the availability of set-off as "security" against insolvency is unpredictable. Like security, set-off is futile if it is not available on insolvency. This could be specially disruptive for netting schemes and for markets and exchanges which rely on cash deposits as margin.

Most commercial countries allow insolvency set-off but an important group of countries do not, except for bank current accounts and connected cross-claims. The allowing countries include English-based jurisdictions, Austria, Canada, Denmark, Finland, Germany, Japan, Sweden, Switzerland and the United States. The refusing countries include France, Belgium, Greece, Luxembourg, Portugal, Spain, South Africa, and most Latin American countries (except Panama). Set-off is discussed in detail in another volume in this series of works on international financial law.

11–30   The broad position appears to be that those countries which allow insolvency set-off do not compromise it on rehabilitation proceedings. The policy appears to be that insolvency set-off, like security, is much too important a creditor protection to be interfered with. Further, the asset lost to the debtor is cash, as opposed to some assets special to the business, such as a factory, and the future financing of the business ought to be dealt with as a separate problem and not achieved by destroying acquired set-offs. In any event Britain does not negate set-off under the administration procedure and this is also generally true of the US Chapter 11, although here set-offs are subject to the automatic stay but with the benefit of the "adequate protection" rules, so that, for example, the debtor can use bank deposits free of the set-off subject to adequate protection. The German *Vergleichsordnung* does not stay set-offs, nor does the Japanese Corporate Reorganisation Law. But in Japan, the claims must be eligible for set-off by maturing prior to the time that reorganisation claims must be reported: CRL, Art 162. There is no stay on set-offs under the Italian *concordato preventivo* but there may be a stay under the Italian *amministrazione straordinaria* and a longer stay under little-used provisions in the Swiss Banking Law in relation to banks suffering a liquidity crisis.

11–31   The stay on set-off may arise because of a freeze on acceleration rights, e.g. as under the Canadian BIA 1992. If the creditor cannot accelerate a loan, for example, he cannot set it off against a maturing deposit. If the maturity of the loan is postponed by a creditor approved plan, but the deposit has matured, the creditor must pay in the deposit – there is no accrued claim to set off against it. This situation occurred in *Re A Debtor, ex p Peakhill Goldfield Ltd* [1909] I KB 30, CA where the debtor's debentures were postponed by a debenture-holders' resolution. This would result in discrimination against the creditor with a set-off when compared to other unsecured creditors, and one would expect the affected creditor to be able to apply to the court on grounds of unfair prejudice which is generally available in statutes such as the British IA 1986 and the Canadian BIA 1992. Any plan should seek to avoid this clear unfairness.

On the other hand, countries which refuse insolvency set-off will usually also refuse it in the case of rehabilitation proceedings, as with the French *redressement*.

Contract cancellation and lease forfeitures

The object of preserving contracts and leases is to assist the continuance of   **11-32** the debtor's business, e.g. supplies of essential raw materials, the right to intellectual property, franchise and distributorship licences, and the right to charters and equipment leases.

From the point of view of contracting counterparties, the object of "*ipso facto* clauses" allowing cancellation on the debtor's insolvency are: (1) the clause is anticipatory in the sense that on insolvency it is only a matter of time before the debtor actually defaults (rescue proceedings have a very low rate of success); (2) the debtor should not be able to enforce contracts profitable to him but cancel those which are loss-making since this results in "cherry-picking" and destroys netting – the debtor is in a better position than the counterparty; and (3) in volatile markets, the counterparty should not be subject to unpredictability and a potential increased loss.

Nullification of cancellation clauses operating solely on insolvency (as opposed to actual breach) affects an enormous range of contracts – sales of land, commodities, foreign exchange or securities, building contracts, agency contracts (securities brokers, estate agents, commodities brokers, bank agency for collection), custodianship of goods or securities, charters and transportation contracts, leases of land or equipment, licences of intellectual property rights, software, franchises and distributorships, loan commitments and accelerations, subscription and underwriting agreements. The nullification would work both ways – to seller or to buyer, to builder or employer; to principal or agent; to bailor or bailee, to carrier or owner; to lessee or lessor, to insurer and insured. It can be extremely difficult to achieve a fair balance in all these cases without excessive complexity.

An **English administration** does not nullify *ipso facto* clauses nor does the   **11-33** **Australian voluntary administration**. But an English administration stays a landlord's right to re-enter for non-payment of rent: *Exchange Travel*

Agency v Triton Property Trust plc [1991] BCC 341. However *ipso facto* clauses are nullified in the case of the **US Chapter 11**, the **Canadian commercial reorganisation**, the **French** *redressement* (Art 37 of the 1985 Law) and the **New Zealand statutory management**, subject in the US, Canada and France to various exceptions. The US stay leads to very complex carve-outs as is inevitable where so many different contracts are caught. The landlord's repossession for non-payment of rent is stayed under BC 1978 s 362(a)(3): *Construction Clearing House Inc v Mulkey of Mo Inc*, 5 Bankr 15, 2 CBC 2d 966, 6 BCD 310 (Bankr WD Mo 1980). Probably one of the most extensive uses of the stay is as follows:

> In *Re Sportfame of Ohio Inc*, 40 Bankr 47 (Bankr ND Ohio 1384), a supplier refused to sell cash on delivery to the debtor in Chapter 11 unless the debtor paid another debt owed to the supplier. *Held*: the supplier would be obliged by injunction to sell. In effect this was ordering specific performance of a contract which would not be specifically performable in favour of the buyer if he were solvent.

The US stay does not (usually) apply to claims against third parties such as guarantors of the liabilities of the debtor or against banks which have issued letters of credit for the account of the debtor: this rule appears universal, but there has been some US erosion of this in special circumstances.

11–34   In **Japan** there is no express nullification of *ipso facto* clauses and it is considered that they are effective. There is only the usual right of the receiver to either insist on performance or to disclaim: CRL Art 103(1). If the receiver insists on performance, it is considered that he is subject to an *ipso facto* clause entitling the counterparty to terminate on insolvency if it is a bilateral contract. To protect trade suppliers, there are special provisions allowing a counterparty to return goods sold or their value as a priority claim: CRL Art 104(2). As to the land lease, the result is different in cases where the land lessor is the bankrupt and where the land lessee is the bankrupt. Where the land lessee is the bankrupt, the land lessor may terminate the land lease pursuant to CC Art 621; provided, however, that the land lessor proves a justifying reason for such termination as stipulated under the Law of Land Lease and Building Lease (Law No 90, 1992), if the law is applicable to the relevant land lease contract (see Supreme Court judgment of October 30, 1993, 27 Minshu 1289). Although this Supreme Court judgment was issued in connection with a bankruptcy procedure, the ruling is likely to be applicable to the case of corporate reorganisation.

Where the land lessor is a bankrupt party, there is an appeal court case in which the receiver of the lessor was prevented from terminating the lease pursuant to BA Art 59, which is the equivalent of CRL Art 103: judgment of Tokyo Appeal Court on May 31, 1961, 1's Kaminshu 1246. The ruling of the appeal court is likely to be applicable to the case of a corporate reorganisation. Since there is no other provision relating to the termination of a lease contract in the case of the land lessor's bankruptcy, neither the lessor nor lessee may terminate the land lease contract in such case unless otherwise agreed in the land lease contract.

Most statutes do not prevent cancellation of loan commitments on insolvency, since to compel a creditor to advance money to an insolvent debtor goes to the root of the contract and ought to be consensual. The single exception appears to be the French *redressement*, although post-order credits may qualify for priority treatment, for what this is worth.

For a more detailed discussion, see para 3–11 *et seq*.

Disclaimer and abandonment powers

The procedures whereby a debtor or his insolvency administrator can elect   **11–35**
to disclaim contracts or abandon property is to enable the debtor to rid itself of onerous liabilities and property. The creditor is left with a claim for damages which is subject to the plan. The doctrine is discussed more fully in chapter 3.

Disclaimer applies to the **US Chapter 11** and to the **French *redressement*.** Thus in the US, subject to the approval of the court, the debtor may assume or reject leases of real or personal property (such as equipment leases) and other executory contracts, leaving the creditor to claim as an unsecured creditor for damages. The Bankruptcy Code limits the amounts which may be claimed as a result of the rejection of a lease of real property or of an employment contract. The fact that the debtor can reject executory contracts, and thus get rid of burdens on the estate, gives the debtor the bargaining power to renegotiate their terms. The rejection of collective bargaining agreements is subject to more restrictive standards.

The disclaimer rights do not apply to an **English** administration and there is case law as to whether the administrator can cause the debtor to repudiate contracts.

Under the **Japanese CRL** Art 103 the receiver may either rescind bilateral executory contracts or perform the obligations of the company and demand performance of the other party's obligations. If the receiver performs, the counterparty's claim for payment is a priority claim. If the receiver rescinds, the counterparty may claim damages. The counterparty cannot cancel by reason of non-payment by the company in the case of certain long-term supply contracts: Art 104–2. There are special rules for employment contracts and land leases.

Avoidance of pre-commencement transactions: preferences

11–36   All developed insolvency laws provide for the avoidance of pre-commencement transactions in the suspect period which prejudice creditors of the estate. The international principles are examined in chapters 5 to 7.

The availability of these avoidance powers under rehabilitation statutes receives varied treatment. The argument is that, if a company is insolvent, the principle of non-discriminatory treatment of creditors, which is at the heart of these avoidance powers, ought to come into play and can do so without damaging legitimate expectations, regardless of whether the proceeding is final or rehabilitative.

The normal insolvency powers to avoid pre-commencement transactions as preferences or otherwise apply in an **English administration**, a US **Chapter 11** case (see BC 1928 s 1107(a) – powers exercisable by the debtor in possession), a **French** *redressement* and a **Japanese reorganisation** (being the avoidance powers set out in CRL, Art 78 *et seq*).

Replacement of management

11–37   **General** Where an enterprise is liquidated, its business comes to a stop and accordingly the management is displaced. But in the case of a rehabilitation proceeding the hope is that the business will continue and hence the business has to be managed by somebody.

The factors in favour of overall control by an external administrator include: existing management has usually lost the confidence of creditors and is often not equipped to switch from expansion to restructuring; the prevention of fraud and the dissipation of assets; the need to avoid expensive and time-consuming collisions if there is a division of powers; the benefit of the experience of work-out professionals; and, in countries which prefer the private work-out to the formal proceeding, the desire to discourage the management from insisting on proceedings where they can stay in place.

The factors against overall control by an external administrator include: existing management is familiar with the business; and the expense of external professionals.

Outside the United States, the consensus appears to favour overall control by external administrators, with varying degrees of court or creditor supervision. The rationale appears to be that in practice the administrator of a large business must continue to employ the debtor's executives, but that it is desirable to vest final authority externally.

As a rough generalisation, the English administration is dominated by the insolvency practitioner and the courts discourage their own involvement; the **US Chaper 11** is dominated by the debtor's management; and the **French** *redressement* is dominated by the court.

In an **English administration,** the business is run by the insolvency admin-   11–38
istrator who must be a qualified and licensed insolvency practitioner –
usually an accountant. He has the power to hire and fire directors, and the
broadest management powers: IA 1986 s 14. But technically the board
remains in place until removed.

Under the **US Chapter 11,** management stays in power – known as debtor
in possession: BC 1978 s 1108. One of the purposes of this was to encourage an early resort to Chapter 11 before it was too late: it was found that
corporations were extremely unwilling to use pre–1978 reorganisation procedures that involved leadership by a trustee in bankruptcy and as a result
business corporations delayed instituting relief until they were forced to,
when the situation was often so far gone as to be incapable of resuscitation:
priority was given to the formal process over the private restructuring. But
an unsecured creditors' committee with investigative and other powers is
appointed by the US trustee (much litigation on reimbursement of their
expenses) and there are detailed provisions whereby the management may
be displaced by a court-appointed trustee for cause (s 1104). But in practice,
because of a presumption in favour of debtor in possession, greater resort
has been had to the half-way house of the appointment of an examiner who
leaves the management in place and who does not himself operate the business but enjoys certain limited investigative powers: s 1106. Examiners can
play expanded roles, e.g. mediating in the negotiation of a Chapter 11 plan.
The result is mixed authority between the debtor's management, the investor's committee and officers.

Under the **French** *redressement* the management remains in charge during   11–39
the observation period (six months, but extendible to 18 months) but the
procedure is dominated by the commercial courts staffed by *juge com-
missaires* of the commercial court, who do not necessarily have to have a
legal training but often do and who are in turn overseen by public prosecu-
tors drawn from professional judges. The other participants are the administrator and the liquidator, both court officials appointed by the commercial
court. The administrator prepares the report on the basis of which the court
decides the fate of the business, and supervises management or displaces
them if they are discharged, e.g. for fraud. He is in charge of implementing
the plan.

The liquidator represents the creditors – and is officially known as the
"representative of the creditors" – and also steps in as an actual liquidator if
the continuance of the business proves not to be feasible. The reason for the
divided roles was that pre–1989 experience showed that a trustee who combined both roles tended to prefer to liquidate or sell rather than to run the
business as a going concern. The court plays a prominent role throughout
and the *juge commissaire* conducts the orchestra.

Under the **Japanese reorganisation** the general rule is that the right to administer the business and to manage and dispose of the assets of a company under reorganisation vests exclusively in the receiver: CRL Arts 53, 174. Certain transactions must be authorised by the court: Art 54. The receiver may appoint an operating "agent": Art 98. There can be various creditor representatives: Arts 101, 160. A 1993 amendment to the Commercial Code requires issuers of bonds to appoint a monitoring company which has rights to take legal proceedings and other rights in respect of insolvencies.

Financing the business

11–40 One of the main problems faced by companies in distress which are going through a rehabilitation process is the availability of continuing finance. Any new finance must come (1) from the free cash resources of the debtor (usually nil), or (2) from disposals of assets (the most usual), or (3) from new loans (in practice lenders will be prepared to lend only if they can have an absolute priority in order to assure repayment by the insolvent debtor), or (4) from depriving creditors of secured assets (or their income), assets under title financing, and set-offs. The position with regard to the latter item in (4) is examined above.

If the post-petition contracts and financing have priority over pre-existing unsecured creditors, and the reorganisation fails, the effect is that the unsecured creditors are subordinated and suffer even greater losses. Hence the justification for post-petition priority can be justified only if there is a real likelihood of success which unhappily is often not so in practice and is usually impossible to predict in advance.

11–41   Under an **English administration,** loans to the administrator have super-priority on the unencumbered assets ranking equally with other post-order commitments and employment contracts adopted by the administrator and ranking ahead of the administrator's remuneration: IA 1986 s 19. But super-priority loans ranking ahead of existing security are not possible, except in the case of floating charges if the chargee has not used his power to veto the administration. The raising of priority loans would be subject to the administrator's duty to existing creditors and to an "unfair prejudice" application under IA 1986 s 27.

Under the **US Chapter 11,** administration expenses and costs rank prior: s 503(b)(1). There are detailed provisions regarding post-petition financing of the debtor in possession (DIP loans). See s 364. The upshot is that the DIP loans rank ahead of pre-petition unsecured creditors and can be secured on already encumbered property, subject to "adequate protection" and subject to various controls.

Under the **French** *redressement,* creditors after the opening judgment have priority: 1985 Law Art 40. They rank ahead of secured creditors. They also rank before tax claims, but after employee claims – the employee is always first in this legislation.

The reorganisation plan

The chief issues in this context are: 11–42

- Who prepares the plan – the debtor, the insolvency administrator or the creditors?

- Are there any time limits for the preparation of the plan or can the procedure drag on indefinitely?

- Are there any limits on the scope of the plan? The rules ought to contemplate compositions and postponements of debt, conversions of debt into equity, new loans and equity, a disposal programme, management changes and hive-downs to subsidiaries.

- Must the court approve the plan? This must invariably be the case, not only to control abuse and to protect minorities, but also to give judicial force to the plan.

- Are there any rules as to priorities, e.g. protection of secured creditors, prior payment of preferential creditors and non-discrimination amongst groups of creditors? Almost invariably, the hierarchy of bankruptcy priorities is preserved.

- Does a sale of the business override prohibitions on assignment or novations in contracts or leases? If it does, then counterparties and lessors are forced into a relationship with unknown parties of unknown integrity and credit-standing. On the other hand, transfer restrictions inhibit a sale and might give the counterparty an unfair bargaining power.

- What are the voting majorities – a mere 50 per cent or some special majority, e.g. 75 per cent?

- Is it possible to bind unnotified creditors? In practice, creditors of large companies quickly come to hear of the proceeding.

- Do shareholders have a vote? Usually the equity is wiped out, but there may be a future value.

- Are there onerous disclosure rules? Normally the plan can be set aside for misrepresentation or non-disclosure.

— Are there any excluded creditors, e.g. foreign taxes or tort claims?

— Are there compulsory conversions of foreign currency claims into local currency, as is usually the case on final bankruptcy? Conversion applies under the **French** *redressement* but not the **English administration.**

— Does interest continue to run during the proceedings? Under the **Japanese reorganisation** (CRL Art 122) interest after the commencement of the proceedings is a deferred claim. Interest does not stop in the case of an **English administration.**

11–43   **English administration** The English administration is an open procedure with few rules as to the content of the administrator's proposals. The underlying principle is to preserve the balance of bargaining power – by not crushing creditors too completely but shielding the company from enforcement actions and leaving the rest to negotiation. The administrator formulates his proposals and puts them to a creditors' meeting within three months: IA 1986 s 23. No court or shareholder approval is required and creditor voting does not bind dissentient creditors – although the administrator can use the voluntary arrangement procedure to achieve this under IA 1986 ss 1–7. There are no rules, no priorities, except as already stated in relation to secured creditors. Preferential creditors do not rank prior – but they should be prioritised in the plan. Creditor protection is maintained by a right to apply to the court on the grounds of "unfair prejudice" under IA 1986 s 27. Notwithstanding this, the procedure seems to work – probably because the basic principles of creditor priorities and non-discrimination are so obvious that it would be futile to depart from them.

Interest and rentals do not cease to run. There are no compulsory foreign currency conversions.

11–44   **US Chapter 11** By contrast, the US Chapter 11 plan is the subject of very detailed legislation. The bare bones of the matter are that the debtor in possession has an exclusive right during the first 120 days to formulate and file a plan. This right of the debtor to propose his own version does not apply in England and Japan and has caused much creditor resentment in the US. There must be a disclosure statement followed by creditor voting (for which purpose creditors are divided into priority classes) and confirmation by the court. Broadly the plan has to meet certain basic requirements which broadly reflect the "absolute priority rule" (super-priority creditors, secured creditors, administrative expenses, priority creditors – employees, taxes and the like – ordinary unsecured creditors, junior creditors and finally equity) with no class being impaired unless all creditors of a lower class receive nothing. The court can bind dissentient creditors (the "cram-down") if certain tests are met, based on observance of the absolute priority rule and non-discrimination between creditors of the same class.

Once the plan has been confirmed, the debtor is discharged from all debts which arose prior to confirmation except as provided in the plan so that the confirmed plan governs the obligations of all parties.

French *redressement* There is a compulsory observation period in order to   **11–45** prepare the plan. The administrator prepares the plan. The observation period is initially limited to six months but is extendible to a maximum of 18 months: 1985 Law Art 8(2). The plan either provides for a continuation of the business or its transfer to a third party or its liquidation and the court has a virtually unlimited discretion as to what to approve. A novelty is the draconian power to transfer the entire business to a new owner, notwithstanding contractual restraints on alienation, and to order continued performance by co-contractors so that landlords and suppliers can be forced into contractual relationships with somebody wholly new to them. Employment contracts are transferred automatically. The purchaser may not dispose of any assets until the entire consideration has been paid. The court exercises an interventionist command.

In exceptional cases, the court can authorise a lease agreement (*contrat de location gérance*) in the case of important companies whereby the lessee must operate the business in the meantime for a minimum period of two years – often he is a purchaser. See 1985 Law Art 42(1). Effectively the lessee is a conservator or manager.

Broadly, the options allowed for a plan are: continuation, transfer or liquidation: the legislation is highly prescriptive.

In the case of continuation, the court decides on the length of the postponement of debts. Continuation is unusual because the position is usually hopeless, and nobody will finance the debtor.

Interest stops at the time of the opening judgment: 1985 Law Art 55. Claims unasserted within two months of publication (plus two months for foreign creditors) are cancelled: 1985 Law Art 53. Employee claims may not be postponed or reduced: 1985 Law Art 76.

Japanese reorganisation The provisions in the Japanese Corporate Rehabili-   **11–46** tation Law governing the reorganisation plan are extremely elaborate, even more so than the US version: they occupy Arts 189 to 272, more than a third of the enactment. Voting majorities are higher.

Broadly, creditors are divided into priority groups as follows (Art 159): (1) secured creditors; (2) preferential creditors; (3) general creditors; (4) deferred creditors e.g. post-order interest; and (5) shareholders.

Draft plans may be submitted (within the period specified by the court), by the company, the receiver, the general creditors, the secured creditors and the shareholders. But the receiver is primarily charged with this duty (Art 189). In practice the receiver prepares the plan and the US exclusive right of the debtor to prepare the plan does not apply. The applicable government departments may comment on the plan, as may labour unions. The draft plan is then voted on by the classes of creditors, e.g. two-thirds of votes of general creditors. Shareholders have no vote: CRL Art 129(3). If the resolutions are adopted, the court may approve the plan, provided (amongst other things) that it is "fair, equitable and feasible". If the required consents of a class are not obtained, the court can nevertheless approve a plan with the modifications prescribed by Art 234 to protect the rights of classes of creditors including a power to give "fair and equitable protection" to the creditors. Once approved, the plan takes effect in accordance with its terms and all previous creditor rights fall away. If not approved, broadly the previous rights of creditors revive. As in the US and France (but not England) post-order interest is excluded: CRL Arts 114–16. As in the US, guarantors of the debtor's liabilities are not affected by an approved plan: CRL Art 240(2).

The court has a discretion to order payment to medium and small entrepreneurs for whom the company is a main customer if the continuance of their businesses would be seriously impeded if the claim were not paid: CRL Art 112–2. This is to alleviate distress in small towns if a large employer collapses. The same Article also allows the court to authorise payment of small claims to facilitate the reorganisation.

Liability of administrators

11–47 The question arises as to whether administrators of insolvent companies are subject to the normal rules applicable to corporate managers or have special dispensations. If a company is insolvent, it is difficult, for example, to apply the normal rules as to the avoidance of preferential transfers. In England, an administrator is subject to fiduciary duties towards the company, although this is not expressly codified. He is held to the standards of a professional insolvency practitioner of ordinary skill: *Re Charnley Davies Ltd* [1990] BCC 605, 618.

Exit from the proceedings

11–48 The proceedings will end either in triumph or disaster. In England, administrations have usually ended in a compulsory liquidation following a sale of the company's assets: the proceeds are then distributed to creditors. In one case in 1993, involving the huge Canary Wharf building project in London, the assets of the numerous companies were sold by the administrator with court approval to a holding company owned by the bank creditors, after which the old companies were liquidated. Unsecured creditors were paid a small dividend out of bank money pursuant to a company voluntary arrangement even though the banks had security over all the assets: *Re Olympia and York Canary Wharf Holdings Ltd* [1993] BCC 866.

It is understood that more than 90 per cent of French *redressements* have ended in liquidation.

Chapter 12

JUDICIAL RESCUE PROCEEDINGS: COUNTRY SUMMARIES

Countries covered

12–1 This section contains brief summaries of corporate rehabilitation proceedings in:

- Australia
- Canada
- Italy
- New Zealand
- Spain
- Eight countries in Central and Eastern Europe

Summaries of the following countries are contained in the previous chapter:

- Britain
- France
- Japan
- United States

For traditional compositions, see para 10–6 *et seq*.

Australia

12–2 **Background** In the Corporate Law Reform Act 1992, Australia adopted a mild corporate rehabilitation statute comprising a voluntary administration and deed of company arrangement, brought in after a careful and cautious review of insolvency law in the best Australian tradition. The procedure stays security enforcement for a very short period comparatively (up to 60 days), but, like the British administration but unlike the Canadian BIA of 1992, does not stay the universal floating charge or interfere with set-offs or with most contract rescissions, and (unlike the US Chapter 11) the debtor's management are subject to the overall control of an administrator who is in charge of the plan. Like the 1986 British approach, directors are encouraged to apply by reason of tougher director liability standards.

To go back further in time, in 1961 Australia adopted the South African judicial management for insolvent companies and called it official management. It did not work well from the beginning. First, anyone, even a director of the debtor company, could be the official manager so that the directors could remain in charge. This produced inevitable abuses in that creditors were kept at bay by those who had put them there in the first place. Secondly, the procedure was available only if the creditors considered that the company would pay its debts in full in a prescribed period – something impossible to say. When the debacle occurred, the creditors were blamed. Official management was buried in Australia in 1993. Parallel to the official management was the company scheme of arrangement which, though costly and time-consuming, was used perhaps more than its counterpart in England. Its disadvantage was the absence of an initial stay.

The new regime under CLRA 1992 may now be briefly summarised. The summary is based on seminar papers prepared by Mr Robert Harman.

Entry Any company that is insolvent or likely to become insolvent may   **12–3** initiate the procedure by a simple written appointment of an administrator. There is no requirement for any application to or filing with a court. An appointment may be made by the directors of a company; the liquidator of a company; or by a secured creditor whose security extends to the whole or substantially the whole of the property of a company ("a fully secured creditor").

Automatic stay The main effect is to stay the exercise of rights against the   **12–4** company and property owned, possessed, used or occupied by it. The stay affects all unsecured creditors, secured creditors (with some exceptions) and persons who have an interest, whether as owner or lessor in property in the possession, use or occupancy of the company, e.g. lessors of real or personal property occupied or used by the company and persons who claim title to property in the possession of the company through reservation of title clauses. Enforcement procedures and winding-up petitions are stayed.

A fully secured creditor can continue to enforce a security if the enforcement commenced before the appointment of the administrator or if it is commenced during a 14-day period, commencing from notice of the appointment of the administrator to the secured creditor: s 441A. A security over perishable property may be enforced: s 441A Other secured creditors may only enforce their security if the enforcement process had commenced before the appointment of the administrator but this is subject to a power of the court to order, on the application of the administrator, a restraint on the continued enforcement of the security, subject to adequate protection of the creditor: s 441D. Also, in some circumstances a person holding a fixed or specific security over, for example, land, who has progressed the enforcement of the security to the point of exercising a power of sale of that property, may complete that process.

The administrator may not dispose of property subject to a charge otherwise than in the ordinary course of the company's business, or with the written consent of the chargee, or with the leave of the court; although the leave of the court may not be given unless the court is satisfied that arrangements have been made to adequately protect the interests of the chargee: s 442C.

If the charge is in the nature of a floating charge, subject to those limitations and the superior powers of the person who is entitled to and who is enforcing the charge, the administrator may deal with the company's property which is subject to that charge as though it continued to be a floating charge: s 442B. Additionally, in the case of the company's assets which are subject to a floating charge, the administrator's right of indemnity for administrative expenses out of those assets will enjoy priority to the claims of the chargee subject to exceptions. Hence the partial floating charge appears to be very weak, as in Britain: para 11–16.

There are similar provisions in relation to owners or lessors of property: ss 440, 441. The stay continues for a period anticipated, in many cases, to be not longer than 35 days, but which may be extended by order of the court in a complex or large administration.

12–5   **Administrator and creditors** The administrator has control of the company, acts as its agent and exercises all the powers of its officers.

He must investigate the affairs of the company and form an opinion whether one of three options (a deed of company arrangement, a termination of the administration or a winding up of the company) is in the best interests of the creditors. Creditors decide on the three options. A simple majority in number (and value, if required) will be required for an effective resolution.

12–6   **Deed of company arrangement** The plan of a proposed arrangement between a company and its creditors may be tailored to suit the circumstances. The legislation places little restriction on the form that such an arrangement may take. It may involve continued trading, a sale of part of the assets, a rescheduling of debts, a composition of debts, conversion of debt to equity, a continued moratorium on creditor's rights, or whatever the creditors decide. However, the arrangement must ultimately provide for or deal with the debts and liabilities of the company, by providing for their satisfaction in part or in full.

If the creditors resolve to agree to a deed of company arrangement, the resultant deed will bind all creditors specified in the deed; secured creditors who have executed the deed (but only if they voted in favour); owners or lessors of property possessed, used or occupied by the company who have executed the deed; the administrator of the deed; the company; and the officers of the company. A person bound by the deed cannot take or continue with proceedings against the company or its property or enforce rights against that property: s 444.

The administrator of the deed may apply to the court for an order restraining a secured creditor or owner or lessor of property who declines to become a party to the deed from enforcing rights against any relevant property. The administrator must, however, satisfy the court that the interests of the secured creditor or property owner will be sufficiently protected under the arrangement: s 444F.

There are procedures for varying the arrangement.

If the creditors do not consider that the company's affairs may be suitably dealt with under a deed of company arrangement, they may resolve for the company to be wound up and, in that event, there is an automatic transmission of the company from administration to the regime of a winding-up in insolvency.

One objective was to avoid the need for constant supervision by the court. However, the court has a general jurisdiction to give directions and make relevant orders, but only on the application of the administrator or other persons who might be affected by various aspects of the administration procedure.

Canada

This summary is mainly based on briefings provided by Canadian law firms.   **12–7**

In Canada, there are two parallel rehabilitation proceedings: (1) the older and tougher Companies' Creditors Arrangement Act, dating from the 1930s, intended originally for publicly-held corporations with public debt and now used by the courts as a draconian reorganisation statute for everybody, and (2) the commercial reorganisation under the Bankruptcy and Insolvency Act 1992 (ss 50–66), amending the Bankruptcy Act 1949, previously significantly amended in 1966. Both statutes are Federal. The BIA was to be reviewed by a Parliamentary Committee in 1995.

The BIA evidenced a marked shift from a creditor-orientated bankruptcy procedure to a debtor-orientated rehabilitation and was probably intended to help employees and small businesses, while the CCAA may be regarded as more suitable for larger businesses. But, apart from the very wide automatic stay in the BIA (up to six months), the Act does not appear as tough as the US Chapter 11.

The CCAA is an open procedure with few formal rules. On the one hand, this allows flexibility. On the other hand, it creates unpredictability and much therefore depends on whether or not the signals from the courts are protective of creditor rights and recognise the tendency of reorganisations to fail in most cases.

The BIA was the result of numerous studies of insolvency dating from the 1960s and leading to no less than seven attempts to bring in new insolvency laws from 1975. The catalyst in the 1990s was probably a political regime favourably disposed to employees and to small businesses, coupled with a recession.

12–8 **Opening of proceedings** Under the BIA a proposal can be made by an insolvent person, a receiver, a liquidator, a bankrupt or a trustee. It can be made to creditors generally, either collectively or separated into classes as provided in the proposal. A proposal can also be made to any or all of the secured creditors provided that, if it is made to one or more secured creditors in respect of the secured claims of a particular class who share a "commonality of interest", the proposal must be made to all secured creditors of that class.

Before lodging a copy of a proposal with a licensed trustee, an insolvent person may (but is not obliged to) file a notice of intention to make a proposal ("proposal notice") with the official receiver followed by a cash flow statement prepared by the insolvent person and reviewed for reasonableness by the trustee named in the proposal notice: s 50.

If a proposal notice has been filed, the debtor must file a definitive proposal within 30 days thereafter: s 50.4(8). The trustee must participate in the preparation of the proposal including any negotiations relating to the proposal: ss 50.4(7), 50.5. The initial 30-day stay can be extended by the court for 45-day periods up to a maximum of six months, if the court is satisfied inter alia as to feasibility and no material prejudice to the creditors: s 50.4(9).

The CCAA stay is typically for 60 to 90 days, but some stays have listed up to two years while a plan is prepared. Hence the CCAA may be preferred for larger companies.

12–9 **Automatic stay** On the filing of a definitive proposal or a proposal notice by an insolvent person under the BIA:

(a) no creditor has any remedy against the insolvent person's property nor may any creditor commence or continue any action, execution or other proceeding for the recovery of a claim payable in bankruptcy;

(b) except with respect to the use of, or dealing with, assets that would significantly prejudice the secured creditor, a provision in a security agreement between the insolvent person and a secured creditor will be ineffective that provides, in substance, that on insolvency or default under the security agreement the insolvent person ceases to have such rights to use or deal with the assets secured under the security agreement. Possibly these stays will prevent creditors from perfecting security during the time periods provided for under statutes such as Ontario's Construction Lien Act, Mortgages Act or Personal Property Security Act.

(c) no person may terminate or amend any agreement or claim any accelerated payment under any agreement with the insolvent person by reason only of the insolvency of the person or the filing of a proposal notice or proposal;

(d) with respect to a lease of real property or licensing agreement, there can be no termination, amendment or claim for accelerated payment based on the grounds in (c) or by reason of rent or royalties, or other payments of a similar nature, not having been paid, in respect of the period preceding the filing of either the proposal notice or the proposal where no proposal notice was filed;

(e) no public utility (fuel, water, electricity, telecommunications, garbage etc.) may discontinue service to an insolvent person based on the grounds in (c); and

(f) various rights of the tax authorities are stayed.

Court relief from the stays in (c) and (d) is available if the applicant can   **12–10**
satisfy the court that the stay would cause it "significant financial hardship". There is an exemption for "eligible financial contracts" so as to allow netting. This aspect is described in detail in another volume in this series on financial law. A member of the Canadian Payments Association can cease acting as a clearing agent or group clearer for an insolvent person. The stay does not require the debtor to be supplied with further goods or services other than on a cash only basis. There is no obligation to continue further advances of money or credit to the debtor: s 65.1.

The stay does not prevent a secured creditor who took possession of the secured assets for the purpose of realisation before the proposal notice or proposal was filed from dealing with those assets or prevent a secured creditor who gave a realisation notice to enforce its security more than 10 days before filing of the proposal notice or definitive proposal from realising on its security: s 69. But the debtor could beat the realisation by filing a proposal notice in the 10-day period which is therefore a warning period for the debtor.

There are complex provisions concerning suppliers rights to recover goods.

The court may lift the stay in respect of a creditor if it is satisfied that the creditor is likely to be significantly prejudiced by the continuance of the stay or that it is otherwise equitable to lift the stay: s 69.4.

Under the CCAA, the stay is discretionary, but broad. Courts have limited relief from the stay, prevented the termination of contracts with the debtor, required suppliers to continue to supply (on normal trade terms but without the US priority), and extended the stay to secured creditors.

12–11 **Creditors approval of proposal** The trustee must call a meeting of creditors within 21 days from the filing of the definitive proposal with the official receiver: s 51(1).

A proposal is deemed to be acceptable if all classes of unsecured creditors vote for the acceptance of the proposal by a majority in number and two-thirds (three-quarters under the CCAA) in value of those unsecured creditors who vote on the resolution: s 54(2)(d). Secured creditors of a class that rejects the proposal are free to deal with their security as provided for in their security agreement and need not comply with the requirement for 10 days prior notice of enforcement in Part XI of the Act: s 69.1(6). Secured creditors of a class to whom the proposal was not made need not comply with the 10 days' notice requirement before realising their security: s 69.1(5).

If unsecured creditors refuse a proposal then the insolvent person is deemed to have made an assignment in bankruptcy: s 57.

Non-acceptance of a proposal by a class of secured creditors does not result in an automatic bankruptcy.

If the proposal is accepted by the unsecured creditors the court must approve it. A proposal must provide for the repayment of certain federal and provincial taxes and preferred employee claims.

By contrast the CCAA proposal procedure is much more flexible. There are no specific conditions but court approval is subject to a general fairness test.

12–12 **Repudiation of commercial leases** An insolvent person who is also a commercial tenant may repudiate the lease on 30 days' notice to the landlord at any time after the filing of a proposal notice until the filing of the definitive proposal: s 65.2(1). A proposal repudiating a commercial lease must provide for payment to the landlord, immediately after court approval of the proposal, of an amount equal to the lesser of six months' rent under the lease or the rent for the remainder of the lease from the date on which the repudiation takes effect: s 60(1.5). A landlord cannot terminate a lease or claim any accelerated rent upon the debtor filing a proposal notice or a proposal for any arrears of rent for the period preceding the filing: s 65.1(2)(c). Within 15 days after receiving notice of a lease repudiation the landlord may apply to the court for a declaration that the lease cannot be repudiated.

The landlord can, through the court, stop the repudiation unless the insolvent person can demonstrate that the repudiation of the lease in question and all other repudiated leases is essential to its ability to make a viable proposal: s 65.2(2). If the lease is terminated the landlord cannot claim any accelerated rent against the estate of the insolvent person if the person subsequently goes bankrupt: s 65.2(6). Probably the landlord can file a claim as an unsecured creditor for damages.

Under the CCAA, a debtor can disclaim a lease with court approval.

Voidable preferences The usual avoidance of preferences is available under a BIA reorganisation, but there is no specific provision in relation to the CCAA.

Italy

The substantive description given below is largely based on a most useful   **12–13**
summary by Gian Bruno Bruni in Campbell (ed) *International Corporate Insolvency Law* (1992) Butterworths. The commentary is the author's.

Italy has four composition or rehabilitation proceedings in addition to final bankruptcy under BA 1942:

1. **Preventative composition (*concordata preventativo*)** This is a conventional but little-used composition requiring payment of 100 per cent of preferred debts and 40 per cent of non-preferred debts. The debtor stays in possession but is subject to supervision by a judicial commissioner. Executions are stayed but not set-offs. Interest ceases to run from petition. Secured creditors are not affected. A two-thirds creditor vote suffices for the composition.

2. **Controlled administration (*amministrazione controllata*)** BA 1942 ss 187–193. This is another older-form breathing-space moratorium for up to two years, permissable only if the debtor has temporary difficulties in fulfilling his obligations and the business has real recovery prospects. Entry into the procedure is considered a benefit and is therefore difficult. The debtor's management stays in possession, but may be displaced by a judicial commissioner. Executions are stayed, but interest does not stop. The proposals must be approved by a bare majority of creditors, as to number and value.

3. **Compulsory administrative liquidation (*liquidazione coatta amministrativa*)** BA 1942 ss 194–215 This is an administrative, not a judicial procedure, intended for banks, insurance companies and cooperatives.

12–14 4. **Extraordinary administration (*amministrazione straordinaria*)** Decree Law No 26 of January 30, 1979, as amended. ("EAL 1979") The chief features of this procedure are: (1) it is intended for large groups; (2) the procedure is controlled by the government, not the courts, and therefore overrides judicial control; (3) there appear to be few rules protective of creditors and indeed there are hardly any rules at all, except sweeping statements of the survival objective; and (4) employees are to be kept in work at the expense of the existing creditors and the taxpayer. The procedure was primarily intended to protect employees and takes state dirigism to the most extreme lengths of all the bankruptcy procedures encountered. State officials appear to have complete discretion over creditors' rights. Article 2 of the EAL 1979 provides: "Insofar as is possible and after taking into consideration the interests of the creditors, the programme [prepared by state-appointed officials] will provide for a recovery plan in conformity with the principles of industrial policy". The statute mandates the continuance of trading and allows state guarantees, so that, if trading is at a loss, the existing creditors are subordinated and lose more than they would have done. Express creditor control appears to be virtually nil. The most serious feature of this law is the subjection of the rule of law to the wishes of politicians and trade unions. The law survived a challenge in the Italian Constitutional Court: Judgement of February 13, 1985, No 41.

12–15 To be eligible for this procedure, by Law No. 55, April 3, 1979 s 1,

(1) the company must be indebted towards banks (qualified indebtedness) for not less than L61,264m. This amount is increased yearly by the Ministry of Industry in proportion to the inflation rate;

(2) the company must have had a workforce of at least 300 employees for not less than a year;

(3) the total indebtedness must be in the amount of more than five times the company's paid-in capital, as resulting from its balance sheet approved by the general meeting; and

(4) the company must be insolvent: this condition is to be ascertained by the bankruptcy judge pursuant to BA 1942 ss 5 and 195; and is automatically satisfied when the company has not been able to pay three months' wages to its employees: EAL 1979 s 1.

12–16 The Ministry of Industry, together with the Ministry of Treasury, issue a decree whereby the company is granted the benefits of the extraordinary administration. The Ministry of Industry appoints extraordinary commissioners (from one to three in number) who take over the management of the company from the directors. A committee of creditors is also appointed with three to five members to supervise the commissioners' activity.

The procedure may last for up to two years (which can be extended no more than twice for a total of four years) and, in case of groups of companies, up to five years.

All executions or legal actions against the company are stayed; no right to set off is allowed to creditors. Interest ceases to accrue in favour of creditors. Bankruptcy proceedings are stayed. The company's directors are displaced. The company loses the ability to sue and to be sued. Its organs (board of directors, company's directors, shareholders' general meeting) cease to function. The court's role, in practice, is confined to verifying the correctness of creditors' claims.

The Ministry of Industry is the supreme superintending authority.

The tentacles of the procedure may be extended: 12–17

(1) to the direct or indirect holding company or to the direct or indirect subsidiaries, or to the companies managed or co-owned by the insolvent company; or

(2) to companies that have lent money to, or issued guarantees in favour of, the insolvent company (or any other company among the above categories), when the amount involved exceeds one-third of their total assets: EAL 1979 s 3.

The Ministry of Treasury, at its discretion, may guarantee all or part of the debts contracted by the procedure towards banks. Thus, the taxpayer pays, which in the jargon of the time was called "the socialisation of the crisis of large companies", for financing the day-by-day management of the company: EAL 1979. But this is at the expense of creditors by virtue of the state maximum preference.

The extraordinary commissioners have powers to set aside preferences under BA 1942 Art 67, and the periods of one or two years in Art 67 are extended to five and three years for good measure. They also may sue the insolvent company's previous directors for misconduct, mismanagement, and wrongful or fraudulent trading under CC 2409.

The extraordinary commissioners are responsible for working out a programme aimed at enabling the company (or part of it) to continue its activity. The programme must be authorised by the Ministry of Industry after hearing the opinion of a ministerial committee.

The procedure can be concluded in three ways: 12–18

(1) the "rescue programme" is successful and the business is sold as a going concern or by branches of activity;

(2) the programme fails and the business is sold on an asset-by-asset basis; or

(3) a scheme of arrangement is proposed on the lines of the compulsory administrative liquidation mentioned at para 12–13 above: secured creditors must be paid in full, unsecured creditors in the amount of 25 per cent.

New Zealand

12–19   New Zealand has a broadly pro-creditor bankruptcy culture based on English ideas. But in the centre of this smooth-flowing river lies a rock which seeks to divert the strong current and throws up a mighty splashing in the process: the Companies (Investigation and Management) Act 1989.

This legislation allows the executive to appoint a statutory manager of a New Zealand company in the public interest and has been used either because of suspected misdoings or because of a labyrinthine corporate structure or to protect the public, usually meaning public shareholders or public debt-holders. Creditors have virtually no influence on the proceedings. The manager has very wide powers to run the company. The stay freezes proceedings, executions, winding-up petitions, enforcement by secured creditors, repossessions under retention of title, hire purchase agreements, leases or mortgages, forfeiture of land leases, landlord's distraint, set-offs, and acceleration by secured creditors. Apart from that, the stay apparently does not nullify *ipso facto* clauses in ordinary commercial contracts.

The procedure goes back to 1934 legislation, which was subsequently extended and which was designed to protect the investing public. Between 1958 and 1990, twenty companies were subjected to the procedure which has been much criticised in New Zealand.

It is believed that the procedure has in practice usually been operated by statutory managers with proper attention to acquired rights, consistent with the New Zealand tradition of fairness. But, like the Italian *amministrazione straordinaria*, the procedure raises the question of whether it is right for the political executive to take strong-arm powers on the bankruptcy of ordinary commercial corporations.

Spain

12–20   This summary is largely based on a very full review by Bufete Mullerat and Rosell in Rajak/White (ed), *A Practitioner's Guide to European Corporate Insolvency Law* (1992/93 ed) Westminster Management Consultants Ltd. The commentary is the author's.

In the first Spanish Code in 1829, there was no separate composition. In the 1855 Code, a suspension of payments was introduced as an alternative to bankruptcy and led to much abuse. In order to correct this, a Law of June 10, 1897 required that the debtor should possess sufficient assets in order to pay his debts in full. The procedure was only applicable where the debtor was experiencing a temporary lack of liquidity.

Finally, the Suspension of Payments Law of July 26, 1922 ("SPL 1922"), which is still in force, reintroduced the concept of rehabilitation.

Once suspension of payments is ordered, bankruptcy cannot be applied for (Judgment of November 26, 1976), but once bankruptcy has been declared, then the debtor cannot apply for the procedure of suspension of payments unless the declaration of bankruptcy is opposed for good reason: see Judgment of the Supreme Court, July 3, 1933 (bankruptcy converted to suspension); Judgment of the Territorial Court of Barcelona, March 23, 1977, chamber 2 (suspension disallowed because of debtor fraud).

Directors are jointly and severally liable for the debts of the company if **12–21** they fail to call a creditors' meeting when the company satisfies eligibility for a declaration of bankruptcy to be made. This encourages the directors to apply for an insolvency procedure.

The entry requirements are high. The application must indicate that the liabilities exceed the assets. The debtor must submit accounts, a list of creditors, a report and a proposal for agreement: SPL 1922 Art 2.

The procedure is begun by a judgment of acceptance for processing and followed, usually after a few months, by a formal declaration of suspension of payments.

The "interventores" are appointed by the first ruling. They are the judicial officials (usually expert lawyers or accountants) responsible for handling the suspension and administering the company.

As from the time of the initial judgment for the acceptance of processing, the debtor's management can be removed: SPL 1922 Art 6 or Royal Decree-Law on attachment of administration of companies of October 20, 1969, which allows directors to be appointed in the case of the attachment of companies.

Bankruptcy applications and creditor enforcement actions are stayed, but this does not apply to secured creditors. Proceedings can continue – only enforcement is stayed.

Forty per cent or more in value of the creditors may require bankruptcy proceedings. Employees, social security and tax are not stayed: SPL 1922 Art 15. Two-fifths of the total liabilities may request the cancellation of the proceedings where the insolvency is considered to be definite.

A Salary Guarantee Fund covers salary arrears up to four months in respect of outstanding salaries and for up to one year in respect of compensation for termination of contract. The Fund is subrogated to the preferential rights of the employees.

12–22   *Ipso facto* cancellation clauses in contracts are not nullified, but if contracts are continued, the creditor's claims are preferential and may not be
excluded or made subject to the insolvency procedures. Landlord forfeitures
of leases are not stayed. Spain does not permit insolvency set-off and hence
post-commencement set-offs are not available. Hence the overall impact on
creditor rights is mild.

The plan is approved if more than half of the creditors attending vote in
favour, provided that the amount of their claims represents 60 per cent of
the total liabilities. Any extension of time for payment over three years
requires a 75 per cent vote.

If the debtor is insolvent, preferences may be avoided under Com C Arts
879–882.

Proceedings may be commenced against the management for negligence
or fraud. But the penalties for fraudulent and wilful insolvency in Arts 520
and 529 of the Penal Code are not applicable: Judgment of the Supreme
Court of February 13, 1957.

In addition to the suspension of payments, the state has powers of inter-
vention, based on a right to seize companies providing public services: Com
C Art 939 *et seq*. This law was used in 1979 and again in 1980 when, by
means of decrees, cotton companies were seized. The Supreme Court, in a
Judgment of December 17, 1986, declared the seizure to be compatible with
the Constitution. See also the precautionary measures allowed by the
Decree-Law of October 29, 1969 (passed as a result of the "MATESA"
case), whereby the administration of a company could be granted to the
employees or creditors. These laws appear to be similar to the Italian extraordinary administration, i.e. unsatisfactory abrogation of the rule of law by
the executive.

Central and Eastern Europe

12–23   After the collapse of the Soviet Empire and its satellite regimes at the beginning at the last decade of the twentieth century, 27 new countries appeared
on the legal scene and many of them immediately and with commendable
zeal, set about the task of reconstructing their legal systems. The Central
European countries already had models from the 1930s or before which
they updated. But most countries in Eastern Europe and Asia had nothing
(and many of them still have nothing) and so were obliged to invent their
own statutes. These are inevitably rudimentary since the preparation of
bankruptcy provisions takes most countries decades, if not centuries. Nevertheless bankruptcy laws do not have to be smothered with rules and regulations and procedures for them to work in practice, and it is reasonable for

countries to experiment and to proceed cautiously. This short summary deals only with rehabilitation concepts.

Belarus The Law of Economic Insolvency and Bankruptcy 1991 provides for insolvency (rehabilitation) and total insolvency (liquidation). There is a vague draconian rehabilitation, which is court supervised. The court has broad interventionist powers. The debtor can propose a plan, and defer maturities for three years. There is no formal voting or rules on plans.   **12–24**

Czech and Slovak Republics The Bankruptcy and Composition Act of 1991 as amended, is based on the Austro-Hungarian BA 1914. There is a three month protection period (extendable by three months) with creditor stays. The protection continues if creditors propose a composition under the Act. This is a conventional old European involuntary composition subject to 75 per cent votes. It must pay one third of the debts within one year.

There is also a conventional old European voluntary composition which must pay 45 per cent of the debts in two years. This is unlikely to be popular.

Hungary There is a bankruptcy moratorium under the Insolvency Act 1992. The debtor initiates: it appears to be substantially an extra-judicial procedure. There is a 90-day moratorium, extendible for 30 days. The debtor proposes a plan, but (improbably) all creditors present at the meeting must agree the plan. The creditors can petition for an administrator.

Kazakhstan The Bankruptcy Law 1992 contains very rudimentary rehabilitation provisions – broadly a court-supervised work-out. There are no creditor stays and all creditors must be paid.   **12–25**

Poland The German-based Bankruptcy Law of 1934 was dusted off. The composition is based on the German composition and was amended in 1990. It is available to economic subjects who have ceased to pay their debts because of exceptional circumstances and those beyond their control – a strict entry requirement.

Russia The Law on Bankruptcy of Enterprises 1992 contains broad and vague reorganisation provisions: "sanification". Management is by managers appointed by the court. Sanification is a tender for the business supervised by court (no procedure for plans, no creditor voting). If there is no tender, the debtor is liquidated. The management cannot exceed 18 months.

Ukraine The Bankruptcy Law 1992 contains a rudimentary "sanatio". There are preliminary proceedings with a view to a work-out, but no credi-

tor stay. Rehabilitiation is basically the take-over of the business by a rehabilitator willing to assume the debts: the rehabilitator must apply within one
month. This seems optimistic. Employees may require a lease of the enterprise for a rent (a type of employee buy-out on lease terms), or a transforma-
tion of the enterprise into another enterprise owned by employees.

Insurance companies, banks and other public interest entities

12–26 A number of developed countries have installed special legislation to protect
insolvent insurance companies, banks and other institutions which are
deemed vital to public confidence in the financial system or whose demise
could cause unacceptable political objections, losses to the public or potentially a systemic failure.

For example, in **Britain** insurance companies and building societies are
subject to a special regime, but not banks (where there is a deposit protection scheme).

In **Italy** a compulsory administrative liquidation (*liquidazione coatta
amminstrativa*) is available under BA 1942 where the orderly winding up of
the business is deemed to be in the public interest, e.g. banks and insurance
companies. The procedure is administrative rather than judicial and is primarily a liquidation procedure. The procedure stays executions.

In the **United States**, insured banks are subject to special proceedings
administered by the Federal Deposit Insurance Corporation outside the
Bankruptcy Code of 1978.

The subject is too large except merely to mention it. In practice, probably
the best method of dealing with insolvent banks, insurance companies and
the like is the confidential private sale to another institution, initiated by the
supervisory authorities, and this indeed is what tends to happen in practice.
Any form of bankruptcy proceeding tends to be fatal.

But the same policy questions arise. For example, if the regime freezes set-
offs and contract cancellations, the risks of systemic collapse could be
increased.

CHAPTER 13

INSOLVENCY CONFLICT OF LAWS: INTRODUCTION

Reasons for lack of comity

A number of factors have influenced the comparative lack of comity in rela- 13–1
tion to international bankruptcy law. One is the sharp division between pro-
creditor and pro-debtor bankruptcy policies. Bankruptcy policies are the
fundamental bedrock of law and are adhered to with a fierce intensity so
that they are converted into mandatory rules of public policy.

The main differences include: the scope and efficiency of security and title
finance (retention of title, factoring, hire-purchase, financial leasing, sale
and repurchase and the like); insolvency set-off; toughness of corporate
rehabilitation proceedings; attitudes towards reputed ownership and the
trust; attitudes to the veil of incorporation and director or shareholder liability; ability to rescind contracts on insolvency and forfeit leases; the width
of rules annulling preferential transfers; and priority creditors.

Another reason for the lack of comity is xenophobic protection of local
creditors and a distrust of foreign legal systems, coupled sometimes with a
popular resentment at foreign debtors who have caused loss to local creditors.

A third is the desire to ensure that local assets do not go to pay foreign
taxes or foreign preferential creditors.

The conflicts are now exacerbated by the appearance of corporate 13–2
rehabilitation laws which have as their object the rescue of the debtor and
which must therefore curtail creditor rights more savagely than a final liquidation in the interests of the resurrection. Examples are the US Chapter 11
and the French *redressement*, studied in chapter 11. When these rehabilitation proceedings in one jurisdiction collide with a final bankruptcy proceeding over the same debtor in another, the conflict will often be sharper by
reason of the diverging objectives – an extra layer of difference on top of different underlying pro-creditor or pro-debtor cultures.

These chapters on conflict of laws are primarily concerned with corporate
bankruptcies, not the bankruptcy of individuals.

An EU draft Bankruptcy Convention is currently under consideration.

Territorial and universal theories

13–3   In ideological terms there are two broad approaches, the territorial and universal theories.

The first theory is that bankruptcy is purely territorial and covers only local assets. The second doctrine of the "universality of bankruptcy" or the "unity of bankruptcy" holds that the only courts which have jurisdiction to bankrupt a debtor are the courts of the debtor's domicile or principal place of business. All creditors must resort to that country and no foreign country has jurisdiction to bankrupt that debtor. That state applies its own insolvency law. The bankruptcy applies to all the debtor's assets globally and not just local assets.

Apart from treaties, in practice most developed states adopt a combination of these extremes.

Advantages and disadvantages of single forum

13–4   The advantages of a single insolvency administration include: it avoids the cost and inefficiency of two competing administrations; all creditors are treated equally in accordance with local rules; all international property is pooled; there is a universal restraint on creditor proceedings; and creditors dealing with a domiciliary should expect to be governed by domiciliary law.

One disadvantage is that local creditors are prejudiced by adverse foreign insolvency laws which (except in the case of banks making large loans) they could not be expected to investigate; they may be legally ambushed if they are attuned to a pro-creditor culture but the foreign debtor is subject to a pro-debtor culture. For example, the debtor's forum may upset or interfere with non-possessory security, disallow insolvency set-off, impose the delays and expense of a harsh rehabilitation or moratorium law, expropriate property held in trust on grounds of the reputed ownership of the debtor, insist that a transfer is preferential, and refuse to permit the rescission of contracts by reason of the insolvency. Further disadvantages include: local creditors cannot wind up local assets if there is only one central seat, but have to incur the cost of going abroad; small creditors are prejudiced since they do not have the resources to prove abroad; there may be problems of jurisdiction if several central seats are possible, especially conflict between the place of incorporation and the place where the main business is; exchange controls may prevent payment to foreign creditors; if the creditor's claim is in foreign money, he may be expropriated if he has to convert his claim into the local currency which is depreciating rapidly; creditors assets are used to pay foreign taxes or employee claims; commonly nothing is left for unsecured creditors after these creditors have been paid; it is not always unfair to allow concurrent proceedings, because usually these relate to local assets so that it is equitable to apply the law of the closest connection; and sovereignty, connexity and a reasonable division of labour mitigate against the overreaching effect of local insolvency laws.

In practice it is not unreasonable to contemplate one main and several ancillary proceedings and to leave it to private international law to resolve the conflicts between the sets of parallel proceedings. It is presently too idealistic to achieve anything approaching a satisfactory set of rules in this field which everybody could agree to.

Generally, the usual pattern for large corporations is that creditors commence the bankruptcy proceedings wherever there are assets so as to protect them from the debtor and from piecemeal attachments. Hence an international bankruptcy often takes the form of a main bankruptcy at the principal place of business plus ancillary bankruptcies in foreign parts. The liquidators of each pool sometimes negotiate agreements between themselves which may have to be approved as a composition or scheme of arrangement by creditors and the local courts.

Examples of foreign assets

It is useful at the outset to have in mind examples of the spread of assets of   **13–5** an international corporate debtor. They may include: deposits with foreign banks payable at the office of the foreign bank; investment securities deposited with foreign custodians, such as Euroclear or Cedel; trade receivables owing by foreign buyers; in the case of banks, loans or guarantees owing by foreign debtors; claims against foreign insurers; intellectual property rights registered abroad; goods being imported but still abroad – raw materials or manufactured products or grain; ships or aircraft travelling the world's seas and skies; land, plantations and mines abroad; and foreign branch offices with buildings and land. If the debtor is an international group, its foreign assets will usually be held by subsidiaries in which event the subsidiaries' properties will belong to the subsidiary and not be available to the creditors of the parent, but the parent's foreign asset will be the shares in the subsidiary.

The location of land or goods is not problematic; they are located where they are. But intangible property must be given a notional location, e.g. negotiable instruments are located where they are; bank deposits at the branch of the bank where they are maintained; contract debts where they are primarily recoverable, usually the place of business of the debtor; and registered shares, where the register is kept, usually the place of incorporation of the issuer of the shares.

Classification of jurisdictions

13–6　In comparing the attitude of jurisdictions to comity, there seems little correlation between bankruptcy bias (pro-debtor and pro-creditor) and comity. Pro-debtor states do not appear to be more nationalistic and protective of local creditors. Examples of pro-creditor states which seem to be protective of local creditors include the Netherlands, Norway, and Sweden (although it is doubtful whether this is still the case).

English-influenced states show marked comity. This is because common law traditions had very similar views when there was one big British Empire with the same laws in 80 or so jurisdictions world-wide. But, it is not true to say that there is lesser comity in civil code countries. Nor is it true that comity depends on similarity of legal systems, e.g. local protectionism between similar states in Latin America is strong (even under treaty law).

There probably is a higher degree of comity between developed countries with substantial international business links, in particular acceptance of the concept of local ancillary proceedings which act in aid of the main proceeding elsewhere, e.g. in English-based countries, Switzerland and the United States.

Comity therefore appears to be primarily influenced by legal nationalism; cultural attitudes about foreigners; the degree of respect and courtesy; and by the extent of the involvement in international business which generates creditor pressures to satisfy legitimate expectations.

Organisation of the topic

13–7　Conflicts tend to arise between the main place of business of the debtor and a foreign country where assets are located. Hence it seems best to examine the position first from the point of view of a bankruptcy at the main seat or domicile of a company, and to review the law which will be applied in that bankruptcy. This is the *domiciliary* or *home* or *principal* forum. Then it is necessary to review the likely reaction of foreign jurisdictions – the *ancillary* forum – to the rules of the home forum. The position in the ancillary forum will either be that no bankruptcy proceedings have been commenced there or alternatively parallel proceedings have been instituted.

Complications arise where there are several parallel proceedings which are ancillary, and where there are two or more central seats or pools of assets so that it is impossible to say which is the main forum or centre of economic activity. The incidence of several parallel proceedings is common, but problems of identifying a main domicile are less frequent.

CHAPTER 14

INSOLVENCY CONFLICT OF LAWS: INSOLVENCY JURISDICTION

Introduction

This section summarises the main international bases of insolvency jurisdic- **14–1**
tion and reviews some countries by way of example. The main heads of jurisdiction to institute bankruptcy proceedings are:

- — Locally incorporated company
- — Local branch
- — Local assets
- — Local business activities
- — Local nationality or residence of the creditor

Local company and local branch

It is believed that most, if not all, developed states claim jurisdiction to wind **14–2**
up insolvent companies which are incorporated or have their principal place
of business locally or are domiciled locally or have a local branch.

If the company is solvent, the Brussels Judgements Convention and its
extensions the Lugano and San Sebastian Conventions (intended to apply to
at least 17 European and other countries) may vest exclusive jurisdiction in
the contracting state where the company's "seat" is located: Art 16. These
Conventions do not apply to "bankruptcy proceedings".

In the case of individuals, it is almost invariably the case that the courts
have jurisdiction to bankrupt individuals who are domiciled or resident
locally or carry on business locally.

Long-arm jurisdiction: summary

The important question therefore is whether the courts exercise a long-arm **14–3**
jurisdiction, i.e. an excessive or exorbitant jurisdiction, based on some other
weaker or fleeting connection with the forum.

The main heads of long-arm bankruptcy jurisdiction are

(1) Local assets
(2) Local business
(3) Local physical presence (individuals)
(4) Nationality or residence of the petitioning creditor

These ephemeral jurisdictional bases are sometimes used, not so much as to collect local assets, but rather to secure jurisdiction over debtors (1) to investigate their affairs under far-reaching investigative powers available only on bankruptcy, particularly in the case of fraud, (2) to recover a fraudulent preference, (3) to recover an excess receipt obtained by a creditor in defiance of the home bankruptcy, e.g. by virtue of a foreign attachment or repossession, (4) to impose liability on a director for fraudulent or wrongful trading, or (5) to recover the debtor's property spirited away by an officer.

Sometimes a single factor on its own is not enough and several connecting factors are required, and often the courts have a discretion. These main grounds are summarised here prior to a more detailed treatment below.

14–4 **Local assets,** however small. Assets jurisdiction was perhaps originally intended to protect local creditors but is now important as a means whereby the administrator in the home forum can protect foreign assets from piece-meal attachment. Local assets may include assets which would arise if the bankruptcy were ordered, e.g. recovery of fraudulently transferred property (Sweden) or a recovery for wrongful trading against a local director (England).

Contrast the ordinary civil jurisdiction over contracts where the presence of local assets is usually not enough, except in the "toothbrush" jurisdictions—e.g. Germany, Japan, Sweden and South Africa but not English-based countries or the Franco-Latin group. In "toothbrush" jurisdictions the courts claim civil jurisdiction (as opposed to bankruptcy jurisdiction) over any person or company which has an asset in the jurisdiction, however small, even though the claim does not concern that asset.

The local rules as to the deemed location of intangible movables will be relevant. An important asset in practice is a bank account within the jurisdiction. Under English law a bank account is generally located for this purpose at the branch where the account is kept.

The "assets" ground of jurisdiction appears almost universal and applies in countries as various as Argentina, England (and many English-based countries), Finland, France, Germany, Sweden and the United States.

Often the jurisdiction, because it is long-arm, is discretionary, e.g. in England and the United States.

But the mere presence of assets may not be enough in a few exceptional states e.g. Denmark, Norway and some Latin American countries (Bolivia, Honduras, Mexico perhaps), where a local branch is required.

Local business, i.e. carrying on business locally either personally or through 14–5
an agent. The objective of this head of jurisdiction is to prevent debtors
from trading locally and then escaping a local bankruptcy by shutting up
shop and departing abroad leaving unpaid trading debts behind. If there are
no local assets as well, the bankruptcy will have no realisations for creditors
and there is usually little point in proceeding, except in special cases, e.g. to
apply fraudulent preference or wrongful trading rules, to secure jurisdiction
over local creditors to compel them to disgorge excess receipts, or to obtain
discovery over officers of the debtor residing locally. This head of jurisdiction is sometimes an extra test if mere local assets are not in themselves
sufficient.

Carrying on business locally is a sufficient jurisdictional link in England
(individuals), in many English-based countries and in Sweden.

The mere entering into of contracts locally is not enough in the absence of
a *main* office (not merely an ancillary branch) in Denmark, Finland (but
local assets are sufficient) or Norway. If neither assets nor carrying on business locally are sufficient, there is a bankruptcy hole.

Local physical presence In the case of individuals, local physical presence at 14–6
the time the petition is served is sometimes a ground of jurisdiction. This is
primarily an English-based rule applying to individual debtors and is subject
to a discretion based on forum non conveniens concepts. In England, the
mere presence of a director of a company locally does not found jurisdiction
over the company.

The presence jurisdiction applies in many English-based countries and in
Finland. But mere physical presence is not enough (except sometimes in
special circumstances, e.g. persons of no fixed abode) in Denmark, Norway
or Sweden.

Local nationality or residence of the petitioning creditor The long-arm juris- 14–7
diction based on the local nationality of the *creditor* applies in France and,
perhaps Belgium and Luxembourg.

Nationality or residence of the *creditor* are irrelevant in Denmark,
English-based countries, Finland, Norway, Sweden, the United States and
(probably) most countries outside the French group. It seems to be a French-
inspired rule.

Whether such countries as Italy and the Netherlands apply their normal
jurisdictional base conferring jurisdiction if the creditor is a local resident is
a matter for investigation.

Local nationality of the *debtor* is enough in Finland, but appears rare elsewhere.

The grounds for opening proceedings

14–8 The grounds for the opening of bankruptcy proceedings, e.g. proof of insolvency and the meaning of insolvency (for example, whether negative net worth is sufficient in addition to inability to pay debts as they fall due) will usually be lex fori and not, for example, any foreign rules prevailing at the foreign domicile of the debtor. But the opening of foreign bankruptcy proceedings may be a sufficient ground for local proceedings. In practice the insolvency is usually obvious.

Compositions and rehabilitations

14–9 The jurisdictional rules for compositions and rehabilitations tend to follow the rules for bankruptcy proceedings, though with some important differences. The US Chapter 11 proceedings and the French *redressement* apply to all debtors, whether domestic or foreign, in accordance with the normal jurisdictional rules for final bankruptcies. But in England, the administration procedure (generally) applies only to British companies. The Japanese position is distinctive: see para 11–6.

Where the rehabilitation jurisdiction applies to foreign companies as well, there is much more scope for confrontation since parallel proceedings are possible in the case of the same company, One proceeding may be a final liquidation and the other a rehabilitation having the different objective of rescue. For example, typical features of rehabilitation which may not apply on final bankruptcy are: stays on security enforcement, subordination of the security to rehabilitation loans and contracts; stays on title finance repossessions; stays on insolvency set-off; stays on contract rescissions and lease forfeitures; and creditor voting to postpone maturities or write-down debt.

Insolvency jurisdiction in England

14–10 **Winding-up of companies** In England and many English-based countries the court has long-arm jurisdiction to wind-up an insolvent foreign company if there are local assets and also if there are persons (English or foreign) who would benefit from the winding-up order, even though there are no local assets of the company itself: there is no point in making a winding-up order to wind up nothing or if creditors have no local advantage. The long-arm jurisdiction is discretionary. It is immaterial that the company did not carry on business in England or that the creditors who stand to benefit are foreign. There are limitations on the English jurisdiction in the case of companies in Scotland and Northern Ireland.

In *Re Compania Merabello San Nicholas SA* [1973] 1 Ch 75, a one-ship Panamanian company had only one asset in England – a claim against an English protection and indemnity mutual insurance club to be indemnified against liability incurred to a shipper for cargo damage. Under the Third Parties (Rights against Insurers) Act 1930 the shipper was entitled to a direct leapfrog claim against the insurer only if a winding up order was made against the company. The company had an asset within the jurisdiction, but it was not one which would come into the hands of the liquidator to be applied towards payment of the company's creditors in general. It would instead vest in a particular creditor and that was indeed the purpose of the shipper's winding-up petition. *Held*: there was jurisdiction to make the order. There was an asset and the petitioning creditor would benefit.

In *Re Eloc Electro-optieck and Communicatie BV* [1981] 3 WLR 176, a Dutch company employed two United States citizens to carry on its business in England. The company had no place of business or assets in England. The two employees were dismissed. They could claim redundancy compensation from the government only if the company was wound up. *Held*: the court had jurisdiction to wind up the company on the petition of the employees since the company had carried on business in England The winding up would produce an asset to pay the employees.

In *Re a Company (No 00359 of 1987)* [1987] 3 WLR 339, a bank lent US$13m to a Liberian company controlled by Greek interests in order to enable the company to finance the acquisition of a new ship. After defaults in payments under the loan agreement, the loan was called in. The bank subsequently obtained judgment in the English courts for the loan. The company had no assets in England. If an order were made, the liquidator would seek to recover from the company's directors (some of whom were resident in England) for fraudulent or wrongful trading. Those amounts would be available for the company's creditors, including the bank. *Held*: the court had jurisdiction if there was a sufficient connection between the case and England and if there was a reasonable possibility that creditors would benefit from the winding up. The connection with England existed because (in particular) the loan agreement was entered into and fell to be performed in England and the company had carried on business in England directly or through agents.

See also *International Westminster Bank plc v Okeanos Maritime Corpn* [1987] 3 All ER 137; *Re Real Estate Development Co* [1991] BCLC 210.

There is also jurisdiction to wind up insolvent foreign companies which have already been dissolved abroad – a jurisdiction stemming from cases on Russian companies dissolved after the 1917 Russian Revolution.

The English courts have jurisdiction to wind up companies incorporated locally. This applies even if the company has no business or assets in England and even though insolvency proceedings have been commenced in a foreign country where most of the assets are: *Re Suresnes Racecourse Ltd* (1890) 90 LT Jo 55 (most of assets in France; French liquidator had been appointed); *North Australian Territory Co Ltd v Goldsborough, Mort & Co Ltd* (1889) 61 LT 716 (most of assets in Australia; liquidation had commenced in Australia).

14–11 **Bankruptcy of individuals** As regards individuals, the English courts have statutory jurisdiction to bankrupt an individual if the debtor is domiciled in England (even though he lives abroad), or was resident in England in the last three years, or has carried on business in England in the last three years, or (under a long-arm rule) was personally present in England when the petition was presented – the "Heathrow petition". Nationality is irrelevant. The granting of the petition is discretionary (IA 1986 s 266), particularly in a long-arm case. For example, the courts may well refuse jurisdiction if the debtor is only temporarily in England and has no other connection with England if it would be unjust to assume jurisdiction. If a debtor has carried on business in England prior to the three-year period but his debts remain unpaid within the three-year period, he is still deemed to be carrying on business in England while his debts remain unpaid: IA 1986 s 265. There is much case law interpreting these concepts under former bankruptcy legislation and in relation to the ordinary civil jurisdiction of the courts and tax litigation. It is thought that similar concepts will apply in many other English-based jurisdictions.

14–12 **Administration of companies** The English rehabilitative administration procedure probably does not apply to foreign incorporated companies. However an administration has been ordered in respect of a foreign company under the special provisions of IA 1986, s 426 relating to insolvency co-operation with designated countries: *Re Sunar Hausenman Inc* (1989) unreported. See also *Re Dallhold* [1992] BCC 994.

Insolvency jurisdiction in Continental Europe

14–13 **France** The courts will exercise jurisdiction if the debtor's registered office or principal place of business is in France (Art 1 of Decree of December 27, 1985) or if it has a local branch.

A further ground of jurisdiction is provided by CC Art 14 whereby a French national who is a creditor may institute bankruptcy proceedings against any debtor, including a foreign company with no assets in France.

The previous case law upholding the proposition has been doubted by commentators because BA 1985 requires a period of observation and there cannot be an investigation and execution of assets unless there are officers of the company within France. Jurisdiction has been assumed where the debtor has assets in France.

These jurisdictional rules apply whether or not the procedure is a final liquidation or a rehabilitation (*redressement judiciaire*). The French procedure is a unified procedure whereby the debtor must first go through an observation period before a decision is made to continue, transfer or liquidate.

Germany It has been held that by virtue of BA 1879 s 238 the courts have bankruptcy jurisdiction over a debtor who carries out business transactions in Germany, but if the proceeding is ancillary it may be limited to German assets. A new German bankruptcy act is in the process of being enacted.

Italy The main stream of case law holds that there must be assets in Italy and the mere fact that an obligation is undertaken and is to be performed in Italy is not enough.

Insolvency jurisdiction in the United States

In the United States, BC 1978 s 109 (a) provides that a US bankruptcy proceeding (including the rehabilitation Chapter 11) can be commenced if the debtor (1) has a residence in the US; (2) is domiciled in the US; (3) has a place of business in the US (which need not be the debtor's principal place of business), or (4) has property located in the US.   **14–14**

US nationality is not enough. Mere physical presence of an individual debtor in the US without any of the above connexity links is not enough – contrary to the English rule.

Any unfairness to the debtor is controlled by the court's discretion – the doctrine of abstention (see BC 1978 s 305). For example, *In Matter of Berthoud*, 231 Fed 529 (1916) the court abstained when the debtor had a bank account in New York but the debtor and the creditors were foreign.

In *Canadian Southern Railroad Co v Gebbard*, 109 US 113 (1895) the Supreme Court conferred US recognition on a Canadian statutory reorganisation of a railroad so that bondholders might be treated equally.

Insolvency jurisdiction in Japan

Japan espouses the Germanic jurisdictional rule whereby the location of assets in Japan grounds jurisdiction over the owner of the assets, irrespective of whether the claim concerns those assets. In Japan, the corporate reorgan-   **14–15** isation law applies to limited companies (*Kabushiki-kaisha*) but is effective only with respect to the company's properties existing in Japan: CRL Art 4. Reciprocally, reorganisation proceedings commenced in a foreign country are not effective with respect to properties situated in Japan: Art 4.2. For this purpose obligations of which demand can be made by way of judicial proceedings under the Code of Civil Procedure are deemed to be situate in Japan: Art 4.3.

Insolvency jurisdiction in Scandinavia

14–16   **Denmark** BA 1977 s 3 confers bankruptcy jurisdiction on the court of the district from which the debtor's business activity is carried on, meaning the main office from which the business is administered as opposed to the main plant. In *Clover Trading Co*, UfR 1982, p 161 H, the court held that it had jurisdiction over a Liberian registered company whose business had been performed solely through a company in Denmark. Permanent residence in Denmark is enough. But if the debtor does not have his "general forum" in Denmark, the mere presence of Danish assets is not enough: *Laurits Michaelsen* UfR 1982, p 220 V. Personal presence is not usually enough. The mere carrying on of a business locally is usually insufficient, if not the main office, so that ancillary bankruptcies would be unusual in Denmark.

Finland BA 1858 s 1 vests bankruptcy jurisdiction at the defendant's domicile. The presence of assets in Finland is enough. Finnish citizenship of the debtor is sufficient — suit at his most recent residence in Finland. Personal presence is enough. Carrying on business locally is insufficient, if not the main office.

Norway BA 1984 s 146 vests bankruptcy jurisdiction in the court where the debtor has its main business establishment. It is doubtful whether the mere presence of assets is enough. Nationality is irrelevant. Personal presence is not usually enough. Carrying on business locally is insufficient if not the main office so that ancillary bankruptcies are not likely in Norway.

14–17   **Sweden** The main jurisdictional rules for both bankruptcies and compositions (*tvangsackord*) are based on the civil jurisdiction rules: see BA 1987 chapter 2 s 1(1), Composition Act 1970 s 6 and Chapter 10 of the Swedish Code of Judicial Procedure 1942. In the case of natural persons, the Swedish courts have jurisdiction if they reside there or, if they have no habitual residence, where they are physically present or, in the case of Swedish citizens abroad, where they last resided in Sweden. In the case of a company, the Swedish courts have jurisdiction if the seat of a board is there or, if no permanent seat, if administrative decisions are taken in Sweden.

As to long-arm jurisdiction, the mere presence of assets of the debtor in Sweden is sufficient, regardless of their value, so long as not fictitious: this is because BA 1987 incorporates the "toothbrush" jurisdiction for ordinary civil suits on debt obligations.

Further, the courts have jurisdiction if the bankruptcy relates to a contract or debt incurred in Sweden.

> In *Katja of Sweden*, NJA 1980, 340, S Ct, a debtor resident in the US who owned no property in Sweden incurred a tax debt in Sweden. The object of the proceedings was to avoid a transfer of Swedish property sold by the debtor as a fraudulent transfer. *Held*: the Swedish courts had bankruptcy jurisdiction, since BA 1987 incorporated the civil jurisdiction rules for debts contained in the Swedish Code of Civil Procedure.

In Sweden, as in English-based and Germanic countries, the nationality and residence of the creditor are irrelevant.

It is understood that the Swedish courts are slow to apply concepts of forum non conveniens to Swedish bankruptcies even in the case of the long-arm jurisdiction. Perhaps the situation is changing.

The same Swedish jurisdiction rules as apply to bankruptcies also apply to compulsory compositions (the *tvangsackord*).

Most of the information in these chapters on insolvency conflicts in Scandinavian law is derived from Michael Bogdan, "International Bankruptcy Law in Scandinavia", 34 ICLQ 50 (1985)

Insolvency jurisdiction in Latin America

Argentina There is the usual jurisdiction over domiciliaries, whether individuals or companies and (broadly) over businesses having their principal establishment (in the sense of controlling centre) in Argentina: see BA 1972 Art 3. Local assets are enough to ground bankruptcy jurisdiction: BA 1972 Art 2. But it may be that transitory assets are not enough, e.g. jewellery of a person in transit. The location of intangibles in Argentina may be enough, e.g. a debt owing by an Argentine company to a foreign creditor may ground jurisdiction over that creditor. **14–18**

Bolivia Local assets are not enough and local autonomous administration in the form of a branch office is required: Com C Art 1492.

Honduras It seems that more than local assets is required, e.g. a local autonomous branch office: Com C Art 1330.

Mexico Mere local assets may not be enough: normally it seems that a local autonomous branch office is necessary: LQ3P Art 13.

For further details as to Latin America, see Fletcher (ed) *Cross-Border Insolvency: Comparative Dimensions,* UK National Committee of Comparative Law (1990) on which the above summary and summaries of Latin American law elsewhere in these chapters on insolvency are based.

Whether principal bankruptcy covers global property

14–19   Where the bankruptcy proceedings are domiciliary – the company's domicile or the individual bankrupt's main place of residence – the insolvency administrator is generally required to collect all the bankrupt's property and to realise it for the benefit of creditors. This is the doctrine of the universality of the bankruptcy. If all creditors can prove locally, they ought to have access to all the property. The international trend in the case of companies is that the duty to collect applies to all the company's property everywhere and not just to local property.

The practical ability of an insolvency administrator to recover foreign assets depends upon whether the state where the assets are located will recognise the status of the administrator as the person entitled to recover the assets.

England An English liquidation impresses the company's property everywhere with a trust for the benefit of persons interested (IA 1986 s 144). But the court may limit the administrator's duties to collect global property in the case of an ancillary insolvency. Similarly an English individual bankruptcy operates as an assignment of all the debtor's property everywhere (IA 1986 s 283; Dicey Rule 161). This includes foreign immovables (unlike the English view of a foreign individual bankruptcy).

United States BC 1978 s 541(a) provides that the bankrupt's estate is composed of property owned by the debtor "wherever located and by whomever held".

14–20   **Argentina** Where the bankrupt is a domiciliary, the Argentine bankruptcy includes all his assets globally.

Denmark The administrator must endeavour to collect global assets, regardless of whether the bankruptcy is domiciliary or non-domiciliary, but the obligation to collect in the case of non-domiciliary bankruptcies will be unusual since the Danish bankruptcy jurisdiction does not usually contemplate ancillary jurisdiction.

Finland It is unclear whether a bankruptcy covers universal property, but perhaps it will do so in the case of a domiciliary bankruptcy.

Norway It seems that the administrator must attempt to collect global assets, regardless of whether the bankruptcy is domiciliary or non-domiciliary, but a non-domiciliary bankruptcy will be unusual because the Norwegian bankruptcy jurisdiction does not normally contemplate ancillary jurisdiction.

Sweden The best opinion of the authors is that a domiciliary bankruptcy is not purely territorial and that the Swedish administrator is under a duty to endeavour to obtain control of foreign assets.

> In *Prosecutor v Bendes,* NJA 1956, 1, S Ct, the bankrupt disposed of assets abroad while subject to Swedish bankruptcy proceedings. *Held*: the bankrupt could be convicted of a punishable offence.

However, Swedish ancillary bankruptcies may be limited to territorial assets.

A few countries limit the bankruptcy to territorial property, e.g. Japan's BA s 3, and a larger number may do so if the local proceeding is ancillary, e.g. England, Germany and Sweden.

CHAPTER 15

INSOLVENCY CONFLICT OF LAWS: RECOGNITION OF FOREIGN INSOLVENCIES

Main options

15–1   If bankruptcy proceedings have been opened at the domicile, the insolvency administrator wishing to collect foreign assets of the debtor must be able (1) to freeze local attachments of the foreign assets, (2) to freeze dealings with the assets by the debtor and (3) to compel a turnover of the foreign assets or their proceeds to the home forum for distribution to creditors. The usual effect of the home proceedings is that the debtor's directors are removed (so that they cannot manage the assets), an individual debtor is dispossessed, and creditor attachments and executions are frozen.

An insolvency administrator has three broad options:

1.   He could attempt to collect foreign assets locally without local proceedings, with or without the aid of the debtor, e.g. by procuring an assignment or power of attorney from the debtor. He would have to be recognised and the home forum freeze on attachments and on the debtor's right of free disposition must have extraterritorial effect.

2.   He could seek the aid of the local court, e.g. by having himself recognised as representing the debtor.

3.   He could commence bankruptcy proceedings locally. These proceedings could either be an ancillary proceeding, or a full bankruptcy proceeding. If a local bankruptcy is instituted, then this is likely to attract local bankruptcy laws, e.g. as to the validity of security, set-off, preferential transfers, priority of unsecured debts and so on.

15–2   Internationally, there is perhaps an increasing tendency to recognise the right of a foreign administrator from the bankrupt's home forum to collect local assets, and an increasing tendency – at least in the legally advanced states – to recognise the freeze on creditor executions, although this may be delayed until local recognition proceedings are taken. But most states will allow concurrent proceedings to be opened, whether an ancillary proceeding or a full bankruptcy, so that in practice the unilateral efforts of the foreign administrator are quickly overtaken by local proceedings which guillotine further attachments. But the effect of the local proceedings is to allow the local jurisdiction to give effect to its own bankruptcy law. The issues then are (1) to decide which law applies, e.g. to security, title finance, set-off, preferential transfers, reputed ownership, the veil of incorporation, compositions and so on; (2) to determine whether local creditors, particularly local priority creditors (taxes, employees) are paid first; and (3) to determine whether the local forum will turn over the local assets to the foreign forum which may go to pay creditors in a different order from that contemplated locally or which may go rather to finance a foreign rehabilitation proceeding as opposed to a final bankruptcy. Very often, if there are concurrent proceedings, the various liquidators settle the matter by pooling agreements, but these too generally have to be approved by creditors or the courts in the various jurisdictions under bankruptcy rules authorising compositions and settlements.

Recognition of home forum proceedings

There are degrees of recognition. The main recognition issues considered in this section are whether the home forum's insolvency administrator is recognised as the debtor's representative entitled to collect local assets, and whether, in the eyes of the local forum, the debtor's right to deal with them and creditor attachments are frozen by the home forum bankruptcy order. The recognition of the home forum's substantive bankruptcy rules are considered separately, e.g. recognition of security, preferential transfers, set-off and director liability.   **15–3**

As to bankruptcy stays on creditor executions, the initial question is whether the freeze applies globally or whether it is purely territorial. The solution follows the usual lines as to whether the home forum treats its bankruptcy laws as having purely territorial effect or universal effect, subject to the practical problems of having the home court's order recognised everywhere in the world.

If the freeze on creditor executions purports to be global, then the home forum has indirect methods of having its views enforced, e.g. equalisation, injunction against creditors subject to the court's jurisdiction, and contempt of court penalties: para 16–1 *et seq.*

Total non-recognition Some countries are not prepared to recognise a bankruptcy at the principal foreign forum or to give it any local effect over local assets in the absence of a treaty.   **15–4**

The effect therefore is that the home forum's administrator has no status to collect assets in the foreign forum, that local attachments of local assets are not stayed, that the debtor can still deal with, dispose of or mortgage his assets in the foreign forum, and there can be no question of an investigation of the debtor's affairs and assets in the foreign forum. The home forum's representative must accordingly prevail upon the debtor to assist in the collection of local assets (see below) or, alternatively and more realistically, prevail upon a creditor to commence local bankruptcy proceedings. As mentioned above, in many countries the presence of local assets is enough to confer bankruptcy jurisdiction so that the bringing of local proceedings is not usually problematic from the jurisdictional point of view. But it attracts local bankruptcy law.

It appears that the following are among the countries which do not recognise foreign bankruptcies and the administrator has no power to collect local assets:

Argentina
Austria (prefers bilateral treaties)
Denmark (perhaps)
Norway (perhaps)

15–5   **Full or partial recognition** In a second group of countries, the domiciliary forum's insolvency proceedings achieve a measure of local recognition in terms of freezes on execution and collection, with or without local recognition proceedings. In order to achieve this limited recognition, it is generally true that certain basic conditions (dealt with in more detail below) are satisfied:

– the domiciliary forum had bankruptcy jurisdiction in the eyes of the foreign local forum. This generally means that the proceedings must have been opened at the debtor's domicile or the seat of a company or its principal place of business;

– the domiciliary forum's decree was final and conclusive;

– the domiciliary forum's decree does not conflict with the foreign local forum's views of public policy;

– (sometimes) proof of reciprocity.

As regards the powers of the domiciliary administrator to collect foreign assets, a distinction needs to be made between individual bankruptcies and corporate bankruptcies. In the case of an individual bankruptcy, the displacement of the bankrupt's powers to deal with his assets in favour of his administrator receives lesser recognition, perhaps because there is no embedded consensus rule that domicile governs capacity.

But whatever the position with regard to individual bankruptcies, the rationale for recognising a foreign liquidator of a company must be that he is the person who now is in control of the company and he is its manager: jurisdictions ought to look to the *lex societas* to determine the rightful manager. Commonly the directors will have been removed and so, if the liquidator is not recognised as being able to act, then nobody is left who can act for the company. It follows that an administrator appointed at the domicile of the company should be recognised as the legitimate representative entitled to control the property of the company everywhere.

The position ought to be the same in the case of corporate rehabilitation proceedings. Thus the English administration expressly constitutes the administrator as agent of the company, in effect its managing officer. The problem does not arise where the management stays in place, as in the US Chapter 11. An English court has recognised a US Chapter 11 proceeding over a Delaware corporation: *Felixstowe Dock & Ry Co v US Lines Inc* [1989] QB 360.

Provided the local conditions of recognition are met, broadly there are four degrees of recognition in this group of states. The detail is reviewed later.   **15–6**

1. **Immediate recognition without proceedings** The foreign local forum recognises the home forum's bankruptcy immediately without formal recognition proceedings locally. This recognition entitles the foreign insolvency representative to collect local assets, and it freezes creditor attachments of local assets and the powers of the debtor to dispose of local property. The effect is to recognise the immediate universality of the home principal bankruptcy so far as property of the estate is concerned. This is the general rule in countries such as **Belgium, El Salvador** (Com C Art 511), **Germany** and **Luxembourg**. It is also the general rule in **England** and **English-based states** and in the US, subject to qualifications, but in all cases the opening of local ancillary proceedings is usually preferable.

2. **Retroactive recognition proceedings** The foreign local forum requires formal recognition proceedings to be taken locally before the foreign representative can collect local assets but the recognition order is retroactive for the purpose of avoiding attachments of local assets by creditors after the opening of the foreign home forum's proceeding which imposes a freeze on attachments. The debtor's dispositions are also nullified. The result is that creditors and transferees may have to disgorge assets, subject presumably to good faith defences. The order prevents the debtor from disposing of his assets locally. The effect is to recognise the immediate universality of the principal bankruptcy so far

as the property of the estate is concerned but to require a formal local recognition procedure. Retroactivity is or may be available in **France**, and possibly in **Greece** and **Italy**.

3. **Non-retroactive recognition proceedings** The foreign local forum requires formal recognition proceedings before the foreign representative can collect local assets and this recognition order is not retroactive, so that prior attachments by creditors of local assets in defiance of the home forum's freeze and prior dealings with the assets by the debtor are effective. This is often a serious disadvantage because the *exequatur* process is commonly costly and time-consuming, e.g. six months, so that in the meantime assets may be dissipated. This is the position in **Mexico, Honduras, Panama** and **Colombia**, although it is possible that in some cases retroactivity is allowed. The effect is to recognise the universality of the principal bankruptcy as regards the property of the debtor but only from the time that the formal local recognition order is made.

4. **Recognition limited to asset collection** The foreign forum is not prepared to recognise the bankruptcy at the principal forum or to give it any effect over local assets so that debtor transfers and creditor attachments are not stayed. But the foreign forum may grant the insolvency representative powers to collect local property, especially in the case of a company where the directors no longer have powers of control. This appears to be the position in **Denmark** (possibly – position unclear), **Finland** (possibly – position unclear), the **Netherlands, Norway** (possibly – position unclear) and **Sweden**.

Conditions of recognition

15–7   A number of conditions generally have to be satisfied before there can be any question of recognition in those countries which confer full or partial recognition. These are primarily: (a) jurisdiction of the domiciliary forum; (b) domiciliary forum decree is final and conclusive; (c) no conflict with public policy; and (d) (sometimes) reciprocity. Some of these may now be examined in summary.

Conditions of recognition: jurisdiction In the case of companies, it seems to be a near universal rule that the foreign forum will recognise the home bankruptcy proceedings only if those proceedings are instituted at the main seat or domicile of the company. In the case of individuals, the test has to be more flexible but domicile and principal place of residence are key factors. The general trend therefore is for foreign states to require a higher threshold of connexity for the purposes of recognition of the jurisdiction of the domiciliary state than the foreign state claims so far as local proceedings are concerned. In particular it is unusual for foreign states to recognise long-arm jurisdictional bases even though they claim them for themselves, e.g. mere presence of assets, mere fleeting presence of the debtor, or the nationality or residence of the *creditor*. The general effect of this is that *ancillary* proceedings in the home state will often not be recognised in the foreign state.

Conditions of recognition: public policy Invariably a state will not recognise   15-8
a foreign bankruptcy proceeding if it conflicts with local ideas of public
policy. For example:

- **Expropriation** Where the bankruptcy is in reality a concealed confiscation without compensation, foreign courts may see through the transparent veil of the false bankruptcy and apply their own rules as to non-recognition of foreign expropriatory decrees purporting to affect local property. Few states give effect to foreign expropriations purporting to transfer assets outside the territorial sovereignty of the expropriating state. The international law of expropriation is reviewed in another volume in this series of works on international financial law.

  In the Swedish Supreme Court case of *Horowitz v Lehner*, NJA 1942, 385, the Nazis confiscated assets of a Jewish firm, and formally placed it under a Nazi administrator and declared it bankrupt. The administrator and the exiled Jewish owner claimed assets in Sweden. *Held*: the Jewish owner was entitled to the assets. The Nazi measures were a confiscation and could have no effect on assets in Sweden. The bankruptcy was irrelevant.

- **Natural justice** It may also be a public policy requirement that the debtor was duly served with process and that the rules of natural justice were observed, e.g. the debtor had a right to be heard. This requirement may be dispensed with in the case of an absconding debtor who has effectively surrendered his right to due process: see *Re Behrends* (1865) 12 LT 149. Naturally it is to be expected that a decree obtained by fraud will receive short shrift abroad.

- **Taxes** Recognition may be refused if the main creditor in the home pro-   15-9
  ceedings is the taxman. The problem with this approach is that the claims by foreign insolvency administrators whose foreign bankruptcy proceedings are recognised will almost invariably be used to pay foreign taxes which are commonly a priority claim on the assets. If the rule were rigorously applied, a forum administrator would never have title to claim foreign assets. An alternative possibility would be for the turnover of assets to be subject to a condition that they are not to be used to pay foreign taxes. Such conditions have been imposed in other contexts,

e.g. an Australian court has allowed assets to be turned over provided they are not used to pay secured creditors in the foreign state in circumstances where the security was void in the state where the assets were: *Re Australian Federal Life & General Insurance Co Ltd* (1931) VLR 317.

The English rule is perhaps that the claim will not be admitted if the moneys are to be used solely to pay the foreign revenue claim but will be admitted if there are both revenue and non-revenue claims. If a local administrator in England seeks to recover assets in England to remit to a foreign country for the purposes only of enabling a foreign administrator to pay death duties, it is considered that generally the claim would be unenforceable in England. See *Bath v British & Malayan Trustees Ltd* [1962] 2 NSWR 114; *Jones v Borland*, 1969(4) SA 29. Contrast *Re Hollins*, 139 NYS 713 (1930) affirmed 106 NE 1034 (1940).

In **Ireland** an insolvency representative may not recover a claim which he would use for the purpose of satisfying a foreign state's claim for taxes due from the company.

In *Peter Buchan Ltd v McVey* (1950) Supreme Court of Eire, reported as a note in *Government of India v Taylor* (1955) AC 491 and cited with approval by Lord Keith at 510, the liquidator of a Scottish company sought to recover assets from a director who had absconded to Eire. The dominant creditor of the company was the UK Inland Revenue for unpaid taxes so that the assets would be used to pay these taxes. *Held*: the liquidator's claim could not be enforced since it was an indirect claim for the taxes of a foreign state.

An **Isle of Man** court has given assistance to a foreign court even though the assets would partly be used to pay foreign taxes: *Re Tucker* (1988) FLR 1988. A **Scottish** court has remitted assets of a deceased's estate which would be used partly to pay Swedish inheritance tax: *Scottish National Orchestra v Thomson's Executors*, 1969 SLT 325. In **Australia** in *Ayres v Evans* (1981) 39 ALR 129, the court allowed a New Zealand trustee to recover Australian assets even though 60 per cent of the moneys claimed were due to New Zealand revenue authorities.

Similarly in the **South African** case of *Priestley v Clegg*, 1985 (3) SA 955, the South African court lent assistance to an English trustee in bankruptcy even though the UK Revenue debts were estimated at 94 per cent of all claims in the English proceedings.

15–10 **Conditions for recognition: reciprocity** Some countries require that the foreign forum where the proceedings are first instituted would recognise the recognising court's bankruptcy proceedings in similar circumstances. Reciprocity is not usually a requirement in England (and hence probably many English-based countries or in the US), but is in Belgium and Switzerland.

Concurrent proceedings in foreign local forum

Even if the home forum's proceeding is recognised, it is generally true that   **15–11**
this will not prevent creditors from initiating a bankruptcy proceeding in the
foreign ancillary forum so that there can be, and often are, parallel proceedings in two jurisdictions. Apart from treaties, it is believed that few, if any,
courts adopt the theory of the "unity of bankruptcy" whereby all creditors
must resort to the bankruptcy at the debtor's domicile or principal place of
business and no other foreign court has jurisdiction to bankrupt the debtor.
Hence most countries allow local concurrent proceedings. This being so, it
is one of the main objects of private international law in this area to regulate
the conflicts where there are parallel proceedings and two or more pools of
assets.

The main initial object is to preserve the assets from creditor attachments
and the debtor's powers of disposition and then hopefully to collect them
for return to the home forum. But, as mentioned, the effect of a full ancillary
bankruptcy proceeding may attract the full local bankruptcy regime, e.g. as
to preferential transfers; compulsory investigation of the debtor's affairs;
set-off; security; stays on the rescission of contracts or forfeiture of leases;
compulsory post-order compositions; recovery from defaulting directors
and bankruptcy penalties and disqualifications; the priority of preferential
creditors (taxes, employees); the proof and allowance of unsecured claims;
the conversion of foreign currency claims into local currency; the deferment
or subordination of certain creditors; and local discharge of the debtor. On
all these matters, the local forum may have very different views from the
foreign home forum.

Full and ancillary proceedings The concurrent proceedings may be either an   **15–12**
ancillary proceeding or a full bankruptcy proceeding. An ancillary proceeding, which is generally limited to local property and allows a turnover of
recoveries to the main forum after payment of local priority creditors and
(sometimes) creditors proving locally, is found in **England** and many other
English-based countries, such as Australia and New Zealand; **Switzerland**;
and the **United States.** See below.

Key questions are the extent to which the effects of a full bankruptcy
apply, whether the local administrator will turn over assets to the foreign
administrator and whether the local priority creditors (taxman, employees,
etc.) must first be paid. These questions have received much attention in
English-based states, Switzerland and the United States, amongst others.

Whether the local bankruptcy is a full bankruptcy or an ancillary bankruptcy, a question arises as to whether all creditors can claim in the local
proceedings or whether only local creditors can claim. If all creditors can
claim (which is the usual case), then there must be some mechanism in both

bankruptcies for compelling creditors to bring into account what they have received in the other bankruptcy. This involves the concept of equalisation discussed at para 16–1 *et seq*.

Turnover may be conditional. An example of a conditional turnover is an Australian case which allowed a turnover on condition that assets were not used to pay secured claims which were void locally: *Re Australian Federal Life and Gnl Insurance Co Ltd* (1931) VLR 317 (Victoria). In a New York case, small creditors were entitled to file the claims with an agent locally: see *Re Stoddard & Norske Lloyd Insurance Co*, 151 NE 159 (NY Court of Appeals 1926).

Recognition in England and English-based countries

15–13　**Generally** English attitudes to recognition differ according to whether the insolvency is of an individual or a company. But in all cases the English courts may refuse to recognise the foreign bankruptcy or liquidation if (probably, although there is little supporting authority):

– the foreign proceedings are not final; or

– the foreign proceedings constitute a fraud (in the sense of dishonest conduct) or are in breach of natural justice, e.g. the debtor was not given notice of the proceedings, although this is not conclusive: see *Re Behrends* (1865) 12 LT 149 (Hamburg bankruptcy without service on absconding debtor outside Germany not a breach of natural justice); or

– the foreign proceedings are contrary to public policy, e.g. they are an attempt to enforce a foreign penal or revenue demand.

Reciprocity is not a requirement for English recognition: see *Williams v Rice* (1926) 3 DLR 225 (Manitoba).

15–14　**Recognition of foreign jurisdiction** A liquidation at the place of incorporation will always be recognised in England: see for example *Baden, Delvaux & Lecuit v Société Générale pour Favorisor le Développement etc.* [1983] BCLC 325. In the case of companies it is perhaps the case that a foreign liquidation will not be recognised unless it is instituted under the law of the place of incorporation – unless the liquidation at the place of incorporation is improbable or impossible, e.g. because the company has been dissolved there. In other words an ancillary foreign liquidation will not be recognised in England. But it is possible that a liquidation at the principal place of business abroad will be recognised in England in an appropriate case, e.g. where the company is a mere brass-plate at its place of incorporation. But England will probably not recognise a foreign liquidation of an English incorporated company with the result that the foreign liquidator will have no power to collect assets in England: see *N Australian Territory Co v Goldsborough Mort & Co* (1889) 61 LT 716.

The disadvantage of recognising liquidation only at the country of incorporation is that many companies are incorporated in one jurisdiction, but carry on their principal business elsewhere. This is true of tax-haven countries or shipping jurisdictions such as Panama and Liberia. It would seem odd therefore to refuse recognition of a liquidation where the main assets are located.

Recovery of property Foreign liquidators appointed under English-recog-   **15–15**
nised foreign proceedings have been held to be entitled to recover the company's property in England: *Macaulay v Guaranty Trust Co of New York* (1927) 44 TLR 99 (Delaware company).

In the same vein, courts in **Ontario** have recognised the ability of a Luxembourg administrator to sue in Ontario.

> In *Re ITT* (1975) 58 DLR (3d) 55, a Luxembourg legal entity known as an "indivision", which is a type of mutual investment fund, went into liquidation in Luxembourg. The Luxembourg administrator sought to recover property in Ontario. *Held*: the effect of the Luxembourg liquidation was to vest the Ontario assets of ITT in the liquidators who could accordingly sue for them in Ontario.

After-acquired property As regards companies, a recognised foreign liquidator can recover after-acquired property of the foreign company in England. But if a subsequent English liquidation has been commenced it is thought that only the English liquidator will be entitled to recover after-acquired property in England.

Creditor attachments In England the principle developed in relation to   **15–16**
foreign bankruptcies of individuals is that an English execution which takes effect after a foreign bankruptcy assignment (where that bankruptcy is recognised in accordance with the English recognition rules) will be ineffective in England except so far as it relates to immovables in England. This is because, if England recognises the foreign assignment, it recognises that the assignment has the effect of depriving the individual of his movables everywhere so that there is nothing to attach. No formal recognition proceedings are necessary.

As regards foreign *companies*, the position is possibly different and the English courts might not restrain English executions even though winding up proceedings have been commenced at the foreign domicile of the company.

In *Re Suidair International Airways Ltd* [1951] 1 Ch 165, a South African incorporated company carried on business in England. A winding up order was made in South Africa. Thereafter an English creditor levied execution on the company's property in England. Subsequently a winding-up order was made in England. *Held*: although the execution was void under South African law, this was not material in deciding whether the creditor should be allowed to keep the fruits of his English execution against the English liquidator.

But in the *Felixstowe* case summarised below, the court would not have permitted creditors to attach a bank account on a final judgment in defiance of a US Chapter 11 stay. The *Suidair* case is considered doubtful. In *Felixstowe* the court permitted a conservatory injunction (the Mareva injunction) but on the basis that the foreign US proceedings would result in discrimination against the English creditors. The case was a good example of conflict between a final bankruptcy and a rehabilitation proceeding.

In *Felixstowe Dock & Ry Co v US Lines Inc* [1988] 2 All ER 77, a US company was subject to Chapter 11 proceedings. Creditors sought a Mareva injunction in England against English assets (a credit balance at a bank) contrary to the US freeze on attachment proceedings. *Held*: the potential prejudice to the English creditors if the injunction were discharged outweighed the prejudice to the debtor company if the injunction were continued. The court applied its normal balancing policies to injunctions. Under the Chapter 11 plan of reorganisation the intention was for the debtor company to close down its European business and concentrate its activities in North America. The reorganisation plan would therefore inevitably give preferential treatment to North American creditors if it was to be successful. If the credit balance in the English bank account were transferred to the US, they would be used for that purpose, to the prejudice of the English creditors.

The interests of the debtor company and its other creditors would not, on the other hand, be adversely affected by continuance of the injunction. The credit balance would remain frozen at the bank where the account was held. In accordance with established law, the court would not allow the English creditors to obtain a garnishee order against the bank in order to enforce any judgment they might obtain if they would thereby get priority over other creditors. Moreover, the judge made it a condition of continuing the Mareva injunction that the creditors undertake not to take any steps to release the frozen funds without giving a reasonable period of notice to the debtor company. In that way, the debtor company would be able to apply for a winding-up order in England before the funds were taken by the English creditors. The funds could then be administered and distributed in an English winding up ancillary to the US Chapter 11 proceedings. Hence the court struck a balance. The creditors were not to be prejudiced by a foreign proceeding which was not a process of universal distribution but rather a process of deliberately preferential distribution. On the other hand, the creditors would not be permitted to proceed to execution. To prevent them from gaining an unfair advantage over other creditors, an ancillary winding-up in England would be conducted. Foreign creditors, including US creditors, would be able under English law to prove in the English proceedings.

In **Manitoba** the courts will give effect to a foreign bankruptcy freeze on   **15–17** executions if that foreign bankruptcy is recognised in Manitoba.

> In *Brand v Green* (1900) 13 Man R 101, a New York corporation went into receivership. A week later creditors attached debts of the corporation in Manitoba. *Held*: the prior insolvency in New York precluded the later attachment of assets in Manitoba.

The courts in **South Africa** have stayed local executions in defiance of an earlier English liquidation order in respect of an English company: *Allen & Shaw v King*, 1912 CPD 115.

Concurrent proceedings Where the principal liquidation is proceeding at the   **15–18** main forum of the place of incorporation, the English courts may order an ancillary liquidation with limitations on the liquidator's powers. The courts must have jurisdiction over the debtor in accordance with the rules already discussed.

The English courts may prefer instead simply to recognise the foreign administrator's right to recover the assets locally.

> In *Re Matheson Brothers Ltd* (1884) 27 CLD 225, a New Zealand company was being wound up in New Zealand. Creditors petitioned to wind up in England. *Held*: no winding-up in England, but the court would accept an undertaking of the company's directors not to dispose of the English assets.

In the **Singapore** case of *Tong Aik (Far East) Ltd v Eastern Minerals & Trading (1959) Ltd* (1965) 2 MLJ 149, the court refused to wind up a Malaysian company on the ground that the Malaysian court was more appropriate.

The general approach of the English courts however is to order an ancil-   **15–19** lary winding-up in order to protect the assets in England. A local winding-up increases the costs.

There are numerous cases going back to the nineteenth century where the English courts have declared their proceedings to be ancillary to the main proceedings in a foreign country: see for example the co-operation between English, Scottish and Queensland courts in *Re Queensland Mercantile Agency Co Ltd* (1888) 58 LT 878.

> In *Re Federal Bank of Australia Ltd* (1893) 62 LJ Ch 561, a company in Victoria was in voluntary liquidation in Victoria and a compulsory winding-up

order was made in South Australia. The company had a branch and assets in England. *Held*: the English court could order a winding-up in England, but limited the power of the Official Receiver to getting in English assets and setting a list of English creditors. See also the Australian case of *Re Alfred Shaw & Co Ltd* (1897) 8 QLJ 93.

The English ancillary procedure and the degree of co-operation depends entirely on the circumstances and the courts have a flexible discretion. The usual procedure in the case of an English ancillary winding-up is that the English liquidator is restricted to collecting the English assets and settling a list of creditors in England: *Re Hibernian Merchants Ltd* [1958] Ch 76. But foreign and home creditors can usually prove pari passu so that the English assets are available to creditors generally. The English assets are not ear-marked solely for English creditors, other than preferred creditors who are paid first after secured creditors. If a creditor has proved abroad, then equality is established by the rule that he must bring his foreign dividends into account in proving locally. If there are surplus assets in England, it is probably the case that the English liquidator may remit them to the foreign liquidator. If there are conflicting claims for assets from two foreign liquidators, the English court should conduct its own winding-up.

In the Manitoba case of *Re National Benefit Assurance Co* [1927] 3 DLR 289, an English company was liquidated in England. An ancillary liquidation was commenced in Manitoba. *Held*: the Manitoba liquidation was ancillary to the English main liquidation. The Canadian assets should be paid over to the English liquidator after payment of preferred creditors in Canada and the costs of the ancillary liquidation. The court followed English authorities on the point.

15–20   The English courts have indicated in various dicta that they will not hand over the proceeds of English assets gathered in an English ancillary winding-up if the foreign proceedings are regarded as discriminatory of English creditors but it is as yet unclear what circumstances would be regarded as discriminatory.

The courts may not remit proceeds if they would then be caught by a charge which is invalid in England as the country of the ancillary jurisdiction but valid in the country of the main liquidation since this would defeat unsecured creditors in the country of the ancillary liquidation. This, at least, is the conclusion reached in Australia.

In *Re Northland Services Pty Ltd* (1978) 3 ACLR 371, a company incorporated in South Australia was being liquidated in that state. An ancillary liquidator was ordered in the Northern Territory. A charge valid in South Australia was void for lack of registration in the Northern Territory. *Held*: the Territory assets would be distributed to all creditors proving in the Territory (which could include S Australian creditors). They would not be remitted to S Australia because they would be caught by the S Australian charge.

Alternatively the court may accept an undertaking from the foreign liquidator not to use the remitted assets to pay the secured creditor: see *Re Australian Federal Life and General Insurance Co Ltd* (1931) VLR 317 (Victoria).

Scotland has recognised an ancillary liquidation at a place of business of the   **15–21** company other than at the place of incorporation: *Queensland Mercantile & Agency Co Ltd v Australian Investments Co Ltd* (1888) 15 R 935 (recognition of English ancillary liquidation of Australian company).

South Africa The Transvaal courts have followed principles similar to those applying to an English ancillary winding-up.

> In *Re African Farms Ltd*, 1906 TS 375, the Transvaal court recognised the authority of an English liquidator of an English company to deal with assets in the Transvaal, movable and immovable, subject to conditions protecting, inter alia, local preferred creditors.

Rehabilitation proceedings The English courts will recognise (though per- **15–22** haps partially) a foreign rehabilitation proceeding carried out under the laws of the company's place of incorporation. Thus a US Chapter 11 proceeding in respect of a US company has been recognised by the English and Hong Kong courts: *Felixstowe Dock & Ry Co v US Lines Inc* [1989] QB 360 (Delaware corporation in Chapter 11); *Modern Terminals v States Steamship Co* (1979) HKLR 512 (Nevada corporation in Chapter 11).

Special British reciprocal jurisdiction: IA 1986 s 426 There is a wider juris- **15–23** dictional base in IA 1986 s 426 which provides:

> "The courts having jurisdiction in relation to insolvency law in any part of the United Kingdom shall assist the courts having corresponding jurisdiction in any other part of the United Kingdom or any relevant authority or territory."

The relevant designated territories are: Channel Islands, Isle of Man, Anguilla, Australia, Bahamas, Bermuda, Botswana, Canada, Cayman Islands, Falkland Islands, Gibraltar, Hong Kong, Republic of Ireland, Montserrat, New Zealand, St Helena, Turks and Caicos Islands, Tuvalu, British Virgin Islands.

The court may apply the insolvency law "applicable to either court in relation to comparable matters falling within its jurisdiction" but the court "shall have regard in particular to the rules of private international law". In other words, the courts must have regard to the English conflicts rules applicable to bankruptcy and not slavishly apply the laws of the foreign bankruptcy forum, e.g. to preferences, set-off, freezes on security, directors liability and the like.

These provisions do not override the common law rules as to insolvency co-operation which continue to apply to debtors in other jurisdictions and indeed to the designated jurisdictions.

15–24   **Recognition of foreign jurisdiction to bankrupt individuals** As regards foreign bankruptcies of **individuals**, England will regard the foreign state as having jurisdiction over the debtor only if he was domiciled there, or submitted to the jurisdiction by petition or appearing or (possibly) if he was resident there or carried on business there: Dicey Rule 164. There are special rules for Scotland and Northern Ireland. Other long-arm bases will probably not be sufficient, such as those claimed by England for itself (presence in England at the time of the petition or English assets) and such as those not claimed by England but claimed elsewhere, e.g. nationality of the petitioning creditor (France).

15–25   **Effect of recognition** In England (apart from special rules for Scotland and Northern Ireland), a foreign individual bankruptcy within the jurisdiction of the home forum will, if the home forum's jurisdiction is recognised by England in accordance with the above rules, operate as an assignment of all movables in England (but not immovables) according to the earliest in date if the home bankruptcy assignment has extraterritorial effect according to the home forum's rules: Dicey Rules 166 to 168. The courts probably ignore the fact that the home bankruptcy may not strictly be an assignment but rather an assumption of control by the trustee in bankruptcy. No court declaration is required to give effect to this. The foreign administrator can however reap the fruits of land because the courts may be willing to appoint the foreign trustee as receiver of the income from English immovables: *Re Osborn* (1931–32) B & Cr 189, approved in *Re A Debtor* [1981] Ch 384. The court may also authorise the foreign trustee to sell the land and remit the proceeds abroad so that effectively immovables are covered and all that is required is a court order: *Re Kooperman* (1928) WN 101. The foreign trustee can also sue in England if he has a right to sue in his own name under foreign law.

The effect of the above rule is that (a) the foreign trustee is entitled to the assets in England, (b) an attachment in England by a creditor contrary to the foreign freeze on attachments is ineffective, and (c) the debtor can no longer mortgage or dispose of his movable assets located in England (other than exempt property).

A foreign trustee in bankruptcy of an individual appointed under an

English-recognised foreign proceeding has title to sue in England to recover the bankruptcy's movable property, e.g. a debt due to the bankrupt. There are numerous cases affirming this, stemming from the 19th century.

In *Alivon v Furnival* (1834) 1 Cr M&R 277, French syndics of a French merchant bankrupt in France sought to recover a French judgement debt in England. *Held*: the syndics were entitled to sue in England.

The court does not investigate whether the foreign bankruptcy rules are the same or different: the only relevant facts are whether the foreign court had jurisdiction in English eyes and whether the foreign administrator has the power under foreign law to collect assets abroad and to sue for them.

The same is true in *Scotland (Obers v Patons Trustees* (1897) 24 R 719)   **15–26**
and in *Australia (Re Young* (1955) St R Qd 254).

Courts in other countries have also assisted foreign trustees to gain control of local immovable property on the basis of principles similar to those applying in England, e.g. Scotland: *Araya v Coghill* 1921 SC 462; South Africa: *Re Free State Colliery Co* (1895) 12 Cape LJ 309; and Ireland: *Re Bolton* [1920] 2 IR 324.

After-acquired property In England the title of a foreign assignee to move-   **15–27**
ables in England also extends to after-acquired property of the bankrupt: see, for example, *Re a Debtor, Ex parte Viscount of the Royal Court of Jersey* (1981) Ch 384.

Concurrent individual bankruptcies in England The jurisdiction of the   **15–28**
English courts to bankrupt an individual debtor is not precluded by the fact that the debtor has already been adjudged bankrupt by the court of a foreign country: Dicey Rule 160. English law does not espouse the principle of the unity of bankruptcy whereby all creditors must have recourse to the courts of the debtor's domicile or his principal place of business and no other court has jurisdiction to bankrupt the debtor.

In *Re Artola Hermanos* (1890) 24 QBD 640, CA, a partnership consisting of five brothers, probably all domiciled in Spain, carried on business in France and England. The firm was declared bankrupt in France. There were debts and assets in England. *Held*: the firm could also be bankrupted in England. See also *Ex p McCulloch* (1880) 14 Ch D 716, CA.

But the fact that the debtor has been adjudicated bankrupt abroad may be a ground for exercising a discretion not to bankrupt him in England, especially if there are no assets in England: *Ex p Robinson* (1883) 22 Ch D 816, CA. Special delimiting provisions apply as between bankruptcies in parts of the UK, i.e. England, Scotland or Northern Ireland.

Recognition in Switzerland

15–29 In Switzerland the matter is governed by the Swiss Private International Law Act of 1987 Arts 166–175.

The Swiss system is based upon separate but parallel insolvency proceedings with regard to the foreign debtor's assets situate in Switzerland and is similar to the English and US ancillary procedures in some respects i.e. is a satellite liquidation of the Swiss assets.

Swiss courts will recognise a foreign decree of bankruptcy or other insolvency procedure upon a petition by the foreign administrator or any of the debtor's creditors if the following conditions are satisfied:

– the foreign decree was rendered by the competent court or other authority at the debtor's domicile or "seat" (principal place of business);

– the foreign decree is final and conclusive ("executable");

– the foreign decision does not obviously contravene Swiss public policy, the debtor had been duly heard and was subject to "fair trial", the creditors had been duly notified of the proceedings and insolvency proceedings had not been previously opened in Switzerland;

– reciprocity is granted by the state where insolvency proceedings have been opened.

When the foreign administrator or any creditor petitions for recognition of the foreign bankruptcy decree, the Swiss court will order on request all provisional measures necessary for the immediate preservation of the bankrupt's assets situate in Switzerland: Art 168.

If the debtor has a branch-establishment in Switzerland, an independent Swiss bankruptcy may be opened: Art 166.

15–30   Formal recognition of the foreign bankruptcy decree by the Swiss court attracts Swiss insolvency law with regard to the debtor's assets located in Switzerland: Art 170. The debtor's claims against third parties are deemed to be located at the domicile of the third party. For example, the debtor's bank account with a Swiss bank is deemed to be located at the bank's place of business.

Vulnerable transactions may be set aside according to the rules of Swiss law: Art 171. The Act also provides for a "hotch-pot" rule: Art 172(3).

Since this is a satellite proceeding with regard to the Swiss assets, there is no creditors' assembly and no creditors' committee for the auxiliary Swiss proceeding. Secured and privileged creditors (according to Swiss insolvency law) may only prove in these proceedings if they are domiciled or have their principal place of business in Switzerland: Art 172 (1). Since Swiss insolvency law does not provide for tax priorities, the bulk of these prior claims will comprise secured claims, and employee and social insurance claims.

Article 173 provides that any surplus remaining after the satisfaction of the creditors entitled to prove in the Swiss proceedings will be turned over to the foreign administrator for distribution among all creditors in the principal bankruptcy procedure.

But before turning over those assets the Swiss court must have examined and recognised the foreign plan of distribution among all creditors; the plan must provide for a distribution which is "fair and equitable" amongst all creditors. Otherwise the court will not turn over the proceeds but will distribute them among all ordinary creditors in Switzerland. All these provisions are applicable by analogy to insolvency procedures other than bankruptcy: Art 175.

Recognition in the United States

Generally Where the debtor is subject to a foreign bankruptcy proceeding   **15–31** outside the United States and the foreign creditors wish to place the US assets under the control of a foreign insolvency representative, there are three options:

1. **No US proceedings** The foreign representative may seek to recover US assets as representative of the foreign creditors but without resorting to US bankruptcy proceeding.

    In *Re Enercons Virginia Inc*, 812 F 2d 1469 (4th Cir 1987), the court recognised an Italian bankruptcy trustee as the sole party entitled to file a claim on behalf of foreign creditors when this action was authorised by the Italian court.

    But attempts by foreign administrators to repatriate US assets without resorting to a local bankruptcy proceeding often do not succeed since the local courts regard prejudice to US interests (e.g. the inconvenience and expense which would be suffered by US creditors having to prove abroad) as of paramount concern at both the state and federal levels.

    In *Disconto Gesellschaft v Umbreit*, 208 US 570 (1908), a German bank Disconto had a lien on assets of a German debtor residing in the US as a result of a Wisconsin judgment. The debtor was extradited to Germany where he filed for bankruptcy. Disconto as a member of the creditors court committee brought proceedings in Wisconsin to recover moneys deposited by the debtor in a US bank. Umbreit, the debtor's attorney, claimed an interest in the funds. *Held* by the US Supreme Court: Umbreit had a prior right. The court said that a country has the right to "first protect the rights of its own citizens in local property before permitting it to be taken out of the jurisdictions for administration in favour of those residing beyond their borders". In this, the court followed the not dissimilar landmark Supreme Court case of *Hilton v Guyot*, 159 US 113 (1895) (French liquidator unsuccessful in enforcing French judgments against debtor's US assets).

It is nevertheless true that US cases have more recently since the 1970s shown greater comity.

2. **Concurrent bankruptcy** The foreign representative may commence a full US bankruptcy proceeding on one or other of the jurisdictional bases mentioned above: see BC 1978 s 303. This is often a costly and cumbersome alternative. Unlike an ancillary liquidation, the bankruptcy estate comprises all property owned by the debtor "wherever located and by whomever held": BC 1978 s 541. Foreign creditors are permitted to prove, subject to equalisation in respect of receipts abroad: see para 16–1. The debtor himself may file a petition in the US even though proceedings are current elsewhere: *Re Florida Peach Corpn*, 63 BR 833 (B Ct ND Fla 1986) where it was held that an involuntary Panamanian bankruptcy did not prevent the debtor from filing a voluntary petition in Florida.

In the US the foreign administrator may instead commence a further case, e.g. a Chapter 7 liquidation case or a Chapter 11 rehabilitation case. The foreign administrator may choose to commence a full case instead of the s 304 proceeding if there are substantial assets in the United States in order to trigger the automatic stay against creditor proceedings and attachments, against set-offs, against the rescission of contracts, against the enforcement of security, or against the repossession of leases, or in order to invoke wider avoidance powers for preferences under US law. For example, a court may allow the opening of a full Chapter 7 liquidation case to invoke the US avoidance powers and then grant a suspension of the proceeding and a turnover of assets to the foreign estate.

In *Re Axona International Credit & Commerce Ltd*, 88 Bankr 597 (Bankr SDNY 1988), the Hong Kong liquidator of a Hong Kong debtor filed a petition in the US under Chapter 7 pursuant to powers in BC 1978 s 303 in order to utilise the US trustee's avoidance powers. Axona had a bank account in the US. Subsequently, after settling with US prepetition transferees and recovering assets from them, the trustee sought to suspend the Chapter 7 case and to turn over all the US assets to the Hong Kong liquidators for distribution to the creditors. *Held*: the court would order the turnover.

3. **Ancillary proceeding** The foreign representative may commence an ancillary administration under BC 1978 s 304. This important section requires a more detailed discussion.

Ancillary proceedings under BC 1978 s 304 This section allows a foreign   15–32
insolvency administrator to commence a US ancillary proceeding. Section
304 provides:

"(a) A case ancillary to a foreign proceeding is commenced by the filing
with the bankruptcy court of a petition under this section by a foreign
representative.

(b) Subject to the provisions of subsection (e) of this section, if a party in
interest does not timely contravene the petition, or after trial, the court
may:

  (1) enjoin the commencement or continuation of
    (A) any action against
        (i) a debtor with respect to property involved in such
foreign proceeding; or
        (ii) such property; or
    (B) the enforcement of any judgment against the debtor with respect
to such property, or any act or the commencement or continuation of any judicial proceeding to create or enforce a lien
against the property of such estate;

  (2) order turnover of the property of such estate, or the proceeds of
such property, to such foreign representative; or
  (3) order other appropriate relief.

(c) In determining whether to grant relief under subsection (b) of this section, the court shall be guided by what will best assure an economical
and expeditious administration of such estate, consistent with

  (1) just treatment of all holders of claims against or interests in such
estate;
  (2) protection of claim holders in the United States against prejudice
and inconvenience in the processing of claims in such foreign proceedings;
  (3) prevention of preferential or fraudulent dispositions of property of
such estate;
  (4) distribution of proceeds of such estate substantially in accordance
with the order prescribed by this title;
  (5) comity; and
  (6) if appropriate, the provision of an opportunity for a fresh start for
the individual that such foreign proceedings concerns."

This section is a mixture of universalism and priority for local interests: it
recognises that aid can be given to other states but limits the aid according
to locally-orientated policies. Prior to s 304, the US was hostile to the recognition of foreign bankruptcies and favoured domestic creditors.

15–33   Since bankruptcy law is largely determined by federal law in the United States, most of the substantive aspects of bankruptcy law are covered by the United States Bankruptcy Code and do not depend upon the vagaries of 50 different state laws. But state law is often involved, e.g. labour law, maritime law, property law or land law. Further it may still be necessary to commence s 304 proceedings in the various states where assets are located (subject to possible consolidation of actions), a complicating factor which does not apply to a full bankruptcy proceeding in the US. The relief under s 304 is discretionary, is intended to be flexible and depends upon the factors listed in the section. Comity has been held to be the most important factor. Reciprocity is relevant but has been held not to be essential.

BC 1978 s 304 is an ancillary proceeding in aid of the foreign bankruptcy and does not involve a full US bankruptcy case. Hence, in contrast to a full bankruptcy case, s 304 does not, according to US case law:

—   establish a trustee or debtor in possession;
—   make available the Code's avoidance provisions for preferential transfers;
—   culminate in a discharge of the debtor.

Although it does not trigger the automatic stay on attachments and other creditor actions in BC 1978 s 362, s 304 allows an official representative of a foreign bankrupt to petition the US Bankruptcy Court for an order staying commencement or continuation of any proceeding initiated by an American against the foreign debtor or his property held in the United States pursuant to the foreign stay. The court may also stay the enforcement of any lien or judgment obtained by US creditors.

> In *Cunard Steamship Co v Salen Reefer Services AB*, 49 Bankr 614 Bankr SDNY 1985, US creditors attached US assets of a Swedish debtor after the commencement of Swedish bankruptcy proceedings. The attachment was prejudgment. The Swedish administrator applied for BC 304 relief. *Held*: the US attachments should be vacated. They would not have been vacated if the attachment had preceded the Swedish bankruptcy: see *Re Toga Manufacturing Ltd*, 28 BR, 165 (B Ct ED Mich 1983). A similar result to *Cunard* was reached in *Victrix Steamship Co v Salen Dry Cargo*, 825 F 2d 709 (2d Cir 1987).

15–34   A s 304 procedure cannot be used unless there is property of the debtor in the United States, unless the relief does not concern property but is, for example, an order for discovery: see *Re Gee*, 53 BR 891 (B Ct SDNY 1985).

The foreign representative, by applying for s 304 relief, does not subject himself to US jurisdiction for other purposes and so is not ambushed into general US jurisdiction: see BC 1978 s 306. A debtor can initiate a full bankruptcy case after the commencement of a BC 1978 s 304 proceeding, but the court can refuse the full case under BC 1978 s 305 and has done so.

The s 304 procedure is available only in relation to a foreign proceeding defined in BC 1978 s 101(22) which must be a proceeding in a foreign country "in which the debtor's domicile, residence, principal place of business, or principal assets were located at the commencement of such proceeding" so that mere ancillary proceedings in a foreign country based on a long-arm rule, such as minimal assets, will usually be excluded. The case may be filed by the foreign representative. A receiver of an English type floating charge – which is the remedy of a single secured creditor – is probably not within the scope of the definition.

The following are amongst the types of other ancillary relief given by   **15–35** courts under s 304. A foreign representative has been permitted by the case law: to attach assets located in the US; to challenge alleged preferential transfers under the law of the home forum, not the US BC 1978; to file a proof of claim in a US bankruptcy case; to pursue discovery; and to file an involuntary bankruptcy petition against a debtor.

The foreign representative may request that any property that the debtor held in the United States be turned over to him for administration and distribution in an insolvency proceeding in the debtor's home country so that the foreign representative will have all the assets available to him in his home proceeding. In such cases, United States creditors are relegated to seeking satisfaction of their claims in the foreign proceeding under foreign law.

Most of the cases on the question of priority of creditors agree that general US creditors should not receive priority over general creditors in the foreign proceeding. But certain US claims may receive priority, e.g. super-liens for environmental clean-ups under state statutes and US employee claims.

The exercise of discretions regarding the turnover of assets is perhaps the   **15–36** most sensitive matter because US creditors will be compelled to claim abroad and be subject to foreign bankruptcy laws. The present case law is somewhat inconclusive: see, e.g. *Re Lineas Areas de Nicaragua SA*, 10 Bankr 709 (Bankr SD Fla 1981). In *Re Culmer*, 25 Bankr 624 (Bankr SDNY 1982) the court authorised the turnover of US assets of an insolvent Bahamian bank to a Bahamian liquidator.

The turnover has respectable ancestry in the State of New York:

> In *Re People of State of New York (Norske Lloyd Insurance Co)*, 242 NY 148, 151 NE 159 (1926), the New State insurance superintendent wished to disburse the balance of a security fund deposited by a Norwegian insurer to US creditors. *Held*: a separate administration was not justified and, in the interests

of efficient administration, the assets located in the US should be turned over to the Norwegian receiver.

BC 1978 s 304 effectively codifies this decision.

An important factor in determining whether the US court will defer to a foreign court under s 304 is whether the foreign insolvency law will treat claims in substantially the same manner as US law. The foreign law need not be the same as US law but must share similar policies. The laws of many states have been found to satisfy either this "substantially similar" test or the requirements of comity: Sweden, Bermuda, Cayman Islands, Italy, Hong Kong, Luxembourg, France, Netherland Antilles, Bahamas, Ecuador (banking law), Dubai (even though Dubai bankruptcy law was undeveloped) and Canada, but possibly not the Spanish suspension of payments.

Recognition in Continental Europe

15–37   **Austria** Austria does not regard foreign bankruptcies as having any effect on movables located in Austria, preferring to negotiate bilateral treaties – a less liberal attitude introduced by the Austrian Bankruptcy Act of 1982.

Belgium and Luxembourg In Belgium and Luxembourg, if the proceedings are opened at the debtor's domicile or the main seat of the company, the administrator's authority is immediately recognised locally and he may collect the bankrupt's assets located locally. Strictly no formal recognition proceedings are required. The debtor is not permitted to dispose of his assets locally and the debtor's creditors cannot attach the debtor's property individually and thereby secure preferential treatment. But in Belgium (and probably Luxembourg) the foreign bankruptcy will only have this effect if the foreign courts would grant reciprocity to the local forum in similar circumstances in reverse: Tribunal de Commerce de Bruxelles, Jurisprudence commercial de Belgique, 1976–IV–629.

15–38   **France** An *exequatur* is required for recognition but is retroactive.

Concurrent proceedings may be opened in France even though the debtor is being bankrupted at the principal place of business abroad. The courts will exercise bankruptcy jurisdiction over a local branch even if it is being wound up at its principal office, e.g. *Maus v Herrisay*, Cass Comm January 19, 1988, D 1988 J 565 (West German entity with branch in France). The bankruptcy is ancillary, but foreign creditors may prove in the bankruptcy, but subject to deduction of what they received abroad by way of dividends in the main proceeding abroad. As to attachments, the court in the *Kleber* case backdated the *exequatur* to the date of the foreign opening and thereby nullified an intervening attachment in France.

> In *Société Kleber v Frics Hansen* (Cass civ Ire, February 25, 1986) a French credi-
> tor, Société Kleber, presented its claims in Danish bankruptcy proceedings
> against a Danish company and attempted at the same time to ensure the recovery
> of its debts by seizing property located in France and having an interim mortgage
> registered over it. It brought an action in France against the Danish company for
> payment of its debts and validation of the interim mortgage. *Held*: the court
> rejected the action on the grounds that the foreign decision, which had been
> recognised by French courts, took effect from the date it had been rendered by
> the foreign court, subject to public policy considerations. The Cour de Cassation
> held that termination of individual proceedings and of registration of securities
> and rejection of claims for payment of prior debts were effective in France from
> the date of foreign judgement, i.e. before it had been recognised in France.

Germany The position summarised below may be altered by the pending   **15–39**
new German bankruptcy legislation, scheduled to come into effect at the
end of the 1990s. As to recognition of foreign jurisdiction, the German
courts will regard the foreign court as having jurisdiction only if the debtor
had his principal place of business there or was domiciled there and provided that the local bankruptcy law does not fundamentally depart from
German insolvency notions, are not poisoned by lack of due process or were
not really insolvency proceedings but were, e.g. a concealed confiscation:
see the Supreme Court judgment, BGH July 11, 1985. The German courts
have not expressed a view on foreign reorganisation proceedings, such as
the French *redressement*, US Chapter 11 or the Italian *amministrazione
straordinaria*. Reciprocity is probably not a requirement.

As to the effect of recognition, if Germany recognises the jurisdiction of
the foreign court, the foreign administrator has recognised ability to collect
and dispose of assets in Germany: Federal Supreme Court, July 11, 1985,
IPR spr 1985 no 218, BGHZ 95, 256. If the foreign administrator is a liquidator of a company, he is recognisable because he is the manager of the
company according to the *lex societas*, e.g. Federal Supreme Court,
December 7, 1961, IPR spr 1960/61 no 157.

As to creditor attachments in Germany a recognised foreign bankruptcy
which stays actions globally will stay an execution in Germany.

> A decision of July 11, 1985 (BGH 95, 256) overturned a century of previous
> territorialism. The simplified facts were: in 1976 bankruptcy proceedings were
> opened concerning the property of a company with its seat in Belgium and the
> plaintiff was appointed by the Belgian court as administrator. The Belgian
> bankrupt had a claim against two companies with their seats in the Federal
> Republic of Germany. The administrator pursued this claim in an action before

a German court. *Held*: an individual execution in Germany is only permissible in the case of a foreign bankruptcy if the creditor was already in a position to enforce judgement before the opening of proceedings, but not if after the opening.

As to concurrent proceedings in Germany, the recognition of the foreign proceedings does not prevent a German proceeding which will then take priority. But the extraterritory may not be universal if the debtor's main operations are not in Germany and there is only slight connection, i.e. German ancillary proceedings are limited to German assets.

15–40 **Greece** An *exequatur* on the lines of the French system is required: CCP Arts 780, 905. The *exequatur* requires that the foreign court had jurisdiction in Greek eyes, i.e. the court was at the debtor's principal place of business or seat of a company, and that the decree was conclusive and not contrary to Greek public policy. The *exequatur* freezes Greek attachments. Whether the *exequatur* is retroactive appears uncertain.

Italy *Exequatur* proceedings (*delibazione*) are required for the foreign bankruptcy decree to be recognised in Italy. The recognising order entitles the foreign administrator to collect assets in Italy. Whether he has a right of action before then is unclear. The *exequatur* stays foreign proceedings but it is not clear if it is retroactive.

Liechtenstein Liechtenstein recognises foreign insolvency proceedings (e.g. on movables in Liechtenstein) if reciprocity is shown (Liechtenstein BA s 5).

15–41 **Netherlands** In the Netherlands, foreign insolvency proceedings have no local effect in the absence of a treaty so that foreign proceedings are regarded as territorial. But the foreign administrator has a right to sue in the Netherlands if the debtor has lost his capacity to do so under foreign law.

Spain In Spain, an *exequatur* is required and reciprocity is required. But a 1983 draft law (which may not yet be in force) provides for a parallel bankruptcy proceeding in Spain opened by the authorities of the country of the debtor's domicile if no full Spanish bankruptcy proceedings have been opened and if the foreign proceedings are recognised (debtor's domicile, conclusive, debtor was heard in time and no conflict with Spanish public policy). This parallel proceeding applies to assets in Spain and evidently involves the legal effects of a full Spanish bankruptcy but limited to local assets. A Spanish administrator is appointed. The court can order protective measures prior to the grant of this recognition procedure.

Recognition in Scandinavia

Denmark In Denmark foreign insolvency proceedings do not prevent the   **15–42**
debtor's creditors from levying execution over assets situate in Denmark:
see, e.g. *Forsikrings A/S Norske Lloyd A/S v Forsikrings National*, UfR
1930, p 8, H. However s 6 of the Danish Bankruptcy Act of 1977 provides
that the Minister of Justice may allow foreign insolvency proceedings to
have effect in Denmark by ministerial ordinance.

> In *Keller & Reiner v Hecksher*, UfR 1911, p 105 LOHS, a German firm bank-
> rupted in Germany attempted to collect a debt in Denmark. *Held*: the firm
> could not do so since it had already been bankrupted and the firm had not been
> authorised by the German administrator to collect the debt. In other words, the
> German bankruptcy order effectively rendered the trustee as the only person
> entitled to collect assets in Denmark. See also *V Herredshovding F Nilsson af
> Malmo v Firmaet Thoger From*, UfR 1878 p 776 SH: foreign bankruptcy
> administrator entitled to reclaim Danish assets on basis of actio pauliana under
> the foreign bankruptcy law.

Concurrent Danish ancillary proceedings are unlikely since there is no
bankruptcy jurisdiction based on mere assets or doing business locally:
generally the main office must be in Denmark. The result is a possible
vacuum unless the Danish courts allow the foreign representative to collect
local assets on behalf of the estate.

Finland Finland does not recognise that foreign insolvency proceedings have
any effect locally in the absence of a treaty. Finland recognises asset jurisdiction.

Norway Norway does not recognise that foreign insolvency proceedings
have any effect locally in the absence of a treaty. But opinions appear to be
divided on whether attachments are stayed.

As to concurrent proceedings, since Norway tends not to claim jurisdiction to bankrupt unless the main office is in Norway, ancillary bankruptcies appear unlikely. Nevertheless some effects of foreign bankruptcies have
been recognised in Norway.

> In *Bjercke v Alcock*, N Rt 1896 p 465 (S Ct) an Englishman declared bankrupt
> in England sued for money owing to him in Norway. *Held*: he could not do so,
> since he could not show that his trustee in bankruptcy had authorised him to do
> so.
>
> In *Wells Konkursbo v Kristiania Bank*, N Rt 1887, p 465 (S Ct) the English
> trustee of an English bankrupt sought to recover assets in Norway. *Held*: the
> trustee's request should be granted. To the same effect, *Wells Konkursbo v
> Halls*, N Rt 1891, p 329 (S Ct).

In *Hannevigs Konkursbo v Hannevig*, N Rt 1925, p 517 (S Ct), a US bank-ruptcy administrator petitioned for a Norwegian bankruptcy. *Held*: the pet-ition should be granted. Note however that the petition was accompanied by petitions of individual creditors.

15–43 **Sweden** In Sweden, the foreign proceedings do not have local effect but it is probably the case that the courts will recognise the powers of a foreign insol-vency administrator in his capacity as the controller of the company if he is appointed under the law of the company's principal place of business abroad.

In *Morska Centrala Handlowa v Kozicki*, NJA 1951, 753, S Ct, a Polish com-pany was bankrupted. *Held*: the Polish administrator could recover assets in Sweden, since he had replaced the original management.

Concurrent bankruptcy proceedings may be opened, but if they are ancil-lary (e.g. because the debtor is not a domiciliary) it is possible that the bank-ruptcy is limited to Swedish assets.

In *Melsom & Holth v Andersson*, NJA 1915, 561 (decided before the Nordic Bankruptcy Convention), a Norwegian debtor was bankrupted in Norway. He moved to Sweden. *Held*: he could also be bankrupted in Sweden. See also *A/S The United Pitwood Exporters Ltd*, NJA 1922, 318.

Sweden still adheres to the territorial view that the foreign bankruptcy does not stay local proceedings.

In the Swedish Supreme Court decision of *Scandinavian Baltic Company A/S v AB Svenska Fryserierna*, NJA 1938, 322, a Danish debtor was being liquidated in Denmark. A creditor attached assets in Sweden. *Held*: the Danish liquidation was not relevant. But the distraint order was quashed for other reasons.

Recognition in Japan

15–44 A bankruptcy procedure commenced outside Japan is not effective with respect to the properties located in Japan: Art 3(2). In addition the Japanese Bankruptcy Law does not provide for any mechanism for recognising a foreign bankruptcy procedure. But the courts have signalled a relaxation of this regime.

In *Kabushiki Kasiha International Management Business v Fincamera SA* (Tokyo Court of Appeal, decision of January 1, 1981, 83 Hanrei-jiho 994), a receiver was appointed with respect to Fincamera by a court in Geneva in 1979. IMB, which was a creditor of Fincamera, provisionally attached in Japan a trade mark of Fincamera registered with the Patent Agency of Japan. The receiver of Fincamera obtained another court order to release the provisional attachment on its trade mark by depositing cash as designated by the court with a competent legal bureau. IMB filed an objection to the court order releasing the provisional attachment, alleging that the receiver of Fincamera was not entitled to file a lawsuit on behalf of Fincamera because the bankrupt order issued by the court of Geneva was not valid in Japan pursuant to BA Art 3(2). *Held*: BA Art 3(2) does not deny the authority of a receiver appointed by a foreign court to manage and dispose of the properties of the bankrupt located in Japan. The nature and the scope of the authority of the foreign receiver must be examined in accordance with the laws of the foreign jurisdiction and the foreign receiver may exercise that authority in accordance with the laws of Japan in respect of property located in Japan. Since under Swiss law the receiver was authorised to manage and dispose of all the properties vested in the bankrupt at the time of commencement of the bankruptcy procedure, the receiver of Fincamera could validly apply for a court order to release the provisional attachment on the trade mark of Fincamera.

However, in a decision of the Osaka District Court, Judgement of September 30, 1983 (139 Hanrei-times 516) the court held that the fact that a bankruptcy order had been issued by a court in Hong Kong with respect to the defendant did not constitute a ground for the motion to dismiss a court procedure whereby an Indian bank sought payment of an overdraft owed by the defendant. Academic and practitioner opinion in Japan appears to favour the greater comity accorded by the Tokyo court to the narrower view of the Osaka court.

Recognition in Latin America

Argentina is worth special study because it is one of the few remaining coun-   **15–45**
tries which still clings to the prior payment of local creditors.

As to recognition proceedings, the powers of a foreign representative are not recognised in Argentina if there are any local creditors who would enjoy priority if there were a local proceeding: *Panair do Brasil* case, CSJN, July 5, 1972, ED, 45–739. It follows that a foreign bankruptcy order will generally have no effect in Argentina.

Concurrent bankruptcy proceedings in Argentina are possible. The foreign bankruptcy order is an act of bankruptcy by the debtor sufficient to ground an Argentine petition and it is not necessary to establish a separate cessation of payments in Argentina, although possibly the order must be of a court at the debtor's domicile or principal place of business. The petition must be by the debtor or by a creditor whose debt is payable in Argentina.

The effect of the Bankruptcy Reform Act of 1983 is that, if there are dual bankruptcy proceedings, one Argentine, the other foreign, then creditors whose debts are payable in Argentina will be paid before creditors whose debts are payable externally. Nationality is not relevant. The object seems to be to protect local creditors and has a long history in Argentina. The subordination of foreign creditors not only leads to a long delay in payment while the proceedings take their course, but may effectively result in no payment at all. If the local creditors accept a composition (on which the foreign creditors cannot vote), the foreign creditors have to wait until local creditors have been paid.

The domicile of payment will be decided by Argentine law and an optional Argentine place of payment may be deemed to be evasive and hence unsuccessful.

> In *Banco Europeo para America Latina v Cura Hinos*, SA CSJN, September 8, 1983, ED 105–593) a mortgage provided that the creditor was to be paid abroad, but payments could be made to an intermediary in Buenos Aires. There were concurrent proceedings in Argentina and abroad. *Held* by the Supreme Court: the alternative place of payment evaded the application of the national priority subordination and the creditor was not admitted to participate in the Argentine proceedings. [Author's note: this case may not be correctly stated.]

Although the position appears not entirely clear, the foreign representative can prove for the remnant after all local creditors have been paid: if he cannot, the foreign creditors can prove for this remnant (if any) themselves.

If there are only local Argentine proceedings and no foreign proceedings, creditors whose debts are payable abroad can (since 1983) prove pari passu with local creditors, but only if the foreign creditors prove reciprocity, i.e. that in their country debts payable abroad would be provable pari passu with debts payable locally.

15–46   In **Bolivia** a foreign bankruptcy is strictly territorial. A foreign domiciliary bankruptcy order is an act of a bankruptcy in **Brazil** on which a petition may be founded: see Com C Art 1489 para 30. The position is similar in **Costa Rica, Paraguay, Peru** and **Uruguay**.

But in other states, foreign domiciliary bankruptcies can be recognised subject to a local *exequatur*, e.g. **Colombia, El Salvador** (it seems – Com C Art 511), **Honduras, Mexico**.

CHAPTER 16

INSOLVENCY CONFLICT OF LAWS: PARTICULAR ASPECTS

Equalisation and other indirect remedies

Generally

Bankruptcy is necessarily territorial even if the home forum claims that its **16–1** proceedings have global impact. A foreign forum has no power to seize local assets or to enforce a local freeze unless the local forum permits it to do so. But the foreign forum may have indirect methods of enforcing its views over creditors within its own jurisdiction. It may achieve this by three main methods:

- **Equalisation,** i.e. obliging a creditor who obtains more abroad than he would have done locally to return the excess to the home bankruptcy.

- **Injunction,** i.e. forbidding a creditor within the jurisdiction, from taking action abroad contrary to the home forum's bankruptcy rules, e.g. from attaching the debtor's property abroad contrary to a local freeze. For example, the English courts have a general jurisdiction to restrain a person by injunction from commencing or continuing legal proceedings abroad contrary to an English insolvency freeze, but this is available only when the creditor is subject to the English jurisdiction: *Re Vocalion (Foreign) Ltd* [1932] Ch 196. They will restrain a creditor resident in England from suing abroad (*Re Distin, ex p Ormiston* (1871) 24 LT 197) but will not restrain a creditor resident abroad from suing abroad: *Re Chapman* (1873) LR 15 Eq 75.

- **Contempt of court,** i.e. imposing penalties on creditors within the court's jurisdiction who act contrary to the home form's rules, e.g. by attaching the debtor's property abroad. This is the most draconian penalty.

Equalisation

The principle is that a creditor who obtains more in a foreign jurisdiction **16–2** than he would in the local jurisdiction should be obliged to equalise in the

---

local proceedings by accounting for what he received abroad. Thus if he receives 30 of his claim of 100 abroad, he should not receive any dividends locally until other creditors have received 30 locally. The doctrine is sometimes known as marshalling or the hotch-pot rule.

The rule is necessary where there are several concurrent proceedings and creditors at home and abroad prove in them all.

The doctrine does not apply in the rare case where the home forum regards its insolvency proceedings as being purely territorial, e.g. Japan BA s 3.

Examples of excess receipts

16–3   Examples of excess receipts might include: a foreign attachment contrary to the home forum's freeze; foreign realisation of security contrary to the home forum's freeze or invalidity of the security under the rules of the home forum; foreign set-off if there is no insolvency set-off in the home forum; the transaction was a preference according to the home forum's rules and should be avoided; and the creditor has received dividends in a foreign bankruptcy.

Enforcement of equalisation

16–4   An important issue is how the bankruptcy forum will enforce equalisation. There are three main possibilities:

- The creditor must equalise only if he proves in the home forum so that he is free not to equalise if he chooses not to avail himself of a double proof.

- The creditor can be sued for return of the foreign excess receipt if the home forum courts have jurisdiction over the creditor. This leads to competing jurisdictions, especially if there are several concurrent proceedings. Note that the EU Brussels Judgment Convention and the related Conventions do not apply to bankruptcy proceedings.

- The creditor is subject to local penalties, e.g. contempt of court.

Country survey of equalisation

16–5   The requirement for equalisation in principle seems to be very common.

In **England**, an unsecured creditor who levies execution on the debtor's property abroad after the commencement of an English winding-up may, if he is subject to the jurisdiction of the English court, be compelled to surrender the fruits of his execution for the general benefit of creditors, at least if he proves in the English liquidation for other debts owed to him: *Re Oriental Inland Steam Co* (1874) LR 9 Ch App 557. A creditor who proves in an English bankruptcy and who has received part of the bankrupt's property abroad will not be allowed to prove unless he brings the part so acquired into the common fund: see, e.g. *Banco de Portugal v Waddell* (1880) 5 App Cas 161. The rule is similar in Scotland: see e.g. *Clydesdale Bank v Anderson* (1890) 27 SC LR 493. Even if the creditor does not prove in the English bankruptcy it is probably the case that he can be compelled to contribute what he received abroad if he is subject to the jurisdiction of the English courts, e.g. because he is resident in England.

In England equalisation may also be supported by the rule of retainer (or the rule in *Cherry v Boultbee*) whereby a person who is liable to contribute to the assets of the estate and who is also a creditor of the estate is not entitled to share in the estate until he has accounted for his contribution. His share is generally calculated at what it would have been if he had paid his contribution to the fund so as notionally to swell the fund and then deducting from his dividend from that swelled fund the property of the estate he already holds. The doctrine has not so far been applied in England in this context but there is no reason why it should not. It has, for example, been applied in cases where a shareholder is entitled to surplus assets on liquidation but is also a debtor to the estate: *Re Kowloon Container Warehouse Co Ltd* [1981] HKLR 210; *Re Peruvian Ry Co* [1915] 2 Ch 144; *Re West Coast Gold Fields Ltd, Rowe Trustee's Claim* [1906] 1 Ch 1. It has also been applicable where a creditor is overpaid a dividend (*Re Searle Hall & Co* [1924] 2 Ch 25) and in numerous cases where a director of a company is both a creditor of the company and a misfeasant liable to contribute or disgorge assets to the company.

Argentina requires that a non-priority creditor who receives a dividend or   16–6
any other payment abroad is to credit that recovery to his share in the Argentine insolvency proceedings. As already noted, foreign creditors whose debts are not payable exclusively in Argentina may in addition be subordinated to creditors whose debts are, if there are concurrent proceedings abroad (but not if there are no foreign proceedings).

In **France** and **Germany**, a creditor who has received dividends abroad must bring them into account when claiming in the local bankruptcy.

> In BGHZ 88, 147 ss (1983) a debtor became insolvent in Germany. A creditor attached his bank account in Zurich. *Held* by the Federal Supreme Court: the creditor must deliver the proceeds of the attachment to the German trustee in bankruptcy. Otherwise the creditor would be unjustly enriched.

16–7   In the **Netherlands** the Bankruptcy Act Art 203 imposes a duty on the creditor to reimburse the Dutch estate if he receives payment of his claim separately abroad from the debtor's assets.

In **Sweden,** although there is no case law, the consensus of the writers is that, if a creditor recovers assets abroad after the opening of a domiciliary proceeding in Sweden, the recovery is deductible from Swedish dividends. Possibly a direct repayment claim against the creditor is available if the creditor is subject to Swedish jurisdiction and the creditor has attached assets abroad in defiance of the Swedish freeze, but not if the creditor has merely received dividends in a foreign parallel bankruptcy.

In **Switzerland** the Act on Private International Law of 1987 Art 172(3) requires crediting towards dividends where a creditor has obtained partial satisfaction for his claim "in a foreign proceeding connected with the debtor's insolvency"

16–8   In the **United States** the matter is governed by BC 1978 s 508(a): if a creditor receives, in a foreign proceeding, payment of, or a transfer of property on account of, a claim allowed under the BC, in effect he cannot claim a dividend in the US proceedings until all creditors of the same class have received the same per cent in a US proceeding. This section only limits the distributions in the US proceedings. It does not authorise the court to take positive steps to compel foreign creditors to disgorge recoveries received abroad which are in excess of what they would have been in the US.

Where a creditor receives dividends in two or more parallel bankruptcy proceedings, these should not be recoverable by direct action or contempt of court penalties because the creditor is acting properly in proving in the foreign collective proceedings. The excess dividends should only be counted against the local dividend: this is the German position (OLG Koln, January 31, 1989, ZIP 1989, 321) and is also the position in France. Perhaps Sweden will also follow this principle, but there is no case law. As to England, see *Banco de Portugal v Waddell* (1880) 5 AC 161

Discovery of foreign assets

16–9   Of some importance is the ability of the administrator from the home forum to obtain testimony from foreign officers of the debtor company and to obtain the production of books and records in foreign parts relating to the insolvent. The purpose of this investigation is to discover the assets of the debtor and to ascertain facts which may led to the avoidance of pre-commencement transactions or the liability of directors or fraud. The duties of the administrator in this respect in the home forum will be governed by the home forum's rules.

The reaction of the foreign local forum will depend on recognition of the insolvency administrator and of the home forum's bankruptcy jurisdiction. Even if the foreign forum does recognise the home forum's administrator, banks in the foreign local forum may impose their bank secrecy rules.

The English courts have restrictively construed the 1970 Hague Convention on the Taking of Evidence Abroad in Civil and Commercial Matters and do not allow it to be used for the purposes of foreign insolvency investigations.

> In *Re International Power Industries NV* (1985) BCLC 128, the trustee of a Netherlands Antilles company which was in Chapter 11 proceedings in the United States applied for an order of the English court under the Evidence (Proceedings in Other Jurisdictions) Act 1975 (which introduced the 1970 Hague Convention into English law). The application was for examination of an officer of the company who was resident in England, and of the company's former English solicitors. The trustee was apparently concerned to obtain information about the management and control of the company and its assets. *Held*: the application should be refused. The court held that the Convention and the Act were not intended to serve as fact-finding machinery for the purpose of investigating companies in insolvency proceedings. The court's approach is consistent with other English decisions (outside insolvency) concerning the Convention: see especially *Rio Tinto Zinc Corp v Westinghouse Electric Corp* [1978] AC 547.

If the debtor is also bankrupted in the foreign local forum, the local powers of investigation are brought into play. Thus in the **United States**, the BC 1978 s 304 proceeding for ancillary relief (para 15–31 *et seq*) may be used to obtain an order for discovery even though the debtor has no assets in the US: *Re Gee* 53 BR 891 (B Ct, SDNY 1985) (Grand Cayman liquidation).

Insolvency set-off

General

One group of states permits insolvency set-off while another group does not 16–10 except in the case of connexity or current accounts. Those which do are mainly in the common law, Germanic and Scandinavian groups. Those which do not are mainly in the Franco-Latin group. In addition:

1. states which allow insolvency set-off usually restrict the preferential build-up of set-offs in the twilight;

2. US law stays set-offs as from an insolvency petition;

3. a set-off may be affected by a moratorium on or a discharge of the claim owed by the debtor on his bankruptcy or by virtue of a composition.

Set-off is discussed in another volume in this series of works on international financial law.

16–11 The position is complicated because of the large number of possible situations. Broadly there are twelve basic situations. The two base cases are, for example: (1) the bank is owed a loan by the home forum of the debtor and owes a deposit for the benefit of the foreign branch of the debtor; and (2) (in reverse) the bank owes a deposit for the account of the home forum of the debtor but is owed a loan for the account of the foreign forum where a branch of the debtor is located.

These basic cases must be examined in three situations, namely, (1) where both jurisdictions allow the set-off, (2) where the home forum does allow set-off, but the foreign forum does not, and (3) where the home forum does not allow set-off, but the foreign forum does.

Then the position has to be examined (1) from the point of view of the home forum and (2) from the point of view of the foreign forum.

Of course one could take the analysis further and posit cases where proceedings have been commenced in one forum but not the other, hence multiplying the permutations to a total of 24. This is one reason that set-off law is so crushingly complex. One cannot go through all these, but one can review some of them to suggest the guiding principles.

Home forum rules

16–12 It seems to be generally true that the home forum will apply its own rules to the availability of set-off on insolvency, including its rules as to preferential build-ups (but see below as to fraudulent preferences) and stays on set-off. This is so in England.

Home forum permits set-off, but foreign forum forbids set-off One may take first the case where the home forum permits insolvency set-off, but the foreign forum does not. If the creditor could have proved for his claim in the English proceedings, then, by the language of the insolvency set-off clause in IR 1986, r 4.90, he is entitled to the set-off even if the foreign forum prohibits set-off. This should be so even if the claim owed to the creditor was incurred through a foreign branch of the debtor. Thus if a bank is owed a loan through the French branch of an English-incorporated debtor and owes a deposit to the debtor in England, then it is considered that the bank could set off the loan against the deposit, even though France prohibits insolvency set-off: the bank is entitled to prove for the loan in the English proceedings. The governing law of the claims is irrelevant.

If conversely the loan is owed through the English office, but the deposit is for the account of the French branch, the result is the same, even though France might maintain that the deposit is a local asset which should be available in an ancillary proceeding in France. This should be so even if the bank is French because the French bank can prove in England. If both states allow a set-off, then the English courts will permit the set-off: consider *Macfarlane v Norris* (1862) 2 B & S 783 summarised below.

> In the English case of *Re Hett, Maylor & Co Ltd* (1894) 10 TLR 412, a company in liquidation in England owed a debt to its bank (apparently in England although this is not clear from the report) and the bank owed the company a credit balance at its Manila branch. *Held*: set-off.

However, if the foreign forum prohibits the set-off, then the creditor may be subject to the foreign forum's sanctions to recover the amount set off, e.g. equalisation, injunction or recovery suit against the creditor.

Home forum forbids insolvency set-off, but foreign forum allows set-off   16–13
The converse case is where the home forum forbids insolvency set-off, but the foreign forum allows it. If the bank creditor owes a deposit for the account of the home forum of the debtor and is owed a loan through a foreign branch of the debtor, then one can expect the home forum to disallow the set-off. If the bank nevertheless sets off, the home forum can claim the unpaid deposit from the bank if it has jurisdiction over the bank.

If the bank creditor is owed the loan for the account of the home office and owes the deposit to the foreign office, then in the eyes of the home forum the bank is entitled to a dividend on the loan because set-off is disallowed. The home forum is interested in the deposit held for the account of the foreign forum because it may be entitled to a turnover of foreign assets, including the deposit, and a set-off would deprive the home forum of the eventual proceeds of the deposit.

The upshot of the rules is that creditors should ensure that the set-off is available in all applicable jurisdictions, because, even though the relevant forum may allow the set-off, the creditor may be subject to recovery measures if he sets off when he should not have done so in the eyes of the prohibiting forum.

If a foreigner nevertheless sets off contrary to a home prohibition, the home forum is left with indirect methods of enforcement, e.g. equalisation, injunction or recovery suit against the creditor if subject to the jurisdiction, and contempt of court or other penalties: para 16–1 *et seq.*

Attitude of foreign local forum to home forum rules on set-off

16–14 This question concerns the attitude of the foreign local forum to the rules on set-off of the home forum where the debtor company is subject to bankruptcy proceedings at its seat or domicile.

The home forum's views will be of no impact in the foreign local forum if the local forum does not recognise the home forum's bankruptcy proceedings at all.

No concurrent proceedings in foreign local forum If the home forum allows insolvency set-off and bankruptcy proceedings have not been commenced in the foreign local forum, there will not usually be a conflict because the set-off is not stayed in the foreign local forum where normally solvent set-off rules will apply. All countries appear to allow solvent set-off. It is true that the solvent setoff rules may not be as wide, e.g. no set-off of unconnected claims where one of them is unliquidated – but the creditor claiming the set-off can get it, one way or another, e.g. by claiming the set-off in the home proceedings.

> In *Macfarlane v Norris* (1862) 2 B&S 783, a creditor was indorsee and holder of bill of exchange accepted by the debtor. The debtor became bankrupt in Scotland. The creditor owed the bankrupt the proceeds of sale of goods sold by the creditor on behalf of the bankrupt. Under the law of Scotland, there was an insolvency set-off. The Scots trustee sued the creditor in the English courts. *Held*: set-off. There would have been a set-off under both English and Scots law, but it seems that the court applied Scots law as the law of the place where the bankruptcy proceedings were taking place.

Where the home forum does not allow insolvency set-off and no bankruptcy proceedings have been commenced in the foreign local forum which allows a solvent set-off, the proper solution is for the foreign local forum, if it recognises the home bankruptcy, to apply the law of the claim for which the home forum's administrator sues because this is a matter of discharge. If that is governed by the home forum's law, then the local forum should forbid the set-off. If it is governed by some other system of law which allows set-off, then the local forum should allow the set-off. But the principles are obscure and the English courts might apply the lex fori. There is some international support for the cumulative law amongst academic writers but not in the case law.

A German court has applied a foreign bankruptcy prohibition on set-off to deny the German creditor's set-off.

> In a German BGH decision of July 11, 1985, a Belgian debtor became bankrupt in Belgium. A German creditor had a set-off in respect of a debt governed by German law. Set-off was prohibited on a Belgian insolvency but was permitted under German law, including German bankruptcy law. *Held*: the Belgian bankruptcy was universal and the set-off should be disallowed.

Concurrent proceedings in foreign local forum If there are concurrent pro-   16–15
ceedings in the local forum and the home forum allows insolvency set-off, then it is to be expected that the local forum will not permit the administrator to sue for a debt locally in defiance of his own set-off: see *Macfarlane v Norris* (1862)2 B&S 783 summarised above.

It would be extraordinary if in a situation where both jurisdictions permit insolvency set-off, the foreign local forum should refuse set-off. They presumably would only do so if a claim is owed for the benefit of a local branch, if that claim would be removed by the set-off (so that local creditors do not get the benefit of it) and the policy of protecting local creditors overrides the set-off policy. This would discriminate against foreign creditors and would show a strong xenophobic policy in favour of local creditors and a weak set-off policy. This is not the English view.

As for the various other permutations, the principles discussed above in relation to the home forum's approval should apply with appropriate modifications to reflect the ancillary nature of the local proceedings.

The British comity provision in IA 1986 s 426, which requires the English courts to give assistance to courts in designated countries, is unlikely to override the English conflicts rules because the section specifically requires that the court has regard to the rules of private international law. As it happens, most of the designated countries also allow insolvency set-off so the question is less pressing. The US comity provision in BC 1978 s 304, is not expressly limited by a requirement that the courts have regard to the rules of private international law.

Security and title finance

The conflicts rules as regards the impact of bankruptcy on security are   16–16
examined in another work in this series of books on financial law. The position as regards title finance or vendor-lessor security, e.g. retention of title and finance leases, may well be similar to that applying to security.

Rescission of executory contracts and leases

Generally

16–17 In some jurisdictions, the ability of a counterparty to rescind an executory contract or forfeit a lease or licence on the bankruptcy of the other party may be nullified and an administrator has power to compel performance of or to disclaim contracts, leases and other property. See para 3–1 *et seq*.

Home forum

It is probably the case that the home forum will apply its own rules as to:

1. the nullification of forfeiture clauses on bankruptcy which fail because the contract is an asset of the estate;

2. disclaimer of contracts, leases and other property, unless real property is involved and this is situated abroad.

Apart from mandatory rules, the question of whether an insolvency operates as an implied repudiation of a contract should be determined – at least in England – according to the governing law of the contract, since this is a matter of discharge and is not a bankruptcy question.

Whether a foreign counterparty cancels a contract contrary to a home forum's mandatory bankruptcy rule that it be performed, the home forum is left with indirect methods of enforcement of its views – equalisation, injunction or recovery suit against the creditor if he is subject to the jurisdiction, and contempt of court and other penalties: para 16–1.

Attitude of foreign local forum to home forum

16–18 If the foreign local forum does not recognise the home forum's bankruptcy, the foreign local forum will plainly not give effect to any bankruptcy rule of the home forum regarding the rescission of contracts or disclaimer.

If the local forum does recognise the home forum's bankruptcy, then, if the local forum is England, the English courts should apply the governing law to questions of rescission, nullification of rescission or forfeiture clauses, and disclaimer, and not the bankruptcy rules of the home forum. This would be consistent with their attitude to bankruptcy discharges: para 16–30 *et seq*. Hence if the home forum law provides for a forced cancellation of the contract, the English should only recognise it if the governing law of the contract is the home forum's law, but not if governed by some other system of law. If the home forum avoids the rescission by providing for a stay on termination rights, the proper law should govern. But there appears to be no case law in England.

Priority, pari passu and deferred creditors

Priority creditors

Generally In all developed jurisdictions, certain creditors rank prior to other   16–19
ordinary unsecured creditors: these are mainly tax and employee claims but may include others: para 1–36 *et seq.*

The prior payment of another state's taxes to the detriment of local creditors and the payment of employees located in another state is bound to be a sensitive matter.

Home forum Generally the home forum applies its own bankruptcy rules to the prior payment of preferential creditors. This is certainly the rule in **England** and the **United States.** Thus in the US case of *Re Florida Peach Corpn*, 87 BR 700 (B Ct MD Fla 1988), it was held that the priority ranking of lawyers fees relating to a Panamanian bankruptcy must be determined by the US rules in BC 1978 s 507. As to employees, it should not matter whether the employee is home or foreign. Foreign taxes are generally not recoverable: para 1–54. The revenue authorities in a foreign forum are left to recover out of local assets in their own forum.

Pari passu creditors

The general rule appears to be that the home forum will apply its own rules   16–20
as to the allowability of unsecured creditors. This will affect such matters as the provability of tort claims, the valuation of contingencies, the rule against double proof, the discounting of future debts, the conversion of foreign currency debts into local currency, and the admissibility of the claims of foreign creditors. But the home forum should apply ordinary contract conflicts rules to such questions as the validity of a contract claim (e.g. the impact of usury or wagering laws). This is considered to be the position in England: Dicey Rule 165.

As to a foreign local forum, assuming it recognises the home forum's bankruptcy jurisdiction, the position of creditors whose claims are disallowed, e.g. because they filed claims too late or because they are non-provable tort claims, should be governed by the ordinary non-bankruptcy rules of the forum. Thus in England, principle indicates that the discharge of a contract debt by a foreign bankruptcy or by the foreign dissolution of an insolvent company should be determined by the proper law and perhaps this rule should also apply to torts by applying the proper law of the tort.

Deferred creditors

16–21   These deferred creditors primarily comprise creditors whose loans are similar to equity and so should be subordinated and US equitably subordinated creditors who are subordinated, e.g. because of culpable interference in the management of the debtor.

The home forum may apply its own rules to these matters, regardless of the governing law of the claim.

Equity shares

16–22   The liability of shareholders to contribute to the assets of a debtor company on bankruptcy and the ranking of share capital are in England governed by the law of the place of incorporation of the company both as regards the home forum and any foreign forum: Dicey Rule 156(2).

Preferences

16–23   The issue here is the rules which should govern the avoidance of pre-commencement transactions as a fraudulent preference or as prejudicial to creditors. The main conflicting issues are likely to be (1) whether a transaction prejudices creditors (on which there is a substantial international consensus); (2) the length of the suspect period (on which there is little agreement); and (3) the defences, e.g. in favour of good faith creditors unaware of the bankruptcy or protecting creditors if the debtor did not intend to prefer – where again there is little agreement. See chapters 4 to 7.

Home forum

The home forum generally applies its own rules as to the avoidance of transactions.

If a foreign forum ignores the home forum's rules, the home forum is left to indirect means of enforcement – equalisation, injunction or recovery action against a creditor subject to the jurisdiction, and contempt of court or other penalties.

In many countries, the preference rule is not regarded as limited to territorial transfers but applies to transfers wherever they are made, e.g. where the debtor makes a payment abroad to a creditor abroad within the home suspect period. This is because preferential transfers should be available to all creditors, local or foreign, as part of the assets. In one class of situation the debtor transfers locally to a foreign transferee who then removes the asset abroad. This should clearly be caught by local law. In another case, the transfer and the asset are both foreign. Often the preference is by a payment through a bank account. In all cases the administrator is left with the task of reclaiming assets situated abroad and transferred to a foreign transferee.

In **England,** the courts apply English preference rules to property within   **16–24** England of a person bankrupt in England.

> In *Re A Debtor (No 199 of 1922)* [1922] 2 Ch 470, CA, a petition was served on a debtor in England who applied for a sequestration in Scotland. Under the law of England, a settlement made by the debtor was void as a preferential transfer, but not under Scots law. *Held:* the courts had jurisdiction to adjudge the debtor bankrupt.

As to preferential transfers abroad, the courts have a discretionary power to apply the English avoidance rules to external transactions, e.g. a payment by the debtor to a bank located abroad: *Powdrill v Hambros Bank (Jersey)* [1992] 3 WLR 690, CA (payment by English company to discharge an overdraft at its bank in Jersey).

Courts in **Australia** have held that their preference sections are not territorially limited, e.g. *Re Merchant & Industrial Finance Ltd* [1975] Qd R 46 (Queensland liquidator could recover payment made preferentially in New South Wales).

Similarly in **Scotland:**

> In the Scottish case of *White v Briggs* (1843) 5 Dunlop 1148, the Scottish bankrupt paid creditors in England within the Scots suspect period. *Held:* the Scottish rule applied to enable the Scottish trustee to recover from the creditors so paid. The court said that the avoidance rule was intended to protect all creditors, not just Scottish creditors.

Legal opinion in **Sweden** appears to favour the view that, in the case of a domiciliary bankruptcy, the avoidance power is global.

In at least two **Argentine** decisions, the court held that the Argentine courts have jurisdiction to avoid preferential transactions performed by the bankrupt in a foreign country.

In the *Federal Case* (1987) (Rev ED, April 10, 1989, p 2, fallo no 41,493) an Argentine company Federal was bankrupted. It owned 98 per cent of the shares of a Brazilian subsidiary, but two months prior to the bankruptcy, the subsidiary issued shares to third parties with the connivance of the parent, Federal, thereby reducing Federal's holding to 8 per cent without compensation. *Held*: the transaction was void as a preference and the Argentine syndic was authorised to attach and sell the new shares.

Attitude of foreign local forum to home forum's avoidance

16–25   Assuming the foreign local forum recognises the home forum's bankruptcy proceedings, one sees a wide variation of attitudes to a home forum avoidance.

If the foreign local forum does not recognise the home forum's bankruptcy, then plainly any avoidance powers under the home forum's rules will not be given any effect in the foreign local forum. For example, several Latin American countries will not recognise foreign bankruptcies and so the foreign preference rules will have no effect locally, e.g. **Bolivia, Costa Rica, Panama, Paraguay, Peru** and **Uruguay**. Hence the question arises only if the local forum recognises the home forum's bankruptcy.

Where the transfer is fraudulent on any analysis, e.g. because it was intentionally made to defeat creditors, there is no conflict and hence there is likely to be a general willingness to give effect to a foreign recovery action. The basic Paulian action, which has found its way into the laws of many developed states, does not necessarily depend on the commencement of bankruptcy proceedings: para 4–19 *et seq.*

If the transferred asset is land it is to be expected that the local forum where the land is situate will be slow to recognise an avoidance under the law of a home forum transferring the land back to the estate.

16–26   The position in England appears uncertain if there are no proceedings in England. If bankruptcy proceedings have commenced in England, the courts will usually apply the English rules and not the foreign rules.

A **British Columbia** court has applied foreign rules of a preferential transfer.

In *Williams v Meeker Cedar Products (1967) Ltd* (1973) 10 CBE (NS) 76, the British Columbia court applied the law of Oregon to a preferential transfer in respect of an insolvent Oregon corporation. See also *Re Premium Plywood Products Inc* (1967) 19 CBE (NS) 76 (BSc).

A similar result was reached in **Manitoba**.

In *Williams v Rice* (1926) 3 DLR 225, the owner of a US firm stripped assets of the firm, some of which were transferred to his brother, a Canadian resident. The US firm went into bankruptcy in the US and the US trustee sought to recover in Manitoba from the Canadian resident. *Held*: the US trustee was entitled to recover the fraudulently transferred property. But this was a serious and obvious fraudulent transfer.

In two decisions in **Denmark** the foreign bankruptcy administrator was held entitled to reclaim Danish assets by means of an *actio pauliana* in accordance with the law of the home forum: *Herredshoving F° Nilsson af Malmo v Firmaet Thoger From*, U 1878 p 776 SH; *Frederikshalds v Morek*, UfR 1908, p I65SH.

In **Germany**, the courts have applied a foreign avoidance rule if the home forum's bankruptcy is recognised: OLG Ham October 25, 1976, IPR spr 1976 no 211.

If ancillary proceedings are begun in **Switzerland**, then the Swiss rules apply: Act on Private International Law of 1987 Art 171.

In the **United States**, BC 1978 s 304 allows the court in an ancillary pro- **16–27** ceeding to turn over property to the foreign administrator and the courts have applied the foreign forum's avoidance rules. Note that if a full bankruptcy case is commenced in the US instead of the BC 304 ancillary proceeding, the US avoidance provisions would apply.

In *Re Metzeler*, 78 BR 674 (Bankr SDNY 1987) a German trustee brought an action seeking to recover allegedly preferential and fraudulent transfers made by the foreign bankrupt immediately before bankruptcy proceedings were instituted against them in West Germany. The German trustee alleged that the German corporation made voidable transfers to a New York bank at a time when the bankrupt was insolvent. Generally, the suspect period in the United States is 90 days. *Held*: German law should be applied to decide whether or not the payment was voidable. The German suspect period reaches back one year from the filing of the bankruptcy petition. The German period governed the US action, not the US period. The court said that "foreign preference and fraudulent transfer actions seeking to recover property located here are a sufficient basis on which to ground a Section 304 petition". All that a foreign trustee must do is show that the elements required in Germany for a turnover were present. He need not show that a transfer is voidable under United States bankruptcy law.

But the courts have not always applied the foreign avoidance law in a s 304 ancillary proceeding. The alternative is for the foreign representative to commence a full US bankruptcy proceeding (attracting US avoidance law) or to proceed directly against the transferee in state or federal non-bankruptcy courts.

Involuntary gap creditors

16–28   Gap creditors are those who enter into transactions in the period between petition and order: they may not be protected.

The home forum is likely to apply its own rules to this question but may extend special protections to third parties who receive assets of the bankruptcy abroad in good faith and without notice of the home forum's proceedings. This rule seems desirable since bankruptcies tend not to achieve official foreign publicity.

As regards the foreign local forum, it may be that similar rules should apply to those which apply to the avoidance of pre-commencement transfers since the underlying policies are similar.

In **Germany** a person who in ignorance of foreign proceedings performs a contract in favour of the debtor is discharged: LG Munchen, December 2, 1986, IPR spr 1986 no 209.

Bankruptcy procedure

16–29   Procedural matters should always be governed by the law of the place where the bankruptcy proceedings are brought. This will apply to such matters as the mode of appointment, qualifications and powers of the administrator, the manner and venue of petitioning, the time within which proofs must be filed and the establishment and powers of creditors committees.

Moratoriums and discharges

16–30   An individual bankruptcy usually results in the discharge of the debtor. A corporate winding-up has the same effect because the company disappears. A judicial composition may result in a moratorium or remission of the debts covered by the composition. A US Chapter 11 leads to a discharge of pre-confirmation debts except to the extent provided in the confirmed plan. The root question therefore is whether a foreign country will allow its creditors to have their debts written off by a domiciliary discharge or composition.

Home forum

Generally the home forum will apply its rules as to discharge or moratorium or remission as a mandatory bankruptcy policy regardless of whether the law governing the debt is home or foreign and regardless of whether the creditor is home or foreign.

Thus in England a bankruptcy discharge is effective despite the fact that the debt may be governed by a foreign law: Dicey Rule 163. Similarly an English moratorium, e.g. under a corporate voluntary arrangement, should be effective in England despite the fact that the postponed debts were governed by a foreign law.

Foreign local forum attitude to home forum

If the foreign local forum recognises the insolvency proceedings at the home forum, then the effect of the home forum's discharge or moratorium in the foreign local forum falls to be considered.   **16–31**

If the local forum refuses to recognise the discharge, then the debtor is still liable to pay, even though he has lost his assets in the bankruptcy. He must pay out of his newly-acquired assets and hence loses the opportunity of a fresh start. In the case of companies which have been liquidated and dissolved, the rule is of little importance because the company is gone: there is nobody to sue unless there are still local unliquidated assets and the local forum will wind them up – this is possible in England.

As regards compositions or rehabilitation plans, a creditor who claimed in the proceedings ought to be bound by a domiciliary composition even though he did not vote in favour, since he must do so in the knowledge that the composition is intended to bind all creditors.

In **England** (apart from special rules for Scotland and Northern Ireland) a   **16–32** foreign bankruptcy discharge is effective only if it is a discharge under the law governing the debt. Thus if the debt is governed by the law of the home forum effecting the discharge, then England will recognise that discharge. If the debt is governed by English law, England will not recognise it. Hence the discharged debtor remains liable to pay in the English courts even though he has lost his assets to pay his creditors in the home forum's bankruptcy proceedings.

> In *Gardiner v Houghton* (1862) 2 B&S 743, a debtor was indebted to a creditor under a contract governed by the law of Victoria. The debtor was made bankrupt in Australia and obtained an order of discharge under the Australian bankruptcy law. *Held*: the discharge was a good defence to an action by the creditor against the debtor in England to recover the debt.
>
> In *Bartley v Hodges* (1861) 1 CBNS 375, the debtor was indebted to a creditor under a contract governed by English law. The debtor was made bankrupt in Australia and obtained an order for discharge under the Australian bankruptcy

law. *Held*: the discharge was not a good defence to an action by the creditor against the debtor in England to recover the debt.

There is Scottish and Commonwealth authority for the proposition that if a creditor, who claims that a foreign discharge was not effective, himself participated in the foreign proceedings, he should not be able to insist that the discharge was ineffective.

The same proper law rules apply to a foreign moratorium. The matter is governed by the proper law of the contract and the moratorium is effective (or recognised) only if it is effective under the proper law of the contract.

In *Gibbs v Société Industrielle des Metaux* (1890) 25 QBD 399, CA, a creditor who carried on business in England agreed under an English contract to sell copper to a debtor, a French company, carrying on business in France. The French debtor refused to accept and pay for copper tendered by the English creditor. Subsequently the debtor was placed under judicial liquidation in France and, as a result, its liability was by French law deemed to be discharged. *Held*: the French debtor was held still liable in damages to the creditor in England because the French discharge did not operate under the proper law of the contract which was English law.

In **Germany**, a court has given legal effect in Germany to a discharge of a Swiss corporation in a Swiss bankruptcy case: Decision of May 27, 1993, IX ZR 254/92.

16–33   In **Denmark** a foreign discharge will be recognised if it arises under the governing law of the debt.

In *Petersen, Moller & Hoppe v d'Auchamp*, U 1867, p 977 LOHS, an English domiciliary was discharged after completion of his English bankruptcy. *Held*: the English discharge was ineffective in Denmark mainly because the debt concerned was governed by Danish law and an English discharge could not reach it.

But it is possible that Denmark will now recognise a discharge effected by a domiciliary bankruptcy.

As to foreign compositions, Denmark might possibly recognise a foreign domiciliary compositions.

In *Johansen & Mooller v Hansen*, U 1895 p 163 LOHS, a Swedish domiciliary debtor obtained a court composition in Sweden. He moved to Denmark where certain creditors, who had not participated in the Swedish proceedings, sued him for the full amount of their debts. *Held*: they could not do so since the Swedish domiciliary composition was binding.

In **Finland** the position on a bankruptcy discharge is unclear but the   16–34
writers have asserted that a foreign discharge is not effective in Finland,
since that relief is available only in the country of the bankruptcy. This may
also be the case as regards foreign compositions. In **Norway** there appears
to be little authority, but it may be that a foreign bankruptcy discharge
would not be recognised in Norway. Opinions appear divided as to the
effect of a foreign composition. In **Sweden,** the case law on foreign discharges is not altogether conclusive.

> In *Stockholms Enskilda Bank v Knos*, NJA 1897 p 28 (S Ct) an English domici-
> liary bankrupt obtained an English discharge. The Swedish creditor bank sued
> the bankrupt in Sweden six years later for the remainder of the debt unpaid.
> The bank had received a dividend in the English proceedings. *Held*: the bank's
> claim was time-barred. But the lower court had held that, apart from the time
> limitations, the debtor was still liable to be sued in Sweden.

> In *Morrison & Co v Ekengren*, NJA 1905, p 146 (S Ct) a Swedish member of a
> New Zealand bankrupted firm was discharged in New Zealand. The debt was
> governed by New Zealand law. An English creditor sued the Swede in Sweden.
> *Held*: the Swedish member had been discharged and could not be sued. But it is
> unclear whether the reason was that the debt was governed by New Zealand
> law or that New Zealand law governed the responsibility of a member for the
> debts of a firm.

As to foreign compositions, an old case has denied a foreign composition's effect in Sweden.

> In *Stalhand v Orre*, NJA 1900, p 163 S Ct, a French firm became subject to a
> French court-approved composition. A creditor sued in Sweden for the full
> amount of his claim. He had filed a claim in the French composition but had
> not voted in favour. *Held*: the creditor was not bound by the French compo-
> sition. He had not consented to it.

Veil of incorporation

This issue involves the following questions, amongst others: 16–35

– The liability of directors or shadow directors to contribute to the assets
  for fraudulent or wrongful trading.

– The liability of the management for failing to call a meeting of shareholders if more than half the capital is lost or for failing to petition if the
  company is insolvent.

— The liability of shareholders for the debts of the company on a stripping of the veil of incorporation or on a consolidation of companies.

See chapters 8 and 9.

Home forum

16–36   As regards proceedings in the home forum, the liability of a director to contribute should apply to foreign directors as well as home directors. As to foreign companies, in England it has been held that liability for wrongful trading applies to directors of foreign companies: *Re A Company (No 00359 of 1987)* [1988] Ch 210 (Liberian company).

The liability of shareholders to contribute should be a matter for the law of the place of incorporation: see *Risdon Iron & Locomotive Works v Furness* [1906] 1 KB 49.

Foreign local forum attitude to home forum rules

16–37   If a foreign local forum recognises the home forum's bankruptcy, its attitude may depend upon whether it characterises the director's liability as a penalty imposed by the home forum in which event it will presumably not recognise it.

Bankruptcy penalties and disqualifications

16–38   It is suggested that foreign states will never recognise a criminal penalty or disqualification imposed by the law of the home forum on the ground that criminal jurisdiction is national. Whether an extradition treaty might apply would be a matter for investigation.

CHAPTER 17

INTERNATIONAL
INSOLVENCY TREATIES

General

Because of the confrontations created by conflicting bankruptcy laws, a   **17-1**
favoured solution has been to negotiate international treaties to resolve the
conflicts.

Current bankruptcy treaties include the following:

- Council of Europe

- Nordic Convention 1933

- Bustamente Code of Private International Law of 1928

- Montevideo Treaties

- Germany-Austria 1979, effective 1985

- Franco-Swiss Convention of June 15, 1869

- Franco-Belgium Convention of July 8, 1899

- Franco-Italian Convention of June 3, 1930

- Franco-Monaco Convention of September 15, 1950

- Franco-Austrian Convention of February 21, 1979

There may be the following treaties: Belgium-Netherlands 1925;
Belgium-Austria 1969; Germany-Netherlands 1962.

There are various early nineteenth century treaties between German
states and Swiss cantons but it is uncertain if these are still in force.

Bankruptcy treaties have a long history. For example, Verona and Trent
concluded a treaty in 1204 that governed the transfer of a debtor's assets,
and Verona and Venice reached an agreement in 1306 which sanctioned the
extradition of fugitive debtors.

French conventions

17–2   The main French conventions are:

— Franco-Swiss Convention of June 15, 1869

— Franco-Belgium Convention of July 8, 1899

— Franco-Italian Convention of June 3, 1930

— Franco-Monaco Convention of September 15, 1950

— Franco-Austrian Convention of February 21, 1979

All the French Conventions – with qualifications with regard to the Austrian Convention – acknowledge the validity of the original court decision whereby a person is adjudicated bankrupt. The acknowledgement is subject to a domestic order (*exequatur*) whereby the foreign court decision is deemed valid and enforceable, but under these Conventions the national judge may not review the merits of the case upon which the person was adjudicated bankrupt.

The **Franco-Swiss Convention** governs not only the bankruptcy of a French national's branch in Switzerland, and that of a Swiss national's branch in France, but also that of any foreigner established in either of the two countries who has French or Swiss creditors and assets in either country. The court having jurisdiction is that where the principal place of business is located, and the jurisdiction of the court and the applicability of its insolvency law are general, except with regard to real property.

The **Franco-Belgian Convention** governs the bankruptcy of either French or Belgian traders established in either of the two countries or even in a third country.

The **Franco-Italian Convention** provides rules only for the acknowledgement of the validity of a court decision made in either of the two countries, the court having jurisdiction being that of the domicile or principal place of business or head office, and the applicable national law being that of that court except for the realisation of the assets and the payment of guarantees, foreclosure of mortgages, and other matters.

The **Franco-Monaco Convention** is very similar to the Franco-Italian Convention.

On the other hand, the **Franco-Austrian Convention** gives a broad definition of the proceedings which it governs and includes preventive proceedings (which had raised problems where the Franco-Swiss Convention was applicable). It grants jurisdiction to the court of the country where the debtor is established. This jurisdiction also covers the bankruptcy of the shareholders or partners and of the managers.

Nordic Bankruptcy Convention of 1933

This Convention applies between the following countries: **17–3**

    Denmark
    Finland
    Iceland
    Norway
    Sweden

Later amendments may not have been accepted by Iceland and Norway although the amendments have not changed the basic features of the Convention.

The Convention is a good example of a bankruptcy convention between countries which share similar attitudes to insolvency policies and hence have confidence in the suitability of each other's legal systems.

The basic feature of the Convention is that a bankruptcy in a member state is accorded recognition in all the member states provided it is a domiciliary bankruptcy. Each state reserves its non-domiciliary bankruptcy jurisdiction as regards the other states, but a non-domicilary bankruptcy is outside the Convention. Hence there could be two non-domicilary concurrent bankruptcies in two states.

No recognition procedure is required in other member states for a domiciliary bankruptcy, and the bankruptcy's effects on property in other states is recognised, e.g. the home administrator can collect it and creditor attachments are stayed. The Convention does not create new harmonised substantive bankruptcy rules and the bankruptcy laws of the domiciliary state apply.

By way of exception the law of a state where an asset is located governs special preferences (such as liens) and the securities attached to that asset.

The Convention provides for publicity measures in the other states. As regards non-secured priority or preferred creditors, such as employees, the domiciliary bankruptcy law applies although there is a special regime for taxes. This was acceptable because the local regimes for preferential creditors are very similar.

The Convention applies similar rules to domiciliary compositions. There has been little case law on the Convention.

Montevideo and Bustamente Conventions: Latin America

The Montevideo Treaty of 1889 covers bankruptcies in Chapter X. This   **17–4** treaty governs relations between:

    Argentina
    Bolivia

Colombia
Peru

The up-dating Montevideo Treaty of 1940 covers bankruptcies in Chapter XII. This treaty governs relations between:

Argentina
Paraguay
Uruguay

The Code Bustamente (Convention on Private International Law of 1928) covers bankruptcies in Chapter IX. The Code has been ratified (often with reservations) by 15 countries:

Bolivia
Brazil
Costa Rica
Cuba
Chile
Ecuador
El Salvador
Guatemala
Haiti
Honduras
Nicaragua
Panama
Peru
Republica Domenicana
Venezuela

Note that the Bustamente list does not include Argentina, Colombia, Mexico, Paraguay or Uruguay.

Bolivia and Peru are members of both Montevideo 1889 and Bustamente, but apparently prefer Montevideo, presumably because Montevideo priorities local creditors but Bustamente does not.

Note that Mexico is not a member of any of these Conventions.

The precise application of the Conventions in each country should be checked.

All three conventions cover other private international law matters as well. The contract rules, for example, could be relevant to determining the validity of a claim.

17–5 **Montevideo 1889** The relevant provisions of this treaty give bankruptcy jurisdiction to the commercial domicile of the debtor. But if there are multiple independent commercial establishments in different states the treaty adopts the local priority rule then in force in the contracting states, i.e. local creditors (those whose debts are payable in that country) can initiate a separate local bankruptcy. Each bankruptcy is then conducted separately in accordance with local rules: Art 39. Only the surplus remaining in one bankruptcy is to be turned over to the other: Art 41. The debtor is discharged only when all the states where bankruptcies are opened have granted the discharge: Art 45.

If there is only one bankruptcy, the law of the opening state applies and all creditors must prove there: Art 42. There is provision for advertisement of a bankruptcy in all states where property of the bankrupt is located: Art 38. Provisional preservation orders are available in all states when a bankruptcy has been opened in one of them: Art 37 and these measures are also available if there are plural bankruptcies. If there is only one bankruptcy, the administrator of that bankruptcy is to be recognised in all the states: Art 45. Secured creditors enforce their rights in the state where the property is located: Art 43.

Montevideo 1940 This treaty sought to up-date Montevideo 1889. Rules   **17–6** regarding the bankruptcy of non-merchants, not included in the 1889 treaty, were now included in the new treaty. Broadly, Montevideo 1889 was not much changed in spirit. The local priority rule is extended in that local creditors enjoy priority of payment out of local assets even if there is only one bankruptcy. In Montevideo 1889, this protectionist rule applied only if there were plural bankruptcies. The treaty extends the rules to judicial liquidations, judicial compositions, suspensions of payment and similar remedies: Art 53. Effectively Montevideo 1940 has so many exemptions to the unity of the bankruptcy that the treaty is almost a denial of the principle. This is because as soon as the bankruptcy becomes international by the presence of separate commercial establishments, each state goes its own way and applies its own laws with minimal cooperation between them.

Bustamente The bankruptcy provisions of this Code do not adopt the local   **17–7** protectionist rules of the Montevideo treaties whereby local creditors (those whose debts are payable locally) are paid first. A single bankruptcy is declared by the court of the debtor's domicile and has effect in all contracting states, subject to any registration or publication requirements of local law: Arts 414, 416. But there may be as many bankruptcies as there are establishments if the debtor has "diverse economically entirely separate commercial establishments": Art 415. Again, the result is to deny the principle of the unity of the bankruptcy at the domicile of the debtor and to require all other states to cooperate by freezing local attachments and by turning over the debtor's assets to the bankruptcy centre.

But in the case of a single bankruptcy, the trustee's powers are extended to all the treaty states: Art 418. Only for acts of execution is a local *exequatur* (recognition proceeding) necessary.

The avoidance powers of the opening court apply in all the states: Art 419. But land and other mortgages, property rights and retention of title clauses are subject to local law: see Art 420. Agreements between the bankrupt and his creditors have extraterritorial effect except for creditors with real rights who have not accepted the agreement: Art 421.

Bankruptcy treaties not in force

17–8   The following bankruptcy conventions either failed or are still in draft:

1.   Hague Bankruptcy Convention of 1925. This was not ratified by any country.

2.   Draft US-Canada Bankruptcy Treaty 1979

3.   An EU Bankruptcy Convention was begun in 1963 and a first draft was presented in 1970 which attempted a single bankruptcy law for all member states. This was unrealistic and was replaced by a second draft in 1980. This recognised that the first draft was too ambitious and so attempted a set of principles of conflicts of laws. It gives primary exclusive jurisdiction to the courts of the state where the debtor's "centre of administration" is located, provides for recognition of that bankruptcy judgment throughout member states and finally provides that the local law of member states as to various specified matters should apply to assets within that state. By the end of 1994, work on this treaty was far advanced.

4.   Benelux Convention of 1961, not yet ratified (Belgium, Luxembourg, the Netherlands)

CHAPTER 18

PRIVATE RESTRUCTURING AGREEMENTS: INTRODUCTION

Introduction

Private restructuring agreements are debt composition or rescheduling con-   **18-1**
tracts negotiated privately between the debtor and his creditors, or a major
group of creditors. The jargon term is "work-out".

Plainly there are endless variations in these agreements and it is proposed
to describe principally the practice for substantial restructuring agreements
involving large companies with many bank and other creditors and to refer
to practice in other contexts where appropriate.

Advantages and disadvantages

Any private consensual work-out has to be assessed against the backdrop of   **18-2**
insolvency proceedings and in particular the effect which insolvency proceedings would have upon creditor recoveries. This will usually require a
detailed review of both the law and the facts, and different conclusions may
be reached according to the jurisdiction. Nevertheless some general points
may be made.

A private work-out has some very considerable advantages over a formal
insolvency proceeding, whether the proceeding is a final liquidation or a
rehabilitation proceeding. But these advantages are available only if the
debtor can be saved and can survive – something which it is very difficult in
many cases to predict in advance.

The paramount and overriding advantage of the private work-out compared to any insolvency proceeding is the ability to avoid the trauma and
taint of insolvency and the effect that insolvency proceedings have upon a
business.

Once a debtor is announced to the world to be formally insolvent the
world is less inclined to deal with the victim of his debts. For example, in the
case of a manufacturing company in a rehabilitation proceeding, customers
will be sceptical about the ability of the insolvent to perform contracts, par-

ticularly if they are long-term, and will take much convincing about the maintenance of quality and safety standards and about the ability of the debtor to provide after-sales service and replacements and to comply with quality and performance warranties. They will be less disposed to place advance deposits for new work. Suppliers will ask for cash on delivery so that the business must always pay cash. Sales representatives may give up. Banks will not wish to advance new money without an absolute assurance of payment. Management will be disheartened and demotivated. If the debtor is a financial institution, it will not be able to take money from customers. Nobody will insure with an insurance company which is in formal proceedings. These "public interest" companies may lose their official authorisation to do business. These fatal consequences can be avoided if the restructuring is private and confidential.

The main disadvantage of a work-out, as compared to, say, a rehabilitation proceeding, is the need for unanimity amongst the participating creditors. Unanimity is needed because a class of creditors will not in practice agree to postpone or reduce their debts unless all creditors of that class agree likewise. Many work-outs involve only bank creditors without involving the general body of creditors, such as trade creditors, so that it is easier to achieve this unanimity. But, if the banks are not prepared to finance other creditors and bear the burden on their own, or the situation is so serious that other creditors, notably public bondholders, must also agree to the private composition to lift the load of debt, then the difficulties of achieving a consensus are increased and often rendered impossible. If one bank holds out in order to get paid and vetoes the work-out, then the work-out cannot proceed. In such a case the only alternative is an insolvency proceeding.

In determining whether to attempt a work-out, the creditors must assess the alternatives. The main alternatives are: (1) final liquidation; and (2) a rehabilitation or composition proceeding, if available.

The first task then is to list the main factors which have to be taken into account in carrying out this assessment.

Final liquidation compared to private restructuring

18–3   **Disadvantages of final liquidation** The disadvantages of a final liquidation compared to a consensual work-out include: business stops and fireside sale price apply; there may be a cascade of knock-on insolvencies; and there can be no conversion of debt to equity, with future recovery or upside possibilities. Further, the debtor's estate available for unsecured creditors may be diminished by realisations by secured creditors, repossessions by vendor/lessor title financiers, set-offs and the cancellation of valuable contracts. Priority creditors (e.g. taxes and employees) may consume the estate to the detriment of ordinary unsecured creditors. Periodic payments, such as interest and rentals on leases of real property or equipment, generally cease to run. Foreign currency debts are usually compulsorily converted into local currency so that there is an exchange risk if the local currency is depreciating. Tax liabilities may crystallise on the cessation of the business, e.g. capital allowances previously granted for the purchase of capital assets: these may rank as priority claims ahead of unsecured creditors. International assets may be lost to local creditors and go to pay foreign creditors in priority: cross-border conflicts tend to increase the expense and delay. Finally, formal proceedings are usually extremely costly in terms of the professional fees of insolvency representatives and lawyers.

Advantages of final liquidation But there may be some advantages to creditors, depending on the jurisdiction and the circumstances. Sometimes the advantages run in favour of one group of creditors at the expense of another. For example, the liquidation may crystallise the personal liability of directors to contribute to the assets: the practical value of this depends on the credit of the directors and any insurance they may have. In special cases, the veil of incorporation may be lifted and shareholders or other group companies rendered liable to contribute to the assets or liable for the debts of the debtor company. Transfers to creditors in the suspect period may be avoided as preferences and hence augment the assets; guarantees may be set aside as gifts or transactions at an undervalue. The doctrine of equitable subordination may subordinate the claims of insiders, shareholders and lenders so as to increase the dividends available to other creditors. Insolvency set-off may be prohibited so as to increase the assets available for distribution to unsecured creditors: this favours the unsecured creditors. In civil code jurisdictions, third parties who are beneficially entitled to assets held by the bankrupt e.g. in custodianship, may be deprived of their assets on the ground that possession or apparent ownership by the bankrupt gave rise to false credit so that the assets should be deemed to belong to the bankrupt: this deprivation is a windfall to the debtor's estate. And finally security which has not been perfected by filing or registration is liable to be avoided on insolvency. **18–4**

Judicial rehabilitation proceedings compared to private restructuring: generally

If there is a possibility of survival, the comparison from the point of view of creditors is between a consensual private work-out and a formal judicially-supervised composition or rehabilitation proceeding instead of a final liquidation. **18–5**

The relative merits of the two alternatives depend fundamentally upon the style of the rehabilitation proceeding available in the jurisdiction. It has been seen from chapter 15 that these can be broadly divided into three classes:

- Traditional compositions, available in most jurisdictions. These have been rarely used, mainly because of the high opening requirements, e.g. that the debtor makes an immediate minimum payment (varying typically from 25 per cent to 40 per cent) in excess of what most debtors can realistically pay (Austria, Brazil, the Italian *concordato preventivo*, Norway, Sweden), or that the debtor's assets must ultimately exceed his liabilities on a balance sheet basis, even though he does not have the liquidity to pay his debts as they fall due, or because the debtor must prove misfortune rather than negligence (Belgium, Luxembourg).

- Mild rehabilitation proceedings which impose a protective freeze on creditor actions so as to give the debtor a breathing-space, but do not fundamentally distort creditor rights by staying set-off, contract cancellations and the like and do not leave the management in charge. Examples are the British administration combined with a creditor's voluntary arrangement, the Japanese corporate reorganisation and the Irish examinership.

- Tough rehabilitation proceedings which significantly erode the rights of creditors so as to augment and preserve the debtor's estate and possibilities of survival, e.g. the Canadian commercial reorganisation, the United States Chapter 11, the French *redressment* and the New Zealand statutory management.

The attributes of these proceedings are discussed in chapter 11. One can disregard the traditional composition proceedings, which have been shown to be of very limited value, so that essentially one should compare the workout with the rehabilitation proceedings available in, say, Britain, Canada, Ireland, France, Japan, Italy, New Zealand and the United States.

Advantages of judicial rehabilitation

18–6   A judicial rehabilitation can only be contemplated if there is a possibility of survival. If not, the debtor must go into final liquidation.

The main advantage of a judicial rehabilitation compared to a final liquidation is the fact that the business can be kept going and it is not necessary to stop trading immediately. The business does not have to be broken up, so that potentially the cataclysmic fall in values commonly experienced on a fire-side bankruptcy sale is not so serious – although serious enough. The group structure is maintained. In addition, the rehabilitation plan can usually accommodate a conversion from debt to equity so the creditors can benefit from a recovery, if it occurs. There is a lesser risk of a cascade of insolvencies. A sale of a going concern can be arranged behind a protective curtain.

When compared to a work-out, the attractiveness of a judicial rehabilitation might involve an assessment of the following factors, amongst others.

Stay on creditor attachments If the proceedings stay actions by unsecured   18–7
creditors to attach or levy execution over assets, the debtor has a breathing-space to reorganise its affairs or to arrange a sale without being threatened by piece-meal seizures disturbing the equal treatment of ordinary unsecured creditors. The stay usually needs to be immediate: the absence of an immediate stay is a weakness of English-based judicial schemes of arrangement for companies. One question is whether the stay applies to unpaid government taxes.

By contrast, one of the most serious risks for a work-out is the destabilisation of the plan or the negotiations by individual creditor enforcement actions or threats to enforce.

Dissentient creditors The formal proceedings may be the only way to bind dissentient creditors, especially disaffected trade creditors, public bond-holders (effectively in the US, Chapter 11 is the only method of binding minority bondholders), dissentient banks who are not prepared to agree to a consensual standstill, counterparties to large burdensome contracts, tort litigants (especially in the US), shareholders who do not recognise that they have lost everything, and labour unions. The compulsory overriding of dissents is achieved by majority creditor voting on a plan, with or without court confirmation, and with or without a court power to impose a plan. The formal proceedings can be used to confirm a pre-packaged plan.

Preferences The institution of the proceedings may crystallise the prefer-   18–8
ence rules allowing the estate to recover assets transferred preferentially to creditors in the suspect period. The preference rules apply in a British administration and the US Chapter 11.

Stays on creditor rights The proceedings may stay other creditor rights, notably: the enforcement of security; set-offs; repossessions of leased equipment or real property or assets held under retention of title clauses; the cancellation of contracts and intellectual property licences by reason of the insolvency procedures; and the withholding of supplies by utilities until they are paid.

Disclaimers Whether it is possible in a work-out for the debtor to disclaim onerous contracts and prevent the disappointed creditor from suing pursuant to the stay on proceedings, depends on the jurisdiction. In a work-out, a rejection of contracts may lead to counterparty retaliation.

Finality A rehabilitation proceeding is often intended to be final – one reason that they take so long. Work-outs may be short-leash, i.e. give only short-term relief so as to maintain creditor control and to enable the creditors to see how the situation develops so that they do not give too much initially. This may lead to a series of crises of confidence and a series of restructurings.

Lender liability The proceedings may mitigate the risks of lender liability experienced in a work-out.

Chaos The debtor's situation may be so chaotic that only the legislative hand can impose a stop.

Disadvantages of judicial rehabilitation

18–9   Against these advantages, one must weigh potential disadvantages which, as always, depend on the jurisdiction.

> **Trauma of insolvency** Any formal public insolvency proceeding involves the trauma of insolvency, the loss of goodwill and a reluctance of other parties to continue to deal with the insolvent debtor. The paramount advantage of a work-out is that it tends to avoid this result, even if there is a breach of confidentiality and resulting media attention.

> **Management** Compared to a consensual work-out, management in a formal proceeding – if they stay in place – tends to be disheartened and it is more difficult to attract competent executives who understand the business. Except in the United States, management is usually displaced in favour of an insolvency representative. In the case of a work-out, management usually remains in place, with or without strengthening, but can often be influenced by creditors. If management is uncooperative or unrealistic, the only alternative may be a proceeding.

18–10   **Loss of control** Practical control of the situation by the process of negotiation is lost in favour of creditors committees and, ultimately, of the court so that there is less flexibility.

> **All creditors involved** All creditors are inevitably involved in a formal proceeding, whereas in the case of a work-out, especially a restructuring

of bank debt, this is often not the case. The result of total creditor involvement is increased complication and confrontation, increased delay and increased cost. Work-outs tend to be limited to bank creditors and occasionally other financial creditors so that the process of the adjustment of rights tends to be simpler.

Security Once formal proceedings have begun, it is not possible for creditors to improve their security for existing debt. But in the case of a work-out, bank creditors can, and commonly do, take security and cross-guarantees for their existing debt and hope to outlive the suspect period.

Debt/equity conversions Debt/equity conversions are probably easier and simpler to negotiate in the context of a work-out. A judicially supervised conversion as part of a plan tends to be more confrontational and formal.

Cost Formal proceedings tend to be more costly than consensual work-outs. This follows from the heavy involvement of professionals – lawyers, accountants and consultants – and the confrontations and litigation caused by a rigid statutory framework, by the compulsory quelling or divestment of creditor rights, and by the involvement of creditors committees and the court, in place of direct creditor negotiation.

Time Formal proceedings tend to take longer than a consensual work-out by banks. This is partly because more parties are involved and partly because of the judicial involvement. Work-outs take time and patience, but the ability to cut corners and compromise facilitates a speedier resolution. **18–11**

New money Because of the trauma of formal insolvency, it may be more difficult in a judicial proceeding to raise new money to keep the business going. In the case of a work-out, the stability of the business is less threatened by the taint of insolvency.

Erosion of creditor rights The degree to which rights are eroded depends on the jurisdiction. The main rights to be considered are stays on security enforcement, set-off and repossessions of leased or sold assets. In practice, the parties to a consensual work-out will commonly agree not to exercise these rights. As regards security, the stay on security enforcement may lead to loss of interest, erosion in the value of the security, legal costs, carrying costs and insurance costs. The court may have a power to substitute security: the US insistence of the "indubitable equivalent" may not be sufficient because of erosion of values during the proceeding or court attitudes which are protective of the debtor.

Contract cancellation The commencement of insolvency proceedings may spark off *ipso facto* clauses on the commencement of insolvency proceedings and entitling parties to cancel or forfeit contracts, franchises, distributorships, agency agreements, leases of land or equipment, intellectual property licences and concessions. A mere consensual work-out may not have this effect, unless there are other contractual grounds for cancellation, e.g. cross-defaults or actual balance sheet insolvency.

Statutory disclosure of information Since all creditors are involved in a formal proceeding, there usually has to be a statutory disclosure of information. Banks in a work-out require information, but the risks and liabilities involved in a formal regulated disclosure – which is subject to more onerous duties to protect the public – can increase the cost and delay and result in additional exposures.

Other factors

18–12   Other factors influencing the choice include:

– Whether it is compulsory for a debtor to petition for his bankruptcy or a rehabilitation proceeding if he is insolvent, or whether management is required to call a meeting of shareholders if, usually, one-half of the capital has been lost. These mandatory rules, where they exist, pre-empt a voluntary work-out and leave no choice.

– Whether the jurisdiction imposes penalties on directors for continuing to incur debts while insolvent. If the directors are easily made personally liable or subject to criminal penalties or disqualifications, it will be more difficult to persuade them to agree to a work-out.

– Whether the creditors can be adequately secured. If they can, this will tend to incentivise banks to agree on rescheduling, thus enabling trade and other creditors to be paid out. Factors include the scope of the security on offer: some jurisdictions allow comprehensive universal business charges, e.g. the original floating charge, while others allow very limited security except over land, or make the security cumbersome or of reduced practical value, e.g. because of enforcement problems or because the security is primed by taxes and wages.

– Whether security for pre-existing debt is inevitably a preference so that the work-out must survive the suspect period. In most countries, this security is automatically deemed preferential. England is an exception. In practice, banks taking security hope to survive the suspect period through a successful work-out and hence this is a factor only if the suspect periods are very long – anything over six months.

– Whether there are problems in taking guarantees, e.g. from other companies in the group. Typical problems would be corporate benefit rules, the treatment of guarantees as gifts and therefore liable to avoidance on insolvency as a preference, problems with financial assistance by a company in connection with the purchase of its shares, and consumerist protections in favour of guarantors.

Jurisdictional attitudes

Some jurisdictions favour the work-out as a means of restructuring debt   18–13
while others discourage the private composition consensually agreed
between creditors (or this is the effect of the insolvency laws, whether or not
intended).

Factors relevant to the extent to which a jurisdiction favours formal proceedings include:

– Whether the directors are penalised or are personally liable if they continue or must compulsorily commence formal proceedings on insolvency; the ability to bind dissentient bondholders; and the non-availability of security, especially security for pre-existing debt.

– In practice, one of the key determinants showing a legal bias in favour of formal proceedings is the attractiveness of formal court-supervised rehabilitation proceedings to the debtor. One criterion is the ease of entry, e.g. costs of the court application; whether there is a high opening requirement that the debtor must pay an impractical proportion of his debts as a condition of the composition; whether actual insolvency must be proved, or only threatened insolvency, or no insolvency, whether a substantial likelihood of survival must be shown. Another test of attractiveness to the debtor is the immediacy of the freeze on creditor enforcement proceedings so that the debtor has a breathing-space to assess its position and formulate a plan with its creditors. If management can retain its position and is not displaced by an insolvency administrator, this will appeal to the directors: this is a crucial factor in practice. The debtor will also be influenced by the extent of the restrictions on other creditor rights – enforcement of security, repossession of leased assets or assets held under retention of title, set-off, or cancellation of contracts or forfeiture of real property leases. This interference will be unattractive to the affected creditors, but attractive to the general body of creditors and the debtor. Other features might include the avoidance of preferences, the avoidance of personal liability on directors, and the compulsory conversion of foreign exchange liabilities. Again, the importance of these rules will depend upon the amount of the debts which are affected.

If the formal composition or rehabilitation proceeding is unattractive or cumbersome, then creditors are faced with the choice between a work-out and the nuclear bomb of a final liquidation. This may tend to incentivise them to agree a work-out.

Any ranking of jurisdictions must be regarded with great caution because of the problem of weighting the various criteria and the impracticability of comparing the actual experience of work-outs in the countries concerned. But some tentative assessments may be made.

18–14 Traditional English countries which have not substantially changed their insolvency laws from those pertaining in England prior to 1986 appear favourable to work-outs. This is because there is no compulsory petition on insolvency, a tolerant test of director's personal liability based on fraudulent trading only, the absence of an attractive composition or rehabilitation proceeding so that the only realistic alternative is final liquidation, a judicial tendency to uphold bondholder trust deed provisions in the widest terms whereby dissentient bondholders can be bound by majority votes, the availability of the universal floating charge and quick enforcement of security, the potential validity of security for pre-existing debt, and inhibitions on guarantees which do not go beyond the normal. Countries such as Austria, the Netherlands and Switzerland are also probably favourable to work-outs.

By contrast, France seems the other way. Debtors must file if they are insolvent. Directors are very vulnerable to personal liability for the debts of the company: possibly this incentivises them to stop earlier, although the contrary view is that it does the opposite and incentivises them to avoid insolvency proceedings of any kind at all costs. In any event, the rehabilitative *redressment judiciaire* is readily available, although on the other hand the complete loss of control to the court might make it unattractive to directors and hence improve the advantages of a work-out. Dissentient bondholders can be bound. But security is very weak and limited in scope; security for pre-exempt debt is automatically preferential and there is a long suspect period of 18 months.

In the United States there is no compulsory duty to file if the debtor is insolvent and management is largely shielded from personal liability for the company's debts. On the other hand, there are expansive notions of equitable subordination and lender liability which may discourage some creditors. The debtor has many incentives to file for a Chapter 11 proceeding, including substantial stays on creditor enforcements, set-off, contract cancellations and repossessions, and the ability of management to stay in place. The latter is a major factor encouraging a formal proceeding in the US. Dissentient bondholders can be effectively bound only by a Chapter 11 proceeding. But security has a wide scope and, although security for pre-existing debt is preferential, the federal suspect period of three months is short by international standards – a factor which is weakened by the presence of longer suspect periods under state insolvency laws.

Although Japan has a reorganisation law based on the pre–1978 US model, it is believed that work-outs are preferred to formal reorganisations.

Participants in a work-out

Some comments may be made on the list of potential participants in a work-   **18–15**
out and their likely attitudes.

Banks

The main participants will be the debtor's banks. These may include deposit banks and banks with varying facilities, e.g. bilateral credits, revolving loans, term loans, syndicated loans, and foreign exchange, trade letters of credit, bonding and guarantee facilities.

Their debts are eminently suitable for rescheduling. The banks are well-organised and sophisticated. They hold most of the debt. Their provisioning policies may lead to a desire to advance new money for interest to keep the loan current, without a special reserve impacting on bank profits and balance-sheets.

But there can be serious divisive factors. The banks may be international banks without a special relationship with the borrower and less susceptible to local official or public pressures. They may be lending to different group companies in different countries. If they are sub-participants, the lead bank may not have an adequate clause permitting it to reschedule the debt or to convert debt to equity or to manage the debt without fear of liability to the sub-participant. They may be secured or subordinated so that the very presence of tiering increases competitive pressures and collisions of interest. Difference of provisioning policies, influenced by management, auditors or their regulator, might provoke contrary attitudes to the acceptability of the work-out, e.g. if one bank would have to recognise a bad debt and reserve against it in its accounts, but the others would not.

Individual banks may be in a position to veto aspects of the work-out by virtue of contract clauses, e.g. negative pledges; prohibitions on disposals or change of business; and borrowing ratios. Events of default comprising change of control (debt/equity conversion), cross-default and "material adverse change" may increase their bargaining power – for what it is worth.

Bondholders

18–16   Bondholders may hold bearer or registered bonds, with or without a trustee or voting provisions.

They are difficult to reschedule. This may be because of legal bars on binding a dissentient minority (US and consumerism), the non-recognition of the trust locally or limitations on the voting powers of bondholder communities to bind dissentients. Trustee conservatism is a factor, as well as institutional bondholder conservatism (especially if they are pension funds, insurance companies, fiduciaries, or not able to invest in equity). Bondholders are difficult to organise and often lack sophistication. The need for public confidence in the bond market may lead to public and official pressures. The original managers of the issue may feel vulnerable and hence press for a protective pay-out with a vehemence born of anxiety or embarrassment.

But the contract vetos they wield are less than those of banks. Commonly bonds are closer to non-voting preference shares. They often have weak negative pledges, no financial ratios and weak disposal and "change of business" clauses, if they appear at all. Although cross-default clauses are standard in bonds, "material adverse change" events of default are not. Potentially divisive factors are the presence of senior and subordinated bonds, as well as levels of sophistication and international spread. The involvement of clearing-houses and custodians may complicate the voting process.

It must usually be possible to bind dissentient bondholders to the composition or to the restructuring of the debt or the postponement of maturities or to a conversion of the debt to equity.

If it is not possible to bind minority bondholders, then if the bondholders are essential to a restructuring, e.g. because the debtor will not be able to pay them even if the banks agree to postpone their debt, the result is that formal proceedings must be commenced which will compel them to be bound by a composition or by court confirmation of a plan.

In most jurisdictions there are arrangements whereby dissentient bondholders can be bound. For example, in the English-based jurisdictions it is generally true that provisions in a trust deed constituting a bond issue to the effect that the bondholders can by voting in a meeting alter the terms of the bonds are generally binding on minority bondholders in the absence of secret deals, discrimination or obvious oppression.

A similar effect is achieved by bondholders statutes in many civil code countries which provide that meetings can by voting settle a broad range of matters, including debt postponement. But there are many solutions as to which bondholder rights are entrenched and which are not.

However in a small group of states there are consumerist laws which effectively entrench the rights of bondholders and prevent any changes without their individual consent which in practice it is not usually possible to obtain from every single bondholder. Thus in the United States, the Trustee Indenture Act of 1939 provides that it is not possible to postpone a bondholder's entitlement to be paid without his consent. This can only be achieved in a Chapter 11 formal proceeding where a plan confirmed by the court will override the minority in the class.

Details of bondholder voting are given in another volume in this series on international finance.

Secured creditors

If there is significant secured debt, the enforcement powers of the secured **18–17** creditors may destabilise the restructuring.

Any secured creditors will usually be banks. Most large corporations borrow unsecured on the strength of a negative pledge, but property, shipping, airlines and private companies may borrow secured.

The attitude of secured creditors may be affected by the character of their security. A creditor secured on receivables of the debtor may face set-offs and debtor resistance if liquidation ensues. A creditor secured on inventory may rely on the continuation of the business to complete the manufacturing process. Creditors secured on shares over group companies are subordinated to the creditors of those companies and so will generally get nothing on a liquidation. A creditor with security over a contract may find that it is cancelled by the counterparty because of the default. A liquidation will almost invariably have a disastrous effect on the value of the security, even if it is a factory.

Enforcement is likely to be cumbersome. A bankruptcy freeze on enforcement may erode the cover by reason of insurance and custodial costs, and the accruing of interest. A creditor in the United States may become subject to environmental clean-up costs under environmental legislation.

Lessors

Small or large equipment may be leased. Big ticket lessors might be suitable **18–18** for rescheduling. They tend to be well-organised and sophisticated, but they are secured in substance. Their attitude may depend on whether the continued business will improve the value of the equipment and on the tax effect of a cancellation. A formal proceeding may lead to a stay on repossessions.

Factors

Factoring companies are relevant only if the factoring was with recourse. Effectively they are secured, but the bankruptcy of the debtor may affect collectability, and give rise to debtor set-offs.

Trade creditors

18–19 These are suppliers and key contractors, and include parties with important contracts, notably franchises, distributorships, intellectual property licences, concessions and charterparties which may be cancelled on a bankruptcy and stop the business.

Suppliers are difficult to reschedule: there are usually too many of them and their debts are too small and not essential for survival. Since they are not financial creditors, they are unaccustomed to work-out procedures, and because their debts are often relatively small individually, they have less incentive to reschedule. Their power may come from an ability to withhold further supplies, but on the other hand they may be dependent on the debtor for continued business.

Litigants

The presence of tort or contract litigation may well lead to delays and unpredictability because of the uncertainty of liability and its amount.

Tax authorities

The fiscal authorities are usually a prior creditor on insolvency. They are not usually rescheduled, but may be subject to political pressures (to maintain employment) and so agree to postpone the tax. Although they are usually primed by work-out security, the work-out may assure payment of arrears.

Employees

18–20 Employees are obviously not rescheduled. They are preferred creditors on bankruptcy. There may be political pressures from labour unions. A Chapter 11 stay on the cancellation of collective bargaining agreements is possible in the United States.

Management

The objective of management is to survive. Their views may be affected by whether or not they can stay in place if formal proceedings commence and by their potential personal liabilities if they continue. Management is often ill-equipped to cope with a work-out, especially if they were orientated towards business expansion, and incapable of taking the hard long-term decisions – to cut employees or favoured projects. They are frequently demoralised and exhausted by the stress of the insolvency and overloaded by administrative tasks forced on them by the departure of staff. The best executives leave the sinking ship.

Shareholders

The shareholders are relevant only if the debtor is a public company. They   18–21
are sometimes unrealistic about the state of the company.

Work-outs must take into account the rules applicable to publicly listed companies and which are the responsibility of the management, notably the need for public announcements to prevent a false market in the shares (leading possibly to panic sales), or a suspension of the listing. Any substantial disposal of assets may require a circular to or approval by shareholders as required by stock exchange regulations. The restructuring agreement with the banks will almost invariably be a material contract which is disclosable in the circular. The approval of shareholders will generally be needed for any new issue of shares resulting from a debt conversion

Types of corporate debtor

The work-out is of course fundamentally affected by the type of debtor. The   18–22
main categories may be listed.

Public and private/large and small

A large public company has group companies, potentially with lenders to subsidiaries spread internationally. Groups often have many bank lenders (who may be non-homogeneous or non-relationship or sub-participants), public bondholders, and duties to public investors (disclosure, false markets, insider trading). They may be subject to shareholder approval of a debt-equity conversion; be of national importance (economy, employment);

or be conglomerates (management problems, disposal of non-core businesses).

Public interest businesses

18–23   Public interest businesses include banks, insurance companies and travel agents. Their insolvency is a threat to public confidence, because of losses to small investors and savers, with a potential political dimension. They may be subject to a special insolvency regime and to bonding and depositor protection schemes. Financial companies in the leasing, bonding, discounting, and equipment finance sectors, are not usually in this "public interest" bracket because their funding comes from institutions, not public depositors.

Asset-based companies

18–24   These include property, shipping and aviation companies. Work-outs of shipping and aviation companies have an international dimension with consequent enforcement complications. Commingling by one-ship companies is not uncommon.

Compare "no asset" service companies: recruitment, securities, brokers, cleaning, estate agents, advertising, travel agents, franchisees in leased premises, consumer rental, and advisory (financial services, brokers, accountants, lawyers). These companies depend on goodwill which tends to vanish on an insolvency.

CHAPTER 19

STANDSTILL AND SUPPORT AGREEMENTS

Standstill Agreements

Usually the first signs of trouble come from creditor self-help in the form of restricted bank credit at higher interest rates, demands for security and guarantees, and insistence on cash on delivery by suppliers. The debtor may be late in producing its financial statements. Banks and other creditors become involved through breach of bank covenants and through default clauses (especially a cross-default in term loans, leases, bonds, licences, distributorships or mortgages), financial ratios, a "material adverse change" clause, a negative pledge, or a prohibition on disposals. A material adverse change clause in a commercial paper programme or revolving credit leads to a refusal by creditors to roll-over and a misrepresentation or non-disclosure risk for borrowers. There may be a refusal to roll-over e.g. because of the announcement of sharply reduced profits. All those factors precipitate the crisis.

19–1

Informal standstill

The first stage is generally a temporary standstill agreed by the major creditors, usually banks, in order to give the debtor company a breathing space, to ensure that no bank creditor is preferred, to allow a feasibility review to take place, and to allow the restructuring to be negotiated.

19–2

Proper practice is for the request for a standstill to come from the debtor company, with or without an invitation to do so, so that the work-out is not seen as a solution imposed upon the debtor.

Steering committee

The initial phase is generally inflamed by crisis and can only be properly dealt with by experienced work-out specialists and strong creditor leadership. Banks with the largest exposures will usually establish a steering

19–3

committee or co-ordinating committee, led by a lead or co-ordinating bank with the necessary experience and resources. Other committees may be formed, e.g. of trade creditors or bondholders or shareholders.

The roles of the bank committee are to act as a point of liaison between the debtor and its major creditors; to negotiate the initial standstill; to commission accountants' reports; to collect information about the creditors and the debtor's situation; and to negotiate the restructuring documentation.

Steering committee members should bear in mind the responsibilities of their position. From the liability point of view, they should avoid acting as agents for creditors (attracting fiduciary duties of due diligence, no conflicts of interest, no secret profits). Their role is not advisory, but administrative. Care should be taken to minimise liability for negligent statements or omissions (ordinary due diligence plus exculpation clauses). They should be aware of the problem of insider information leading to insider trading in the company's securities. Any secret bargains, e.g. fees, prepayments, security or other kick-backs, should be avoided: creditors who make secret bargains in connection with creditor arrangements are vulnerable: see *Re EAB* [1902] 1 KB 457; *Re Milner* (1885) 15 QBD 605, CA. The committee should be aware of potential liability for the tort of procuring a breach of a contractual relations, e.g. by demanding non-payment of other creditors or the grant of security in breach of another lender's negative pledge, or the disposal of assets contrary to an anti-disposal clause, and of the risks of shadow directorship or (in the US) equitable subordination. Any advice to management should not be intrusive or preemptory.

The members of the committee should disclose potential conflicts if appropriate, e.g. if they are an agent bank and also a sole lender, a secured lender, or a lender which has delegated management to sub-participants.

Prospectus requirements imposed by securities regulation should be considered in relation to circulars to creditors. These would be rare because of the usual exemptions in favour of sophisticated investors or existing creditors or because a bank loan is not a "security" or an "investment" within the legislation. The US exemptions are more restricted.

Terms of standstill agreement

19–4   As mentioned, generally a standstill will be agreed between the major bank creditors and the debtor to allow time for information to be collected and the restructuring agreement to be negotiated. Typical terms of a standstill letter include those listed below.

1.   **Equality of treatment of creditors and no improvement of creditor positions**

- No prepayments or repayments unless pro rata (allowance being made for fluctuating overdrafts and revolving lines of credit)

- No new security or guarantees to any creditor or other preferential arrangements not available to other creditors

- No intra-group transfers which might deplete one debtor company and its creditors and improve the position of lenders to another group company

- No preferential increases in interest or commission rates in favour of individual creditors

- Permitted disclosure of information between creditors which might otherwise breach bank confidentiality rules

- No disposals of assets

2. **Banks hold their positions** 19–5

- No loan acceleration or demand or close-out of swaps, foreign exchange contracts

- No termination of facilities (overdrafts, rollover lines, foreign exchange, acceptances, letters of credit) but no duty to increase exposure over a previously agreed limit

- No enforcement of security or calling of guarantees

- No set-offs

- No petition or filing for insolvency proceedings and no attachments or executions

- (Sometimes) no assignments, transfers or sub-participations (to control the identity of creditors)

The standstill date may be retrospective to freeze exposures at particular point in time so as to negate last-minute improvements in position by individual creditors – this is a voluntary reflection of preference laws.

3. **New money** 19–6

- Any new money will be advanced on a LIFO basis; the bankers agree in principle that new money will enjoy prior security. Inevitably, the debtor will need fresh financing. Note the relevance of borrowing limits in constitutional documents or loan agreements, and the directors' potential responsibility for new liabilities under wrongful trading rules.

- Immediately available security to be provided to the banks pending more complete security.

4. **Short-leash controls**

- All facilities are placed on demand, which is controlled by a bank majority.

- Interest to be kept current (or rolled-up).

- Termination of standstill on certain defaults, including material adverse change decided by a bank majority.

19–7 5. **Other provisions**

- Debtor to pay fees and expenses of steering committees, accountants, valuers

- Confidentiality, except as required by law or regulation (e.g. stock exchange requirements)

- An exculpation and indemnity in favour of the steering committee (e.g. for fees incurred)

- A reservation of the rights of lenders under their existing agreements and a "no-waiver" declaration

- A provision that the agreement comes into effect only if, before a prescribed date, 90 per cent (or some smaller per cent) of the eligible bank creditors have acceded to the agreement.

A striking feature of those typical provisions is how closely the voluntary agreements reflect the mandatory provisions of a judicial rehabilitation proceedings on the lines of the US Chapter 11 or French *redressement judiciaire*, e.g. breathing space, no enforcement, no contract cancellation, no set-off, no security enforcement, priority moratorium loans, and a measure of creditor democracy. But, as discussed, judicial proceedings have disadvantages.

Management changes

19–8 Rightly or wrongly, the financial distress of a company usually leads to a loss of creditor confidence in the existing management.

Creditors can initiate discussion on management changes but not so as to control them, notably because of the shadow director problem.

If the creditors promote the appointment of a company doctor, he may require an indemnity from the banks (because of wrongful trading) and performance-related remuneration and share options. The problem for new management is that they have to deal with a crisis as well as learn about the business.

Review of debtor's position

A review of the debtor's position – either before or after a standstill agreement is essential for a properly informed restructuring. This will usually involve a review of the following: the corporate tree, joint ventures, affiliates, management, and inter-company transactions; the debt position by company (security, leases, guarantees, covenants, defaults, commitments to lend, schedule of existing facilities); the asset position by company (inventory, real estate, intellectual property, receivables analysis, machinery and equipment, availability of security); copies of all banking and financial documents; cash flow projections, budgeting, medium term forecasts; tax analysis (overdue obligations, liability of officers); special contracts (supply and sale contracts; lease, franchise, licensee and distributorship contracts, defaults and cancellation rights; warranty liabilities); licences, and permits and potential cancellations by regulatory authorities; litigation and attachments; employees and unionisation; key employees; compulsory redundancy payments; pension plan liabilities.

19–9

All work-out specialists emphasise the importance of shared information. There must be equality of information in a creditor group. Misinformation leads to irrational decisions.

Information should be kept confidential so as not to create panic. This conflicts with the need to protect investors. Publicity may be enforced by duties to make an announcement to prevent a false market in the debtor's securities, and by the filing of financial statements.

The lenders generally appoint accountants to investigate the prospects of the debtor company during the initial temporary standstill period. These are not usually the auditors, but an independent firm so as to avoid any real or imagined taint and to forestall problems if the existing auditors were negligent. They will usually report direct to the steering committee so that their responsibility is direct: English case law has restricted the scope of auditors' duties to third parties, e.g. *Caparo Industries v Dickman* [1989] 2 WLR 316. Their terms of reference are usually: to investigate the financial viability of the debtor; to describe its business and financial position; to prepare projected cash-flows, prospects and forecasts (a three-year forecast is unsafe and anything over five years very suspect), to indicate the debtor's borrowing requirements, the feasibility of a disposals programme and strategic plan; to comment on the value of the security on offer; and to comment on management and controls.

London Approach

19–10   In 1990 the Bank of England issued a paper entitled "The Provision of Financial Support for Companies with Liquidity Problems" in which it outlined the "London Approach" to the orderly management of work-outs. The key features are (a) a responsible and supportive attitude by bank lenders towards companies experiencing financial difficulty, (b) the continued role of the Bank of England as a neutral chairman and intermediary (which may involve some arm twisting), (c) a lending standstill so that a proper analysis can be made of whether continuing support – and particularly additional financing – is justifiable, (d) the gathering of the fullest possible information to support that analysis and the subsequent judgment, and (e) the important role for the lead bank, which needs to ensure that all interested bank creditors are informed of the company's position at the earliest possible stage, and are kept informed. These guidelines are not legally binding, but they create expectations and indeed reflect good banking practice.

Support agreements

19–11   Support agreements are variously called "restructuring", "rescheduling" or "support" agreements.

Override and consolidated agreements compared

A support agreement can consolidate all the credits into one agreement or be an override or overlay agreement setting out additional terms applying to all the credits but without otherwise altering the original credit agreements. Override agreements are common in major corporate restructurings but consolidated agreements are typical of sovereign debt reschedulings. State insolvency is reviewed in another volume in this series on international financial law.

The advantage of a consolidated agreement is that the same financial and documentary terms apply to all creditors. But the disadvantages include the time and difficulty of re-documenting large numbers of different facilities in one document and the possible adverse impact of a reconstitution of debt on existing security or on existing guarantees.

Restructured debt

The eligible debt which is subject to the restructuring will usually be that **19–12** owed to financial institutions, notably bank credits (term loans, overdrafts); acceptance credits; foreign exchange facilities; guarantee and bonding facilities; documentary letters of credit; interest swaps, interest caps, floors and collars.

The agreement will not usually cover the following (but may do so exceptionally): public debt (such as debentures and eurobonds these are dealt with separately, if at all); commercial paper; supplier and other trade debt: para 18–15 *et seq.*

Insider debt (such is that owing to controlling shareholders or associated companies) may be subordinated.

Terms of support agreements

Financial terms The financial terms of the restructuring may defer repay- **19–13** ment instalments and extend maturities, roll-up interest, provide for a debt to equity conversion increase margins and commitment fees, and provide for up-front fees and the expenses of the restructuring.

Standstill clause The agreement generally provides that, unless prescribed majorities so consent, the lenders agree: (1) to maintain their facilities at the agreed levels and exposures as at the initial standstill commencement date and not to cancel them, e.g. overdrafts, foreign exchange facilities; and (2) not to petition for insolvency proceedings or enforce payment, or accelerate loans, or close out swaps, foreign exchange contracts and the like, or enforce security or exercise set-offs.

The standstill typically continues only for a limited period subject to a unanimous extension by the creditors – this is the short-leash approach.

Most favoured debt clause To enforce equality, the debtor usually agrees that, if it pays or prepays debt involved in the support agreement or eligible for inclusion (even though not included), it will prepay the included debt equally and rateably.

Interest and fees Usually there is an uplift in interest margins on existing debt to compensate for the increased risk. There is generally also a front-end fee for the work involved and as a sweetener to the bank creditors.

New money The support agreement will provide for any new money that may be required. This will be syndicated on the conventional basis, and is usually given priority on the security on the "last in, first out" principle. The commitments are commonly fixed by reference to exposures on the standstill commencement date and not by reference to actual outstandings on that date. Overdraft outstandings are arbitrary since they depend on the pattern of operational receipts and payments.

Representations and warranties The support agreement will contain usual representations and warranties, e.g. as to the legal status of the borrower, powers, constitutional documents, legal validity, the status of the security (title to secured assets, first priority of security and validity), the correctness of information supplied as a basis for the standstill, and the absence of litigation. The purposes of these are: (a) they are investigatory; (b) they constitute an express event of default if incorrect; and (c) they allow a suspension of new money drawdowns if incorrect. The topic is reviewed in another work in this series on international financial law, as are other term loan provisions discussed below, notably covenants and events of default.

19–14 **Covenants** The agreement usually contains very detailed covenants, most of them building on the conventional practice for term loan agreements.

The covenants will normally include an elaborate information clause (including monthly management accounts), and a tight negative pledge (even though the rescheduled debt is secured).

Invariably there will be stringent control of disposals of all kinds (sales, leases, options etc.) except in accordance with any agreed asset disposal programme. The presence of security over the assets confers a high degree of control in any event.

Support operations almost invariably include a disposal programme, identifying proposed disposals and setting out a timetable for the disposals. The objects of a disposal programme are to rid the company of loss-making assets or to enable the company to retrench to its core activities, or to reduce the debt in an orderly fashion. The dangers are that a disposal will result in saleable, profit-making assets being disposed of, leaving only a rump of loss-making assets. The disposals may spark off severance pay claims and involve contract damages.

All individual disposals are usually controlled by the majority creditors, e.g. to ensure that the price is fair, that it is reviewed by the creditors and that the disposal does not result in risks, e.g. the credit risk of the buyer if the price is deferred or if there are potential warranty claims against the debtor as seller.

Disposals proceeds will be applied first to LIFO new money and then pro rata to existing debt.

Ring-fencing The ring-fence is a series of covenants intended to prevent leakage of assets from the debtor companies to subsidiaries or other related companies who are not involved in the security package (e.g. because security is not available abroad or because of a foreign creditor veto) or who are not included in the restructuring agreement.

The main restrictions control transfers and other disposals to the non-included companies; loans, credit and other financial assistance, including guarantees or security, in favour of those companies; and a prohibition on or no material changes in inter-company pricing.

Events of default Generally the standstill is cancellable on demand subject to   **19–15**
majority bank control. The protection to the debtor company is that a bank consensus is required before the arrangement can be brought to a halt. The directors may properly require a non-legally binding letter of comfort from the banks that they do not presently intend to exercise their powers to cancel so that the directors can continue trading without incurring personal liability and to forestall the need for stock exchange announcements to prevent a false market in the shares.

If specific events of default are included, they will cover those normally found in term loan documentation, i.e. non-payment, non-compliance with covenants, breach of representation or warranty, cross-default, creditor processes (execution, attachment etc.), insolvency, liquidation, receivership and the like, and a wide material adverse change clause. The appropriate events of default will also extend to subsidiaries and guarantors.

It is common also to include an event of default or mandatory prepayment clause if a single person, or persons acting in concert acquire control of the debtor (e.g. by reference to a 30 per cent test), or there are changes in key management not previously approved by the majority banks.

Other provisions These may include: protections for the steering committee   **19–16**
and agent banks; indemnities against defaults, including breakage costs; default interest; the usual boiler-plate e.g. expenses, fees, stamp duties, notices, waivers, provisions for assignments and transfers by creditors, currency indemnity, set-off, governing law and jurisdiction.

Creditor decision-making Decisions by creditors tend to be tiered between: (1) bank unanimity (such as increases in exposure, extensions of time, reductions in rates, material reductions in security); (2) majority banks (acceleration, cancellation, waivers of important covenants); (3) steering committee (minor and administrative decisions); and (4) agent bank or co-ordinator (decisions delegated by the banks).

Majorities may be defined so that a few banks with large exposures do not dominate the group, e.g. some compound of majority by number and by exposures

Security for restructured debt

19–17   The security will generally comprise an omnibus package of cross-guarantees from all members of the group, plus security to the extent available. In English-based countries, the security will generally comprise fixed and floating charges over all the assets of the group.

Some limitations on the security should be noted:

1.   Security for pre-existing debt granted in the suspect period may be vulnerable as a preference: para 5–17 *et seq*. But it is better to have potentially valid security than not to have it at all.

2.   Guarantees may be vulnerable on insolvency as a gift or transaction at an undervalue (see IA 1986 s 238) or because of "corporate benefit" rules or because they conflict with borrowing limits.

3.   Overseas subsidiaries may not be able to grant security because of objections by overseas creditors or because the security is not available as a matter of law or because of negative pledges held by creditors not participating in the support agreement.

4.   Where a work-out results from a buy-out whereby the shell buy-out company bought an operating group, the operating group may be prevented from granting security by reason of rules prohibiting the grant by a company of financial assistance for the purchase of its own shares, e.g. the British Companies Act 1985 s 151. The subsidiary may not be able to satisfy the tests allowing it to give the security, e.g. if they would become insolvent by reason of the cross-guarantees.

As regards timing, one possibility is to take immediately available security over the core companies at once, i.e. at the time of the original standstill agreement, and require the debtor to supplement it with further security as required by the majority banks or co-ordinating committee. A framework agreement could cover these matters, together with bank decision-making, prior to the completion of further documentation.

A trustee is useful to hold the benefit of the security for the benefit of all creditors.

Maximising the security

19–18   A number of techniques can be used in England and other English-based countries to maximise the security:

–   Floating charges for pre-existing debt must survive a long suspect period. But the floating charge can be "purified" by roll-over of the debt in a current account: *Re Yeovil Glove Co Ltd* [1965] Ch 148. On this theory, payments into the account discharge the old debt, and payments out are treated as new debt and hence the security is to that extent not vulnerable as being security for pre-existing debt. One could reorganise the group current accounts into direct accounts with operating subsidiaries so as to facilitate this process. But the roll-over of debt or re-routed debt which does not swell the assets, or (sometimes) money subject to strings so that the company effectively never has the use of the money, are not new money, for the purpose of purifying a floating charge. For an explanation of these situations, see para 5–21 *et seq.*

— Floating charges should, so far as possible, be converted to fixed charges, e.g. over shares, capital equipment, intellectual property rights, major contracts, book debts. In England, fixed charges have a shorter preference period than floating charges, are not automatically preferential even if for pre-existing debt, and are not subordinated to the prior payment of preferential creditors.

— The main relationship bank should establish a wages account since advances for wages are subrogated to the preferential position of employee wages on insolvency: para 1–42. Proceeds of sale of the fixed security should be appropriated to the non-preferential claims of the bank, so as to procure the priority of the preferential claims in case the security is insufficient to cover both. The validity of this device was confirmed by *Re William Hall (Contractors) Ltd* [1967] 2 All ER 1150

— Floating charges securing guarantees are not for purified new money under IA 1986 s 245 so one should consider reorganising the debt. For an explanation, see para 5–21 *et seq.*

Loss sharing agreements

Loss sharing agreements compared to pro rata sharing clauses

The banks may enter into a loss-sharing agreement. These are different from 19–19 priority arrangements between two or more creditors holding security from a common customer or from normal forms of pro rata sharing clauses in syndicated credits.

Normal pro rata sharing clauses provide that if one bank receives a greater pro rata share than the other banks (by reason of set-off, guarantee, execution proceeds or security), it must pay the excess to the agent bank who redistributes to the syndicate banks pro rata and the paying bank is subrogated to the claims paid. The conventional pro rata sharing clause may allow "double-dipping". For example, a bank has 140 deposit and 100 loan. The bank sets off 100 of deposit, leaving 40 of deposit; it shares the 100 with other banks as a result of which it acquires additional debt by subrogation which it then sets off against the remaining 40. The efficacy of double-dipping depends on the circumstances.

The differences are that in a loss-sharing clause in a restructuring agreement: (1) the sharing formula differs according to whether the receipt is pre- or post-enforcement; (2) losses are calculated on exposures at the standstill commencement date (such as agreed overdraft lines), not on actual outstandings; (3) the debtor is not bound by the redistribution; and (4) there is no double-dipping.

Sharing formula

19–20   Loss-sharing contracts vary greatly, but a typical arrangement divides the tiering into pre-enforcement recoveries and post-enforcement recoveries by the banks.

Pre-enforcement recoveries are applied first to the pro rata payment of principal and interest on new money LIFO loans, and then to pro rata payment of principal and interest on pre-existing loans and credits.

Any disposal proceeds may be applied pro rata according to standstill exposures. Any proceeds of disposals by a subsidiary may be used to pay the creditors of that subsidiary (to avoid the legal complications of transfers of the proceeds from that subsidiary to other members of the group) on the basis that any resulting inequalities between creditors are corrected by post-enforcement loss-sharing.

Post-enforcement recoveries are often applied in the following order: (1) any priority creditors by law, e.g. wages; (2) principal and interest on new money loans; (3) principal on old money loans; and (4) interest on old money loans.

The sharing is usually calculated on the basis of the standstill date exposures of the banks, as opposed to actual outstandings (because the overdraft outstandings may be arbitrary). Contingencies, such as bonds and guarantees, will have to be valued. The close-out of foreign exchange contracts and swaps may produce a net amount so that the exposure is net and not gross for valuation purposes.

Sometimes the loss-sharing order of payments is tiered and not pari passu. For example, lenders to operating companies may bargain for a higher priority than lenders to the holding company who are effectively subordinated creditors if the assets are in the subsidiaries. Often more time is spent on resolving tiering disputes between creditors than any other aspect of the restructuring.

CHAPTER 20

PRIVATE RESTRUCTURING AGREEMENTS: DEBT/EQUITY CONVERSIONS

Conversion of debt into equity

Introduction

Some work-out plans involve an agreement by creditors to convert their   **20–1**
debt into shares so that they become shareholders in the debtor instead of
creditors. The conversion is technically achieved either by the creditors
releasing their debt to the extent of the subscription price for the new shares
of setting off their debt against their liability for the subscription price on
the shares.

Debt eligible for conversion

The main classes of creditor in the case of a commercial company would   **20–2**
typically include: banks, bondholders, lessors, sellers of large assets on
credit, trade suppliers, and intercompany creditors and it needs to be considered which debt is eligible for conversion.

The practicalities of the situation usually lead to the result that, even
though these creditors would rank equally on a final liquidation, it is not
feasible to require all of them to convert on the same terms. A second
important reality is that, if negotiations are difficult or long drawn-out, the
expense will increase and the debtor may collapse in the meantime. One
may comment on each class of creditor in turn.

Banks Banks and similar financial institution are usually creditors for loans
to the debtor, for guarantees, bonds and letter of credit issued on behalf of
the debtor and for foreign exchange facilities.

Bank debt is usually the most amenable to conversion. Firstly, the banks
are generally a relatively small group who are well-organised and who can

---

act more or less as a coherent homogeneous group so that it is easier to negotiate with them than with a large population of small creditors. Secondly, they are commonly sophisticated and so better equipped to assess a complex structure and to make an informed and rational decision. Third, their credits frequently dwarf the exposures of other creditors so that conversion of all or part of the bank debt is sufficient to stabilise the debtor. Finally, banks are more susceptible to official pressures from their regulators; this encourages unanimity.

In practice, therefore, if a debt conversion is warranted, the banks will commonly be participants.

20–3   **Bondholders** It is much more difficult in practice to persuade bondholders to convert. Since they may be numerous and may include a large number of small creditors, it is cumbersome to organise them and to negotiate with them. This difficulty is compounded if there is no trustee acting as their representative, in which event the negotiations have to be conducted with large holders and the scheme advertised to the remainder in newspapers and notified in formal notices to the bondholders with unpredictable results. Bondholders are not susceptible to official pressures. The local legal regime may, by public protective statutes, inhibit or outlaw a compulsory debt conversion decided by a majority so that unanimity by overriding a dissenting minority cannot be achieved. The topic is reviewed in another volume in this series. It is hardly surprising that one bondholder will not convert if all his fellows do not also convert: the result would be that the non-converting bondholders would achieve priority of payment even though they are the same type of creditors.

20–4   **Lessors** This class comprises primarily lessors of equipment, such as aircraft, ships, machinery, or computers. In substance, they are secured creditors who are able to cancel the lease on a default by the lessee-debtor, repossess the equipment and sell it. Apart from lessors of small items – vehicles, office equipment and the like – these lessors are commonly financial institutions with whom negotiations can conveniently be conducted. However, since they are effectively secured, it will often be difficult to persuade them to convert unless the leased asset is worthless. Any freeze on repossession by them of the leased equipment on insolvency proceedings (as in the case of the US Chapter 11, the British administration or the French *redressement judiciaire*) may be a weakly persuasive factor.

In the unlikely event that they do convert, there are two alternatives. Either the lessor would terminate the lease, sell the equipment and convert the unpaid balance of the net present value of future rentals uncovered by the sale proceeds, plus accrued unpaid rentals. Or the lessor would sell the leased equipment to the lessee and convert the uncovered balance as above plus accrued unpaid rentals. A sale to the lessee would often be undesirable since in many jurisdictions a sale to the lessee destroys the tax advantages of leasing, i.e. the deductibility of all or a portion of the capital purchase price of the leased equipment from the lessor's taxable profits (capital allowances).

Conversion by a lessor of land is probably rare – although theoretically possible.

Large sellers This class comprises non-trade sellers of large assets to the **20–5**
debtor on deferred credit terms, as where the debtor has bought a company with the purchase price deferred or has bought a factory on credit. It may be possible to persuade these sellers to convert alongside the banks.

Trade suppliers This class comprises numerous unpaid suppliers. It would be rare for them to convert. They are normally small creditors and it is generally not worth the trouble. Often there are many of them, so negotiation is cumbersome and unpredictable and would be expensive and time-consuming. They are commonly short-term creditors and may resent being classed with medium-term financial institutions. The debtor's business may depend upon the continued goodwill of its trade suppliers.

Intercompany debt Intercompany debt is debt owed by one company in a **20–6**
group of companies to another, e.g. a loan owed by a subsidiary to its parent. Capitalisation of intercompany debt is frequent and can (usually) be achieved without the involvement of outside parties. If the debtor is the parent, the subsidiary cannot usually convert since many company statutes prohibit a company from holding shares in its parent company: see, for example, the British Companies Act 1985 s 23. In such a case, the subsidiary should subordinate its credit to other creditors.

In the case of companies owing debt to large shareholders or directors, these connected persons would usually be expected to convert.

Advantages of conversion

The conversion of debt into equity is not a procedure which creditors gener- **20–7**
ally view with approbation: they prefer to keep their credits in the form of debt. But on occasion, notably where the debtor is hopelessly insolvent and the debt almost valueless, they may be persuaded to do so – but only if there is a light at the end of the tunnel.

The reasons which may lead creditors to convert may be briefly listed.

Wrongful or fraudulent trading If a corporate debtor is insolvent, then in many jurisdictions including England, continued trading and the continued incurring of debts may expose the directors of the debtor to personal liability for fraudulent or wrongful trading. In other jurisdictions, insolvency law may impose a duty on management to initiate insolvency procedures if the company is insolvent: para 8–14 *et seq*. Hence if the creditors do not convert to a sufficient extent to restore solvency, the directors must stop trading and in practice insolvency proceedings will or must commence, so that the private work-out will have failed. The unhappy choice may therefore be forced upon the creditors.

Interest burden If the debtor is so seriously insolvent that it is not even able to pay interest as it falls due, let alone principal, the conversion will relieve the company of its interest burden. Dividends on shares are generally payable only out of profits or other distributable reserves and not out of capital, and universally a company may not pay dividends while it is insolvent. The elimination of interest can thus at a stroke convert a loss-making company to a profitable company. For example: a company has profits of 100, but interest of 300: loss 200. If the creditors convert, the loss of 200 is converted into a profit of 100.

Solvency ratios Banks, insurance companies, investment dealers and others may be required to maintain certain solvency ratios if they are to maintain their official authorisation to do business. Once the licence is gone, the business is gone. Conversion – or subordination – is therefore often the only alternative.

Share in the upside If there is a light at the end of the tunnel, conversion into equity keeps alive the possibility that the debtor's fortune will recover, in which event the converting creditors stand to benefit from the future potential gain. This may be more attractive than an immediate write-off or debt reduction.

20–8 **New money** If creditors are prepared to convert, this may increase the possibility of new money from senior creditors or a rights issue from existing shareholders so as to provide the necessary continuing finance for the debtor.

Supplier confidence The conversion may be desirable to maintain supplier confidence and continuing credit from suppliers.

Voting On conversion, the creditors may be entitled to exercise votes for management and hence effectively control or influence the choice of directors. Attempts by creditors to control the directors while they are creditors might run the hazard of converting the creditors into shadow directors who may be personally liable for a debts of the company in certain circumstances: para 21–15 *et seq*.

Public relations Banks may seek to foster continued public esteem if they convert instead of bayoneting the wounded in the eyes of the public.

Disadvantages of conversion

The disadvantages of conversion will need to be balanced against the advantages. 20–9

Timing The conversion of shares into equity, notably in the case of a public company whose shares are listed, is time-consuming. This is because negotiations tend to be more difficult as creditors weigh up the pros and cons of conversion, because more parties are involved, e.g. existing shareholders who will be diluted and who are not prepared to accept that they have lost everything, or bondholders who cannot be contacted or crammed down by majority resolution. Formal circulars to shareholders up to prospectus standard may have to be prepared and formal meetings called and held. During this period, the debtor may collapse from lack of finance. If the debtor is on its last legs the only alternative may be a rehabilitation proceeding (if available) which keeps the creditors at bay. These proceedings suffer the disadvantage of any formal insolvency proceedings, e.g. loss of goodwill and values, collapse of supplier and management confidence, and expense.

Loss of security A company cannot grant security for share liabilities, so that a potentially super-priority senior secured claim can rank only as a junior unsecured claim on liquidation.

Loss of guarantees On conversion, creditors will generally lose any guarantees. Often banks lending to a holding company of a group will have guarantees from subsidiaries. These have to go on conversion of the debt into shares of the holding company, since in many, if not most, developed jurisdictions, a company may not give financial assistance in connection with the acquisition of its own shares or those of its holding company: a subsidiary guarantee of the parent company's liabilities on its shares would generally offend the rule.

Loss of priority A converting creditor becomes a shareholder and therefore 20–10 ranks after creditors of the company: he becomes a subordinated claimant.

No mandatory interest The creditor loses his contractual right to interest: instead he is relegated to a claim for a dividend. Dividends are payable only if management so decides and, generally, only if there are sufficient net profits. Everywhere, dividends are not payable if the company is insolvent. Hence if the fortunes of the company recover to some extent, the creditor is in a worse position as regards the remuneration on his investment.

Exit The recovery of the debt may be more problematic if the debtor's fortunes improve: debt is repayable when due, but shares are not generally redeemable except in narrow circumstances. The exit from a shareholding is generally by a sale: if the converting creditors will form a large bloc, a sudden sale by existing former creditors may depress the price. There may also be agreed sale restrictions between the banks in a special shareholders agreement in order to avoid this result, or, more usually, to maintain equality between the banks.

Insolvency petitions A creditor can unilaterally petition for insolvency proceedings, and so retains dominant control of his investment in this regard. But a shareholder cannot petition on his own: usually a vote is required, e.g. 75 per cent.

20–11 **Tax deductibility** Interest is generally deductible in computing taxable profits, but dividends are not. Naturally, this is relevant only if there will be profits.

Provisioning If debt is converted, then the banks may, under local provisioning policies, be obliged to write off the debt completely in their books, at the time of conversion. If the debt is simply rescheduled, the provision may be partial only so that it can be written off in stages and hence the impact on the bank's balance sheet is cushioned by a periodic write-off of instalments, instead of a single lump-sum. If a bank's balance sheet is damaged, then naturally its financing costs tend to rise to reflect its reduced credit-standing.

Securities violations Under s 15 of the US Securities Act of 1933, a controlling person is liable jointly and severally with the controlled person for certain securities law violations, unless the controlling person acted in good faith and did not directly or indirectly induce the violation.

Other implications of conversion

20–12 There are inevitably manifold other implications of a conversion from debt to equity and manifold obstacles in the path. This section lists some of the points which may need to be considered.

Restrictions on equity holdings by banks In some jurisdictions, e.g. the United States and Japan, banks may be restricted from holding equity investments in a company above certain thresholds to distinguish ordinary investments in marketable securities from dominant or influential holdings. The original objective of the legislator was to prevent monopolies by financial institutions, an objective overtaken by the regulatory desire to restrain banks from investing in risky equities which might threaten their stability and solvency, e.g. the US Glass-Steagall Act. The regulatory authority may be prepared to allow conversions where forced on a bank as part of a workout or there may be a specific exception in favour of temporary holdings acquired in collecting debt previously contracted in good faith (US). The detail is too complex and ephemeral to consider here, but the threshold may be as low as 5 per cent for voting equity securities (US).

Other restrictions on equity holdings If the converting creditors are foreign, e.g. foreign banks, local law may restrict foreign investment in local companies above certain thresholds as part of a policy aimed at limiting foreign ownership. This may be especially so in key industries, e.g. defence, energy, natural resources and utilities.

Change of control or the establishment of influential or dominant holdings in regulated industries, e.g. banks or insurance companies, may require an official consent in order to supervise the competence, integrity, and suitability of controlling shareholders. An example is the UK Banking Act 1987 which has thresholds of 15 per cent, 50 per cent and 75 per cent for shareholdings in authorised institutions which lead either to notification duties or rights of objection by the Bank of England.

Changes of control If the shareholding control of the company changes as a   **20–13** result of the conversion, it may no longer be possible for the company to carry forward tax losses and to set them against future profits (as in the US). A tax review is desirable. Further, contracts of the company may allow a counterparty to cancel or terminate a contract if there is a change of control to a party or parties acting in concert. These clauses may be found in concessions, franchises or intellectual property licences and in bond issues or loan agreements (where they are known as a "poison pill"). The object of the clauses in bond issues and loan agreements is that, if the borrower is taken over, the credit status of the borrower may be fundamentally altered. In other contracts, such as concessions and franchises, the objective of the clause may be inspired by a desire to ensure that the ultimate controllers are acceptable persons to the other contracting party or to prevent seepage of know-how or confidential information to competitors.

Merger and anti-trust legislation If the converting creditors will have a substantial stake, compliance or anti-trust legislation should be considered. The materiality test may be as low as 15 per cent or less.

Mandatory bid The conversion may give rise to a duty to make a mandatory bid for all the shares of the company. Thus under Rule 9 of the British Takeover Code (which is not legally binding but which is backed by compelling market sanctions), a person must make a takeover offer for all the shares of the company if he and persons acting in concert with him acquire shares carrying 30 per cent or more of the voting rights of a listed company and certain other companies. The Panel on Takeovers and Mergers will generally grant a dispensation in the case of a work-out provided that shareholder approval is obtained.

20–14   **Shareholder approval** Generally shareholder approval by resolution will have to be obtained. This will usually be required because the authorised capital must be increased to accommodate the conversion, or because the shareholders have pre-emption rights by statute or in company law or in the rules of the stock exchange or in guidance rules set by large institutional investors (as in the UK), or because shareholder approval is required for an allotment of shares, or because existing shareholder class rights are affected.

If shareholders have pre-emption rights which they might not choose to disapply, one solution is a rights issue to existing shareholders underwritten by the banks on terms that, if the banks are obliged to subscribe for shares, the subscription price may be paid by release of the bank debt. Another solution is an open offer to existing shareholders and creditors on terms which give the shareholders a prior right to the shares in the event of competition – this is sometimes called a "claw-back"

Although the shareholders of an insolvent company have lost everything, they may not see things in that light and require some sweetener to encourage them to agree the dilution of their equity which flows from a conversion. This sweetener may take the form of the issue to the shareholders of warrants entitling them to subscribe for shares on advantageous terms so that they benefit from any recovery of the company.

20–15   **Approval of convertible bondholders** If there are any convertible bond issues outstanding, a bondholder approval may be required. Convertible bonds generally contain anti-dilution clauses whereby the conversion price is adjusted downwards if there are fresh issues of shares. But bondholder approval will normally be necessary because convertible bonds invariably prohibit the issue of senior or more favourable share capital ranking ahead of the bondholders conversion rights, unless bondholder approval is obtained.

Loss of listing Many stock exchanges predicate the continued listing of shares on a large portion of the shares of the company being held by the public, as opposed to a holding by a single shareholder or persons acting in concert. One objective is to maintain liquidity so that investors have access to a market in the shares. Another objective is to prevent prejudice to investors by the presence of a dominating shareholder who can persistently out-vote the public.

Transactions with shareholders Transactions with large shareholders may be controlled by company law or stock exchange regulations in order to prevent conflicts of interest leading to transactions which are detrimental to the company. A shareholder approval may be required.

Insider dealing Insider dealing occurs when a privileged insider of a company, such as an officer or a financial adviser or a bank, has access to unpublished price-sensitive information about the securities of the company gained by virtue of his relationship with the company, and exploits that information to make a profit or avoid a loss by dealing in the securities in circumstances where the price of the securities would be materially altered if the information had been disclosed. The classic example is the director who buys shares in a target company for which he knows his own company is about to make an offer. Many developed states have specific or general legislation to counter insider dealing. The topic is discussed in another volume in this series of works on financial law. 20–16

Banks who convert (or individuals in the banks) may be caught by the legislation in two main situations. The first is where the bank trades securities of the debtor at a time when it is negotiating a debt-equity swap as a result of which it has material price-sensitive information from the debtor company (such as an accountant's report) which is given to it to enable it to evaluate the work-out but which is not available to the public. The second case is where the bank trades after it has converted and where it has special insider information flowing from its rights under a rescheduling agreement for the unconverted portion of its debt, e.g. information about planned disposals or information drawn from internal management accounts supplied to the banks. In the UK a mere agreement to convert debt should not constitute a dealing in securities for the purposes of the insider dealing prohibitions in the Criminal Justice Act 1993 as the security will not at that time have been admitted to dealing on a regulated market.

One potential solution is for the bank to erect a Chinese wall between its lending officers and its securities trading division, i.e. an arrangement to prevent the flow of information between the two departments. If the Chinese wall is not legally recognised (on the grounds that knowledge of one department of the bank is imputed to the bank as a whole), there is little that can be done. Some banks hive off their securities dealing activities into separate subsidiaries which are separately managed, separately staffed and separately located: this will generally resolve the problem.

20–17   **False markets** As mentioned above, the general law, statute, stock exchange regulations or director's fiduciary obligations may require that public announcements be made to prevent a false market in shares. A false market arises where the company's actual situation, if known, would substantially depreciate the value of the company's securities traded in the market.

Section 47 of the Financial Services Act 1986 lays down criminal liability for dishonest concealment of material facts in relation to dealings in certain investments.

It is usually the responsibility of the company and its board to decide when an announcement should be made: they must balance carefully the need for announcement when the banks know of the proposals but shareholders do not, as against the dangers of premature announcements before the proposals have gained general acceptance amongst creditors: an announcement of a proposal which subsequently flops could create even worse confusion, as could attempts to inform shareholders of every twist and turn in the subsequent negotiations. A general warning announcement could be considered if the proposals have gone far enough.

20–18   **Conflicts of interest** The banks may suffer a conflict of interest between their role as shareholders and their role as creditors. In Britain the usual rule is that, in voting, a shareholder or creditor may vote in accordance with his own selfish interests provided there is no unconscionable abuse of a minority, no discrimination between those of the same class, and no secret bribes or other benefits.

Consolidation of debtor If the converted debt is substantial in relation to the existing equity, the debtor may become a subsidiary or associated company of the converting creditor which must be consolidated on its balance sheet. The thresholds vary, but suffice it to say that if the debtor is a subsidiary, then usually the debtor would have to be consolidated in the accounts of the converting creditor – an alarming prospect which could impact prejudicially on the financial condition of the creditor as shown in consolidated accounts, if the debtor has very substantial liabilities.

In such a situation, it may be possible for the converting creditor to convert into non-voting preference shares so as to avoid the debtor being treated as a subsidiary, or to adopt an alternative share structure which does not lead to control within the meaning of company law or accounting regulation.

20–19   **Disclosure of shareholdings** In many commercial jurisdictions, control of shares above a prescribed amount in public companies (e.g. 3 per cent in Britain) must be disclosed to the company. Disclosure may also be required by stock exchanges. It may be necessary to aggregate the holding of converted debt with other normal investment holdings – a point of importance for banks. Breach may result in a freeze on the shares and on rights and earnings flowing from the shares.

Board control and lender liability If the banks control the board or appoint nominee directors, this may increase lender liability risks: para 20–15.

No issue of shares at a discount Commonly shares may not be issued at a discount, e.g. British Companies Act 1985 s 100. An example is converting debt of £750 into shares having a nominal par value of £1,000. But the conversion is not at a discount merely because the debt happens to be worthless: see *Re Mercantile Trading Co, Schroder's Case* (1871) LR 11 Eq 13.

Types of securities

Any amount of financial engineering may be exercised on designing the type   20–20
of security into which the creditors may convert, e.g. preference shares entitled to a fixed dividend which cumulates if not paid in any year, redeemable preference shares (which by company law can generally only be redeemed out of profits or reserves or the proceeds of a fresh issue of shares, or, perhaps, in a case of some companies, notably private companies, if the company is certified to be solvent), or preference shares convertible into ordinary shares (to take advantage of a recovery or a take-over offer), or full-voting ordinary shares ranking ahead of existing ordinary shares or common stock.

The issue of the shares may technically require the preparation and public filing of a full prospectus under securities legislation. The circular may require a statement from the banks as to their intentions with regard to the continuance of their non-converted facilities.

In order to incentivise management, the converting creditors may grant management share options over a proportion of the bank's shares if certain performance targets are met.

If the converted holding of the banks is substantial, there may be a shareholders agreement between the banks which would typically regulate voting and restrictions on sales. This typically requires pro rata sales, subject to an individual right to accept a take-over for the whole.

Other possibilities are: subordinated debt with warrants for shares; limited recourse debt; convertible debt; deep discount bonds (no interest); and success fees. These share in the upside, are simple, require no shareholder consent and (usually) present no special regulatory problems. The disadvantages of profit-related securities are (a) the profit may be equated to an unenforceable restriction on the debtor's redemption of the security and (b) possible subordination of the debtor's claim on insolvency (para 1–48).

Transfer to bank holding company

20–21   If a loan is secured, it may be possible to transfer the assets to a newly-formed company either owned by the banks or (if this presents balance sheet consolidation problems) to a company owned by charitable trustees. The objective is to insulate the assets from the insolvent group and to retain the upside potential if there is an upturn in the market. This device is typical of defaulted property development loans.

The sale is achieved by the banks making new loans to Newco which Newco uses to buy the assets from the debtor company which repays the old loans of the banks. Alternatively, if the security covers shares of the borrowing companies, the shares can be sold to Newco leaving the old loans intact, although on restructured terms.

Points to consider include: (a) any potential consolidation of Newco on the balance sheets of the banks, (b) the tax impact of the change of control, (c) lender liability risks (especially if bank nominees are directors), (d) whether the transfer is a foreclosure requiring court approval, (e) preference rules (unlikely to prejudice the transaction if the banks are fully secured because they were doing no more than they are entitled to do), (f) liabilities attached to the assets, e.g. environmental risks, (g) commercial pressures to continue funding Newco to prevent a future insolvency, (h) (if Newco buys the main debtor companies) due diligence on their assets and liabilities, and (i) prohibited financial assistance by a company for the purpose of the acquisition of its shares.

CHAPTER 21

INSOLVENCY AND LENDER LIABILITY

Lender liability

Generally

The potential heads of lender liability appear to be common in all developed   **21–1**
countries, but there is considerable divergence of approach. Many of the
cases arise in connection with insolvency and the main differences appear to
be (1) the degree to which banks are fixed with liability on big pocket principles, regardless of fault, and (2) the expansiveness of the damages awarded
against banks. The main problem in sifting through the international case
law on the subject is to distinguish consumer – orientated cases where the
decision is based upon the weak bargaining power and lack of sophistication of the individual consumer where plainly greater protections are
needed.

    This review considers the principle heads of risk for banks which com-
monly arise in relation to a debt restructuring or of a corporate customer in
financial difficulties. Responsibilities under consumer statutes are outside
our scope.

Breach of contract to lend money

Where a borrower is in financial difficulties, a bank may decline to lend on   **21–2**
the basis that there is no point in throwing good money after bad. The contract of the loan may be an ordinary line of credit or a demand loan or overdraft under the terms of which the bank is on paper entitled to terminate the
obligation to make loans forthwith on notice or after reasonable notice, or
the loan contract may be a term loan which will typically contain events of
default on the occurrence of which the bank is entitled to accelerate any outstanding loans and to cancel its commitment to make further loans and in
which there will usually be a "conditions precedent" clause which provides
that the bank may suspend its commitment to lend so long as there is an
event of default or pending event of default, such as a material adverse

change in the borrower's financial condition, or a cross-default, or a breach of a financial ratio.

In England, if a bank fails to make a loan pursuant to a commitment to do so, the borrower cannot obtain an order for specific performance whereby the court orders the bank to make the loan: *South African Territories v Wallington* [1898] AC 309.

The English courts lean against the award of substantial damages. The damages payable by the bank are, primarily, any extra interest and costs incurred by the borrower in arranging another loan: *Prehn v Royal Bank of Liverpool* (1870) LR 5 Ex Ch 92. But if the borrower is unable to obtain a new loan or can only obtain a new loan at great cost, the lender is not responsible in damages for extra costs which are attributable to a decline in the borrower's credit in the meantime since those damages are not attributable to the bank's failure to lend, but rather to the borrower's financial condition for which it must bear its own responsibility: *Bahamas Sisal Plantation v Griffin* (1897) 14 TLR 139.

21–3   However if the loan was intended to finance a particular venture or contract and the bank could have contemplated that damages would result from its breach of contract, then the bank may be responsible for losses which were specifically contemplated at the time of the contract, e.g. inevitable default by the borrower on a contract being financed by the loan or loss of profit on that contract. But this will only be the case if the bank was expressly on notice when the loan contract was made that the loan is to be used for that contract and of the potential consequences: *Manchester & Oldham Bank v Cook* (1883) 49 LT 674. It is not enough that the losses in fact arise. The borrower must endeavour to mitigate its losses, e.g. by borrowing elsewhere.

The bank may also be responsible where it commits to make a loan without making credit approval a condition precedent to the contract.

> In *Box v Midland Bank Ltd* [1981] 1 Lloyds LR 434, an engineer went to his bank for a loan to finance a project. The local branch manager said that head office approval was required but this was a formality. On the strength of that assurance, the engineer increased his overdraft. Head office turned down the credit approval. The engineer went bankrupt. He sued the bank for £2,500,000 for the lost project. The bank counterclaimed for its overdraft of £40,000. *Held*: the bank should pay the engineer £5000. See also *First Energy (UK) Ltd v Hungarian International Bank Ltd, The Times*, February 24, 1993, CA, a similar case.

21–4   There do not seem to be any cases in England where a bank was held liable to continue to lend by reason of a course of dealing whereby the bank had given the customer an expectation that credit would be given and then abruptly cut-off that expectation, as some US cases have indicated. The English approach is to examine the terms of the contract and to ascertain whether or not the bank was entitled to terminate the credit and then to give effect to that contract, except in the case of gross unconscionability.

> In a Finnish case decided by the Finnish Supreme Court (KKO 1991: 42) the bank's customers had entered into a loan agreement with the bank to finance the purchase of an apartment. The customers bought the apartment and moved in but the bank did not make the loan available as a result of which the customers could not pay the purchase price and the purchase was cancelled. *Held*: the bank was liable to compensate the customers for the penal interest, advertising costs for a new apartment, the costs of moving to and from the apartment and legal costs.

Decisions of this sort follow simple contract breach principles and no doubt illustrations can be found in all the leading jurisdictions to the same effect.

There is a line of cases in some jurisdictions, notably certain civil code **21-5** jurisdictions and the United States, whereby an abrupt, arbitrary and sudden withdrawal of credit is deemed contrary to the fundamental good faith principles in the code.

> In the decision of an Amsterdam court (Rb. Amsterdam October 22, 1991, KG 1991, 371) a company in financial difficulties was in the process of seeking new capital. In order to complete these negotiations, the company needed to keep its business going and required additional credit from the bank. The bank however refused to grant any additional credit on the ground that the limit of the existing credit line had been reached. The security put up by the company was sufficient to cover the extra credit. *Held*: the bank must extend the additional credit in view of the long-standing relationship with the company and because for the company the additional credit was of vital importance. The bank ran no extra risk because of the sufficiency of the security offered to the bank.

Similarly, in a Belgian case of December 4, 1987, decided by a Brussels court (reported in JLMB, 1989) the court held a bank liable for the abrupt termination of a credit, even though the bank was entitled to terminate in accordance with the contract, on the ground that this infringed the principle of good faith. It seems that the Belgian courts will examine whether the right to terminate clearly goes beyond what a normal prudent person would do in the circumstances, e.g. Cass, April 6, 1984, RW 1984–85, 1638; Cass, March 10, 1983, JT 1983, 716; Cass, September 10, 1971, Arr Cass, 1972, 31. There is much case law on the subject. The facts should be examined with care because it does not necessarily follow that they do more than respect the ordinary principle, evident everywhere, that where a bank makes available a credit without specific events of default, the credit is terminable only on reasonable notice: what constitutes reasonable notice must be decided in accordance with the particular circumstances of the case.

21–6   In Canada, case law gave a borrower a reasonable period of days before the bank could appoint a receiver and this was codified in amendments to the Bankruptcy Act in 1992 which provided that a lender must give a borrower 10 days notice before exercising the bank's rights against the security. This was intended to eliminate the uncertainty that surrounded the issue of reasonable notice.

By contrast the English courts leave the bargain to be settled by the parties and will not relieve the borrower against the "forfeiture" of acceleration even if payment is only a day late: see for example *The Brimnes* [1974] 3 All ER 88, CA (forfeiture of ship charter); *The Laconia* [1977] AC 850 (forfeiture of ship charter); *The Angelic Star* [1988] 1 Lloyds Rep 122, CA (acceleration of shipping loan). This follows the English policies of predictability and freedom of contract: it is up to the borrower to negotiate his own grace periods and he will be held to his bargain outside the consumer context. There is no room for some vague "good faith" requirement. But the courts construe the contract strictly and the ability to terminate forthwith must be clear.

> In the English case of *Williams & Glyn's Bank Ltd v Barnes* (1981) Com LR 205, a bank facility letter provided for an increase in the facility so that the customer could pay various bills on their maturity. The facility letter was subject to "usual banking conditions" . *Held*: the bank could not cancel the facility since it was intended to remain in force in order to meet the various bills on maturity. The words "usual banking conditions" were meaningless and did not import a term that money was repayable on demand.
>
> In the unreported decision of *Titford Property Co Ltd v Cannon Street Acceptances Ltd* (May 22, 1975, Goff J), the bank agreed to make a loan to property companies for specified developments. A clause stated that the facility was repayable forthwith on demand. *Held*: the provision in the facility agreement that the facility was intended for a specific project overrode the immediate demand clause.

21–7   An example of a Danish case where a bank was liable for the costs of a customer in connection with an unjustified termination of a loan agreement is to be found in a judgment reported at U 87. 963 V.

The US courts, too, have implied a covenant of good faith.

> In *KMC Co v Irving Trust Co*, 757 F 2d 752 (6th Cir 1985), the bank's credit agreement in favour of a family-owned wholesale grocery business with annual

sales of $100,000,000 provided that the loan was repayable on demand and the bank would make advances in its sole and absolute discretion. But the documents also contained provisions whereby the bank agreed to advance upon a formula based upon accounts receivable and inventory. The bank was not content with the company's management and refused to make an advance of $800,000 to cover cheques which were about to be presented, even though the bank was fully secured. The cheques were bounced and the company suffered such a blow to its reputation that it was liquidated. *Held*: the abrupt termination of the line of credit without notice was a breach of the bank's obligation of good faith. The jury awarded the company $7.5 million in damages.

Less disapproving views have been taken in other US cases, e.g. *Kham & Nate's Shoes No 2, Inc v First Bank of Whiting*, 908 F 2d 1351 (7th Cir 1990).

21–8 As to set-off, the English rule is that the bank may effect a set-off of current accounts without notice unless there was an express or implied agreement to keep the accounts separate: see, e.g. *Garnett v McKewan* (1872) LR 8 Ex 10. Implied agreements not to set-off are common, e.g. where there is a loan account and a wages account. New York's Banking Law provides in s 9–g that a bank must give notice of the set-off to the depositor prior to the set-off or on the same business day.

The withdrawal of credit is similar to wrongful dishonour of a cheque, but with the essential difference that the dishonour of a cheque is published to the holder of the cheque so that the customer's reputation is instantly called into question. In England where the customer is a trader he is entitled to recover substantial general damages without proof of special damage where the bank wrongfully fails to honour a cheque which is covered by a credit balance or an agreed overdraft. This was established as long ago as *Marzetti v Williams* (1830) 1 B&Ad 415. Because the holder of the cheque is informed of the dishonour, the bank may also be liable to the customer for damages for libel. The case law has held that words such as "not sufficient", "refer to drawer" and "present again" were either defamatory or capable of being defamatory. See, e.g. *Baker v Australian and New Zealand Bank Ltd* (1958) NZLR 907, *Jayson v Midland Bank Ltd* (1968) 1 Lloyds Rep 409, CA.

21–9 Liability to third parties for the abrupt withdrawal of credit – which could have been used to pay third parties such as suppliers – seems to be rare.

US examples are where a bank, by continuing credit, induces customers to place advance deposits for goods or services which the bank knows will never be supplied and the bank uses the deposits to repay its loan, where a bank induces a junior secured creditor or a subordinated creditor not to take action by assurances that the lender does not propose to enforce, while the lender is improving its own collateral or procuring repayment. Where the bank is secured, suppliers may supply goods to the debtor on credit which the bank then uses to repay its loans: the bank may be liable to the supplier in such a case under Netherlands law: *Erba v Amsterdamsche Bank NV* (NJ 1957, 514 and 1959, 581).

If the bank raises the interest rate to reflect the worsening credit, this may be contrary to the rate of interest agreed in the contract and reasonable notice may be required.

Abusive credit and false wealth

21–10   Here and there, the idea has surfaced that a bank may be liable to third party creditors of the debtor if the bank continues to give credit to an insolvent debtor without informing the third parties of the true situation, thereby, it is said, inducing false credit. This is yet another branch of the curious false wealth doctrine: this has struck down the trust in civil code jurisdictions and has given rise to the reputed ownership doctrine (that assets in the possession of the debtor and apparently belonging to him are deemed to belong to his creditors even though they are beneficially owned by someone else) and to the necessity to publicise security interests, either by possessory pledges or by registration systems. The basic premise is that, where a debtor has many possessions but a few assets, he invites false credit. This is now extended to the proposition that, where a bank in some way aids and abets the debtor's appearance of wealth when he is insolvent, then the bank should be liable to third parties as a culpable participant.

The notion is that the bank is abusively supporting the debtor to the detriment of other creditors. The difficulties which lie in the way of this idea are several. First it would seem unfortunate if the jurisdiction imposes penalties on the abrupt termination of credit, yet imposes penalties on the continuance of credit giving an appearance of false wealth. Second, the bank is subject to secrecy. Thirdly, the causation seems thin: it is not the bank's grant of credit which results in the other creditor's loss: it is the debtor's insolvency which results in the loss.

In any event, the doctrine of abusive support seems rare.

> In the US case of *Monsen v Consolidated Dress Beef Co*, 579 F2d 793 (3d Cir 1978), the debtor's employees bought notes of the debtor company every week under an employee programme. The bank had security over the assets so that the notes were junior. The company was in difficulties, but the bank encouraged the company to continue the programme, using the proceeds to improve its position. *Held* (in a jury case): the bank was liable as an aider and abetter of a securities fraud, even though it had had no direct contact with the

noteholders: the bank had actively encouraged the continuance of the note programme in the knowledge that the employees were endangered.

Austrian case law has imposed liability on state-owned banks which con- **21–11**
tinued to extend loans to insolvent subsidiaries, thereby creating an impression that those subsidiaries were still solvent. But these cases are evidently explicable on the ground that the debtor's management were liable for fraudulently incurring credit and the bank as the owner was liable on account of its participation in the management. The sole bank stockholder not only materially influenced the management's formulation of its objectives but also itself negligently consented to the obstruction of a necessary bankruptcy which would inevitably follow and was thus a contributory accomplice to the negligent offence against the bankruptcy law. See the decision of the Austrian Supreme Court of July 14, 1986, 1 Ob 57/86 J Bl 1986 713; W Bl 1988 129, cited in the Campbell study noted in the Bibliography to this work.

A similar idea appears where it is alleged that a bank which does not prevail upon a debtor company to inform the market of its true condition, but which nevertheless continues to support the company by further credit, is aiding and abetting a false market and is therefore liable to shareholders who buy the shares in the expectation that all was well. Such a liability would not arise in England since the duty to notify shareholders through stock exchange or other channels is a duty of management, not the lending banks.

Bank as adviser

Where a bank has held itself out as advising the borrower on the suitability **21–12**
of the loan or a transaction to be financed by the loan, the bank may be liable for negligent advice. Most of the cases have arisen in the consumer context where an unsophisticated individual enters into a transaction with the bank which is clearly most unwise: many have concerned guarantees given by aged mothers to support the business loans of their impecunious and foolish sons who are already in default and where the bank failed either to disclose the wayward child's financial condition to the parent or failed to point out to the parent what the consequences would be if the son's business were to fail and the bank then enforced over the parent's home given as security for the guarantee. The classic English case is *Lloyds Bank v Bundy* [1975] QB 326 and there have been many English cases before and since. Those are paralleled by the notorious Australian foreign exchange cases, e.g. *Foti v Banque Nationale de Paris* (1990) ATR 81–025.

In these cases farmers and other unsophisticated individuals took out foreign currency mortgage loans from banks without being advised that, in the event of a depreciation of the Australian currency as against the foreign currency of the loan, the debtors would have to pay substantially increased amounts, as indeed turned out to be the case. The banks incurred liability, primarily under s 52 of the Australian Trade Practices Act (Commonwealth) 1974 which provides in a draconian section that in trade or commerce "a corporation shall not engage in misleading or deceptive conduct or conduct likely to mislead or deceive", regardless of intent to mislead and regardless of knowledge of falsity.

So far as English law is concerned, a bank is not normally responsible for advising a potential borrower about the nature or prudence of the proposed borrowing: see *Williams & Glyns Bank Ltd v Barnes* (1981) Com LR 205.

Credit references

21–13　An area for particular risk for banks where the customer is in financial difficulties is in the giving of credit references since, on the one hand the bank has an interest in encouraging the continuance of transactions and avoiding panic, while on the other hand the bank may incur responsibility if the credit reference is incorrect. There are numerous international decisions on negligent credit references which do no more than exhibit the ordinary liability for negligent misrepresentation.

> The leading English case is *Hedley Byrne & Co Ltd v Heller & Partners Ltd* [1964] AC 465, HL. One bank, on behalf of a customer, enquired of another bank whether the latter's customer was good for a particular contract, to which the bank responded that the company was considered good for its ordinary business engagements. The contract was awarded but the company concerned went into liquidation causing loss to the customer. The bank giving the reference had been negligent. *Held*: the bank was liable for the negligent credit reference. However it had disclaimed responsibility and this was effective in the absence of fraud.

An American example is as follows:

> In *First Va Bankshares v Benson*, 559 F2d 1307 (5th Cir 1977), a prospective purchaser of a debtor's securities relied on the lender's suggestion that relations with borrowers were orderly and normal. But the lender was over-advanced and it knew that the financial statements were grossly inaccurate. *Held*: the bank was liable to the purchaser for his loss. The lender should have refrained from giving investment advice.

A bank may buy time by giving satisfactory trade references so as to allow the bank to collect, see, e.g. *Re American Lumber Co*, 5 BR 470 (D) Minn (1980). The bank should refer the enquiry to the debtor or require the enquirer to "reply on independent enquiries".

An Australian example is *Compafina Bank v Australian and New Zealand Banking Group Ltd* (1984) ATR 80–546 where the bank, with splendid loyalty but imprudent imprecision, described their customer as "an entrepreneur extraordinaire of the highest repute and integrity". A Canadian authority is *Mason Construction Ltd v Bank of Nova Scotia* (1985) 16 DLR (4th) 598 (Supreme Court of Canada).

> A contractor sought assurances from a bank that the bank's customer would have sufficient financing to cover the construction of a proposed development. In reliance on this assurance the plaintiff entered into a contract with the bank's customer. The bank did not advance sufficient funds and eventually exercised its power of sale as mortgagee and sold the development. *Held*: the bank was liable to the contractor for negligent misrepresentation because the customer had signed the contract in reliance on the bank's assurance of adequate funding. The bank had not revealed that the loan arrangement which the bank had with its customer did not assure adequate financing.

Bank credit references are usually given "without responsibility" or some other exculpation, and in England this is effective to exclude liability for negligence but not of course for fraud. Numerous Austrian decisions have upheld the liability exclusion in the Austrian General Business Conditions of banks for incorrect credit references unless there was flagrant gross negligence by the bank. See, e.g. the Supreme Court's ruling of Evbl 1985/98. See also RZ 1958, 52.

Misrepresentation liability

Apart from credit references, other possible areas where a bank may incur **21–14** liability for misrepresentation are:

- Liabilities under securities laws for misrepresentation or non-disclosure

- Aiding and abetting non-disclosure of financial information. Liability is unlikely in England because this is a company responsibility.

- Misrepresentation in a circular to shareholders that bank will maintain its lines when it does not intend to.

- Insider dealing

- Liability for overcharging interest to the borrower. In the US "prime rate cases", the bank said it would charge interest at a spread above its prime rate which was its rate for its best and most creditworthy customers, but allegedly was not. This gave rise to treble liability under the Racketeer Influenced and Corrupt Organisations Act intended to impede infilt-ration by organised crime into business, but used to punish banks in ordinary commercial transactions on the basis that the bank was obtain-ing money by fraudulent pretences.

Liability as agent bank to a syndicate or to a sub-participant for non-dis-closure pursuant to fiduciary duties. This topic is discussed in another volume in this series of works on financial law.

Control of debtor

21–15   This head of liability arises through the exercise of control through directors appointed to the board by the bank, intrusive interference in management, economic coercion, control via pledged stock, or a clause allowing the lender to approve or veto management. Jurisdictions differ on the extent of interference or dominance necessary to satisfy control criteria. It has been said that the US leads the field because of "big pocket" concepts and jury trials prone to emotional verdicts.

Heads of potential liability include:

–   The bank is in control of management and therefore is liable as a manager or is a shadow or de facto director thereby incurring personal liability for wrongful or fraudulent trading: chapter 8.

–   The bank is liable to indemnify a bank nominee on the board who incurs personal liability as a director.

–   The bank procured a breach of contract by the debtor, e.g. on loan or supply contracts.

–   The bank's loan is equitably subordinated, as where the bank exercises dominant interference in the debtor's management and thereby causes loss. This appears to be an exclusively US doctrine: para 9–12 *et seq.*

–   The bank is an insider or connected person under preference laws: para 6–5.

–   The bank becomes an owner or operator for the purpose of environment laws; see, e.g. *US v Mirabile*, No 84–2280 (ED Pa, Sept 4, 1985).

–   The bank controls the company and is liable as a controlling person under Federal securities laws (e.g. under a prospectus) to the same extent as the controlled person unless the controlling person acted in

good faith and did not directly or indirectly induce the act or acts constituting the violation. This too seems to be an exclusively US doctrine.

Liabilities of secured creditor

A secured creditor may incur liability under the following heads: **21–16**

– Enforcement when the creditor is not entitled to enforce

– Failure to obtain a reasonable price on a sale. The English standard is
  tolerant.

– Liability as mortgagee in possession or via a receiver in English-based
  countries, especially for ships, aircraft or for tort liability

– Misrepresentation to purchasers as to the value of the assets

– Environmental liability: see below

Security is reviewed in another volume in this series of works on financial
law.

Lender liability for environmental pollution

Introduction

Lenders inevitably face the risk that environmental liability incurred by their   **21–17**
borrowers may impact on the ability to repay since the borrower may
become subject to an unexpected clean-up liability which renders it insolvent. This is part of the credit risk which has to be evaluated.

Lenders are less familiar with the prospect of incurring primary liability
for the environmental problems of their borrowers. Outside the US, this
liability is rare outside three situations, namely (1) where the lender is an
owner under title finance transactions, (2) where the lender as secured creditor takes possession of the security through a receiver and the receiver himself causes pollution, or (3) where the lender intrusively interferes in
management and itself becomes a director or itself is instrumental in causing
the pollution: outside the US the degree of intrusion must normally be very
great. Merely taking security or making a loan is almost invariably not
enough. If the liability does arise, it could far exceed the loan or any security
for the loan.

Categories of environmental liability

21–18   Statutory provisions expressly imposing liability on lenders are rare. In Belgium a duty of care is imposed on lenders to operators of environmentally sensitive projects to supervise compliance by the borrower with applicable environmental legislation. In the Australian state of Victoria recent amendments to the Environmental Protection Act 1970 expressly impose liability on mortgagees in possession or control for the cost of making sites safe and abating any environmental hazards, but make it clear that, except as indicated above, lenders are not liable as occupiers when acting solely as the holder of a security interest, as a mortgagee in possession or as the appointer of a receiver who assumes control of the business. As to the US position, see below.

Four broad categories of potential lender liability may be identified. These are:

(1) involvement in management
(2) occupation
(3) ownership
(4) operational control or responsibility

Each is examined in turn.

Involvement in management

21–19   This may be expressed as "involvement", as in Denmark, France, Luxembourg, the Netherlands, Portugal and Spain, as being "concerned in management" (Australia) or may be described as involvement in day-to-day management (UK) or as acting as a "shadow director". It may also be expressed as "having charge, management or control", as in parts of Canada. There is potential for both secured and unsecured lenders to fall into this category, particularly in refinancing and loan work-out situations. The usual care should be exercised to avoid intrusive interference in management.

Liability provisions in many jurisdictions, including continental European civil law systems, the US and the common law countries, often extend liability to directors and officers. A typical provision in common law countries extends criminal liability to directors and senior officers where the company's offence was committed with the consent or connivance, or was attributable to any neglect on the part of directors and officers.

In any event, personal liability as manager or criminal liability as a director may catch nominee directors of lenders on the boards of borrowing companies or directors of orphan or special purpose companies in securitisations.

Occupation

Occupation, which need not necessarily involve physical occupation but   21–20
may arise when there is possession and control, is a popular category for the
imposition of environmental liability. It forms a key role in liability provisions in Australia and in the United Kingdom. This risk may arise where a
secured lender takes possession on a default: see below.

Ownership

Some form of ownership, whether of real property, chattels or contami-   21–21
nants, features as a category in the environmental liability laws of most
countries, including the United States, United Kingdom, Australia and
Canada. This risk is most likely to arise in relation to title finance where the
financier is owner, either as lessor or vendor, such as financial leasing, sale
and leaseback and conditional sale.

Operational control or responsibility

This is more of an all-embracing category which has many variants.   21–22
Examples include being the operator (US); the person carrying on a process
(UK); the person discharging pollutants or depositing waste; the person
causing or permitting (Australia), (sometimes "knowingly" causing or permitting (UK)); having charge, management or control of a pollutant or del-
eterious substance (Ontario, Canada) and more remotely, persons assisting
by their conduct in the breach of environmental laws or licences by a principal (Germany): this is unlikely to involve mere lending for ordinary business
purposes. In Canada the party liable must usually have "possession, dominion or control" of the polluting property.

In Ontario, in *Attorney General v Tyre King Tyre and Recycling Ltd*
(1992) 8 CELR (NS) 202 9 OR (3d) 318, a mortgagee not in possession was
held not to be liable for clean-up costs where there had been no actual exercise of the power of management and control or, indeed, any circumstances
placing the mortgagee in a liability category, such as occupier, owner or
operational control or responsibility.

When a lender enforces security in common law countries by going into
possession, it is likely to attract the liabilities attached to owners and occupiers for contamination while it is in possession. Examples include the UK,
Canada ("ownership or control") and Australia (New South Wales and
Victoria), the liability in the latter case being limited to making the site safe
and abating any environmental hazards. Similarly, in the US, the lender will
become a deemed owner for the purposes of CERCLA liability (see below).

In civilian jurisdictions such as Belgium, Greece and Italy however, enforcement will generally take the form of a court sale of the secured assets. As a result the lender will never become the owner and will therefore avoid liability. Similarly, in Germany the lender enforcing avoids liability, except in the case of moveable property, by never assuming ownership.

A lender enforcing security may also incur liability by virtue of assuming operational control or responsibility. In Canada, for example, there are state provisions which attach liability to those in possession or control of a source of contamination. In the US, being the operator of a vessel or facility attracts liability, whilst in Germany liability can arise where the lender goes into possession and operates a plant.

The appointment of a receiver may give rise to personal liability of the appointee for which he is likely to seek an indemnity from the lender.

In the UK an administrative receiver is likely to become the occupier and person in operational control and responsibility. This means that he may incur liability for "knowingly permitting" the continuation of a contamination problem, as well as for breaches of environmental regulations occurring after appointment.

Priority of environmental clean-up orders and costs

21–23   In the absence of specific powers to the contrary, clean-up orders and claims for clean-up costs will generally rank as unsecured debts behind secured lenders. However, Canadian cases are of interest:

> In *Panamericana v Northern Badger Oil and Gas Ltd* (1991) 81 DLR (4th) 280, a receiver of oil wells was seeking to pay off secured creditors and his own fees, leaving unsatisfied an order requiring him to carry out a shut-down and clean-up operation. The secured creditors and the receiver claimed priority. *Held* by the Alberta Court of Appeal: the receiver was under a clean-up duty in accordance with "the general law" and had a public duty to fellow citizens under laws enacted to protect the environment and the health and safety of all citizens. The regulatory authority imposing the clean-up order was not to be regarded as a creditor. It was a public authority given a duty of enforcing public law and there was therefore no question of subverting the insolvency statutes. Note that the case related to an order for clean-up, rather than a claim for clean-up costs already incurred by the regulatory authority. In the latter case, presumably the claim would have been treated as an unsecured debt ranking after those of the secured creditors.

> In an Ontario decision of *King (Township) v Rolex Equipment Co* (1992) 8 OR (3d) 457, it was held that a local township could appoint a receiver over a property abandoned by its owner and that the receiver could properly expend money on cleaning up the site, despite the fact that such receivership costs

would have priority over a secured lender which had not gone into possession and was already facing a substantial loss. The decision was justified on the basis that receivership costs may be incurred at the expense of prior mortgagees where they are for necessary preservation or improvement of the property or where there are public interests involved which might outweigh the detriment to the mortgagee.

In England a claim for clean-up costs already incurred would normally   **21–24** rank as an unsecured debt. However, it is possible for certain clean-up costs incurred to be registered as local land charges.

In Victoria and New South Wales statutory charges and restriction orders relating to the environment may have priority over the security of financiers and in Ontario the Attorney-General has a lien on properties for clean-up costs which takes priority over a mortgagee's claim: see *AG v Tyre King Tyre & Recycling Ltd* (1992) 8 CELR (NS) 2029 or (3d) 318.

CERCLA

The potential for primary lender liability became a serious issue in the   **21–25** United States, following enactment of the Comprehensive Environmental Response Compensation and Liability Act 1980 (CERCLA). This Act introduced a comprehensive clean-up scheme for land contamination known as "Superfund". Under the scheme the US Environmental Protection Agency is given power to clean up contaminated sites using moneys from a substantial environmental trust fund. The Agency may then seek to recover the costs from "potentially responsible parties". Clean-up costs average $25 million per site and frequently exceed the site's value.

CERCLA imposes strict, retroactive and joint and several liability. The list of potentially responsible parties is a long one. It includes present and some past owners and operators and those who arrange to have hazardous substances or waste disposed of or treated at the site. Stockholders, officers and managers may also be liable.

Following the enactment of CERCLA, lenders faced the prospect of incurring liability as owners or operators for the full clean-up costs in relation to any site over which they took possession. Lenders sought to avoid new transactions involving security over industrial property and to avoid taking possession of such properties where they already had security, pending site investigations.

Ironically, given the impact it was later to have on lenders, CERCLA included a secured creditor exemption covering activities falling short of going into possession. This exemption states that secured creditors "who without participating in the management of a vessel or facility hold indicia of ownership primarily to protect a security interest" are not to be included in the definition of owner or operator.

It was the subsequent judicial interpretation of this statutory exemption, notably in the case of *US v Fleet Factors*, 901 F 2d 1550 (11th Cir 1990), which gave lenders cause for alarm. In the *Fleet Factors* case it was held that a secured lender's capacity to influence, as well as its actual involvement in the borrower's business activities, is sufficient to be regarded as "participation in management", thus taking the lender outside the statutory exemption. In this case, the lenders participation in the financial management of a facility was said to have been of "a degree indicating a capacity to influence the borrower's treatment of hazardous wastes".

The effect of this judicial interpretation of the secured creditor exemption in CERCLA was to bring into question actions commonly taken by lenders to protect security – such as monitoring operations, requiring compliance with regulations and other compliance-related activities, providing financial advice and being involved in refinancing or loan work-out arrangements.

21–26   In view of the adverse impact on lending to industrial enterprises, in April 1992 the US Environmental Protection Agency (EPA) published a set of lender liability rules which aimed to clarify when lenders would and would not be liable under CERCLA but these rules were set aside by a US Appeals Court on the basis that the Agency exceeded its authority in promulgating them.

The advent of lender liability in the US under CERCLA was probably a manifestation of a deep pocket philosophy. It was born of the determination to see that clean-up was undertaken even if, in order to ensure success, this meant penalising innocent but financially well-endowed parties – whether they be existing owners or operators not responsible for the existence of contamination or lenders.

SELECT BIBLIOGRAPHY
ON INTERNATIONAL INSOLVENCY

There is a very substantial and excellent literature on the domestic insolvency laws of the leading countries. This list comprises mainly comparative and international works. The article literature is not included and this list is not at all comprehensive.

Allen & Overy	*Butterworths International Insolvency Law* (1995) Butterworths (contains translations of the insolvency laws of nine leading jurisdictions)
David Botwinik and Kenneth Weinrib (eds)	*European Bankruptcy Laws* (2nd ed 1986) American Bar Association
Dennis Campbell (ed)	*International Corporate Insolvency Law* (1992) Butterworths (country reports)
Dennis Campbell and Anthony Collins (eds)	*Corporate Insolvency and Rescues: the International Dimension* (1993) Kluwer
J H Dalhuisen	*International Insolvency and Bankruptcy* (1982) Matthew Bender
Ian Fletcher (ed)	*Cross-Border Insolvency: Comparative Dimensions* (1990) United Kingdom Comparative Law Series Vol 12
Richard A Gitlin and Rhona R Mears (eds)	*International Loan Workouts and Bankruptcies* (1989–)
Harry Rajak (ed)	*A Practitioner's Guide to European Corporate Insolvency Law* (1992–93) Westminster Management Consultants Ltd (country reports)

In addition, accountants' firms have published international guides, such as *Touche Ross Guide to International Insolvency* (1989) Probus Publishing, Deloitte Touche Tohmatsu International, *Guide to Insolvency in Europe* (1993) CCH; Klynveld Peat Marwick Goerdeler, *International Insolvency Procedures* (1988).

See also:

Campbell/Meroni (eds)	*Bankers' Liability: Risks & Remedies*, (1993) Kluwer

| Donald L Rome | *Business Workouts Manual* (2nd ed 1992) Warren, Gorham & Lamont, Inc. Cumulative supplements |
| Weil, Gotshal & Manges | *Restructurings* (1993) Euromoney Books |

The English literature on insolvency is substantial. Without being comprehensive, one may mention: Ian F Fletcher, *The Law of Insolvency* (1990) Sweet & Maxwell; Ian M Fletcher, John Higham, William Trowe, *The Law and Practice of Corporate Administrations* (1994) Butterworths; Roy M Goode, *Principles of Corporate Insolvency Law* (1990) Sweet & Maxwell; James R Lingard *Corporate Rescues & Insolvencies* (2nd ed 1990) Butterworths; Robert R Pennington *Pennington's Corporate Insolvency Law* (1991) Butterworths; Harry Rajak, *Insolvency Law: Theory and Practice* (1993) Sweet & Maxwell; Philip St J Smart, *Cross-Border Insolvency* (1991) Butterworths; Gordon Stewart, *Administrative Receivers and Administrators* (1987) CCH Editions; Peter Totty and Michael Jordan, *Insolvency* (1986) Longman. There are many other first-class works. A standard work on personal bankruptcy is Muir Hunter and David Graham, *Williams & Muir Hunter on Bankruptcy* (19th ed 1979) Stevens, since supplemented by *Muir Hunter on Personal Insolvency* (1987–) Sweet & Maxwell.

In the United States, the literature is also substantial. See, for example, *Collier's Bankruptcy Manual* (loose-leaf) Matthew Bender; Richard F Broude, *Reorganisations under Chapter 11 of the Bankruptcy Code* (1986–) Law Journal Seminars – Press; Thomas H Jackson, *The Logic and Limits of Bankruptcy Law* (1986) Harvard University Press; Robert D Albergotti, *Understanding Bankruptcy in the US* (1992) Blackwells.

LIST OF RESEARCH TOPICS

This list contains a list of topics which could be considered for a research thesis or a shorter article. The topics relate to the areas covered by this book. Research topics in relation to the areas covered by other books in this series on international financial law will be found in the volumes concerned.

The selection is based on relative originality and usefulness. Topics which have already been extensively covered by the legal literature are not included. In many cases there is an existing literature on the listed topics, but further work is considered worthwhile to develop what has already been achieved or to explore a new approach. It is possible that some of the listed topics may not be at all original and the author is simply unaware of the work which has already been done. If the chosen titles do not appeal, it is hoped that they will be suggestive of those which do. Some of the titles are no more than pointers which would have to be developed into a proper topic.

The author would be very glad to receive a copy of any essays which may be written and which are derived from this list.

- Pro-debtor and pro-creditor classifications of insolvency law

- Insolvency law and economic development

- Individual and corporate insolvencies compared

- Compromises between competing interests in insolvency law

- Investigation of delinquent managers of failed corporations: conflict of laws

- Comparative insolvency conflict of laws in common law countries

- Comparative insolvency conflict of laws in Germanic and Scandinavian countries

- Comparative insolvency conflict of laws in Franco-Latin countries

- Comparative insolvency conflict of laws in Islamic jurisdictions

- Nationalism and foreign creditors in insolvency conflicts

- Roman insolvency law from the classical period to Justinian

- Comparative history of insolvency law: 1100 to 1500

- Comparative history of insolvency law: 1500 to 1800

- Comparative history of insolvency law: 1800 to 1900
- Comparative history of insolvency law in Italian states: 1100 to 1800
- Insolvency law in emerging countries (mainly former Communist countries)
- Creditor equality in insolvency law
- Jurisprudence and insolvency: the ethics of insolvency law
- Insolvency law and political policies
- Insolvency law as the foundation of commercial law
- Insolvency law and fairness to debtors and creditors
- Insolvency law and freedom of contract
- Legal and economic approaches to insolvency
- Economic influences on insolvency law
- The impact of recessions on insolvency law
- Direct actions and other leapfrog claims as a protection against insolvency (see chapter 1)
- Divided ownership and the trust in commercial and financial law: international survey
- Custodianship of securities and insolvency: comparative law
- Restitution and unjust enrichment on insolvency: comparative law
- Fungibility of goods, contract debts and investment securities: sale, security interests
- Insolvency practitioners: comparative review
- Cancellation of contracts on insolvency: comparative law
- Comparative law of forfeitures on insolvency
- Comparative history of the law of fraudulent and other preferential transfers
- Payments in the suspect period and preferential transfers: comparative law
- Financial assistance to purchase the company's own shares: comparative law
- Classification of jurisdictional attitudes to the veil of incorporation as a protection against insolvency

- Maintenance of corporate capital: international survey

- Comparative law of director liability for fraudulent and wrongful trading and negligent management

- Consolidation of corporate groups on insolvency: comparative law

- Corporate disclosure as a protection against insolvency

- International history of insolvency compositions and judicial rescue proceedings

- Comparative law of corporate rehabilitation proceedings

- Success or failure of the survival concept in insolvency law

- Banks: international survey of insolvency rehabilitation proceedings

- Insurance companies: international survey of insolvency rehabilitation proceedings

- Insolvency of unincorporated commercial trusts

- Private consensual debt restructuring agreements and judicial corporate rehabilitation proceedings: comparative approaches

- History of insolvency conventions and treaties

- Conflict of laws and preferential transfers

- International conflicts between final liquidations and corporate rehabilitation proceedings

- Comparative law of ancillary insolvency proceedings

- Conflict of laws and insolvency set-off

INDEX

All references are to paragraph number

Abusive support doctrine, 21–10 to
   21–11
Actio Pauliana. *See under* Preferences
Advertisement,
  bankruptcy, of, 1–3
Africa. *See* Kenya; Liberia; Nigeria;
   South Africa; Zambia; Zimbabwe
  fraudulent trading, 8–9
  insolvency set-off, 1–25
  pro-creditor/pro-debtor attitudes,
   1–13
  public and private companies, 8–6
Agency,
  deposits and sale proceeds, 2–36 to
   2–38
  insolvency of agent, 1–32
  misapplication of money, 1–27
  undisclosed principal, 1–30 to 1–32
   false wealth and, 1–31
   jurisdictions allowing, 1–30 to
    1–32
Aircraft finance,
  aircraft liens, 1–19
Appropriation,
  trust property, 2–29
Argentina. *See also* Latin America
  companies, types of, 8–6
  custodianship, 2–7
  directors' duty to call shareholders
   meeting on loss of capital, 8–17
  equalisation in, 16–6
  foreign insolvencies, recognition of,
   15–4, 15–45
  insolvency jurisdiction, 14–18
   global property, 14–20
   local assets, 14–4
  insolvency set-off, 1–25
   current-account set-off, 1–26
  preference rules, 4–12, 7–2
   conflict of laws, 16–24
  trusts, 2–7
Assignment of debts,
  generally, 2–39 to 2–40

Assignment of debts—*cont.*
  jurisdictional attitudes, 2–1
  late notification of, 5–25
  less than full value, for, 1–46
  notice of, 2–1, 2–39 to 2–40
Attachments,
  exempt assets, 1–58, 2–1
  generally, 1–1, 1–2
  stays on, 18–7
Australia,
  credit references, 21–13
  directors,
   liability of, 8–28
   standard of care, 8–23
  environmental liability, 21–18,
   21–19, 21–20, 21–22, 21–24
  fraudulent trading, 8–9
  insolvency set-off, 1–24
  judicial rescue proceedings,
   administrator, 12–5
   automatic stay, 12–4
   contract cancellation, 11–33
   creditors, 12–5
   deed of company arrangement,
    11–1, 12–2, 12–6
   entry, 12–3
   generally, 12–2
   ipso facto clauses, 11–33
   official management, 11–8, 12–2
   voluntary arrangement, 11–1
  lender liability,
   bank as adviser, 21–12
   credit references, 21–13
   environmental pollution, 21–18,
    21–19, 21–20, 21–22, 21–24
  preference rules, 4–7, 7–1
   compensating contracts, 5–29
   conflict of laws, 16–24
   current accounts, net improvement
    test, 5–14
  pro-creditor, as, 1–11
  public and private companies, 8–6
  veil of incorporation, 8–7
  voluntary compositions, 10–5

Australia—*cont.*
  wrongful trading, 8–11
Austria,
  abusive credit, 21–11
  assignment of debts, notice of, 2–40
  bank bankruptcies, 1–62
  companies, types of, 8–6
  contracts, rejection/performance on
     insolvency, 3–2
  direct action, 1–32
  foreign currency creditors, 1–55
  foreign insolvencies, recognition of,
     15–4, 15–37
  Franco-Austrian Convention, 17–2
  fungible securities, co-ownership of,
     2–23, 2–24
  insolvency set-off, 1–24, 11–29
  preference rules,
     Actio Pauliana, 4–19
     gifts, 5–5
     preferential intent, 6–8
  preventive compositions and
     moratoriums, 10–7, 10–8
  private debt restructuring, 18–14
  security, attitude to, 1–20, 11–12
  shareholders, group liability, 9–9
  veil of incorporation, 8–7
  wrongful takings of money, 2–13
Avoidance. *See* **Preferences**

Bahamas,
  insolvency set-off, 1–24
Bahrain,
  insolvency set-off, 1–25
     current-account set-off, 1–26
Bailment. *See* **Custodians** *and* **Trusts**
     and trustees
Bank deposit,
  current account set-off, 1–26, 21–8
Bank depositors,
  priority on insolvency, 1–40
Bank liability. *See* **Lender liability**
Bankruptcy. *See* **Insolvency**
Bankrupt's property. *And see*
     Proprietary claims on insolvency
     and **Trusts and trustees**
  deprivation on insolvency, 2–1
  exempt assets, 1–58, 2–1
  false wealth. *See* **False wealth**

Bankrupt's property—*cont.*
  family home, 1–58
  pension, 1–58
  reputation, 1–58
  salary, 1–58
  seizure of, 1–1
  tools of the trade, 1–58
Banks,
  bankruptcies of, 1–62
  Chinese walls, 20–16
  conflicts of interest, 20–18
  credit references, 21–13
  current account set-off, 1–26, 21–8
  equity holdings, restrictions on,
     20–12
  floating charges and, 1–5
  insider dealing, 20–16
  insolvency set-off, 1–22
  judicial rescue proceedings, 12–26
  liability. *See* **Lender liability**
  loss sharing agreements, 19–19
  misrepresentation by, 21–14
  mistaken payments to customers,
     1–28
  private debt restructuring. *See* **Private**
     debt restructuring
  solvency ratios, 20–7
  standstill agreements, 19–3, 19–4
  wages accounts, 19–18
Belarus,
  bankruptcy law, 1–13
  judicial rescue proceedings, 12–24
  preference rules, 7–3
Belgium,
  assignment of debts,
     late notification of, 5–25
     notice of, 2–40
  contracts, termination on insolvency,
     3–2
  directors' duty to call shareholders
     meeting on loss of capital, 8–16,
     8–17
  environmental liability, 21–18
  foreign insolvencies, recognition of,
     15–6, 15–37
  Franco-Belgian Convention, 17–2
  fungible securities, co-ownership of,
     2–7, 2–23, 2–24
  insolvency jurisdiction, 14–7
  insolvency set-off, 1–25, 11–29

Belgium—*cont.*
 lender liability
  breach of contract to lend money,
   21–5
  environmental pollution, 21–18
  negligent management, 8–21
  preference rules, 4–12, 7–1, 7–4
  Actio Pauliana, 4–19
  compensating contracts, 5–29
  roll-over of secured current
   accounts, 5–19
  security over after-acquired assets,
   5–20
  suspect period, 6–4, 6–6, 7–1, 7–4
 preventive compositions and
  moratoriums, 10–7, 10–8
 pro-debtor jurisdiction, as, 1–11
 security, attitude to, 1–20, 11–12
 trusts and, 2–7
 veil of incorporation, 8–7
Bermuda,
 insolvency set-off, 1–24
 negligent management, 8–26
Big pocket liability,
 directors and shareholders, 8–2
 lenders, 9–17
Bills of exchange. *See* **Negotiable
 instruments**
Bolivia,
 foreign insolvencies, recognition of,
  15–46, 16–25
 insolvency jurisdiction, 14–18
Bondholders,
 private debt restructuring, 18–16
 debt/equity conversions, 20–2
Brazil. *See also* **Latin America**
 companies, types of, 8–6
 custodianship, 2–7
 foreign insolvencies, recognition of,
  15–46
 insolvency set-off, 1–25
 preference rules, 4–12, 7–5
  transfer of business, 5–31
 preventive compositions and
  moratoriums, 10–8
 trusts, 2–7
Britain. *See* **United Kingdom**
Building contracts. *See* **Construction
 contracts**

Bulk sales. *See* **Preferences**
Bustamente Code, 17–4, 17–7

Canada,
 contracts,
  ipso facto clauses, 3–12
 credit references, 21–13
 direct action, sub-contractors, 1–34
 directors, liabilities of, 8–30
 environmental liability, 21–19,
  21–21, 21–22, 21–23
 equity creditors, 1–48
 insolvency set-off, 1–24, 11–29
 judicial rescue proceedings
  automatic stay, 12–9 to 12–10
  Bankruptcy and Insolvency Act,
   11–2, 12–7
  commercial reorganisation, 11–2,
   12–7
  Companies' Creditors Arrangement
   Act, 11–2, 12–7
  creditors approval of proposal,
   12–11
  freeze on acceleration rights, 11–31
  generally, 12–7
  ipso facto clauses, 11–33
  opening of proceedings, 12–8
  repudiation of commercial leases,
   12–12
  set-off, 11–31
  voidable preferences, 12–12
 lender liability, 9–19
  breach of contract to lend money,
   21–6
  credit references, 21–13
  environmental pollution, 21–19,
   21–21, 21–22, 21–23
 Manitoba, foreign insolvencies,
  recognition of, 15–17
 mechanics liens, 1–34
 negligent management, 8–24
 preference rules, 4–7, 7–1
  conflict of laws, 16–26
 pro-debtor/pro-creditor attitudes,
  1–10, 1–11
 Quebec, insolvency set-off, 1–24,
  5–28
 security interests, public registration
  of, 2–4

Cancellation. *See* Termination
Caribbean. *See* Bahamas; Bermuda;
    Cayman Islands
Cascade/domino insolvencies, 1–16,
    1–23, 3–15, 18–3
Cayman Islands,
    insolvency set-off, 1–24
    pro-creditor jurisdiction, as, 1–11
Central and Eastern Europe. *See also*
    Belarus; Czech Republic; Hungary;
    Kazakhstan; Poland; Russia;
    Slovak Republic; Ukraine
    generally, 1–13, 12–23
Charters,
    creditors, priority of, 1–19
Cheque,
    dishonour of, 21–8
Chile. *See also* Latin America
    companies, types of, 8–6
    insolvency set-off, 1–25
        transaction set-off, 1–26
    preference rules, 4–12
China,
    bankruptcy laws, 1–13
    insolvency set-off, 1–24
Chinese walls,
    insider dealing, 20–16
Clearing houses. *See* Custodians
Co-ownership,
    securities, of, 2–7, 2–23, 2–24
    tenancy in common, imposition of,
        2–31
Collection. *See* Deposits for sale or
    collection
Colombia. *See also* Latin America
    companies, types of, 8–6
    directors' duty to call shareholders
        meeting on loss of capital, 8–17
    foreign insolvencies, recognition of,
        15–6, 15–46
    insolvency set-off, 1–25
Comity,
    attitudes to, 13–6
    developed countries and, 13–6
    influences on, 13–6
    jurisdictions, classification of, 13–6
    pro-creditor/pro-debtor attitudes,
        13–6
    reasons for lack of, 13–1 to 13–2

Commingling,
    accidental, 2–14
    shareholders' liability, 9–3 to 9–6
Composition. *See* Judicial rescue
    proceedings
Conflict of laws,
    bankruptcy penalties and
        disqualifications, 16–38
    bankruptcy procedure, 16–29
    comity. *See* Comity
    contempt of court, 15–3, 16–1,
        16–13
    contracts, rescission of, 16–17 to
        16–18
    creditors,
        deferred creditors, 16–21
        equity shares, 16–22
        gap creditors, 16–28
        pari passu creditors, 16–20
        priority creditors, 16–19
    deferred creditors, 16–21
    discharges, 16–30 to 16–31
    discovery of foreign assets, 16–9
    disqualifications, 16–38
    equalisation
        country survey, 16–5 to 16–8
        enforcement of, 16–4
        excess receipts, examples of, 16–3
        generally, 16–1, 16–2
    equity shares, 16–22
    examples of foreign assets, 13–5
    executory contracts, rescission of,
        16–17 to 16–18
    foreign insolvencies, recognition of.
        See also under individual
        countries, *e.g.* England
    concurrent proceedings in foreign
        local forum,
        full and ancillary proceedings,
            15–12
        generally, 15–11
    conditions of recognition,
        generally, 15–7
        jurisdiction, 15–7
        public policy, 15–8
            expropriation, 15–8
            natural justice, 15–8
            taxes, 15–9
        reciprocity, 15–10

Conflict of laws—*cont.*
foreign insolvencies, recognition of—
cont.
generally, 15–1 to 15–2
home forum proceedings,
recognition of
full or partial, 15–5
generally, 15–3
immediate, without
proceedings, 15–6
limited to asset collection,
15–6
non-retroactive recognition
proceedings, 15–6
retroactive recognition
proceedings, 15–6
total non-recognition, 15–4
gap creditors, involuntary, 16–28
global property, 14–19 to 14–20
injunction, 15–3, 16–1
insolvency jurisdiction. *See also under*
individual countries, *e.g.* **England**
compositions, 14–9
eligible debtors, 14–9
global property, 14–19 to 14–20
grounds for opening proceedings,
14–8
local branch, 14–2
local company, 14–2
long arm jurisdiction,
generally, 14–3
local assets, 14–4
"toothbrush" jurisdictions,
14–4
local business, 14–5
local nationality or residence of
petitioning creditor, 14–7
local physical presence, 14–6
rehabilitations, 14–9
insolvency set-off
generally, 16–10 to 16–11
home forum rules
attitude of foreign local forum
to, 16–14
concurrent proceedings in
foreign local forum,
16–15
no concurrent proceedings in
foreign local forum,
16–14
generally, 16–12

Conflict of laws—*cont.*
insolvency set-off—*cont.*
home forum rules—*cont.*
home forum forbids set-off,
foreign forum allows, 16–13
home forum permits set-off,
foreign forum forbids,
16–12
leases, rescission of, 16–17 to 16–18
moratoriums, 16–30 to 16–31
pari passu creditors, 16–20
penalties, 16–38
preferences, 16–23 to 16–27
rescission of executory contracts and
leases, 16–17 to 16–18
security, 16–16
single forum, advantages and
disadvantages, 13–4
territorial theory, 13–3
title finance, 16–16
universal theory, 13–3
veil of incorporation, 16–35 to 16–37
Consents. *See* **Licences**
Consolidation,
insolvent groups, of, 9–16, 20–18
mortgages, of, 1–19
Construction contracts,
mechanics liens, 1–34
sub-contractor claims on insolvency,
1–34
Consumer protection,
generally, 1–17
Contracts,
acceptance on insolvency, 3–2
examples, 3–2
anticipatory repudiation, 3–8
breach of, 3–8
cancellation,
anticipatory repudiation, where,
3–8
breach of contract, where, 3–8
express right of. *See ipso facto*
clauses, *infra*
judicial rehabilitations, 18–11
personal contracts, 3–9
solvent counterparty, by, 3–7 to
3–15
construction contracts, 1–34
creditors with rights of rescission,
1–35

Contracts—*cont.*
  disclaimer of,
    exceptions,
      bankrupt lessors, 3–4
      bankrupt sellers of land, 3–4
      disclaimer is all or nothing, 3–4
      polluted property, 3–4
      generally, 3–3
      judicial rehabilitations, 18–8
  forfeitures,
    examples, 3–16 to 3–17
    rule against, 3–16 to 3–17
      exceptions, 3–19
        contract and lease rescissions, 3–19
        direct actions, 3–19
        rescission, 3–19
  generally, 1–1
  increased liabilities on bankruptcy, 3–18
  insolvency set-off and, 1–22
  interested parties
    debtor, 3–1
    mortgagees, 3–1
    solvent counterparty, 3–1
    sub-contractors, 1–34, 3–1
  ipso facto clauses,
    judicial rescue proceedings and, 11–32 to 11–34, 18–11
    nullification of, 11–33, 12–19, 12–22
    overriding,
      counterparty is monopoly utility, 3–10
      forfeiture of a vested asset, 3–10
      penal forfeiture, 3–10
    statutory nullification of, 3–11 to 3–15
  liabilities increased on bankruptcy, void for, 3–18
  performance
    counterparty, by, 3–2, 3–5
    debtor's estate, by, 3–5 to 3–6
      case law, 3–6
    personal, 3–9
  rejection on insolvency, 3–2
    examples, 3–2
  rescission on insolvency, 1–1, 1–35, 2–1
    conflict of laws, 16–17 to 16–18
    forfeitures, 3–19

Contracts—*cont.*
  set-off and, 1–22
  solvent counterparty rights,
    cancellation,
      anticipatory repudiation, where, 3–8
      breach of contract, 3–8
      express right of. *See ipso facto* clauses, *supra*
      generally, 3–7
      personal contracts, 3–9
    termination on insolvency, 1–1, 1–35, 2–1
    void
      examples of provisions, 3–16 to 3–17
      increased liabilites on bankruptcy, 3–18
Conventions. *See* **Treaties**
Corporate charges,
  public registration of, 1–20, 2–5
Corporate insolvency,
  classes of corporation, 1–62
  exempt assets, 1–58, 2–1
  generally, 1–1, 1–57
  individual insolvency compared, 1–57 to 1–61
  invisible property, 2–4
  limitations on security, 1–59
  preferences, 4–7
  rehabilitation, 1–60
Corporate rehabilitation,
  abandonment powers, 11–35
  contract cancellation, 11–32 to 11–34
  country summaries. *See under* individual countries, *e.g.* **England**
  debtor incentives to commence proceedings, 11–9
  disclaimer powers, 11–35
  ease of entry, 11–7 to 11–8
  eligible debtors, 11–5 to 11–6, 14–9
  exit from proceedings, 11–48
  financing the business, 11–40 to 11–41
  generally, 1–60
  grounds for petition, 11–7 to 11–8
  insolvency set-off, 11–29 to 11–31
  key issues, 11–3 to 11–4
  lease forfeitures, 11–32 to 11–34
  liability of administrators, 11–47

Corporate rehabilitation—*cont.*
mild proceedings, 11–1
preferences, 11–36
reorganisation plan, 11–42 to 11–46
replacement of management, 11–37
to 11–39
security, stay on enforcement of,
11–12 to 11–25
set-off, 11–29 to 11–31
stay on legal proceedings, 11–11
title finance, 11–26 to 11–28
tough proceedings, 11–2
Costa Rica. *See also* **Latin America**
foreign insolvencies, recognition of,
15–46, 16–25
Credit,
abusive, 21–10 to 21–11
reducing cost of, 1–16
set-off and, 1–23
references, 21–13
refusal of, 21–2 to 21–9
Creditors. *See also* **Insolvency claims**
bankruptcy, effect of, 1–2
consensually subordinated creditors,
1–50
deferred creditors
conflict of laws, 16–21
consensually subordinated
creditors, 1–50
equitably subordinated creditors,
1–49
equity creditors, 1–48
generally, 1–47
no *escritura publica*, 1–50
post-insolvency interest, 1–50
direct action, with. *See* **Direct action**
equitably subordinated creditors,
1–49
equity creditors, 1–48
equity shareholders, 1–51
conflict of laws, 16–22
expropriated creditors, 1–52 to 1–56
foreign creditors, 1–53
foreign currency creditors, 1–55
foreign penal demands, 1–54
foreign revenue authorities, 1–54
gap creditors, 16–28
ladder of payment, 1–14
late claimants, 1–53
life insurance policy holders, 1–40

Creditors—*cont.*
mistaken payments by, 1–28
owners wrongfully deprived of
property, 1–28
pari passu creditors,
assignments for less than full value,
1–46
conflict of laws, 16–20
discounting, 1–45
generally, 1–2, 1–5, 1–14, 1–44,
5–17
preferences. *See* **Preferences**
priority creditors,
bank depositors, 1–40
conflict of laws, 16–19
employee remuneration and
benefits, 1–39, 1–41
environmental clean-up expenses,
1–40
expenses of insolvency proceedings,
1–37
generally, 1–36
others, 1–40
secured creditors and, 1–41
subrogation to priority claims,
1–42 to 1–43
taxes, 1–38
priority unsecured, France, in, 1–20
rescission rights, with, 1–35
secured creditors, 1–16. *See also*
Security
limitations on, 1–19
priority creditors and, 1–41
private debt restructuring, 18–17
remedies of, 1–19
safe harbours, 1–19
set-off, with. *See* **Insolvency set-off**
shareholders, 1–51
super-priority creditors, 1–15 to 1–35
title finance creditors, 1–27
tort claimants, 1–56
trade creditors, 18–19
Curator. *See* **Insolvency representatives**
Current account set-off, 1–26, 21–8
Custodians. *And see* **Trusts and trustees**
apparent owner treated as absolute
owner, 2–8
clearing-houses, 2–8, 2–22, 3–6
deposits for safe-keeping, 2–7, 2–9
Euroclear. *See* **Euroclear**

Custodians—*cont.*
    false wealth doctrine. *See* **False wealth**
    fungibles. *See* **Fungibles**
    investment securities, 2–8, 2–9
    property claim converted into
        damages claim, 2–26
    reputed ownership. *See* **False wealth**
    securities, 2–8, 2–22 to 2–26
Cyprus,
    insolvency set-off, 1–24
Czech Republic,
    insolvency set-off, 1–24
    judicial rescue proceedings, 12–24
    preference rules, 7–6
    pro-creditor jurisdiction, as, 1–12

Damages,
    administrator's repudiation of
        contract, 1–44
    property claim converted into
        damages claim, 2–26
    secured debt, as, 1–18
Defamation,
    bankrupt's claim for, exempting,
        1–58
Denmark. *See also* **Scandinavian
    jurisdictions**
    assignment of debts, late notification
        of, 5–25
    companies, types of, 8–6
    contracts, rejection/performance on
        insolvency, 3–2
    direct action, 1–32
    directors
        duty to call shareholders meeting
            on loss of capital, 8–17
        liability for financial statements,
            8–28
    discharges, foreign, 16–33
    discounting of unmatured credits,
        1–45
    equity creditors, 1–48
    foreign currency creditors, 1–55
    foreign insolvencies, recognition of,
        15.4, 15.6, 15–42
    fraudulent trading, 8–10
    fungibles, co-ownership of, 2–7
    insolvency jurisdiction, 14–16
        global property, 14–20

Denmark—*cont.*
    insolvency jurisdiction—*cont.*
        local branch, 14–4
        local business, 14–5
    insolvency set-off, 1–24, 5–28, 11–29
    lender liability,
        breach of contract to lend money,
            21–7
        environmental pollution, 21–19
    negligent management, 8–26
    Nordic Bankruptcy Convention,
        1933, 17–3
    preference rules, 4–12
        Actio Pauliana, 4–19
        compensating contracts, 5–29
        conflict of laws, 16–27
        excessive remuneration to
            managers, 5–4
        executions, 5–36
        late registration of security, 5–23
        legal seizures, 5–36
        ordinary course of business
            payments, 5–12
        payment of debts, 5–8
        security for pre-existing debt, 5–17
        suspect period, 6–6
    preventive compositions and
        moratoriums, 10–7, 10–8
    public and private companies, 8–6
    security, attitude to, 1–20
    trusts and, 2–7
Depositories. *See* **Custodians**
Deposits for sale or collection,
    illustrations, 2–33
    proceeds,
        civil countries, in, 2–38
        receipt of,
            agent, by, 2–37
            insolvent, by, 2–35
            sub-agent, by, 2–36
    property held by insolvent *in specie*,
        2–34
Deprivation on insolvency,
    jurisdictional attitudes, 2–1
Direct action,
    building sub-contractors, 1–34
    forfeitures and, 3–19
    generally, 1–29
    insolvency of agent, on
        principal against third party, 1–32
        third party against principal, 1–32

Direct action—*cont.*
  lifting the veil of incorporation, 1–34
  product liability, 1–34
  third party liability insurance, 1–33
  undisclosed principal, 1–30 to 1–32
    jurisdictions allowing, 1–30 to
      1–32
Directors,
  big pocket liability, 8–2
  breach of company law, liability for,
    8–27
    financial statements, 8–28
    ratification by shareholders, 8–29
  business judgment rule, 8–19 to
    8–20, 8–24, 8–26
  corporate preference, participation in,
    6–23
  de facto directors,
    liabilities of, 8–32, 9–18
    shareholders as, 9–7
  direct action against, 1–34
  disqualification, 1–1
    preferences, 4–9, 6–23
    transactions at an undervalue, 4–9
  duty to call shareholders' meeting on
    loss of capital, 8–14, 8–16 to
    8–18
  duty to petition for insolvency, 8–14,
    8–15
  environment liability, 8–31
  financial statements, liability for,
    8–28
  fraudulent trading, 8–9 to 8–10
  liabilities of, 1–11, 8–1 *et seq*
  lifting the veil, 1–34
  misfeasance, 1–28, 5–3, 6–23
  negligent management, 8–19 to 8–26
    business judgment rule, 8–19 to
      8–20
  preferences, 4–9, 6–23
  preferential claims, liability for, 8–30
  secret profits, 2–13
  shadow directors, 21–19
  tort liability, 8–31
  wrongful trading, 8–11 to 8–13
Discharges,
  conflict of laws, 16–30 to 16–31
  generally, 1–60
Disclaimer,
  contracts, of. *See* Contracts

Discovery,
  foreign assets, of, 16–9
Distress. *See* Attachments
Divided ownership. *See* Trusts and
  trustees
Domino/cascade insolvencies, 1–16,
  1–23, 3–15, 18–3

Eastern Europe. *See* Central and Eastern
  Europe
Egypt,
  insolvency set-off, 1–25
  preference rules, 4–12
  pro-debtor jurisdiction, as, 1–13
Eire. *See* Republic of Ireland
El Salvador. *See also* Latin America
  foreign insolvencies, recognition of,
    15–6, 15–46
Employees,
  private debt restructuring and, 18–20
  remuneration and benefits, priority
    on insolvency, 1–39, 1–41
Employer,
  sub-contractors direct rights against,
    1–34
England. *See also* English-based
  countries; United Kingdom
  administration
    building societies, 12–26
    contract cancellation, 11–32
    debtor incentives, 11–9
    disclaimer rights and, 11–35
    ease of entry, 11–7
    eligible debtors, 11–5, 14–9
    end of proceedings, 11–48
    financing the business, 11–41
    foreign insolvencies, recognition of,
      15–5
    grounds for petition, 11–7
    insolvency jurisdiction, 14–12
    insurance companies, 12–26
    interest, 11–42, 11–43
    ipso facto clauses, 11–33
    lease forfeitures, 11–32
    preferences, 11–36
    procedure, 11–43
    rentals, 11–43

England—*cont.*
  administration—*cont.*
    replacement of management,
        11–37, 11–38
    security, stay on enforcement of,
        11–14 to 11–16
    set-off, 11–30
    stay on legal proceedings, 11–11
    title finance, 11–27
  administrator, 11–47
  assets
    exempt, 1–58
    foreign, discovery of, 16–9
  assignment of debts, 2–40
    notice of, 2–40
  bankruptcy of individuals, 14–11
  borrower liability, 9–18
  commodities, deposit of, 2–23
  compositions,
    preventive compositions and
        moratoriums, 10–9
    voluntary, 10–5
  consolidation on insolvency, 9–16
  constructive trust, 2–13
  contracts, disclaimer/rescission/
        performance on insolvency, 3–2,
        3–4
  corporate guarantees, 5–6
  credit references, 21–13
  creditors. *See* priority on insolvency,
        infra
  custodianship of securities, 2–22,
        2–23
  discharges, foreign, 16–32
  discounting of unmatured credits,
        1–45
  discovery of foreign assets, 16–9
  environmental liability, 21–19,
        21–20, 21–22, 21–24
  equalisation, 16–5, 16–8
  equity creditors, 1–48
  expenses of insolvency proceedings,
        1–37
  family home, 1–58
  foreign insolvencies, recognition of,
    concurrent individual bankruptcies
        in England, 15–28
    concurrent proceedings, 15–18 to
        15–21
    creditor attachments, 15–16

England—*cont.*
  foreign insolvencies, recognition of—
        cont.
    effect of recognition, 15–25 to
        15–26
    generally, 15–13
    recognition of foreign jurisdiction,
        15–14
    bankrupt of individuals, 15–24
    recovery of property, 15–15
        after-acquired property, 15–15,
        15–27
    rehabilitation proceedings, 15–22
    requirements for, 15–13
    special British reciprocal
        jurisdiction, 15–23
  fraudulent trading, 8–9
  guarantees, 5–6
  insolvency jurisdiction,
    administration of companies,
        14–12
    bankruptcy of individuals, 14–11
    global property, 14–19
    local assets, 14–4
    local business, 14–5
    winding-up of companies, 14–10
  insolvency set-off, 1–24, 5–28,
        11–29, 11–30
    conflict of laws, 16–12, 16–14,
        16–15
  insurance companies, insolvency of,
        1–62
  judicial rescue proceedings. *See*
        administration, *supra*
  lender liability,
    bank as adviser, 21–12
    breach of contract to lend money,
        21–2 to 21–4, 21–6
    current account set-off, 21–8
    credit references, 21–13
    environmental pollution, 21–19,
        21–20, 21–22, 21–24
    shadow director, 21–19
  moratoriums,
    foreign, 16–32
    preventive compositions, 10–9
  negligent management, 8–22 to 8–23
  post-insolvency interest, 1–50
  preference rules. *See under* **English-
        based countries**
  preventive compositions and
        moratoriums, 10–9

England—*cont.*
  priority on insolvency,
    conflict of laws, 16–19, 16–20,
      16–22
    equity creditors, 1–48
    expenses of insolvency proceedings,
      1–37
    expropriated creditors, 1–53, 1–54,
      1–55
    foreign creditors, 1–53
    foreign currency creditors, 1–55
    foreign revenue and penalties, 1–54
    late claimants, 1–53
    post-insolvency interest, 1–50
    taxes, 1–41
    tort claims, 1–56
    wages, 1–41
  reputed ownership, 2–3
  securities, deposit of, 2–22
  shareholders, group liability, 9–9
  spouse, bankruptcy of, 1–58
  subordinated creditors, 1–49
  trusts
    constructive, 2–13
    express trusts of money, 2–16
    tests of trusteeship, 2–16 to 2–19
  veil of incorporation, 8–7
  winding-up of companies, 14–10
  wrongful trading, 8–11
English-based countries. *See also*
  England
  administration. *See under* England
  assignment of debts, notice of, 2–40
  comity, attitude to, 13–6
  constructive trusts, 2–13
  corporate charges, registration of,
    1–20, 2–5
  creditors. *See* priority on insolvency,
    infra
  direct action
    building sub-contractors, 1–34
    third party against principal, 1–32
    third party liability insurance, 1–33
    undisclosed principal, 1–30 to
      1–32
  directors' liability for debts of
    insolvent company, 1–11, 8–9
  equity creditors, 1–48
  exempt assets, 1–58
  false wealth, 2–3

English-based countries—*cont.*
  floating charge, 1–5, 1–11, 1–41,
    4–10, 5–16, 19–17
    capture of after-acquired assets by,
      5–20
    connected persons, granted to, 6–5
    guarantees, securing, 19–18
    pre-existing debt, for, 5–21 to
      5–22, 19–18
  foreign insolvencies, recognition of.
    See under England
  fraudulent trading, 8–9
  insolvency jurisdiction
    local assets, 14–4
    local business, 14–5
    local physical presence, 14–6
  insolvency set-off, 1–5, 1–11, 1–21,
    11–29
  mortgages, non-possessory chattel
    mortgages, 1–59
  ordinary course of business payments,
    5–11
  preference rules
    Actio Pauliana, 4–7, 4–19, 4–20
    administration, 11–36
    avoidance
      guarantees, revival of, 6–17
      preferred transferee insolvent,
        6–21
      protection of third parties, 6–19
      set-off against repayment claim,
        6–22
      tests for, 4–9
    compensating contracts, 5–29
    conflict of laws, 16–24, 16–26
    corporate bankruptcies, 4–7
    defences, 4–9
    execution judgment, 5–36
    floating charges, 4–11, 5–20, 5–21
    fraudulent conveyances, 4–7
    generally, 4–7, 7–1
    gifts, 4–8 to 4–9
    individual bankruptcies, 4–7
    negotiable instruments, 5–9
    ordinary course of business
      payments, 5–11
    preferential intent, 4–10, 5–24,
      5–29, 6–8, 6–9, 6–14
      negation of, 6–10, 6–11
      onus of proof, 6–12

English-based countries—*cont.*
  preference rules—*cont.*
    recapture, 6–16
    relation back, 4–7, 5–36
    security,
      floating charges for pre-existing
        debt, 5–21, 19–18
      late registration of, 5–23
      over after-acquired assets, 5–20,
        6–20
      pre-existing debt, for, 5–17,
        5–18
      replacement of void security by
        valid security, 5–24
      revival of, 6–18
      roll-over of secured current
        accounts, 5–19
    shareholders, transactions with,
      5–33
    suspect period, connected persons,
      4–10
    tests of a preference, 6–2
    transactions at an undervalue, 4–9
  priority on insolvency,
    equity creditors, 1–48
    taxes, 1–41
    tort claimants, 1–56
    wages, 1–41
  private debt restructuring, 18–14
  pro-creditor, as, 1–5, 1–11, 1–13,
    1–32, 4–6
  public and private companies, 8–6
  registration of corporate charges,
    1–20, 2–5
  reputed ownership, 2–3
  schemes of arrangement, 10–5
  secret ownership, 1–11
  security. *See also* preference rules,
    supra
    attitude to, 1–20, 11–12
  self-help, 1–20
  set-off, 1–5, 1–11, 1–21
  shareholder liability, 9–1
  subrogation to priority claims, 1–42
  suspect period, length of, 6–4
  trusts, constructive, 2–13
  undisclosed principal, 1–30 to 1–32
  universal business charge, 1–20
  universal floating charge. *See* floating
    charge, *supra*
  voluntary compositions, 10–5

Enterprise finance,
  encouraging, 1–16
Environmental pollution. *See* **Lender
  liability**
Equalisation,
  conflict of laws. *See* **Conflict of laws**
  definition, 16.1
Euroclear. *See also* Custodians
  fungible securities, 2–23
European Union,
  directors' duty to call shareholders
    meeting on loss of capital, 8–16
Execution. *See* **Attachments**
Expropriations,
  generally, 1–1

Factoring,
  private debt restructuring and, 18–18
False wealth,
  assignment of debts, 1–11, 2–39
  civil law jurisdictions, 2–8
  common law jurisdictions, 2–4
  France, 1–11
  generally, 2–3
  jurisdictional attitudes, 2–3
  lender liability, 21–10 to 21–11
  prevention of, 1–17
  reputed ownership, 2–3
  secret ownership and, 2–4
  secret profits and, 2–13
  security and, 1–17
  specificity, doctrine of, 1–20
  trusts, 1–11, 2–3
  undisclosed principal and, 1–31
Family home,
  homestead exemption, 1–58, 2–1
  insolvency and, 1–58
Far East. *See* **China; Hong Kong; Japan;
  Korea**
Fiduciary transfers. *See* **Security**
Financial institutions. *See* **Banks**
Finland. *See also* **Scandinavian
  jurisdictions**
  Bankruptcy Convention, 1933, 17–3
  companies, types of, 8–6
  directors' duty to call shareholders
    meeting on loss of capital, 8–16,
    8–18

Finland—*cont.*
discharges, foreign, 16–34
discounting of unmatured credits,
1–45
foreign insolvencies, recognition of,
15–6, 15–42
insolvency jurisdiction, 14–16
global property, 14–20
local assets, 14–4
local business, 14–5
local nationality of debtor, 14–7
local physical presence, 14–6
insolvency set-off, 1–24, 5–28, 11–29
lender liability, 9–19
breach of contract to lend money,
21–4
security, attitude to, 1–20
Floating charges. *See also* **Security**
advantages of, 1–5
avoidance, tests for, 4–10
capture of after-acquired assets by,
5–20
connected persons, granted to, 6–5
disadvantages of, 1–5
English-based countries, 1–5, 1–11,
1–41, 4–10, 5–16, 19–17
guarantees, securing, 19–18
monopolistic scope of, 1–41
pre-existing debt, for, 5–21 to 5–22,
19–18
pro-creditor/pro-debtor jurisdictions,
1–5
security and, 1–18
Foreign currency,
conversion of, 11–42
insolvency claims, 1–55
Forfeitures. *See* **Contracts**
Formalities,
security, 1–18
France. *See also* **Franco-Latin
jurisdictions**
abusive support of insolvent
company, 9–20
assignment of debts, 1–11, 2–40
late notification of, 5–25
companies, types of, 8–6
contracts, *ipso facto* clauses, 3–13,
11–33
Conventions, 17–2

France—*cont.*
corporate rehabilitation. *See*
redressement judiciaire, infra
creditors. *See* priority on insolvency,
infra
current-account set-off, 1–26
direct action,
sub-contractors, 1–34
third party liability insurance, 1–33
undisclosed principal, 1–31
worker against ultimate employer,
1–34
directors,
duty to call shareholders meeting
on loss of capital, 8–18
liabilities of, 1–11
breach of company law, 8–27
environmental liability, 21–19
equalisation in, 16–6, 16–8
expenses of insolvency proceedings,
1–41
false wealth doctrine, 1–11
foreign creditors, 1–53
foreign currency creditors, 1–55
foreign insolvencies, recognition of,
15–6, 15–38
fungibles, co-ownership of, 2–7
insolvency jurisdiction, 14–13
local assets, 14–4
local nationality of creditor, 14–7
insolvency set-off, 1–5, 1–11, 1–25,
11–29, 11–31
current-account set-off, 1–26
lien de connexite['] principle, 1–26
transaction set-off, 1–26
ipso facto clauses, 3–13
judicial rescue proceedings. *See*
redressement judiciaire, infra
late claimants, 1–53
long suspect periods, 1–26
negligent management, 8–21
preference rules, 4–12, 7–1, 7–7
Actio Pauliana, 4–19, 7–7
late registration of security, 5–23
redressement judiciaire, 11–36
roll-over of secured current
accounts, 5–19
suspect period, 6–4, 7–7
priority on insolvency,
employees, 1–41

France—*cont.*
  priority on insolvency—*cont.*
    expenses of insolvency proceedings,
      1–41
    expropriated creditors, 1–53, 1–55
    foreign creditors, 1–53
    foreign currency creditors, 1–55
    late claimants, 1–53
    secured creditors, 1–41
    unsecured creditors, 1–20
  private debt restructuring, 18–14
  pro-debtor jurisdiction, as, 1–11
  redressement judiciaire,
    contract cancellation, 11–33
    disclaimer powers, 11–35
    ease of entry, 11–8
    eligible debtors, 11–6, 14–9
    end of proceedings, 11–48
    financing the business, 11–41
    foreign currency conversion, 11–42
    generally, 1–11, 11–2, 18–14
    grounds for, 11–8
    ipso facto clauses, 11–33
    preferences, 11–36
    reorganisation plan, 11–45
    replacement of management,
      11–37, 11–39
    security interests, 11–22 to 11–24
    set-off, 11–31
    stay on legal proceedings, 11–11
    title finance, 11–28
  rehabilitation law, 1–11
  secured creditors, 1–41
  security, attitude to, 1–11, 1–20,
    11–12
  set-off. *See* insolvency set-off, *supra*
  sub-contractor, direct rights of, 1–34
  transaction set-off, 1–26
  treaties. *See* Conventions, *supra*
  trusts and, 2–7
  undisclosed principal, 1–31
  unsecured creditors, 1–20
  veil of incorporation, 1–11, 8–7
Franco-Latin jurisdictions,
  compensating contracts, 5–29
  direct action, 1–32
  insolvency set-off, 1–21, 1–23, 5–27,
    16–10
  long suspect periods, 1–26
  non-merchants, position of, 1–57

Franco-Latin jurisdictions—*cont.*
  ordinary course of business payments,
    5–13
  preference rules,
    Actio Pauliana, 4–12
    creditor enforcements, 5–36
    creditor ignorance of insolvency,
      6–13
    general preferences, 4–13
    generally, 4–12, 7–1
    negotiable instruments, 5–9
    ordinary course of business
      payments, 5–13
    payment of debts, 5–8
    security for pre-existing debt, 5–17
    suspect period, 6–4, 7–1
    transactions automatically void,
      4–13
  revendication, right of, 3–6
  set-off, 1–21, 1–23, 5–27, 16–10
  trusts, 2–6, 2–7
Fraudulent trading. *See also* Directors
  creditor liable for, subordination of,
    1–49
  debt/equity conversions and, 20–7
  definition, 8–9
  tests for, 8–9
Fraudulent transfer. *See* Preferences
Fungibles,
  co-ownership of, 2–7
  custodianship of securities, 2–9,
    2–22, 2–23, 2–24 to 2–25
    property claim converted into
      damages claim, 2–26
  loans of, 2–25
  securities,
    co-ownership of, 2–7, 2–23, 2–24
    loans of, 2–25
  settlement netting, 5–30
  storage of, 2–20
  test of ownership, 2–20 to 2–21
  trust of, 2–20 to 2–21
  trust of part of, 2–24

Germany,
  assignment of debts, notice of, 2–40
  companies, types of, 8–6
  contracts, performance on insolvency,
    3–2

Germany—*cont.*
  direct action, undisclosed principal,
    1–31, 1–32
  discharges, foreign, 16–32
  discounting of future debt, 1–45
  environmental liability, 21–22
  equalisation in, 16–6, 16–8
  equity creditors, 1–48
  fiduciary transfer, 1–20, 9–20
  foreign currency creditors, 1–55
  foreign insolvencies, recognition of,
    15–6, 15–39
  fungible securities, co-ownership of,
    2–23, 2–24
  future debts, discounting back, 1–45
  gap creditors, 16–28
  insolvency jurisdiction, 14–13
    local assets, 14–4
  insolvency set-off, 1–24, 5–28,
    11–29, 11–30, 16–10
    conflict of laws, 16–14
  moratoriums, 10–9
  negligent management, 8–26
  preference rules, 7–1
    conflict of laws, 16–27
  preventive compositions and
    moratoriums, 10–9
  pro-creditor jurisdiction, as, 1–10,
    1–11, 1–12
  public registration system, lack of,
    1–20
  security, attitude to, 1–20, 11–12
  shareholders, group liability, 9–8
  tracing of money, 2–2
  trusts, 2–2, 2–6
  undisclosed principal, 1–31, 1–32
  veil of incorporation, 8–7
Gifts,
  voidable preferences, as. *See*
    Preferences
Goodwill,
  bankruptcy, effects of, 1–23
Greece,
  companies, types of, 8–6
  direct action, 1–32
  directors liability for preferential
    claims, 8–30
  foreign insolvencies, recognition of,
    15–6, 15–40
  insolvency set-off, 1–25, 11–29

Greece—*cont.*
  preference rules, 4–12
    Actio Pauliana, 4–19
  security, attitude to, 1–20
Guarantees,
  corporate, 5–6
  "cross-stream" guarantees, 5–6
  debt/equity conversions and, 20–9
  floating charges securing, 19–18
  revival of, 6–17
  undervalue transactions, as, 5–6,
    19–17
  "upstream" guarantees, 5–6
Guarantors,
  preferment of, 5–34
Guernsey,
  insolvency set-off, 1–24

Hidden ownership. *See* **Secret
  ownership**
Hire purchase. *See* **Title finance**
Home. *See* **Family home**
Homestead exemption, 1–58, 2–1
Honduras. *See also* **Latin America**
  foreign insolvencies, recognition of,
    15–6, 15–46
  insolvency jurisdiction, 14–18
Hong Kong,
  fraudulent trading, 8–9
  insolvency set-off, 1–24
  pro-creditor jurisdiction, as, 1–11
  public and private companies, 8–6
Hotch-pot. *See* **Equalisation**
Hungary,
  bankruptcy law in, 1–12
  companies, types of, 8–6
  judicial rescue proceedings, 12–24
  shareholders, group liability, 9–8

India,
  insolvency set-off, 1–24
  pro-creditor jurisdiction, as, 1–11,
    1–13
  public and private companies, 8–6
Indonesia,
  pro-creditor jurisdiction, as, 1–13
Information,
  statutory disclosure, 18–11

Insider dealing,
debt/equity conversions and, 20–16
Insolvency,
advertisement of, 1–3
application for, 1–3
assets, exempt, 1–58, 2–1
causes of, 1–63
conflict of laws. *See* **Conflict of laws**
corporate. *See* **Corporate insolvency**
creditors. *See* **Creditors**
definition, 6–1
discharge, 1–60
effects of, 1–1, 1–23
essential features of, 1–2
exempt assets, 1–58, 2–1
expenses of proceedings, 1–37
family home and, 1–58
general principles of, choice, 1–1 *et
seq*
goodwill and, 1–23
hierarchy. *See* **Creditors**
individual
corporate insolvency compared,
1–57 to 1–61
discharge and rehabilitation, 1–60
exempt assets, 1–58, 2–1
generally, 1–57
limitations on security, 1–59
matrimonial property, 1–61
preference rules, 4–7
reputed ownership, 2–3
international treaties. *See* **Treaties**
judicial rescue proceedings. *See*
Judicial rescue proceedings
jurisdiction. *See* **Conflict of laws**
liabilities increased on, contract void
for, 3–18
matrimonial property, community of,
1–61
non-merchants, position of, 1–57
pensions, exemption from seizure,
1–58
petition for, 1–3
procedure, 1–3
proceedings, expenses of, 1–37
publication of, 1–3
purpose of, 1–1
salaries, exemption from seizure,
1–58

Insolvency—*cont.*
set-off. *See* **Insolvency set-off**
spouse, of, 1–58
tools of the trade, exemption from
seizure, 1–58
trauma of, 18–9
Insolvency administrator. *See*
Insolvency representatives
Insolvency claims,
creditors. *See* **Creditors**
direct action. *See* **Direct action**
Insolvency representatives,
appointment of, 1–3
Insolvency set-off,
advantages of, 1–23
banks, 1–22
bar on, 1–25
circuitry, avoidance of, 1–22, 1–23
compensating contracts, 5–29
conflict of laws. *See* **Conflict of laws**
contracts and, 1–22
countries allowing, 1–24, 5–28,
11–29
countries disallowing, 1–25, 5–27,
11–29, 11–30
exceptions to bar, 1–26
current account set-off, 1–26, 21–8
debt-purchasing, 1–46
effects of, 1–22
English-based countries, 1–5, 1–11,
1–21
Franco-Latin jurisdictions, 1–21,
1–23
generally, 1–21, 5–27
policies of, 1–23
preferences and, 5–27 to 5–29
pro-creditor/pro-debtor attitudes,
1–5, 1–21
purchase of debts, 1–46
repayment claim, against, 6–22
security function of, 1–22, 11–29
transaction set-off, 1–26
unpublicised security interest, as,
1–23
Insurance,
policy-holders, priority on insolvency,
1–40
third party liability insurance, 1–33
Insurance companies,
bankruptcies of, 1–62

Insurance companies—*cont.*
  judicial rescue proceedings, 12–26
  solvency ratios, 20–7
Interest,
  overcharging, 21–14
  post-insolvency, 1–50
  test of trusteeship, 2–18
  usury, 1–13, 1–17
Ipso facto . See Contracts
Ireland. *See* Northern Ireland; Republic
    of Ireland
Isle of Man,
  foreign insolvencies, recognition of,
    15–9
  insolvency set-off, 1–24
Israel,
  insolvency set-off, 1–24
  pro-creditor jurisdiction, as, 1–13
  public and private companies, 8–6
Italy,
  assignment of debts,
    late notification of, 5–25
    notice of, 2–40
  companies, types of, 8–6
  contracts, performance on insolvency,
    3–2
  direct action, undisclosed principal,
    1–31
  discounting of unmatured credits,
    1–45
  foreign currency creditors, 1–55
  foreign insolvencies, recognition of,
    15–6, 15–40
  Franco-Italian Convention, 17–2
  insolvency jurisdiction, 14–13
  insolvency set-off, 1–24
  judicial rescue proceedings
    compulsory administrative
      liquidation (*liquidazione
      coatta amministrativa*), 12–13
      banks, 12–26
      insurance companies, 12–26
      public interest, 12–26
    controlled administration
      (*amministrazone controllata*),
      12–13
    extraordinary administration
      (*amministrazione
      straordinaira*), 11–2, 11–30,
      12–14 to 12–18

Italy—*cont.*
  judicial rescue proceedings—*cont.*
    generally, 12–13
    preventative composition
      (*concordato preventivo*),
      11–30, 12–13
    set-off, 11–30
  negligent management, 8–26
  preference rules, 7–8
    Actio Pauliana, 4–19, 7–8
    creditor ignorance of insolvency,
      6–13
    gifts, 5–5
    security for pre-existing debt, 5–18
  preventive compositions and
    moratoriums, 10–7, 10–9
  pro-debtor jurisdiction, as, 1–11
  security, attitude to, 1–20, 11–12
  undisclosed principal, 1–31
  veil of incorporation, 8–7

Japan,
  assignment of debts,
    late notification of, 5–25
    notice of, 2–40
  business judgment rule, 8–26
  companies, types of, 8–6
  contracts, rejection/performance on
    insolvency, 3–2
  corporate reorganisation,
    contract cancellation, 11–34,
      11–35
    ease of entry, 11–8
    eligible debtors, 11–6, 14–9
    generally, 11–1, 11–6
    grounds for application, 11–8
    interest, 11–42
    ipso facto clauses, 11–34
    lease forfeitures, 11–34
    preferences, 11–36
    reorganisation plan, 11–46
    replacement of management,
      11–39
    security, 11–25
    set-off, 11–30
    stay on legal proceedings, 11–11
  discounting unmatured debts, 1–45
  fiduciary transfer, 1–20, 9–20
  foreign insolvencies, recognition of,
    15–44

Japan—*cont.*
insolvency jurisdiction, 14–15
local assets, 14–4
insolvency set-off, 1–24, 5–28, 11–29
judicial rescue proceedings. *See*
corporate reorganisation *supra*
negligent management, 8–25, 8–26
preference rules, 7–9
corporate reorganisation, 11–36
creditor ignorance of insolvency,
6–13
security for pre-existing debt, 5–18
private debt restructuring, 18–14
pro-creditor jurisdiction, as, 1–12
security, attitude to, 1–20, 11–12
veil of incorporation, 8–7
Jersey,
fraudulent trading, 8–9
insolvency set-off, 1–24
Judicial rescue proceedings,
classification of, 10–5 to 10–9
compositions and moratoriums. *See*
also **Moratoriums**
country examples, 10–8 to 10–10
moratoriums, 10–7
preventive composition
proceedings, 10–6
voluntary compositions, 10–5
corporate rehabilitation. *See*
Corporate rehabilitation
country summaries. *See under*
individual countries, *e.g.* **England**
generally, 10–1
ipso facto clauses and, 11–32 to
11–34, 18–11
private debt restructuring. *See* **Private**
debt restructuring
rehabilitations. *See* **Rehabilitations**

Kazakhstan,
bankruptcy law, 1–13
judicial rescue proceedings, 12–25
Kenya,
pro-creditor jurisdiction, as, 1–13
Korea,
assignment of debts,
late notification of, 5–25
notice of, 2–40
companies, types of, 8–6

Korea—*cont.*
discounting unmatured debts, 1–45
insolvency set-off, 1–24
preference rules, creditor ignorance of
insolvency, 6–13
pro-creditor jurisdiction, as, 1–12
Kuwait,
bankruptcy law, 1–13
insolvency set-off, 1–25

Latin America. *See also* **Argentina;**
Brazil; Chile; Colombia; Costa
Rica; El Salvador; Honduras;
Mexico; Panama; Paraguay; Peru;
Uruguay
assignment of debts, notice of, 2–40
Bustamente Code, 17–4, 17–7
comity, attitude to, 13–6
companies, types of, 8–6
directors' duty to call shareholders
meeting on loss of capital, 8–16
insolvency jurisdiction, 14–18
local branch, 14–4
insolvency set-off, 1–24, 1–25, 11–29
Montevideo Treaty, 1889, 17–4,
17–5
Montevideo Treaty, 1940, 17–4,
17–6
preference rules, 4–12
late registration of security, 5–23
pro-debtor jurisdictions, 1–12
security, attitude to, 1–20, 11–12
sociedad anónima, 8–6
trusts, 2–7
Leases,
acceptance/rejection on insolvency,
3–2
bankrupt lessor, 3–4
creditors, priority of, 1–19
interested parties
debtor, 3–1
mortgagees, 3–1
solvent counterparty, 3–1
sub-contractors, 1–34, 3–1
ipso facto clauses. *See* **Contracts**
private debt restructuring, 18–18
debt/equity conversions, 20–4
rescission of, 1–35, 2–1
conflict of laws, 16–17 to 16–18

Leases—*cont.*
 rescission of—*cont.*
  forfeitures, 3–19
Lender liability,
 abusive credit, 9–20, 21–10 to 21–11
 agent banks, 21–14
 bank as adviser, 21–12
 big pocket liability, 9–17
 breach of contract to lend money,
  21–2 to 21–9
  liability to third parties, 21–9
 cheque dishonour, 21–8
 control of debtor, 21–15
 credit, withdrawal of, 21–2 to 21–9
 credit references, 21–13
 environmental pollution for,
  categories of environmental
   liability, 21–18
  CERCLA, 21–25 to 21–26
  generally, 21–17
  involvement in management,
   21–19
  occupation, 21–20
  operational control or
   responsibility, 21–22
  ownership, 21–21
  priority of environmental clean-up
   orders and costs, 1–40, 21–23
   to 21–24
 false wealth, 21–10 to 21–11
 generally, 9–17, 21–1
 interference in management, 9–18 to
  9–19
 judicial rehabilitation, 18–8
 misrepresentation liability, 21–14
 overcharging interest, 21–14
 secured debtor, liabilities of, 21–16
Liberia,
 insolvency laws, 1–13
 insolvency set-off, 1–24
Licences,
 creditors, priority of, 1–19
 patent licence, 1–35
 rescission of, 1–35
Liechtenstein,
 foreign insolvencies, recognition of,
  15–40
 insolvency set-off, 1–24
Lien,
 aircraft lien, 1–19
 maritime lien, 1–19, 1–41

Lien—*cont.*
 mechanics lien, 1–34
 possessory, 5–15
 vendor's lien, 3–6
Life insurance. *See* **Insurance**
Lifting the veil,
 direct action against directors or
  shareholders, 1–34
 shareholder liability. *See* **Shareholders**
 United States, in, 9–4 to 9–5
Liquidator. *See* **Insolvency**
  representatives
Loans,
 equity creditors, 1–48
Loss sharing agreements. *See* **Private**
  debt restructuring
Luxembourg,
 assignment of debts,
  late notification of, 5–25
  notice of, 2–40
 environmental liability, 21–19
 foreign insolvencies, recognition of,
  15–6, 15–37
 fungible securities, co-ownership of,
  2–7, 2–23, 2–24
 insolvency jurisdiction, local
  nationality of creditor, 14–7
 insolvency set-off, 1–25, 11–29
  current-account set-off, 1–26
 negligent management, 8–21
 preference rules, 4–12
  suspect period, 6–4, 6–6
 preventive compositions and
  moratoriums, 10–7, 10–9
 pro-debtor jurisdiction, as, 1–11
 security, attitude to, 1–20
 trusts and, 2–7

Malaysia,
 insolvency set-off, 1–24
Mandate. *See* **Agency**
Manitoba. *See* **Canada**
Maritime lien, 1–19, 1–41
Marshalling. *See* **Equalisation**
Matrimonial property,
 community of, 1–61, 2–6
Mexico. *See also* **Latin America**
 companies, types of, 8–6
 custodianship, 2–7

Mexico—*cont.*
    direct action, principal against third
        party, 1–32
    foreign insolvencies, recognition of,
        15–6, 15–46
    insolvency jurisdiction, 14–18
    insolvency set-off, 1–25
        transaction set-off, 1–26
    trusts, 2–7
Middle East. *See* Bahrain; Cyprus;
    Egypt; Israel; Kuwait; Qatar; Saudi
    Arabia; Turkey
Misrepresentation and non-disclosure,
    liability for, 21–14
Mistaken payments,
    proprietary claims on insolvency for,
        2–14
Montevideo Treaty 1889, 17–4, 17–5
Montevideo Treaty 1940, 17–4, 17–6
Moratoriums,
    conflict of laws, 16–30 to 16–31
    preventive compositions and, 10–7,
        10–8, 10–9
    secured debt, on, 1–19
    super-priority moratorium loans,
        1–19
Mortgages,
    collateral, to secure debt of third
        parties, 5–15
    consolidation of, 1–19
    disclaimer and, 3–5
    foreign currency, 1–18
    hire-purchase recharacterised as,
        1–27
    new money mortgages, 5–15
    non-possessory chattel mortgage,
        1–18, 1–20, 1–59
    purchase money mortgages, 5–15
    scope of assets, 1–18
    second mortgage, 1–19
    secret ownership and, 2–4
    wrongful disposal of mortgaged
        securities, 2–13

Napoleonic code,
    trusts and trustees, 2–6
Negotiable instruments,
    payment of as voidable preference,
        5–9

Netherlands,
    assignment of debts, notice of, 2–40
    bank bankruptcies, 1–62
    companies, types of, 8–6
    contracts, performance on insolvency,
        3–2
    direct action, 1–32
    directors,
        diligence duties, 8–25
        liability for preferential claims,
            8–30
    discounting unmatured credits, 1–45
    equalisation in, 16–7
    fiduciary transfer, 1–20, 9–20
    foreign insolvencies, recognition of,
        15–6, 15–41
    fraudulent trading, 8–10
    fungible securities, co-ownership of,
        2–7, 2–23, 2–24
    insolvency set-off, 1–24
    lender liability,
        breach of contract to lend money,
            21–5
        environmental pollution, 21–19
        negligent management, 8–25, 8–26
    preference rules, 7–10
        Actio Pauliana, 4–19
        creditor ignorance of insolvency,
            6–13
        ordinary course of business
            payments, 5–12
        security over after-acquired assets,
            5–20
        security for pre-existing debt, 5–18
    preventive compositions and
        moratoriums, 10–7, 10–10
    private debt restructuring, 18–14
    pro-creditor jurisdiction, as, 1–12,
        4–6
    security, attitude to, 1–20, 11–12
    tracing of money, 2–2
    trusts and, 2–2, 2–7
    veil of incorporation, 8–7
Netting,
    agreements, bar on insolvency set-off
        and, 1–25
    settlement netting, 5–30
New money,
    new money mortgages, 5–15

New money—*cont.*
  private debt restructuring and, 19–6,
    19–13, 19–18, 20–8
  security for, 5–15
New Zealand,
  credit references, 21–13
  exempt assets, 1–58
  family home, protection of, 1–58
  fraudulent trading, 8–9
  insolvency set-off, 1–24, 5–28
  ipso facto clauses, 3–12, 11–33,
    12–19
  judicial rescue proceedings, 12–19
    ipso facto clauses, 11–33, 12–19
    statutory management, 11–2,
      12–19
  lender liability, credit references,
    21–13
  preference rules, 4–7, 7–1
  pro-creditor/pro-debtor attitudes,
    1–11, 12–19
  public and private companies, 8–6
  shareholders, group liability, 9–10
  spouse, bankruptcy of, 1–58
  voluntary compositions, 10–5
Nigeria,
  insolvency set-off, 1–24
  pro-creditor jurisdiction, as, 1–13
Non-merchants,
  no bankruptcy of, 1–57
Nordic Bankruptcy Convention 1933,
  17–3
Northern Ireland. *See also* **English-
  based countries; United Kingdom**
  foreign insolvencies, recognition of,
    15–24
  insolvency set-off, 1–24
Norway. *See also* **Scandinavian
  jurisdictions**
  companies, types of, 8–6
  direct action, 1–32
  directors liability for preferential
    claims, 8–30
  discharges, foreign, 16–34
  discounting of unmatured credits,
    1–45
  foreign insolvencies, recognition of,
    15–4, 15–6, 15–42
  fraudulent trading, 8–10
  insolvency jurisdiction, 14–16

Norway—*cont.*
  insolvency jurisdiction—*cont.*
    global property, 14–20
    local branch, 14–4
    local business, 14–5
  insolvency set-off, 1–24, 5–28
  negligent management, 8–25, 8–26
  Nordic Bankruptcy Convention,
    1933, 17–3
  preference rules, 4–12
    excessive remuneration to
      managers, 5–4
    executions, 5–36
    negotiable instruments, 5–9
    payment of debts, 5–8
    recapture, 6–16
    security over after-acquired assets,
      6–20
    security for pre-existing debt, 5–17
    suspect period, 6–4
  preventive compositions and
    moratoriums, 10–6, 10–10
  security, attitude to, 1–20
Notarial bond. *See* **Security**
Notice,
  assignment of debts, of, 2–1, 2–39 to
    2–40

Pakistan,
  insolvency set-off, 1–24
  pro-creditor jurisdiction, as, 1–13
  public and private companies, 8–6
Panama. *See also* **Latin America**
  discounting of unmatured credits,
    1–45
  foreign insolvencies, recognition of,
    15–6, 16–25
  insolvency set-off, 1–24, 11–29
  pro-creditor/pro-debtor attitudes,
    1–12
Paraguay. *See also* **Latin America**
  foreign insolvencies, recognition of,
    15–46, 16–25
Pari passu creditors. *See* **Creditors**
Patent licence,
  termination on insolvency, 1–35
Pauline action. *See* **Preferences**, Actio
  Pauliana
Payments,
  preferences, as. *See* **Preferences**

Pension,
exemption from seizure, 1–58
Personal injury,
bankrupt's claim for, exempting,
1–58
Peru. *See also* **Latin America**
foreign insolvencies, recognition of,
15–46, 16–25
preference rules, 7–11
Petitions,
insolvency, 1–3
Philippines,
bulk sales rules, 5–31
creditors without *escritura publica*,
1–50
custodianship, 2–7
direct action, 1–32
pro-creditor/pro-debtor attitudes,
1–13
trusts, 2–7
Poland,
insolvency set-off, 1–24
judicial rescue proceedings, 12–25
pro-creditor jurisdiction, as, 1–12
Portugal,
assignment of debts,
late notification of, 5–25
notice of, 2–40
custodianship, 2–7
direct action, 1–32
directors liability for preferential
claims, 8–30
environmental liability, 21–19
fungibles, co-ownership of, 2–7
insolvency set-off, 1–25, 11–29
negligent management, 8–25, 8–26
preference rules, 4–12
trusts and, 2–7
Possessory management. *See* **Security,**
enforcement
Preferences,
Actio Pauliana, 4–19 to 4–21, 7–7,
7–8, 7–13, 7–16
available outside bankruptcy, 4–21
creditor collusion, 4–21, 5–17, 6–8
English-based countries, 4–7, 4–20
Franco-Latin jurisdictions, 4–12
insolvency not required, 4–21

Preferences—*cont.*
Actio Pauliana—*cont.*
intent to hinder, defeat or delay,
4–19, 5–16, 5–17
prejudice to creditors, 4–21
security for pre-existing debt, 5–17,
5–18
United States, 4–16
actual insolvency of debtor, 6–1 to
6–2
avoidance and recapture,
avoidance procedure, 6–15
guarantees, revival of, 6–17
preferred transferee insolvent, 6–21
protection of third parties, 6–19
recapture, 6–16
security
over after-acquired assets, 6–20
revival of, 6–18
set-off against repayment claim,
6–22
bulk sales, 4–5, 5–1, 5–31
compensating contracts, 5–29
composition proceedings, 6–6
conflict of laws, 16–23 to 16–27
connected persons, 6–5
corporate rehabilitations, 11–36
creditor enforcements, 5–35 to 5–36
defences
creditor ignorance of insolvency,
6–13 to 6–14
preferential intent. *See* preferential
intent, *infra*
summary, 6–7
deliberate concealment, 4–1
deterrence, 6–23
excessive remuneration to managers,
5–4
fraud. *See also* Actio Pauliana, *supra*
prevention of, 4–2
general preferences, 4–5
gifts, 4–5, 4–8 to 4–9, 4–13, 5–3 to
5–5
corporate, 5–3
examples, 5–4
guarantees,
revival of, 6–17
undervalue transactions, as, 5–6,
19–17
guarantors, preferment of, 5–34
honouring commitments and, 4–3

Preferences—*cont.*
  insiders, 6–5
  insolvency set-off, 5–27 to 5–29,
    6–22
  intent. *See* preferential intent, *infra*
  intent of debtor. *See* preferential
    intent, *infra*
  intentionally fraudulent transfers. *See*
    Actio Pauliana, *supra*
  intentionally prejudicial transfers,
    4–5
  involuntary transfer by debtor, 4–5
  judicial executions, 5–35 to 5–36
  judicial rehabilitations, 18–8
  jurisdictions, 4–6 to 4–18. *See also*
    under individual countries, *e.g.*
    England
    pro-creditor/pro-debtor, 4–6
    ranking, main issues, 4–6
  law. *See* rules, *infra*
  negotiable instruments, 5–9
  netting, 5–30
  Pauline action. *See* Actio Pauliana,
    supra
  payments,
    abnormal means, by, 5–29
    current accounts, 5–14
      net improvement test, 5–14
    existing debts, of, 5–8
    indirect payments, 5–8
    negotiable instruments, 5–9
    ordinary course of business
      payments, 5–10 to 5–13
    prepayments, 4–13, 5–8
    triangular payments, 5–8
  penalties, 6–23
  policies, 4–1 to 4–3
    avoidance of insolvency and, 4–3
    debtor harassment, prevention of,
      4–2, 5–17
    equality, 4–2
    fraud, prevention of, 4–2
    honouring commitments and, 4–3
    objectives of, 4–2
    predictability and, 4–3
  predictability, need for, 4–3
  preferential intent, 4–10, 4–13, 6–8
    advantages, 6–9
    classification of jurisdictions, 6–8
    disadvantages, 6–9

Preferences—*cont.*
  preferential intent—*cont.*
    negation of
      pressure, 6–10
      protection of debtor against
        misfeasance, 6–11
    onus of proof, 6–12
  prejudice to creditors
    Actio Pauliana, 4–21
    case law, 5–1, 5–2
    generally, 5–1 to 5–2
    judicial executions, 5–35 to 5–36
    none, where, 5–2
    payments. *See* payments, *supra*
    preferment of guarantors, 5–34
    security. *See* security, *infra*
    set-off
      compensating contracts, 5–29
      countries allowing, 5–28
      countries disallowing, 5–27
      generally, 5–27
    settlement netting, 5–30
    test for, 5–1, 5–2
    transactions with shareholders,
      financial assistance to purchase
        company's own shares,
        5–33
      maintenance of capital, 5–32
    transfer of business, 5–31
    undervalue transactions,
      gifts, 5–3 to 5–5
      guarantees as, 5–6, 19–17
      subordinations as, 5–7
      transactions at an undervalue,
        5–3 to 5–5
  prepayments, 4–13, 5–8
  pro-creditor/pro-debtor jurisdictions,
    4–5
  recapture. *See* avoidance and
    recapture, *supra*
  relation-back doctrine, 4–4, 4–7,
    5–36
  requirements preferential
    transactions, 4–1
  rules
    categories of,
      bulk sales laws, 4–5, 5–31
      gifts, 4–5
      intentionally prejudicial
        transfers, 4–5

Preferences—*cont.*
  rules—*cont.*
    categories of—*cont.*
      involuntary transfer by debtor,
        4–5
      outline of, 4–5 to 4–6
      payment of shareholders before
        creditors, 4–5
      timely publication of security
        granted by debtor, 4–5
      transfer of debtor's business, 4–5
    pro-creditor/pro-debtor, 4–6
    selected countries, 7–1 to 7–17
  security,
    after-acquired assets, over, 5–20,
      6–20
    assignments, late notification of,
      5–25
    avoided as, 1–19
    floating charges for pre-existing
      debt, 5–21 to 5–22, 19–18
    generally, 1–19
    indirect security, 5–16
    late registration of, 5–23 to 5–24
    new money, for, 5–15
    pre-existing debt, for, 5–17 to 5–18
      automatically void, 5–17
      deliberate intent, 5–17
      no knowledge of insolvency,
        5–18
      not void if intent negated, 5–17
      pre-existing obligation, 5–18
    purchases of unsecured claims by
      secured creditor, 5–26
    roll-over of secured current
      accounts, 5–19
    secured loan to pay off existing
      creditors, 5–16
    triangle transactions, 5–16
  set-off, 5–27 to 5–29, 6–22
  settlement netting, 5–30
  suspect period
    abnormal payments in, 5–29
    connected persons, 4–10, 6–5
    English-based countries, 4–10
    length of, 6–3 to 6–4, 6–6
    payments in, 5–8
    security for pre-existing debt in,
      5–17
    transactions in good faith during,
      4–3

Preferences—*cont.*
  terminology, 4–4
  test of. *See also* defences, *supra*
    actual insolvency of debtor, 6–1 to
      6–2
    balance sheet test, 6–1, 6–2
    creditor ignorance of insolvency,
      6–13 to 6–14
    preferential intent. *See* preferential
      intent, *supra*
    prejudice to creditors. *See* prejudice
      to creditors, *supra*
  transfer of business, 5–31
    bulk sales, 4–5, 5–1, 5–31
  undervalue transactions, 4–9, 4–13,
    5–3 to 5–5
    guarantees as, 5–6, 19–17
    subordinations as, 5–7
Prepayments,
  automatically void transactions, as,
    4–13
  penalties on, 1–19
  preferential, as, 4–13, 5–8
  restriction on, 1–19
Principal. *See* Agency
Priorities. *See* Creditors
Private debt restructuring,
  advantages, 18–2
  banks and, 18–15
    loss sharing agreements, 19–19
    standstill agreements, 19–3, 19–5
  bondholders and, 18–16
  creditors,
    secured, 18–17
    trade, 18–19
  debt/equity conversions,
    advantages of, 20–7 to 20–8
    banks, 20–2
      conflicts of interest, 20–18
      provisioning policies, 20–11
      public relations, 20–8
      solvency ratios, 20–7
    board control, 20–19
    bondholders, 20–3
      bondholder approval, 20–15
    changes of control, 20–13
    consolidation of debtor, 20–18
    debt eligible for conversion, 20–2
      to 20–6
    disadvantages of, 20–9 to 20–11
    disclosure of shareholdings, 20–19

Private debt restructuring—*cont.*
  debt/equity conversions—*cont.*
    equity holdings, restrictions on,
      20–12
    false markets, 20–17
    implications of, 20–12 to 20–19
    insider dealing, 20–16
    intercompany debt, 20–6
    large sellers, 20–5
    lender liability, 20–19
    lessors, 20–4
    listing, loss of, 20–15
    mandatory bid, 20–13
    merger and anti-trust legislation,
      20–13
    no issue of shares at a discount,
      20–19
    provisioning and, 20–11
    restrictions on equity holdings,
      20–12
    securities, types of, 20–20
    shareholders,
      shareholder approval, 20–14
      transactions with, 20–15
    trade suppliers, 20–5
    transfer to bank holding company,
      20–21
  debtor, types of,
    asset-based companies, 18–24
    public interest businesses, 18–23
    public and private/large and small,
      18–22
  disadvantages, 18–2
  employees and, 18–20
  factors and, 18–18
  final liquidation,
    advantages, 18–4
    compared, 18–3 to 18–4
    disadvantages, 18–3
  generally, 10–1, 18–1
  insider debt, 19–12
  judicial rehabilitation,
    advantages, 18–6 to 18–8
    compared, 18–5 to 18–11
    disadvantages of, 18–9 to 18–11
  jurisdictional attitudes, 18–13 to
    18–14
  lessors and, 18–18
  litigants and, 18–19
  London rules, 19–10

Private debt restructuring—*cont.*
  loss sharing agreements
    pro rata sharing clauses compared,
      19–19
    sharing formula, 19–20
  management and, 18–20
  new money, 19–6, 19–13, 19–18,
    20–8
  participants in, 18–15 to 18–21
  secured creditors and, 18–17
  security for restructured debt,
    generally, 19–17
    maximising, 19–18
  shareholders and, 18–21
  standstill agreements. *See* **Standstill**
    agreements
  steering committee, 19–3
  support agreements. *See* **Support**
    agreements
  tax authorities and, 18–19
  trade creditors and, 18–19
Pro-creditor/pro-debtor jurisdictions,
  comity, attitude to, 13–6
  generally, 1–4 to 1–5
  insolvency set-off, 1–5
  preferences, 4–6
    suspect period, 6–4
  scaling of, 1–6 to 1–10
    key determinants, 1–7 to 1–8
    table, 1–9
  security for pre-existing debt, 5–17
  summary survey of, 1–11 to 1–13
  trade creditors, 18–19
  universal floating charge, 1–5
Product liability. *See* **Torts**
Promissory note. *See* **Negotiable**
  instruments
Property of the estate. *See* **Bankrupt's**
  property
Proprietary claims on insolvency. *See*
  also **Bankrupt's property; Trusts**
  and trustees
  accidental commingling, 2–14
  express trusts of money, 2–16
  mistaken payments, 2–14
  special purpose payments, 2–11
    case law examples, 2–12
  wrongful taking of money, 2–13
Public auction. *See* **Security,**
  enforcement

Public interest,
foreign insolvencies, recognition of, 15–8
judicial rescue proceedings, 12–26
private debt restructuring and, 18–23
recognition of foreign insolvencies and, 15–8 to 15–9
special legal regimes, 1–62
Publication and publicity,
bankruptcy, of, 1–3
set-off as unpublicised security interest, 1–23

Qatar,
bankruptcy law, 1–13
Quebec. *See* **Canada**

Rehabilitations,
corporate rehabilitation. *See* **Corporate rehabilitation**
history of, 10–2 to 10–4
individual insolvency and, 1–60
judicial rehabilitation,
advantages of, 18–6 to 18–7
disadvantages of, 18–9 to 18–11
private restructuring compared, 18–5 to 18–11
Remedies,
secured debtor, of, 1–19
Republic of Ireland,
examinership, 11–1
insolvency set-off, 1–24
pro-debtor jurisdiction, as, 1–11
public and private companies, 8–6
veil of incorporation, 8–7
wrongful trading, 8–11
Reputed ownership. *See* **False wealth**
Rescission. *See* **Termination**
Retention of title. *See* **Title finance**
Roman law,
Actio Pauliana, 4–19
pro-debtor, as, 1–12
Russia,
bankruptcy law, 1–13
judicial rescue proceedings, 12–25
preference rules, 7–12

Safe-keeping. *See* **Custodians**
Salary,
exemption from seizure, 1–58
Sale and lease-back. *See* **Title finance**
Sale and repurchase. *See* **Title finance**
Saudi Arabia,
companies, types of, 8–6
directors' duty to call shareholders meeting on loss of capital, 8–16, 8–18
insolvency set-off, 1–24
Scandinavian jurisdictions. *See also* **Denmark; Finland; Norway; Sweden**
companies, types of, 8–6
direct action, 1–32
insolvency jurisdiction, 14–16 to 14–17
insolvency set-off, 1–24, 5–28, 16–10
Nordic Bankruptcy Convention 1933, 17–3
pro-creditor, as, 1–12
self-help, 1–20
undisclosed principal, 1–32
veil of incorporation, 8–7
Scotland. *See also* **English-based countries; United Kingdom**
directors liability for financial statements, 8–28
foreign insolvencies, recognition of, 15–9, 15–21, 15–24, 16–24
insolvency set-off, 1–24
moratoriums and discharges, foreign, 16–32
ordinary course of business payments, 5–13
preferences, conflict of laws, 16–24
pro-creditor jurisdiction, as, 1–12
security, attitude to, 1–20
Secret ownership,
Anglo-American jurisdictions, 1–11
mortgages, 2–4
trusts, 2–4
Secret profits,
delinquent directors, by, 2–13
generally, 2–10
wrongful takings of money, 2–13

Secured Creditors. *See* **Creditors**
Securities clearance systems. *See*
   Custodians
Security,
  after-acquired assets, over, 5–20,
    6–20
  attitudes to, 1–11, 1–20, 11–12
  avoided as preference, 1–19
  bankruptcy, effect of, 1–1, 1–19
  co-ownership, 2–7, 2–23, 2–24
  conflict of laws, 16–16
  corporate charges, public registration
    of, 1–20
  countries hostile to, 1–20, 11–12
  countries sympathetic to, 1–20,
    11–12
  creditors. *See* **Creditors**
  creditors, secured. *See* **Creditors**
  custodianship of, 2–8, 2–9
  damages, 1–18
  debt which may be secured, scope of,
    1–18
  debt/equity conversions and, 20–9
  defensive control, as, 1–16
  document, contents of, 1–18
  enforcement, 1–19
    judicial protectionism, 1–19
    possessory management, 1–20
    private debt restructuring, 18–17
    private sale, 1–20
    public auction, 1–19, 1–20
    self-help, 1–19
    stay on, 1–19, 11–12 to 11–25
  essence of, 1–17
  false wealth and, 1–17
  fiduciary transfers, 1–20
  floating charges. *See* **Floating charges**
  foreign currency mortgages, 1–18
  formalities, 1–18
  fraudulent transfer. *See* **Preferences**
  future debt, 1–17, 1–18
  informal creation of, 1–18
  investment securities, custodianship
    of, 2–8, 2–9
  judicial protectionism, 1–19
  judicial rehabilitations and, 18–10
  jurisdictional classification,
    hostile, 1–20, 11–12
    key issues, 1–18 to 1–19

Security—*cont.*
  jurisdictional classification—*cont.*
    sympathetic, 1–20, 11–12
  limitations on, 1–19, 1–59
  meaning of, 1–17
  mortgages. *See* **Mortgages**
  new money, for, 5–15
  notarised, where, 1–18
  objections to, 1–17
  oral creation of, 1–18
  perfection of, 1–18
  policies of, 1–16
  pre-existing debt, for, 5–17 to 5–18,
    19–17
  preferences. *See* **Preferences**
  prepayments,
    penalties on, 1–19
    restriction on, 1–19
  priorities. *See* **Creditors**
  public registration, 1–18, 1–20, 2–4,
    2–9
  purposes of, 1–16
  rationale of, 1–16
  redemption of, restricting, 1–19
  restructured debt, for. *See* **Private
    debt restructuring**
  revival of, 6–16
  secured creditors. *See* **Creditors**
  set-off. *See* **Insolvency set-off**
  specificity, doctrine of, 1–20
  super-priority moratorium loans,
    1–19
  title finance creditors, 1–27
  universal business charge, 1–20
  writing, in, 1–18
Segregation,
  test of trusteeship, 2–19
Seizure. *See* **Attachments**
Self-help,
  English-based countries, 1–20
  Scandinavian jurisdictions, 1–20
  security, enforcement of, 1–19
Sequestration. *See* **Attachments**
Set-off. *See* **Insolvency set-off**
Shareholders,
  big pocket liability, 8–2
  capital, maintenance of, 5–32, 5–33
  "claw-back", 20–14
  de facto directors, as, 9–7
  debt/equity conversions, 20–14,
    20–15

Shareholders—*cont.*
  deferred, 1–51
  direct action against, 1–34
  equity shareholders, insolvency and,
    1–51
  financial assistance to purchase
    company's own shares, 5–33
  liability,
    commingling, 9–3 to 9–6
    consolidation on insolvency, 9–16
    generally, 8–1, 9–1 to 9–2
    group liability, 9–7 to 9–10
    tax, for, 9–11
    US equitable subordination,
      9–12 to 9–15
    informalities, 9–3 to 9–6
    undercapitalisation, 9–3 to 9–6
  lifting the veil, 1–34
  ordinary, 1–51
  pre-emption rights, 20–14
  preferred, 1–51
  priority on insolvency, 1–51
  private debt restructuring, 18–21
  purchase of company's own shares,
    5–33
Ship finance,
  maritime lien, 1–19, 1–41
Shipbuilding contracts. *See*
  Construction contracts
Singapore,
  administration, 11–1
  foreign insolvencies, recognition of,
    15–18
  fraudulent trading, 8–9
  insolvency set-off, 1–24
  voluntary compositions, 10–5
Slovak Republic,
  insolvency set-off, 1–24
  judicial rescue proceedings, 12–24
  preference rules, 7–6
  pro-creditor jurisdiction, as, 1–12
South Africa,
  foreign insolvencies, recognition of,
    15–9, 15–17, 15–21
  fraudulent trading, 8–9
  impeachable transactions, 4–4
  insolvency jurisdiction, 14–4
  insolvency set-off, 1–24, 1–25, 11–29
  judicial management, 11–8, 12–2
  notarial bond, 1–20

South Africa—*cont.*
  preference rules,
    Actio Pauliana, 4–19
    bulk sales, 5–31
    guarantors, preferment of, 5–34
    negotiable instruments, 5–9
    ordinary course of business
      payments, 5–11
    shareholders, transactions with,
      5–33
  pro-debtor jurisdiction, as, 1–12,
    1–13
  public and private companies, 8–6
  security, attitude to, 1–20
  veil of incorporation, 8–7
South America. *See* **Latin America**
South Korea. *See* **Korea**
Soviet Union,
  former states of. *See* **Belarus;**
    Kazakhstan; Russia; Ukraine
Spain,
  assignment of debts, notice of, 2–40
  companies, types of, 8–6
  creditors without *escritura publica*,
    1–50
  environmental liability, 21–19
  foreign insolvencies, recognition of,
    15–41
  insolvency set-off, 1–25, 11–29
  judicial rescue proceedings, 12–20 to
    12–22
    ipso facto clauses, 12–22
    suspension of payments, 11–1,
      12–20, 12–22
  negligent management, 8–21
  preference rules, 4–12, 7–13
    preferential intent, 6–8
  security, attitude to, 1–20, 11–12
  veil of incorporation, 8–7
Specificity,
  doctrine of, 1–20
Spouses,
  bankruptcy of, 1–58
  matrimonial property, community of,
    1–61
Sri Lanka,
  insolvency set-off, 1–24
Standstill agreements,
  banks and, 19–3, 19–5
  generally, 19–1

Standstill agreements—*cont.*
informal standstill, 19–2
London rules, 19–10
management changes, 19–8
new money, 19–6
review of debtor's position, 19–9
short-leash controls, 19–6
steering committee, 19–3
terms of, 19–4 to 19–7
Stays,
attachments, on, 18–7
automatic, 12–4, 12–9 to 12–10
corporate rehabilitation, in, 11–11
enforcement of security, on, 1–19,
11–12 to 11–25
insolvency conflict of laws, 16–10
Subordination,
consensual subordination, 1–50
equitable subordination, 1–49, 9–12
to 9–15
insider debt, of, 19–12
undervalue transaction, as, 5–7
Subrogation,
priority claims on insolvency, 1–42 to
1–43
Support agreements,
covenants, 19–14
ring-fencing, 19–14
creditor decision-making, 19–16
events of default, 19–15
financial terms, 19–13
insider debt, 19–12
interest and fees, 19–13
most favoured debt clause, 19–13
new money, 19–13
override and consolidated agreements
compared, 19–11
representations, 19–13
restructured debt, 19–12
standstill clause, 19–13
terms of, 19–13 to 19–16
warranties, 19–13
Sweden. *See also* **Scandinavian
jurisdictions**
companies, types of, 8–6
composition, foreign, 16–34
direct action, 1–32
directors,
duty to call shareholders meeting
on loss of capital, 8–16, 8–18

Sweden—*cont.*
directors—*cont.*
liability for preferential claims,
8–30
discharges, foreign, 16–34
discounting of unmatured credits,
1–45
equalisation in, 16–7, 16–8
floating charge, 6–20
foreign insolvencies, recognition of,
15–6, 15–43
insolvency jurisdiction, 14–17
global property, 14–20
local assets, 14–4
local business, 14–5
insolvency set-off, 1–24, 11–29
negligent management, 8–25
Nordic Bankruptcy Convention 1933,
17–3
ordinary course of business payments,
5–12
preference rules, 4–12, 7–14 to 7–15
Actio Pauliana, 4–19
conflict of laws, 16–24
excessive remuneration to
managers, 5–4
executions, 5–36
negotiable instruments, 5–9
payment of debts, 5–8
security over after-acquired assets,
6–20
security for pre-existing debt, 5–18
preventive compositions and
moratoriums, 10–10
sale of goods contracts, 3–2
security, attitude to, 1–20, 11–12
shareholders, group liability, 9–10
Switzerland,
assignment of debts, notice of, 2–40
comity, attitude to, 13–6
companies, types of, 8–6
contracts, performance on insolvency,
3–2
direct action,
insolvency of agent, on, principal
against third party, 1–32
undisclosed principal, 1–31
directors, duties of,
diligence, 8–25
to call shareholders meeting on loss
of capital, 8–16, 8–18

Switzerland—*cont.*
  discounting of unmatured credits,
    1–45
  equalisation in, 16–7
  fiduciary transfer, 1–20, 9–20
  foreign insolvencies, recognition of,
    15–29 to 15–30
  Franco-Swiss Convention, 17–2
  insolvency set-off, 1–24, 11–29
  lender liability, 9–19
  negligent management, 8–25, 8–26
  preference rules, 7–16
    Actio Pauliana, 4–19
    conflict of laws, 16–26
    preferential intent, 6–8
      creditor collusion, 6–8
    security for pre-existing debt, 5–18
    suspect period, 6–4
  private debt restructuring, 18–14
  pro-creditor jurisdiction, as, 4–6
  security, attitude to, 1–20, 11–12
  undisclosed principal, 1–31
  veil of incorporation, 8–7

Taxes,
  foreign insolvencies, recognition of,
    15–9
  priority on insolvency, 1–38, 1–41
Tenancy in common. *See* Co-ownership
Termination,
  contracts, of, 1–1, 1–35, 2–1, 3–2
    solvent counterparty, by. *See*
      Contracts
  creditors with rights of, 1–35
  forfeitures, 3–19
  ipso facto clauses. *See* Contracts
  lease, of. *See* Leases
  patent licence, of, 1–35
Thailand,
  assignment of debts, notice of, 2–40
  insolvency set-off, 1–24
  pro-creditor/pro-debtor attitudes,
    1–13
Title finance,
  conflict of laws, 16–16
  corporate rehabilitation proceedings,
    11–26 to 11–28
  creditors, 1–27
  hire purchase, 1–27, 1–59

Title finance—*cont.*
  recourse factoring, 1–27
  retention of title, 1–27, 2–19
  sale and lease-back, 1–27
  sale and repurchase, 1–27
Title retention. *See* Title finance
Tools of the trade,
  exemption from seizure, 1–58
Torts,
  directors' liability, 8–31
  insolvency claims, 1–56
  interference with goods, 2–26
  product liability, 1–34, 1–56
Tracing. *See* Trusts and trustees
Transaction set-off. *See* Insolvency set-
  off
Transactions at an undervalue. *See*
  Preferences, undervalue
  transactions
Treaties,
  bankruptcy treaties not in force, 17–8
  French conventions, 17–2
  generally, 17–1
  Montevideo and Bustamente
    Conventions, 17–4 to 17–7
  Nordic Bankruptcy Convention 1933,
    17–3
Trustee in bankruptcy. *See* Insolvency
  representatives
Trusts and trustees. *See also* Bankrupt's
    property; Custodians; False wealth;
    Proprietary claims on insolvency
  apparent owner, 2–2
    treated as absolute owner,
      examples, 2–8
  assignment of debts. *See* Assignment
    of debts
  bailees of goods, 2–8
  beneficial ownership, 2–2
  civil code/common law division,
    1–10, 2–2 to 2–5
  commingled property, 2–14. *See also*
    tracing of trust property, *infra*
  constructive trusts,
    accidental commingling, 2–14
    mistaken payments, 1–28, 2–10,
      2–14
    special purpose payments, 2–11 to
      2–12
    wrongful taking of money, 2–13

Trusts and trustees—*cont.*
  custodians. *See* **Custodians**
  deposits for sale or collection. *See*
      Deposits for sale or collection
  express trusts of money, 2–16
  Franco-Latin systems, 2–6, 2–7
  fungibility, 2–20 to 2–21. *See also*
      Fungibles
  Germanic view, 2–6
  jurisdictional attitudes, 2–1, 2–2 to
      2–5
    apparent ownership, 2–2
    beneficial ownership, 2–2
    false wealth/credit, 2–3
    fear of fraud and fraudulent
        preferences, 2–5
    priorities, 2–4
    secret ownership rights, 2–4
    taxation, 2–5
  Napoleonic view, 2–6
  proprietary claims on insolvency. *See*
      Proprietary claims on insolvency
  reputed ownership. *See* **False wealth**
  special purpose payments, 2–11
    case law examples, 2–12
  tests of trusteeship,
    express trusts of money, 2–16
    generally, 2–15
    interest test, 2–18
    presumptions if no express trust of
        money, 2–17 to 2–19
    principle of ownership, 2–15
    segregation test, 2–19
  tracing of trust property,
    appropriation, 2–29
    bona fide purchaser for value, 2–28
    charging property, 2–30
    generally, 2–10, 2–27 to 2–28
    priority claim, 2–32
    tenancy in common, 2–31
  unjust enrichment. *See* **Unjust
      enrichment**
  warehouse keepers, 2–8
Turkey,
  companies, types of, 8–6
  direct action, 1–32

Ukraine,
  bankruptcy law, 1–13

Ukraine—*cont.*
  judicial rescue proceedings, 12–25
  preference rules, 7–17
Undervalue transactions. *See*
    Preferences
Undisclosed principal. *See* **Agency**
United Kingdom. *See also* **England;
    English-based countries; Northern
    Ireland; Scotland**
  administration. *See* **England**
  directors' duty to call shareholders
      meeting on loss of capital, 8–16,
      8–18
  wrongful trading, 8–12
United States,
  assignment of debts, notice of, 2–40
  bank bankruptcies, 1–62
  bank failures, 8–24
  business judgment rule, 8–24
  comity, attitude to, 13–6
  common law jurisdictions,
      undisclosed principal, 1–30,
      1–31
  consolidation on insolvency, 9–16
  contracts
    assumption/rejection on insolvency,
        3–2
    disclaimer, 3–4
    forfeiture, 3–18
    invalid, 3–18
    ipso facto clauses, 3–14 to 3–15,
        11–33
  corporate rehabilitation,
    contract cancellation, 11–33
    disclaimer powers, 3–4, 11–35
    ease of entry, 11–8
    eligible debtors, 11–6, 14–9
    financing the business, 11–41
    generally, 11–2
    grounds for petition, 11–8
    ipso facto clauses, 11–33
    preferences, 11–36
    reorganisation plan, 11–44
    replacement of management,
        11–37, 11–38, 18–9
    security interests, 11–17 to 11–21
    set-off, 11–30
    stay on legal proceedings, 11–11
  credit references, 21–13

United States—*cont.*
  creditors. *See* priority on insolvency, *infra*
  "cross-stream" guarantees, 5–6
  direct action,
    third party against principal, 1–32
    undisclosed principal, 1–30 to 1–32
  disclaimer, 3–4, 11–35
  discovery of foreign assets, 16–9
  environmental liability, 1–40, 21–19, 21–21, 21–22
    CERCLA, 21–25 to 21–26
  equalisation in, 16–8
  equitable subordination, 1–49, 9–12 to 9–15
  exempt assets, 1–58
  foreign currency creditors, 1–55
  foreign insolvencies, recognition of,
    ancillary proceedings, 15–32 to 15–36
    concurrent bankruptcy, 15–31
    generally, 15–6, 15–31
    no US proceedings, 15–31
  fraudulent trading, 8–10
  guarantees, 5–6
  homestead exception, 1–58
  insolvency jurisdiction, 14–14
    global property, 14–19
    local assets, 14–4
  insolvency set-off, 1–24, 5–28, 11–29, 11–30
  insured banks, 12–26
  judicial rescue proceedings. *See* corporate rehabilitation, *supra*
  leases, assumption/rejection on insolvency, 3–2
  lender liability, 9–18, 9–19
    abusive credit, 21–10
    breach of contract to lend money, 21–5
    liability to third parties, 21–9
    credit references, 21–13
    environmental pollution, 21–19, 21–21, 21–22
      CERCLA, 21–25 to 21–26
    overcharging interest, 21–14
  liens, 5–15
  lifting the veil, 9–4 to 9–5
  management buy-outs, 8–24

United States—*cont.*
  matrimonial property, community of, 1–61
  negligent management, 8–24
  preference rules,
    Actio Pauliana, 4–16, 4–19, 5–16
    avoidance,
      conflict of laws, 16–27
      prohibited, where, 4–15, 4–18
      protection of third parties, 6–19
      set-off against repayment claim, 6–22
      tests for, 4–14
    bulk sales, 5–31
    corporate rehabilitation, 11–36
    creditor ignorance of insolvency, 6–14
    execution levies, 5–36
    fraudulent transfers, 4–16
    generally, 4–14 to 4–15
    guarantors, preferment of, 5–34
    involuntary transfers, 5–36
    leveraged buy-out financings, 5–33
    liability of transferee of avoided transfers, 4–17
    ordinary course of business payments, 5–11
    pro-debtor, 4–6
    recapture, 6–16
    security,
      late registration of, 5–24
      new money, for, 5–15
      over after-acquired assets, 5–20
      payment to third party creditors, 5–16
      pre-existing debt, for, 5–17
    State law, 4–18
    suspect period, 6–4
    time limits, 4–17
    transfer of business, 5–31
  priority on insolvency,
    conflict of laws, 16–19, 16–21
    employee remuneration and benefits, 1–39
    environmental clean-up expenses, 1–40
    foreign currency creditors, 1–55
    subrogation to priority claims, 1–43
  private debt restructuring, 18–14

United States—*cont.*
  private debt restructuring—*cont.*
    standstill agreements, 19–3
    pro-creditor/pro-debtor attitudes,
      1–10, 1–11
    preferences, 4–6
    secret ownership, 1–11
    security, 11–17 to 11–21
      attitude to, 1–20, 11–12
    shareholder liability, 9–1
      commingling, undercapitalisation
        and informalities, 9–3 to 9–6
      equitable subordination, 1–49,
        9–12 to 9–15
    standstill agreements, 19–3
    subordination, equitable, 1–49, 9–12
      to 9–15
    trusts, tests of trusteeship, 2–17 to
      2–19
    undisclosed principal, 1–30, 1–31
    "upstream" guarantees, 5–6
    veil of incorporation, 8–4, 8–7, 9–4
      to 9–5
Universal charges. *See* Security
Unjust enrichment,
  accidental commingling, 2–14
  generally, 2–1, 2–10
  jurisdictional attitudes, 2–1, 2–10
  mistaken payments, 1–28, 2–10,
    2–14
  special purpose payments,
    case law examples, 2–12
    generally, 2–11
  wrongful taking of money, 2–13
Unsecured creditors. *See* Creditors
Uruguay. *See also* Latin America
  foreign insolvencies, recognition of,
    15–46, 16–25
Usury,
  historical hostility to, 1–13, 1–17

Veil of incorporation,
  companies, types of, 8–5 to 8–6
  conflict of laws, 16–35 to 16–37
  jurisdictions, scale of, 8–7
  lifting. *See* **Lifting the veil**
  personal liability
    directors. *See* **Directors**
    financing banks, 8–1
    other group companies, 8–1
    regulators, 8–1
    shareholders. *See* **Shareholders**
  policies, 8–2 to 8–4
  private companies, 8–5 to 8–6
  public companies, 8–5 to 8–6
  United States, in, 9–4 to 9–5
Venezuela,
  preference rules, 4–12

Warehouses. *See* **Custodians**
Work-out. *See* **Private debt
  restructuring**
Wrongful trading,
  creditor liable for, subordination of,
    1–49
  debt/equity conversions and, 20–7
  definition, 8–11
  directors, by, 8–11 to 8–13
  reasonableness test, 8–11

Zaire,
  pro-debtor jurisdiction, as, 1–13
Zambia,
  insolvency set-off, 1–24
  pro-creditor jurisdiction, as, 1–13
Zimbabwe,
  pro-debtor jurisdiction, as, 1–13